T0301638

An Arbitrage Guide to Financial Markets

Wiley Finance Series

Hedge Funds: Quantitative Insights
François-Serge Lhabitant
A Currency Options Primer
Shani Shamah
New Risk Measures in Investment and Regulation
Giorgio Szegö (Editor)
Modelling Prices in Competitive Electricity Markets
Derek Bunn (Editor)
Inflation-indexed Securities: Bonds, Swaps and Other Derivatives, 2nd Edition
Mark Deacon, Andrew Derry and Dariush Mirfendereski
European Fixed Income Markets: Money, Bond and Interest Rates
Jonathan Batten, Thomas Fetherston and Peter Szilagyi (Editors)
Global Securitisation and CDOs
John Deacon
Applied Quantitative Methods for Trading and Investment
Christian L. Dunis, Jason Laws and Patrick Naim (Editors)
Country Risk Assessment: A Guide to Global Investment Strategy
Michel Henry Bouchet, Ephraim Clark and Bertrand Groslambert
Credit Derivatives Pricing Models: Models, Pricing and Implementation
Philipp J. Schönbucher
Hedge Funds: A Resource for Investors
Simone Borla
A Foreign Exchange Primer
Shani Shamah
The Simple Rules: Revisiting the Art of Financial Risk Management
Erik Banks
Option Theory
Peter James
Risk-adjusted Lending Conditions
Werner Rosenberger
Measuring Market Risk
Kevin Dowd
An Introduction to Market Risk Management
Kevin Dowd
Behavioural Finance
James Montier
Asset Management: Equities Demystified
Shanta Acharya
An Introduction to Capital Markets: Products, Strategies, Participants
Andrew M. Chisholm
Hedge Funds: Myths and Limits
François-Serge Lhabitant
The Manager's Concise Guide to Risk
Jihad S. Nader
Securities Operations: A Guide to Trade and Position Management
Michael Simmons
Modeling, Measuring and Hedging Operational Risk
Marcelo Cruz
Monte Carlo Methods in Finance
Peter Jäckel
Building and Using Dynamic Interest Rate Models
Ken Kortanek and Vladimir Medvedev
Structured Equity Derivatives: The Definitive Guide to Exotic Options and Structured Notes
Harry Kat
Advanced Modelling in Finance Using Excel and VBA
Mary Jackson and Mike Staunton
Operational Risk: Measurement and Modelling
Jack King
Interest Rate Modelling
Jessica James and Nick Webber

An Arbitrage Guide to Financial Markets

Robert Dubil

John Wiley & Sons, Ltd

Other Wiley Editorial Offices

John Wiley & Sons Inc., 111 River Street, Hoboken, NJ 07030, USA

Jossey-Bass, 989 Market Street, San Francisco, CA 94103-1741, USA

Wiley-VCH Verlag GmbH, Boschstr. 12, D-69469 Weinheim, Germany

John Wiley & Sons Australia Ltd, 33 Park Road, Milton, Queensland 4064, Australia

John Wiley & Sons (Asia) Pte Ltd, 2 Clementi Loop #02-01, Jin Xing Distripark, Singapore 129809

John Wiley & Sons Canada Ltd, 22 Worcester Road, Etobicoke, Ontario, Canada M9W 1L1

Wiley also publishes its books in a variety of electronic formats. Some content that appears
in print may not be available in electronic books.

Library of Congress Cataloging-in-Publication Data

Dubil, Robert.
An arbitrage guide to financial markets / Robert Dubil.
p. cm.—(Wiley finance series)
Includes bibliographical references and indexes.
ISBN 0-470-85332-8 (cloth : alk. paper)
1. Investments—Mathematics.. 2. Arbitrage. 3. Risk. I. Title. II. Series.
HG4515.3.D8 2004
332.6—dc22   2004010303

British Library Cataloguing in Publication Data

A catalogue record for this book is available from the British Library

ISBN 0-470-85332-8

Project management by Originator, Gt Yarmouth, Norfolk (typeset in 10/12pt Times)
Printed and bound in Great Britain by T.J. International Ltd, Padstow, Cornwall
This book is printed on acid-free paper responsibly manufactured from sustainable forestry
in which at least two trees are planted for each one used for paper production.

To Britt, Elsa, and Ethan

Contents

1

The Purpose and Structure of Financial Markets

1.1 OVERVIEW

Financial markets play a major role in allocating wealth and excess savings to productive ventures in the global economy. This extremely desirable process takes on various forms. Commercial banks solicit depositors' funds in order to lend them out to businesses that invest in manufacturing and services or to home buyers who finance new construction or redevelopment. Investment banks bring to market offerings of equity and debt from newly formed or expanding corporations. Governments issue short- and long-term bonds to finance construction of new roads, schools, and transportation networks. Investors—bank depositors and securities buyers—supply their funds in order to shift their consumption into the future by earning interest, dividends, and capital gains.

The process of transferring savings into investment involves various market participants: individuals, pension and mutual funds, banks, governments, insurance companies, industrial corporations, stock exchanges, over-the-counter dealer networks, and others. All these agents can at different times serve as demanders and suppliers of funds, and as transfer facilitators.

Economic theorists design optimal securities and institutions to make the process of transferring savings into investment most efficient. "Efficient" means to produce the best outcomes—lowest cost, least disputes, fastest, etc.—from the perspective of security issuers and investors, as well as for society as a whole. We start this book by addressing briefly some fundamental questions about today's financial markets. Why do we have things like stocks, bonds, or mortgage-backed securities? Are they outcomes of optimal design or happenstance? Do we really need "greedy" investment bankers, securities dealers, or brokers soliciting us by phone to purchase unit trusts or mutual funds? What role do financial exchanges play in today's economy? Why do developing nations strive to establish stock exchanges even though often they do not have any stocks to trade on them?

Once we have basic answers to these questions, it will not be difficult to see why almost all the financial markets are organically the same. Like automobiles made by Toyota and Volkswagen which all have an engine, four wheels, a radiator, a steering wheel, etc., all interacting in a predetermined way, all markets, whether for stocks, bonds, commodities, currencies, or any other claims to purchasing power, are built from the same basic elements.

All markets have two separate segments: original-issue and resale. These are characterized by different buyers and sellers, and different intermediaries. They perform different timing functions. The first transfers capital from the suppliers of funds (investors) to the demanders of capital (businesses). The second transfers capital from the suppliers of capital (investors) to other suppliers of capital (investors). The original-issue and resale segments are formally referred to as:

- *Primary markets* (issuer-to-investor transactions with investment banks as intermediaries in the securities markets, and banks, insurance companies, and others in the loan markets).
- *Secondary markets* (investor-to-investor transactions with broker-dealers and exchanges as intermediaries in the securities markets, and mostly banks in the loan markets).

Secondary markets play a critical role in allowing investors in the primary markets to transfer the risks of their investments to other market participants.

All markets have the originators, or issuers, of the claims traded in them (the original demanders of funds) and two distinctive groups of agents operating as investors, or suppliers of funds. The two groups of funds suppliers have completely divergent motives. The first group aims to eliminate any undesirable risks of the traded assets and earn money on repackaging risks, the other actively seeks to take on those risks in exchange for uncertain compensation. The two groups are:

- *Hedgers* (dealers who aim to offset primary risks, be left with short-term or secondary risks, and earn spread from dealing).
- *Speculators* (investors who hold positions for longer periods without simultaneously holding positions that offset primary risks).

The claims traded in all financial markets can be delivered in three ways. The first is an immediate exchange of an asset for cash. The second is an agreement on the price to be paid with the exchange taking place at a predetermined time in the future. The last is a delivery in the future contingent on an outcome of a financial event (e.g., level of stock price or interest rate), with a fee paid upfront for the right of delivery. The three market segments based on the delivery type are:

- *Spot* or *cash markets* (immediate delivery).
- *Forwards markets* (mandatory future delivery or settlement).
- *Options markets* (contingent future delivery or settlement).

We focus on these structural distinctions to bring out the fact that all markets not only transfer funds from suppliers to users, but also risk from users to suppliers. They allow *risk transfer* or *risk sharing* between investors. The majority of the trading activity in today's market is motivated by risk transfer with the acquirer of risk receiving some form of sure or contingent compensation. The relative price of risk in the market is governed by a web of relatively simple arbitrage relationships that link all the markets. These allow market participants to assess instantaneously the relative attractiveness of various investments within each market segment or across all of them. Understanding these relationships is mandatory for anyone trying to make sense of the vast and complex web of today's markets.

1.2 RISK SHARING

All financial contracts, whether in the form of securities or not, can be viewed as bundles, or packages of unit payoff claims (mini-contracts), each for a specific date in the future and a specific set of outcomes. In financial economics, these are referred to as *state-contingent claims*.

Let us start with the simplest illustration: an insurance contract. A 1-year life insurance policy promising to pay $1,000,000 in the event of the insured's death can be viewed as a package of 365 daily claims (lottery tickets), each paying $1,000,000 if the holder dies on that day. The value of the policy upfront (the premium) is equal to the sum of the values of all the individual tickets. As the holder of the policy goes through the year, he can discard tickets that did not pay off, and the value of the policy to him diminishes until it reaches zero at the end of the coverage period.

Let us apply the concept of state-contingent claims to known securities. Suppose you buy one share of XYZ SA stock currently trading at €45 per share. You intend to hold the share for 2 years. To simplify things, we assume that the stock trades in increments of €0.05 (tick size). The minimum price is €0.00 (a limited liability company cannot have a negative value) and the maximum price is €500.00. The share of XYZ SA can be viewed as a package of claims. Each claim represents a contingent cash flow from selling the share for a particular price at a particular date and time in the future. We can arrange the potential price levels from €0.00 to €500.00 in increments of €0.05 to have overall 10,001 price levels. We arrange the dates from today to 2 years from today (our holding horizon). Overall we have 730 dates. The stock is equivalent to $10,001 \times 730$, or 7,300,730 claims. The easiest way to imagine this set of claims is as a rectangular chessboard where on the horizontal axis we have time and on the vertical the potential values the stock can take on (states of nature). The price of the stock today is equal to the sum of the values of all the claims (i.e., all the squares of the chessboard).

Table 1.1 Stock held for 2 years as a chessboard of contingent claims in two dimensions: time (days 1 through 730) and prices (0.00 through 500.00)

1	2	...	364	365	366	...	729	730	
500.00	500.00		500.00	500.00	500.00		500.00	500.00	500.00
499.95	499.95		499.95	499.95	499.95		499.95	499.95	499.95
499.90	499.90		499.90	499.90	499.90		499.90	499.90	499.90
499.85	499.85		499.85	499.85	499.85		499.85	499.85	499.85
		...							
60.35	60.35		60.35	60.35	60.35		60.35	60.35	60.35
60.30	60.30		60.30	60.30	60.30		60.30	60.30	60.30
60.25	60.25		60.25	60.25	60.25		60.25	60.25	60.25
60.20	60.20		60.20	60.20	60.20		60.20	60.20	60.20
60.15	60.15		60.15	60.15	60.15		60.15	60.15	60.15
60.10	60.10	...	60.10	60.10	60.10	...	60.10	60.10	60.10
60.05	60.05		60.05	60.05	60.05		60.05	60.05	60.05 *Stock*
60.00	60.00		60.00	60.00	60.00		60.00	60.00	60.00 *price*
59.95	59.95		59.95	59.95	59.95		59.95	59.95	59.95 *S*
59.90	59.90		59.90	59.90	59.90		59.90	59.90	59.90
59.85	59.85		59.85	59.85	59.85		59.85	59.85	59.85
59.80	59.80		59.80	59.80	59.80		59.80	59.80	59.80
		...							
0.45	0.45		0.45	0.45	0.45		0.45	0.45	0.45
0.40	0.40		0.40	0.40	0.40		0.40	0.40	0.40
0.35	0.35		0.35	0.35	0.35		0.35	0.35	0.35
0.30	0.30		0.30	0.30	0.30		0.30	0.30	0.30
0.25	0.25		0.25	0.25	0.25		0.25	0.25	0.25
0.20	0.20		0.20	0.20	0.20		0.20	0.20	0.20
0.15	0.15		0.15	0.15	0.15		0.15	0.15	0.15
0.10	0.10		0.10	0.10	0.10		0.10	0.10	0.10
0.05	0.05		0.05	0.05	0.05		0.05	0.05	0.05
0.00	0.00		0.00	0.00	0.00		0.00	0.00	0.00
1	*2*	...	*364*	*365*	*366*	...	*729*	*730*	

Days

A forward contract on XYZ SA's stock can be viewed as a subset of this rectangle. Suppose we enter into a contract today to purchase the stock 1 year from today for €60. We intend to hold the stock for 1 year after that. The forward can be viewed as $10{,}001 \times 365$ rectangle with the first 365 days' worth of claims taken out (i.e., we are left with the latter 365 columns of the board, the first 365 are taken out). The cash flow of each claim is equal to the difference between the stock price for that state of nature and the contract price of €60. A forward carries an obligation on both sides of the contract so some claims will have a positive value (stock is above €60) and some negative (stock is below €60).

Table 1.2 One-year forward buy at €60 of stock as a chessboard of contingent claims. Payoff in cells is equal to $S - 60$ for year 2. No payoff in year 1

1	2	...	364	365	366	...	729	730	Stock price S
0.00	0.00		0.00	0.00	440.00		440.00	440.00	500.00
0.00	0.00		0.00	0.00	439.95		439.95	439.95	499.95
0.00	0.00		0.00	0.00	439.90		439.90	439.90	499.90
0.00	0.00		0.00	0.00	439.85		439.85	439.85	499.85
0.00	0.00		0.00	0.00	0.35		0.35	0.35	60.35
0.00	0.00		0.00	0.00	0.30		0.30	0.30	60.30
0.00	0.00		0.00	0.00	0.25		0.25	0.25	60.25
0.00	0.00		0.00	0.00	0.20		0.20	0.20	60.20
0.00	0.00		0.00	0.00	0.15		0.15	0.15	60.15
0.00	0.00	...	0.00	0.00	0.10	...	0.10	0.10	60.10
0.00	0.00		0.00	0.00	0.05		0.05	0.05	60.05
0.00	0.00		0.00	0.00	0.00		0.00	0.00	60.00 price
0.00	0.00		0.00	0.00	−0.05		−0.05	−0.05	59.95
0.00	0.00		0.00	0.00	−0.10		−0.10	−0.10	59.90
0.00	0.00		0.00	0.00	−0.15		−0.15	−0.15	59.85
0.00	0.00		0.00	0.00	−0.20		−0.20	−0.20	59.80
0.00	0.00		0.00	0.00	−59.55		−59.55	−59.55	0.45
0.00	0.00		0.00	0.00	−59.60		−59.60	−59.60	0.40
0.00	0.00		0.00	0.00	−59.65		−59.65	−59.65	0.35
0.00	0.00		0.00	0.00	−59.70	...	−59.70	−59.70	0.30
0.00	0.00		0.00	0.00	−59.75		−59.75	−59.75	0.25
0.00	0.00		0.00	0.00	−59.80		−59.80	−59.80	0.20
0.00	0.00		0.00	0.00	−59.85		−59.85	−59.85	0.15
0.00	0.00		0.00	0.00	−59.90		−59.90	−59.90	0.10
0.00	0.00		0.00	0.00	−59.95		−59.95	−59.95	0.05
0.00	0.00		0.00	0.00	−60.00		−60.00	−60.00	0.00

S

Days

An American call option contract to buy XYZ SA's shares for €60 with an expiry 2 years from today (exercised only if the stock is above €60) can be represented as a $8,800 \times 730$ subset of our original rectangular $10,001 \times 730$ chessboard. This time, the squares corresponding to the stock prices of €60 or below are eliminated, because they have no value. The payoff of each claim is equal to the intrinsic (exercise) value of the call. As we will see later, the price of each claim today is equal to at least that.

Table 1.3   American call struck at €60 as a chessboard of contingent claims. Expiry 2 years. Payoff in cells is equal to $S - 60$ if $S > 60$

1	2	...	364	365	366	...	729	730	S
440.00	440.00		440.00	440.00	440.00		440.00	440.00	500.00
439.95	439.95		439.95	439.95	439.95		439.95	439.95	499.95
439.90	439.90		439.90	439.90	439.90		439.90	439.90	499.90
439.85	439.85		439.85	439.85	439.85		439.85	439.85	499.85
0.35	0.35		0.35	0.35	0.35		0.35	0.35	60.35
0.30	0.30		0.30	0.30	0.30		0.30	0.30	60.30
0.25	0.25		0.25	0.25	0.25		0.25	0.25	60.25
0.20	0.20		0.20	0.20	0.20		0.20	0.20	60.20
0.15	0.15		0.15	0.15	0.15		0.15	0.15	60.15
0.10	0.10	...	0.10	0.10	0.10	...	0.10	0.10	60.10
0.05	0.05		0.05	0.05	0.05		0.05	0.05	60.05 Stock
0.00	0.00		0.00	0.00	0.00		0.00	0.00	60.00 Price
0.00	0.00		0.00	0.00	0.00		0.00	0.00	59.95 S
0.00	0.00		0.00	0.00	0.00		0.00	0.00	59.90
0.00	0.00		0.00	0.00	0.00		0.00	0.00	59.85
0.00	0.00		0.00	0.00	0.00		0.00	0.00	59.80
0.00	0.00		0.00	0.00	0.00		0.00	0.00	0.45
0.00	0.00		0.00	0.00	0.00		0.00	0.00	0.40
0.00	0.00		0.00	0.00	0.00	...	0.00	0.00	0.35
0.00	0.00		0.00	0.00	0.00		0.00	0.00	0.30
0.00	0.00		0.00	0.00	0.00		0.00	0.00	0.25
0.00	0.00		0.00	0.00	0.00		0.00	0.00	0.20
0.00	0.00		0.00	0.00	0.00		0.00	0.00	0.15
0.00	0.00		0.00	0.00	0.00		0.00	0.00	0.10
0.00	0.00		0.00	0.00	0.00		0.00	0.00	0.05
0.00	0.00		0.00	0.00	0.00		0.00	0.00	0.00

Days

Spot securities (Chapters 2–5), forwards (Chapters 6–8), and options (Chapters 9–10) are discussed in detail in subsequent chapters. Here we briefly touch on the valuation of securities and state-contingent claims. The fundamental tenet of the valuation is that if we can value each claim (chessboard square) or small sets of claims (entire sections of the chessboard) in the package, then we can value the package as a whole. Conversely, if we can value a package, then often we are able to value smaller subsets of claims (through a "subtraction"). In addition, we are sometimes able to combine very disparate sets of claims (stocks and bonds) to form complex securities (e.g., convertible bonds). By knowing the value of the combination, we can infer the value of a subset (bullet bond).

In general, the value of a contingent claim does not stay constant over time. If the holder of the life insurance becomes sick during the year and the likelihood of his death increases, then likely the value of all claims increases. In the stock example, as information about the company's earnings prospects reaches the market, the price of the claims changes. Not all the claims in the package have to change in value by the same amount. An improvement in the earnings prospects for the company may be only short term. The policyholder's likelihood of death may increase for all the days immediately following his illness, but not for more distant dates. The prices of the individual claims fluctuate over time, and so does the value of the entire bundle. However, at any given moment of time, given all information available as of that moment, the sum of the values of the claims must be equal to the value of the package, the insurance policy, or the stock. We always restrict the valuation effort to here and now, knowing that we will have to repeat the exercise an instant later.

Let us fix the time to see what assumptions we can make about some of the claims in the package. In the insurance policy example, we may surmise that the value of the claims for far-out dates is greater than that for near dates, given that the patient is alive and well now, and, barring an accident, he is relatively more likely to take time to develop a life-threatening condition. In the stock example, we assigned the value of €0 to all claims in states with stock exceeding €500 over the next 2 years, as the likelihood of reaching these price levels is almost zero. We often assign the value of zero to claims for far dates (e.g., beyond 100 years), since the present value of those payoffs, even if they are large, is close to zero. We reduce a numerically infinite problem to a finite one. We cap the potential states under consideration, future dates, and times.

A good valuation model has to strive to make the values of the claims in a package independent of each other. In our life insurance policy example, the payoff depends on the person dying on that day and not on whether the person is dead or alive on a given day. In that setup, only one claim out of the whole set will pay. If we modeled the payoff to depend on being dead and not dying, all the claims after the morbid event date would have positive prices and would be contingent on each other. Sometimes, however, even with the best of efforts, it may be impossible to model the claims in a package as independent. If a payoff at a later date depends on whether the stock reached some level at an earlier date, the later claim's value depends on the prior one. A mortgage bond's payoff at a later date depends on whether the mortgage has not already been prepaid. This is referred to as a *survival* or *path-dependence* problem. Our imaginary, two-dimensional chessboards cannot handle path dependence and we ignore this dimension of risk throughout the book as it adds very little to our discussion.

Let us turn to the definition of risk sharing:

Definition   Risk sharing is a sale, explicit or through a side contract, of all or some of the state-contingent claims in the package to another party.

In real life, risk sharing takes on many forms. The owner of the XYZ share may decide to sell a covered call on the stock (see Chapter 10). If he sells an American-style call struck at €60 with an expiry date of 2 years from today, he gives the buyer the right to purchase the share at €60 from him even if XYZ trades higher in the market (e.g., at €75). The covered call seller is choosing to cap his potential payoff from the stock at €60 in exchange for an upfront fee (option premium) he receives. This is the same as exchanging the squares corresponding to price levels above €60 (with values between €60 and €500) for squares with a flat payoff of €60.

Table 1.4   Stock plus short American call struck at €60 as a chessboard of contingent claims. Payoff in cells is equal to 60 if $S > 60$ and to S if $S < 60$

1	2	...	364	365	366	...	729	730	Stock price S
60.00	60.00		60.00	60.00	60.00		60.00	60.00	500.00
60.00	60.00		60.00	60.00	60.00		60.00	60.00	499.95
60.00	60.00		60.00	60.00	60.00		60.00	60.00	499.90
60.00	60.00		60.00	60.00	60.00		60.00	60.00	499.85
				...					
60.00	60.00		60.00	60.00	60.00		60.00	60.00	60.35
60.00	60.00		60.00	60.00	60.00		60.00	60.00	60.30
60.00	60.00		60.00	60.00	60.00		60.00	60.00	60.25
60.00	60.00		60.00	60.00	60.00		60.00	60.00	60.20
60.00	60.00		60.00	60.00	60.00		60.00	60.00	60.15
60.00	60.00	...	60.00	60.00	60.00	...	60.00	60.00	60.05
60.00	60.00		60.00	60.00	60.00		60.00	60.00	60.00
59.95	59.95		59.95	59.95	59.95		59.95	59.95	59.95
59.90	59.90		59.90	59.90	59.90		59.90	59.90	59.90
59.85	59.85		59.85	59.85	59.85		59.85	59.85	59.85
59.80	59.80		59.80	59.80	59.80		59.80	59.80	59.80
...				...				...	
0.45	0.45		0.45	0.45	0.45		0.45	0.45	0.45
0.40	0.40		0.40	0.40	0.40		0.40	0.40	0.40
0.35	0.35		0.35	0.35	0.35		0.35	0.35	0.35
0.30	0.30		0.30	0.30	0.30	...	0.30	0.30	0.30
0.25	0.25		0.25	0.25	0.25		0.25	0.25	0.25
0.20	0.20		0.20	0.20	0.20		0.20	0.20	0.20
0.15	0.15		0.15	0.15	0.15		0.15	0.15	0.15
0.10	0.10		0.10	0.10	0.10		0.10	0.10	0.10
0.05	0.05		0.05	0.05	0.05		0.05	0.05	0.05
0.00	0.00		0.00	0.00	0.00		0.00	0.00	0.00

Days

Another example of risk sharing can be a *hedge* of a corporate bond with a risk-free government bond. A hedge is a sale of a package of state-contingent claims against a primary position which eliminates all the essential risk of that position. Only a sale of a security that is identical in all aspects to the primary position can eliminate all the risk. A hedge always leaves some risk *unhedged*! Let us examine a very common hedge of a corporate with a government bond. An institutional trader purchases a 10-year 5% coupon bond issued by XYZ Corp. In an effort to eliminate interest rate risk, the trader simultaneously shorts a 10-year 4.5% coupon government bond. The size of the short is duration-matched to the principal amount of the corporate bond. As Chapter 5 explains, this guarantees that for small parallel movements in the interest rates, the changes in the values of the two positions are identical but opposite in sign. If interest rates rise, the loss on the corporate bond holding will be offset by the gain on the shorted government bond. If interest rates decline, the gain on the corporate bond will be offset by the loss on the government bond. The trader, in effect, speculates that the credit spread on the corporate bond will decline. Irrespective of whether interest rates rise or fall, whenever the XYZ credit spread declines, the trader gains since the corporate bond's price goes up more or goes down less than that of the government bond. Whenever the credit standing of XYZ worsens and the spread rises, the trader suffers a loss. The corporate bond is exposed over time to two dimensions of risk: interest rates and corporate spread. Our chessboard representing the corporate bond becomes a large rectangular cube with time, interest rate, and credit spread as dimensions. The government bond hedge eliminates all potential payoffs along the interest rate axis, reducing the cube to a plane, with only time and credit spread as dimensions. Practically any hedge position discussed in this book can be thought of in the context of a multi-dimensional cube defined by time and risk axes. The hedge eliminates a dimension or a subspace from the cube.

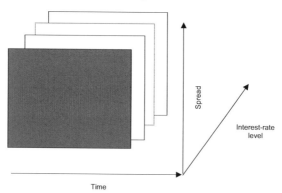

Figure 1.1 Reduction of one risk dimension through a hedge. Corporate hedged with a government.

1.3   THE STRUCTURE OF FINANCIAL MARKETS

Most people view financial markets like a Saturday bazaar. Buyers spend their cash to acquire paper claims on future earnings, coupon interest, or insurance payouts. If they buy good claims, their value goes up and they can sell them for more; if they buy bad ones, their value goes down and they lose money.

When probed a little more on how markets are structured, most finance and economics professionals provide a seemingly more complete description, adding detail about who buys and sells what and why in each market. The respondent is likely to inform us that businesses need funds in various forms of equity and debt. They issue stock, lease- and asset-backed bonds, unsecured debentures, sell short-term commercial paper, or rely on bank loans. Issuers get the needed funds in exchange for a promise to pay interest payments or dividends in the future. The legal claims on business assets are purchased by investors, individual and institutional, who spend cash today to get more cash in the future (i.e., they *invest*). Securities are also bought and sold by governments, banks, real estate investment trusts, leasing companies, and others. The cash-for-paper exchanges are immediate. Investors who want to leverage themselves can borrow cash to buy more securities, but through that they themselves become issuers of broker or bank loans. Both issuers and investors live and die with the markets. When stock prices increase, investors who have bought stocks gain; when stock prices decline, they lose. New investors have to "buy high" when share prices rise, but can "buy low" when share prices decline. The decline benefits past issuers who "sold high". The rise hurts them since they got little money for the previously sold stock and now have to deliver good earnings. In fixed income markets, when interest rates fall, investors gain as the value of debt obligations they hold increases. The issuers suffer as the rates they pay on the existing obligations are higher than the going cost of money. When interest rates rise, investors lose as the value of debt obligations they hold decreases. The issuers gain as the rates they pay on the existing obligations are lower than the going cost of money.

In this view of the markets, both sides—the issuers and the investors—*speculate* on the direction of the markets. In a sense, the word *investment* is a euphemism for *speculation*. The direction of the market given the position held determines whether the investment turns out good or bad. Most of the time, current issuers and investors hold opposite positions (long vs. short): when investors gain, issuers lose, and vice versa. Current and new participants may also have opposite interests. When equities rise or interest rates fall, existing investors gain and existing issuers lose, but new investors suffer and new issuers gain.

The investor is exposed to market forces as long as he holds the security. He can enhance or mitigate his exposure, or *risk*, by concentrating or diversifying the types of assets held. An equity investor may hold shares of companies from different industrial sectors. A pension fund may hold some positions in domestic equities and some positions in domestic and foreign bonds to allocate risk exposure to stocks, interest rates, and currencies. The risk is "good" or "bad" depending on whether the investor is *long* or *short* on exposure. An investor who has shorted a stock gains when the share price declines. A homeowner with an adjustable mortgage gains when interest rates decline (he is short interest rates) as the rate he pays resets lower, while a homeowner with a fixed mortgage loses as he is "stuck" paying a high rate (he is long interest rates).

While this standard description of the financial markets appears to be very comprehensive, it is rather like a two-dimensional portrait of a multi-dimensional object. The missing dimension here is the *time of delivery*. The standard view focuses exclusively on spot markets. Investors purchase securities from issuers or other investors and pay for them at the time of the purchase. They modify the risks the purchased investments expose them to by diversifying their portfolios or holding shorts against longs in the same or similar assets. Most tend to be speculators as the universe of hedge securities they face is fairly limited.

Let us introduce the time of delivery into this picture. That is, let us relax the assumption that all trades (i.e., exchanges of securities for cash) are immediate. Consider an equity investor who agrees today to buy a stock for a certain market price, but will deliver cash and receive the stock 1 year from today. The investor is entering into a *forward buy* transaction. His risk profile is drastically different from that of a spot buyer. Like the spot stock buyer, he is exposed to the price of the stock, but his exposure does not start till 1 year from now. He does not care if the stock drops in value as long as it recovers by the delivery date. He also does not benefit from the temporary appreciation of the stock compared with the spot buyer who could sell the stock immediately. In our time-risk chessboard with time and stock price on the axes, the forward buy looks like a spot buy with a subplane demarcated by today and 1 year from today taken out. If we ignore the time value of money, the area above the current price line corresponds to "good" risk (i.e., a gain), and the area below to "bad" risk (i.e., a loss). A forward sell would cover the same subplane, but the "good" and the "bad" areas would be reversed.

Market participants can buy and sell not just spot but also forward. For the purpose of our discussion, it does not matter if, at the future delivery time, what takes place is an actual exchange of securities for cash or just a mark-to-market settlement in cash (see Chapter 6). If the stock is trading at €75 in the spot market, whether the parties to a prior €60 forward transaction exchange cash (€60) for stock (one share) or simply settle the difference in value with a payment of €15 is quite irrelevant, as long as the stock is liquid enough so that it can be sold for €75 without any loss. Also, for our purposes, futures contracts can be treated as identical to forwards, even though they involve a daily settlement regimen and may never result in the physical delivery of the underlying commodity or stock basket.

Let us now further complicate the standard view of the markets by introducing the concept of *contingent delivery time*. A trade, or an exchange of a security for cash, agreed on today is not only delayed into the future, but is also made contingent on a future event. The simplest example is an insurance contract. The payment of a benefit on a $1,000,000 life insurance policy takes place only on the death of the insured person. The amount of the benefit is agreed on and fixed upfront between the policyholder and the issuing company. It can be increased only if the policyholder pays additional premium. Hazard insurance (fire, auto, flood) is slightly different from life in that the amount of the benefit depends on the "size" of the future event. The greater the damage is, the greater the payment is. An option contract is very similar to a hazard insurance policy. The amount of the benefit follows a specific formula that depends on the value of the underlying financial variable in the future (see Chapters 9–10). For example, a put option on the S&P 100 index traded on an exchange in Chicago pays the difference between the selected strike and the value of the index at some future date, times $100 per point, but only if the index goes down below that strike price level. The buyer thus insures himself against the index going down and the more the index goes down the more benefit he obtains from his put option, just as if he held a fire insurance policy. Another example is a *cap* on an interest rate index that provides the holder with a periodic payment every time the underlying interest rate goes above a certain level. Borrowers use caps to protect themselves against interest rate hikes.

Options are used not only for obtaining protection, which is only one form of risk sharing, but also for risk taking (i.e., providing specific risk protection for upfront compensation). A bank borrower relying on a revolving credit line with an interest rate defined as some spread over the U.S. prime rate or the 3-month C-LIBOR (London interbank offered rate) rate can sell *floors* to offset the cost of the borrowing. When the index rate goes down, he is required to make periodic payments to the floor buyer which depends on the magnitude of the interest rate decline. He willingly accepts that risk because, when rates go down and he has to make the floor payments, the interest he is charged on the revolving loan also declines. In effect, he fixes his minimum borrowing rate in exchange for an upfront premium receipt.

Options are not the only packages of contingent claims traded in today's markets. In fact, the feature of contingent delivery is embedded in many commonly traded securities. Buyers of convertible bonds exchange their bonds for shares when interest rates and/or stock prices are high, making the post-conversion equity value higher than the present value of the remaining interest on the unconverted bond. Issuers call their outstanding callable bonds when interest rates decline below a level at which the value of those bonds is higher than the call price. Adjustable mortgages typically contain periodic caps that prevent the interest rate and thus the monthly payment charged to the homeowner from changing too rapidly from period to period. Many bonds have credit covenants attached to them which require the issuing company to maintain certain financial ratios, and non-compliance triggers automatic repayment or default. Car lease agreements give the lessees the right to purchase the automobile at the end of the lease period for a pre-specified residual value. Lessees sometimes exercise those rights when the residual value is sufficiently lower than the market price of the vehicle. In many countries, including the U.S., homeowners with fixed-rate mortgages can prepay their loans partially or fully at any time without penalty. This feature allows homeowners to refinance their loans with new ones when interest rates drop by a significant enough margin. The cash flows from the original fixed-rate loans are thus contingent on interest rates staying high. Other examples abound.

The key to understanding these types of securities is the ability to break them down into simpler components: spot, forward, and contingent delivery. These components may trade separately in the institutional markets, but they are most likely bundled together for retail customers or original (primary market) acquirers. Not uncommonly, they are unbundled and rebundled several times during their lives.

Proposition All financial markets evolve to have three structural components: the market for spot securities, the market for forwards and futures, and the contingent securities market which includes options and other derivatives.

All financial markets eventually evolve to have activity in three areas: spot trading for immediate delivery, trading with forward delivery, and trading with contingent forward delivery. Most of the activity of the last two forms is reserved for large institutions which is why most people are unaware of them. Yet their existence is necessary for the smooth functioning of the spot markets. The trading for forward and contingent forward delivery allows dynamic risk sharing for holders of cash securities who trade in and out of contracts tied to different dates and future uncertain events. This risk sharing activity, by signaling the constantly changing price of risk, in turn facilitates the flow of the fundamental information that determines the "bundled" value of the spot securities. In a way, the spot securities that we are all familiar with are the most complicated ones from the informational content perspective. Their value reflects all available information about the financial prospects of the entity that issued them and expectations about the broad market, and is equal to the sum of the values of all state-contingent claims that can be viewed as informational units. The value of forwards and option-like contracts is tied to more narrow information subsets. These contracts have an expiry date that is short relative to the underlying security and are tailored to specific dimension of risk. Their existence allows the unbundling of the information contained in the spot security. This function is extremely desirable to holders of cash assets as it offers them a way to sell off undesirable risks and acquire desirable ones at various points in time. If you own a bond issued by a tobacco company, you may be worried that legal proceedings against the company may adversely affect the credit spread and thus the value of the bond you hold. You could sell the bond spot and repurchase it forward with the contract date set far into the future. You could purchase a spread-related option or a put option on the bond, or you could sell calls on the bond. All of these activities would allow you to share the risks of the bond with another party to tailor the duration of the risk sharing to your needs.

1.4   ARBITRAGE: PURE VS. RELATIVE VALUE

In this section, we introduce the notion of *relative value arbitrage* which drives the trading behavior of financial firms irrespective of the market they are engaged in. Relative arbitrage takes the concept of *pure arbitrage* beyond its technical definition of riskless profit. In it, all primary market risks are eliminated, but some secondary market exposures are deliberately left unhedged.

Arbitrage is defined in most textbooks as riskless, instantaneous profit. It occurs when the *law of one price*, which states that the same item cannot sell at two different prices at the same time, is violated. The same stock cannot trade for one price at one exchange and for a different price at another unless there are fees, taxes, etc. If it does, traders will buy it on the exchange where it sells for less and sell it on the one where it sells for more. Buying Czech korunas for British pounds cannot be more or less expensive than buying dollars for pounds and using dollars to buy korunas. If one can get more korunas for pounds by buying dollars first, no one will buy korunas for pounds directly. On top of that, anyone with access to both markets will convert pounds into korunas via dollars and sell korunas back directly for pounds to realize an instantaneous and riskless profit. This strategy is a very simple example of *pure arbitrage* in the spot currency markets. More complicated pure arbitrage involves forward and contingent markets. It can take a *static* form, where the trade is put on at the outset and liquidated once at a future date (e.g., trading forward rate agreements against spot LIBORs for two different terms, see Chapter 6), or a *dynamic* one, in which the trader commits to a series of steps that eliminate all directional market risks and ensures virtually riskless profit on completion of these steps. For example, a bond dealer purchases a callable bond from the issuer, buys a swaption from a third party to offset the call risk, and delta-hedges the rate risk by shorting some bullet swaps. He guarantees himself a riskless profit provided that neither the issuer nor the swaption seller defaults. Later chapters abound in detailed examples of both static and dynamic arbitrage.

Definition   Pure arbitrage is defined as generating riskless profit today by statically or dynamically matching current and future obligations to exactly offset each, inclusive of incurring known financing costs.

Not surprisingly, opportunities for pure arbitrage in today's ultra-sophisticated markets are limited. Most institutions' money-making activities rely on the principle of *relative value arbitrage*. Hedge funds and proprietary trading desks of large financial firms, commonly referred to as *arb desks*, employ extensively relative arbitrage techniques. Relative value arbitrage consists of a broadly defined hedge in which a close substitute for a particular risk dimension of the primary security is found and the law of one price is applied as if the substitute was a perfect match. Typically, the position in the substitute is opposite to that in the primary security in order to offset the most significant or unwanted risk inherent in the primary security. Other risks are left purposely unhedged, but if the substitute is well chosen, they are controllable (except in highly leveraged positions). Like pure arbitrage, relative arbitrage can be both *static* and *dynamic*. Let us consider examples of static relative arbitrage.

Suppose you buy $100 million of the 30-year U.S. government bond. At the same time you sell (short) $102 million of the 26-year bond. The amounts $100 and $102 are chosen through "duration matching" (see Chapters 2 and 5) which ensures that when interest rates go up or down by a few basis points the gains on one position exactly offset the losses on the other. The only way the combined position makes or loses money is when interest rates do not change in parallel (i.e., the 30-year rates change by more or less than the 26-year rates). The combined position is not risk-free; it is speculative, but only in a secondary risk factor. Investors hardly distinguish between 30- and 26-year rates; they worry about the overall level of rates. The two rates tend to move closely together. The relative arbitrageur bets that they will diverge.

The bulk of swap trading in the world (Chapter 8) relies on static relative arbitrage. An interest rate swap dealer agrees to pay a fixed coupon stream to a corporate customer, himself an issuer of a fixed-rate bond. The dealer hedges by buying a fixed coupon government bond. He eliminates any exposure to interest rate movements as coupon receipts from the government bond offset the swap payments, but is left with swap spread risk. If the credit quality of the issuer deteriorates, the swap becomes "unfair" and the combined position has a negative present value to the dealer.

Dynamic relative arbitrage is slightly more complicated in that the hedge must be rebalanced continuously according to very specific computable rules. A seller of a 3-year over-the-counter (OTC) equity call may hedge by buying 3- and 6-month calls on the exchange and shorting some of the stock. He then must rebalance the number of shares he is short on a daily basis as the price of those shares fluctuates. This so-called delta hedge (see Chapters 9–10) eliminates exposure to the price risk. The main unhedged exposure is to the implied volatility differences between the options sold and bought. In the preceding static swap example, the swap dealer may elect not to match the cash flows exactly on each swap he enters into; instead, he may take positions in a small number of "benchmark" bonds in order to offset the cash flows in bulk. This shortcut, however, will require him to dynamically rebalance the portfolio of bonds.

This book explains the functioning of financial markets by bringing out pure and relative value arbitrage linkages between different market segments. Our examples appear complicated as they involve futures, options, and other derivatives, but they all rely on the same simple principle of seeking profit through selective risk elimination.

Definition   Relative value arbitrage is defined as generating profit today by statically or dynamically matching current and future obligations to nearly offset each other, net of incurring closely estimable financing costs.

To an untrained eye, the difference between relative value arbitrage and speculation is tenuous; to a professional, the two are easily discernible. A popular equity trading strategy called *pairs trading* (see Chapter 5) is a good case in point. The strategy of buying Pfizer (PFE) stock and selling GlaxoSmithKline (GSK) is pure speculation. One can argue that both companies are in pharmaceuticals, both are large, and both with similar R&D budgets and new drug pipelines. The specific risks of the two companies, however, are quite different and they cannot be considered close substitutes. Buying Polish zlotys with British pounds and selling Czech korunas for British pounds is also an example of speculation, not of relative value arbitrage. Polish zlotys and Czech korunas are not close substitutes. An in-between case, but clearly on the speculative side, is called a *basis trade*. An airline needing to lock in the future prices of jet fuel, instead of entering into a long-term contract with a refiner, buys a series of crude oil futures, the idea being that supply shocks that cause oil prices to rise affect jet fuel in the same way. When prices increase, the airline pays higher prices for jet fuel, but profits from oil futures offset those increases, leaving the total cost of acquiring jet fuel unchanged. Buying oil futures is appealing as it allows liquidating the protection scheme when prices decline instead of rising or getting out halfway through an increase. This trade is not uncommon, but it exposes the airline to the *basis* risk. When supply shocks take place at the refinery level not the oil delivery level, spot jet fuel prices may increase more rapidly than crude oil futures.

Most derivatives dealers espouse the relative value arbitrage principle. They sell options and at the same time buy or sell the underlying stocks, bonds, or mortgages in the right proportions to exactly offset the value changes of the sold option and the position in the underlying financial asset. Their lives are, however, quite complicated in that they have to repeat the exercise every day as long as the options they sold are alive, even if they do not sell additional options. This is because the appropriate proportions of the underlyings they need to buy or sell change every day. These proportions or hedge ratios depend on changing market factors. It is these market factors that are the secondary risks the dealers are exposed to. The dynamic rebalancing of the positions serves to create a close substitute to the options sold, but it does not offset all the risks.

Relative value arbitrage in most markets relies on a building block of a static or dynamic *cash-and-carry* trade. The static version of the cash-and-carry trade (introduced in Chapters 6–7) consists typically of a spot purchase (for *cash*) and a forward sell, or the reverse. The dynamic trade (introduced in Chapter 9), like in the preceding option example, consists of a series of spot purchases or sales at different dates and a contingent payoff at the forward date. The glue that ties the spot and the forward together is the cost of financing, or the *carry*, of the borrowing to buy spot or lending after a spot sale. Even the most complicated structured derivative transactions are combinations of such building blocks across different markets. When analyzing such trades, focusing on institutional and market infrastructure details in each market can only becloud this basic structure of arbitrage. This book clarifies the essence of such trades by emphasizing common elements. It also explains why most institutions rely on the interaction of dealers on large trading floors to take advantage of inter-market arbitrages. The principle of arbitrage is exploited not only to show what motivates traders to participate *in* each market (program trading of stock index futures vs. stock baskets, fixed coupon stripping in bonds, triangular arbitrage in currencies, etc.), but also what drives the risk arbitrage *between* markets (simultaneous trades in currencies in money markets, hedging mortgage servicing contracts with swap options, etc.).

Many readers view *no-arbitrage conditions* found in finance textbooks as strict mathe-matical constructs. It should be clear from the above discussion that they are not mathematical at all. These equations do not represent the will of God, like those pertaining to gravity or thermodynamics in physics. They stem from and are continu-ously ensured by the most basic human characteristic: greed. Dealers tirelessly look to discover pure and relative value arbitrage (i.e., opportunities to buy something at one price and to sell a disguised version of the same thing for another price). By executing trades to take advantage of the temporary deviations from these paramount rules, they eliminate them by moving prices back in line where riskless money cannot be made and, by extension, the equations are satisfied.

In this book, all the mathematical formulae are traced back to the financial transac-tions that motivate them. We overemphasize the difference between speculation and pure arbitrage in order to bring out the notion of relative value arbitrage (sometimes also referred to as *risk arbitrage*). Apart from the ever-shrinking commissions, most traders earn profit from "spread"—a reward for relative value risk arbitrage. A swap trader, who fixes the borrowing rate for a corporate client, hedges by selling Treasury bonds. He engages in a relative value trade (swaps vs. government bonds) which exposes him to swap spread movements. A bank that borrows by opening new checking deposits and lends by issuing mortgages eliminates the risk of parallel interest rate movements (which perhaps affect deposit and mortgage rates to the same degree), but leaves itself exposed to yield curve tilts (non-parallel movements) or default risk. In all these cases, the largest risks (the exposure to interest rate changes) are hedged out, and the dealer is left exposed to secondary ones (swap spread, default).

Most forms of what is conventionally labeled as *investment* under our definition qualify as *speculation*. A stock investor who does not hedge, or risk-share in some way, is exposed to the primary price risk of his asset. It is expected in our lives that, barring short-term fluctuations, over time the value of our assets increases. The economy in general grows, productivity increases, and our incomes rise as we acquire more experience. We find ourselves having to save for future consumption, family, and retirement. Most of the time, often indirectly through pension and mutual funds, we "invest" in real estate, stocks, and bonds. Knowingly or not, we speculate. Financial institutions, as their assets grow, find themselves in the same position. Recognizing that fact, they put their capital to use in new products and services. They speculate on their success. However, a lot of today's institutional dealers' trading activity is *not* driven by the desire to bet their institutions' capital on buy-low/sell-high speculative ventures. Institutional traders do not want to take primary risks by speculating on markets to go up or down; instead, they hedge the primary risks by simultaneously buying and selling or borrowing and lending in spot, forward, and option markets. They leave themselves exposed only to secondary "spread" risks. Well-managed financial institutions are compensated for taking those secondary risks. Even the most apt business school students often misunderstand this fine distinction between speculation and relative value arbitrage. CEOs often do too. Nearly everyone has heard of the Barings, IG Metallgesellschaft, and Orange County fiascos of the 1990s. History is filled with examples of financial institutions gone bankrupt as a result of gambling.

Institutional trading floors are designed to best take advantage of relative arbitrage within each market. They are arranged around individual *trading desks*, surrounded by associated marketing and clearing teams, each covering customers within a specific market segment. Trading desks that are likely to buy each other's products are placed next to each other. Special *proprietary desks* (for short, called *prop* or *arb desks*) deal with many customer desks of the same firm or other firms and many outside customers in various markets. Their job is to specifically focus on relative value trades or outright speculation across markets. The distinction between the two types of desks—customer vs. proprietary—is in constant flux as some markets expand and some shrink. Trading desks may collaborate in the types of transactions they engage in. For example, a money market desk arranges an issuance of short-term paper whose coupon depends on a stock index. It then arranges a trade between the customer and its swap desk to alter the interest rate exposure profile and between the customer and the equity derivatives desk to eliminate the customer's exposure to equity risk. The customer ends up with low cost of financing and no equity risks. The dealer firm lays off the swap and equity risk with another institution. Hundreds of such intermarket transactions take place every day in the dealing houses in London, New York, and Hong Kong.

Commercial banks operate on the same principle. They bundle mortgage, car loan, or credit card receipts into securities with multiple risk characteristics and sell the unwanted ones to other banks. They eliminate the prepayment risk in their mortgage portfolios by buying swaptions from swap dealers.

1.5 FINANCIAL INSTITUTIONS: ASSET TRANSFORMERS AND BROKER-DEALERS

Financial institutions can be broadly divided into two categories based on their *raison d'être*:

- Asset transformers.
- Broker-dealers.

The easiest way to identify them is by examining their balance sheets. Asset transformers' assets have different legal characteristics from their liabilities. Broker-dealers may have different mixes on the two sides of the balance sheet, but the categories tend to be the same.

An asset transformer is an institution that invests in certain assets, but issues liabilities in the form designed to appeal to a particular group of customers. The best example is a commercial bank. On the asset side, a bank issues consumer (mortgage, auto) and business loans, invests in bonds, etc. The main form of liability it issues is checking accounts, saving accounts, and certificates of deposit (CDs). Customers specifically desire these vehicles as they facilitate their day-to-day transactions and often offer security of government insurance against the bank's insolvency. For example, in the U.S. the Federal Deposit Insurance Corporation (FDIC) guarantees all deposits up to $100,000 per customer per bank. The bank's customers do not want to invest directly in the bank's assets. This would be quite inconvenient as they would have to buy and sell these "bulky" assets frequently to meet their normal living expenditures. From a retail customer's perspective, the bank's assets often have undesirably long maturity which entails price risk if they are sold quickly, and they are offered only in large denominations. In order to attract funding, the bank repackages its mortgage and business loan assets into liabilities, such as checking accounts and CDs, which have more palatable characteristics: immediate cash machine access, small denomination, short maturity, and deposit insurance. Another example of an asset transformer is a mutual fund (or a unit investment trust). A mutual fund invests in a diversified portfolio of stocks, bonds, or money market instruments, but issues to its customers small denomination, easily redeemable participation shares (unit trust certificates) and offers a variety of services, like daily net asset value calculation, fund redemption and exchange, or a limited check-writing ability. Other large asset transformers are insurance companies that invest in real estate, stocks, and bonds (assets), but issue policies with payouts tied to life or hardship events (liabilities). Asset transformers are subject to special regulations and government supervision. Banks require bank charters to operate, are subject to central bank oversight, and must belong to deposit insurance schemes. Mutual fund regulation is aimed at protecting small investors (e.g., as provided for by the Investment Company Act in the U.S.). Insurance companies rates are often sanctioned by state insurance boards. The laws in all these cases set specific forms of legal liabilities asset transformers may create and sound investment guidelines they must follow (e.g., percentage of assets in a particular category). Asset transformers are compensated largely for their role in repackaging their assets with undesirable features into liabilities with customer-friendly features. That very activity automatically introduces great risks into their operations. Bank liabilities have much shorter duration (checking accounts) than their assets (fixed-rate mortgages). If interest rates do not move in parallel, the spread they earn (interest differential between rates charged on loans and rates paid on deposits) fluctuates and can be negative. They pursue relative value arbitrage in order to reduce this *duration gap*.

Broker-dealers do not change the legal and functional form of the securities they own and owe. They buy stocks, currencies, mortgage bonds, leases, etc. and they sell the same securities. As dealers they own them temporarily before they sell them, exposing themselves to temporary market risks. As brokers they simply match buyers and sellers. Broker-dealers participate in both primary sale and secondary resale transactions. They transfer securities from the original issuers to buyers as well as from existing owners to new owners. The first is known as *investment banking* or *corporate finance*, the latter as *dealing* or *trading*. The purest forms of broker-dealers exist in the U.S. and Japan where laws have historically separated them from other forms of banking. Most securities firms in those two countries are pure broker-dealers (investment banking, institutional trading, and retail brokerage) with an addition of asset-transforming businesses of asset management and lending. In most of continental Europe, financial institutions are conglomerates commonly referred to as *universal banks* as they combine both functions. In recent years, with the repeal of the Glass–Steagal Act in the U.S. and the wave of consolidations taking place on both sides of the Atlantic, U.S. firms have the possibility to converge more closely to the European model. Broker-dealers tend to be much less regulated than asset transformers and the focus of laws tends to be on small investor protection (securities disclosure, fiduciary responsibilities of advisers, etc.).

Asset transformers and broker-dealers compete for each other's business. Securities firms engage in secured and unsecured lending and offer check-writing in their brokerage accounts. They also compete with mutual funds by creating bundled or indexed securities designed to offer the same benefits of diversification. In the U.S., the trading on the American Stock Exchange is dominated by ETFs (exchange-traded funds), HOLDRs (holding company despositary receipts), Cubes, etc., all of which are designed to compete with index funds, instead of ordinary shares. Commercial banks securitize their credit card and mortgage loans to trade them out of their balance sheets. The overall trend has been toward *disintermediation* (i.e., securitization of previously transformed assets into more standardized tradeable packages). As burdensome regulations fall and costs of securitization plummet, retail customers are increasingly given access to markets previously reserved for institutions.

1.6 PRIMARY AND SECONDARY MARKETS

From the welfare perspective, the primary role of financial markets has always been to transfer funds between suppliers of excess funds and their users. The users include businesses that produce goods and services in the economy, households that demand mortgage and consumer loans, governments that build roads and schools, financial institutions, and many others. All of these economic agents are involved in productive activities that are deemed economically and socially desirable. Throughout most of history, it was bankers and banks who made that transfer of funds possible by accepting funds from depositors and lending them to kings, commercial ventures, and others. With the transition from feudalism to capitalism came the new vehicles of performing that transfer in the form of shares in limited liability companies and bonds issued by sovereigns and corporations. Stock, bond, and commodity *exchanges* were formed to allow original investors in these securities to efficiently share the risks of these instruments with new investors. This in turn induced many suppliers of funds to become investors in the first place as the risks of holding "paper" were diminished. "Paper" could be easily sold and funds recovered. A specialized class of traders emerged who dealt only with trading "paper" on the exchanges or OTC. To them paper was and is faceless. At the same time, the old role of finding new productive ventures in need of capital has shifted from bankers to *investment bankers* who, instead of granting loans, specialized in creating new shares and bonds for sale to investors for the first time. To investment bankers, paper is far from faceless. Prior to the launch of any issue, the main job of an investment banker or his *corporate finance* staff, like that of a loan banker, is to evaluate the issuing company's business, its financial condition and to prepare a valuation analysis for the offered security.

As we stated before, financial markets for securities are organized into two segments defined by the parties to a securities transaction:

- Primary markets.
- Secondary markets.

This segregation exists only in securities, not in private party contracts like OTC derivatives. In private contracts, the primary market issuers also tend to be the secondary market traders, and the secondary market operates through assignments and mark-to-market settlements rather than through resale.

In *primary markets*, the suppliers of funds transfer their excess funds directly to the users of funds through a purchase of securities. An investment banker acts as an intermediary, but the paper-for-cash exchange is between the issuing company and the investor. The shares are sold either publicly, through an initial public offering or a seasoned offering, or privately through a *private placement* with "qualified investors", typically large institutions. Securities laws of the country in which the shares are sold spell out all the steps the investment bank must take in order to bring the issue to market. For example, in the U.S. the shares must be registered with the Securities and Exchange Commission (SEC), a prospectus must be presented to new investors prior to a sale, etc. Private placements follow different rules, the presumption being that large qualified investors need less protection than retail investors. In the U.S. they are governed by Rule 144-A which allows their subsequent secondary trading through a system similar to an exchange.

In *secondary markets*, securities are bought and sold only by investors without the involvement of the original user of funds. Secondary markets can be organized as exchanges or as OTC networks of dealers connected by phone or computer, or a hybrid of the two. The Deutsche Börse and the New York Stock Exchange (NYSE) are examples of organized exchanges. It is worth noting however that exchanges differ greatly from each other. The NYSE gives access to trade flow information to human market-makers called *specialists* to ensure the continuity of the market-making in a given stock, while the Tokyo Stock Exchange is an electronic market where continuity is not guaranteed, but no dealer can earn monopoly rents from private information about buys and sells (see Chapter 4). Corporate and government bond trading (see Chapter 3) are the best examples of OTC markets. There, like in swap and currency markets, all participants are dealers who trade one on one for their own account. They maintain contact with each other over a phone and computer network, and jointly police the fair conduct rules through industry associations. For example, in the OTC derivatives markets, the International Swap Dealers Association (ISDA) standardizes the terminology used in quoting the terms and rates, and formalizes the documentation used in confirming trades for a variety of swap and credit derivative agreements. The best example of a hybrid between an exchange and an OTC market is the NASDAQ in the U.S. The exchange is only virtual as participants are connected through a computer system. Access is limited to members only and all members are dealers.

Developing countries strive to create smooth functioning secondary markets. They often rush to open stock exchanges even though there may only be a handful of companies large enough to have a significant number of dispersed shareholders. In order to improve the liquidity of trading, nascent exchanges limit the number of exchange seats to very few, the operating hours to sometimes only one per day, etc. All these efforts are aimed at funneling all buyers and sellers into one venue. This parallels the goals of the specialist system on the NYSE. Developing countries' governments strive to establish a well-functioning government bond market. They start by issuing short-term obligations and introduce longer maturities as quickly as the market will have an appetite for them.

The main objective in establishing these secondary trading places is to lower the cost of raising capital in the primary markets by offering the primary market investors a large outlet for risk sharing. Unless investors are convinced that they can easily get in and out of these securities, they will not buy the equities and bonds offered by the issuers (local businesses and governments) in the first place. This "tail wag the dog" pattern of creating secondary markets first is very typical not only for lesser developed nations, but is quite common in introducing brand new risk classes into the market-place. In the late 1980s, Michael Milken's success in selling highly speculative high-yield bonds to investors relied primarily in creating a secondary OTC market by assuring active market-making by his firm Drexel Burnham Lambert. Similarly, prior to its collapse in 2002, Enron's success in originating energy forwards and contingent con-tracts was driven by Enron's ability to establish itself as a virtual exchange of energy derivatives (with Enron acting as the monopolist dealer, of course). In both of these cases, the firms behind the creation of these markets failed, but the primary and secondary markets they started remained strong, the high-yield market being one of the booming high performers during the tech stock bubble collapse in 2000–02.

1.7   MARKET PLAYERS: HEDGERS VS. SPECULATORS

According to a common saying, nothing in life is certain except death and taxes. No investment in the market is riskless, even if it is in some way guaranteed. Let us challenge some seemingly intuitive notions of what is risky and what is safe.

Sparkasse savers in Germany, postal account holders in Japan, U.S. Treasury Bill investors, for most intents and purposes avoid default risk and are guaranteed a pos-itive nominal return on their savings. T-Bill and CD investors lock in the rates until the maturity of the instruments they hold. Are they then risk-free investors and not spec-ulators? They can calculate in advance the exact dollar amount their investment will pay at maturity. After subtraction of the original investment, the computed percentage return will always be positive. Yet, by locking in the cash flows, they are forgoing the chance to make more. If, while they are holding their CD, short-term or rollover rates increase, they will have lost the extra *opportunity* return they could have earned. We are hinting here at the notion of *opportunity cost of capital* common in finance.

Let us consider another example. John Smith uses the $1,000 he got from his uncle to purchase shares in XYZ Corp. After 1 year, he sells his shares for $1,100. His annual return is 10%. Adam Jones borrows $1,000 at 5% from his broker to purchase shares in XYZ Corp. After 1 year, he sells his shares for $1,100. His annual return is 10% on XYZ shares, but he has to pay 5%, or $50, interest on the loan, so his net return is 5%. Should we praise John for earning 10% on his capital and scold Adam for earning only 5%? Obviously not. Adam's cost of capital was 5%. So was John's! His was the nebulous opportunity cost of capital, or a *shadow cost*. He could have earned 5% virtually risk-free by lending to the broker instead of investing in risky shares. So his relative return, or excess return, was only 5%. In our T-Bill or CD example, one can argue that an investor in a fixed-rate CD is a speculator as he gambles on the rates not increasing prior to the maturity of his CD. The fact that his net receipts from the CD at maturity are guaranteed to be positive is irrelevant. There is nothing special about a 0% threshold for your return objective (especially if one takes into account inflation).

In the context of this book, all investors who take a position in an asset, whether by borrowing or using owned funds, and the asset's return over its life is not contractually identical to the investor's cost of capital, will be considered *speculators*. This definition is only relative to some benchmark cost of capital. In this sense both Adam and John speculate by acquiring shares whose rate of return differs from their cost of capital of 5%. An outright CD investment is speculative as the rate on the CD is not guaranteed to be the same as that obtained by leaving the investment in a variable rate money market account. A homeowner who takes out a fixed-rate mortgage to finance a house purchase is a speculator even though he fixes his monthly payments for the next 30 years! When he refinances his loan, he cancels a prior bet on interest rates and places a new one. In contrast, an adjustable rate mortgage borrower pays the fair market rate every period equal to the short-term rate plus a fixed margin.

Most financial market participants can be divided into two categories based on whether their capital is used to place bets on the direction of the market prices or rates or whether it is used to finance holdings of sets of transactions which largely offset each other's primary risks: speculators and hedgers.

Speculators are economic agents who take on explicit market risks in order to earn returns in excess of their cost of capital. The risks they are exposed to through their investments are not offset by simultaneous "hedge" transactions. Hedgers are economic agents who enter into simultaneous transactions designed to have offsetting market risks in such a way that the net returns they earn are over and above their cost of capital. All arbitrageurs, whether pure or relative, are hedgers. They aim to earn nearly risk-free returns after paying all their financing costs. A pure arbitrageur's or strict hedger's returns are completely risk-free. A relative arbitrageur's returns are not risk-free; he is exposed to secondary market risks.

All "investors" who use their capital to explicitly take on market risks are speculators. Their capital often comes in the form of an outside endowment. Mutual funds obtain fresh funds by shareholders sending them cash. Pension funds get capital from payroll deductions. Insurance companies sell life or hazard policies and invest the premiums in stocks, bonds, and real estate. Individual investors deposit cash into their brokerage accounts in order to buy, sell, or short-sell stocks and bonds. In all these cases, the "investors" use their funds (i.e., sacrifice their cost of capital) to bet on the direction of the market they invest in. They "buy" the services of brokers and dealers who facilitate their investment strategies. In order to help these investors improve the precision of the bets they take, broker-dealers who are hedgers by nature invent new products that they "sell" to investors. These can be new types of bonds, warrants and other derivatives, new classes of shares, new types of trusts, and annuities. Often, the division of the players into speculators and hedgers is replaced by the alternative terms of:

- *Buy-side* participants.
- *Sell-side* participants.

Buy-side players are investors who do not originate the new investment vehicles. They choose from a menu offered to them by the sell-side players. The sell-siders try to avoid gambling their own capital on the explicit direction of the market. They want to use their capital to finance the hedge (i.e., to "manufacture" the new products). As soon as they "sell" them, they look to enter into a largely offsetting trade with another counterparty or to hedge the risks through a relative arbitrage strategy. Often the sell-sider's hedge strategies are very imperfect and take time to arrange (i.e., when sell-siders act as speculators). The hedger/speculator compartmentalization is not exactly equivalent to sell/buy-side division. Sell-siders often act as both hedgers and speculators, but their mindset is more like that of the hedger ("to find the other side of the trade"). Buy-siders enter into transactions with sell-siders in order to get exposed to or alter how they are exposed to market risks ("to get in on a trade").

We use quotes around the words "buy" and "sell" to emphasize that the sell-sider does not necessarily sell a stock or bond to a buy-sider. He can just as well buy it. But he hedges his transaction while the buy-sider does not.

Geographically, the sell-side resides in global financial centers, like New York or London, and is represented by the largest 50 global financial institutions. The buy-side is very dispersed and includes all medium and smaller banks with mostly commercial business, all mutual and pension funds, some university endowments, all insurance companies, and all finance corporations. The buy/sell and hedger/speculator distinctions have recently become blurred. Larger regional banks in the U.S. which have traditionally been buy-side institutions started their own institutional trading businesses. They now offer security placement and new derivative product services to smaller banks and thrifts. In the 1990s, some insurance companies established sell-side trading subsidiaries and used their capital strength and credit rating to compete vigorously with broker-dealers. Most of these subsidiaries have the phrase "Financial Products" inserted in their name (e.g., Gen Re Financial Products or AIG FP).

One type of company that can be by design on both the buy- and sell-side is a hedge fund. Hedge funds are capitalized like typical speculators (read: investment companies), similar to mutual funds, but without the regulatory protection of the small investor. Yet almost all hedge fund strategies are some form of relative value arbitrage (i.e., they are hedges). The original capital is used only to acquire leverage and to replicate a hedge strategy as much as possible. Most hedge funds have been traditionally buy-siders. They have tended not to innovate, but to use off-the-shelf contracts from dealers. Sometimes, however, hedge funds grow so large in their market segment that they are able to wrest control of the demand and supply information flow from the dealers and are able to sell hedges to the dealers, effectively becoming sellers of innovative strategies. In the late 1990s, funds like Tiger, AIM, or LTCM, sometimes put on very large hedged positions, crowding dealers only into speculative choices as the supply of available hedges was exhausted by the funds. The early 2000s have seen the return of hedge funds to their more traditional buy-side role as the average size of the fund declined and the number of funds increased dramatically.

1.8 PREVIEW OF THE BOOK

Most financial markets textbooks are organized by following markets for different types of securities: stocks, money markets, bonds, mortgages, asset-backed securities, real estate trusts, currencies, commodities, etc. This is analogous to reviewing the car industry alphabetically by make, starting with Acura, Audi, and BMW and ending with Volkswagen and Volvo. This book is arranged structurally to emphasize the common features of all the segments, analogous to describing the engines first, then chassis and body, and ending with safety features and interior comforts. This allows the reader to fully understand the internal workings of the markets, rather than learning about unimportant institutional details. The book is divided into four parts:

- *Part I: Spot*—trading in cash securities for immediate delivery, arbitrage through spot buying, and selling of like securities that trade at different prices.
- *Part II: Forwards*—futures and forward contracts for future delivery of the under-lying cash assets, arbitrage through static cash-and-carry (i.e., spot buy or sell), supplemented by borrow or lend against a forward sell or buy).
- *Part III: Options*—derivative contracts for contingent future delivery of the under-lying cash assets, arbitrage through dynamic cash-and-carry, or delta-hedge (i.e., continuous rebalancing of the cash-and-carry position).
- *Appendix: Credit Risk*—default-risky delivery (spot, forward, or contingent), arbit-rage through all three strategies using default-risky assets against default-free assets.

The first three represent the fundamental building blocks present in any market. Each part is defined by the delivery time and form of transactions. Each has its own internal no-arbitrage rules (law of one price) and each is related to the other two by another set of no-arbitrage rules (static and dynamic cash-and-carry equations). As we will show, all the no-arbitrage rules, player motivations, and trade strategies of each segment in markets for different securities (stocks, bonds, etc.) are strikingly similar.

The appendix of the book is dedicated to credit risks that cut across all three dimensions of financial markets. This part enjoys the lightest treatment in the book and contains only one chapter (Chapter 11) covering both the math and descriptions. This is because most modeling of credit risks tends to be mathematically advanced. It relies on the already complex option-pricing theory. Like options, credit risks deal with contingent delivery. However, the condition for payoff is not a tractable market price or rate movement, but rather a more esoteric concept of the change in the credit quality of the issuer (as evidenced by a ratings downgrade or default), which in turn depends on mostly unhedgeable variables (legal debt covenants, earnings performance, debt–equity ratios, etc.).

Each of the three parts of the book starts with a chapter containing a technical primer, followed by more descriptive chapters containing applications of the analytics in arbitrage-based trading strategies. The primers, labeled Financial Math I, II, and III, are intensely analytical, but at a mathematically low level. We avoid using calculus and instead rely on numerical examples of real financial transactions. This should help not only novice readers, but also readers with science backgrounds, who often follow the equations, but often find it difficult to relate them to actual money-making activities. The main quantitative tool used is cash flow discounting, supplemented by some rudimentary rate and price conventions. Chapter 2, "Financial Math I", contains a brief summary of present value techniques. It offers definitions of rates and yields, and introduces the concept of a yield curve used to perform cash flow discounting. It then develops no-arbitrage equations for bond, stock, and currency markets. Chapter 6, "Financial Math II", describes the mechanics of futures and forwards trading in commodities, interest rates, equities, and currencies. It then presents no-arbitrage rules that link forwards and futures back to spot markets. These rely on cost-of-carry arguments. Chapter 6 also develops further the concept of the yield curve by showing how forwards are incorporated into it. Chapter 9, "Financial Math III", starts with basic payoff diagrams and static arbitrage relationships for options. It then describes the details of option valuation models that rely on the notion of dynamic cash-and-carry replication of option payoffs. It draws the fundamental distinction between hedgers who manufacture payoffs and speculators who bet on future outcomes. It offers analytical insights into money-making philosophies of derivatives traders. The chapter covers stock, currency, and interest rate options.

The "Financial Math" primer chapters are followed by survey chapters that delve deeper into the specifics of markets for different securities. These describe the players, the role of these markets in the savings–investment cycle, and the special conventions and nomenclature used. They offer sketchy but insightful statistics. They also rely on the knowledge contained in the primers to further develop detailed arbitrage strategies that are considered "benchmark" trades in each market. These are presented mostly as pure arbitrages; their relative value cousins are not difficult to imagine and some are also described. In Chapter 3, we survey spot fixed income markets. We go over money markets securities (under 1 year in maturity) which enjoy the most liquidity and turnover. We cover government and corporate bond markets. We touch on swaps, mortgage securities, and asset-backed securities. In Chapter 4, we describe the markets for equities, currencies, and commodities. Stock markets are most likely the most familiar to all readers, so we focus on more recent developments in cross-listings, basket trading and stock exchange consolidations. Chapter 5 uses the mathematical concepts of Chapter 2 and applies them to the spot securities described in Chapters 3 and 4. It presents pure arbitrage and relative value trades for different bond segments, equities, and currencies. It covers speculative basis trades in commodities. In Part II, following the primer on futures and forwards, Chapter 7 focuses on the cash-and-carry arbitrage and its various guises in currencies (covered interest rate parity), equities (stock index arbitrage) and bond futures (long bond futures basis arbitrage). It also extends the concept of hedging the yield curve using Eurocurrency strip trading and duration matching. Chapter 8 is devoted entirely to swap markets that represent spot and forward exchanges of streams of cash flows. These streams are shown to be identical to those of bonds and stocks rendering swaps as mere repackagings of other assets. This chapter combines the analytical treatment of swap mechanics with some more descriptive material and market statistics. In Part III, following the options primer, Chapter 10 describes a few forms of options arbitrage, admittedly in rather simplistic terms, but it also extends the option discussion to multiple asset classes and option-like insurance contracts. Part IV contains one chapter on credit risk and its relationship to fixed income assets described in prior chapters.

Clearly, the most important, but also the most quantitative chapters in the book are all the primers (Chapters 2, 6, 9, and 11). Readers interested only in the mechanics of markets can read those in sequence and then use other chapters as reference material. For readers interested in the details of various markets, the order of study is very important, particularly in Parts II and III. The descriptive chapters rely heavily on the knowledge contained in their Financial Math primers. This is less so in Part I, where, apart from Chapter 5, we focus more on the description of basic securities and market infrastructure and less on arbitrage.

We hope our audience finds this book as contributing significantly to their deep understanding of today's global financial marketplace.

Part One
Spot

2
Financial Math I—Spot

Cash flow discounting is the basis of all securities valuation. The fundamental value of a stock is equal to the present value of all the dividends and capital gains the owner will be entitled to in the future. The fundamental value of a bond is equal to the present value of all the interest payments and principal repayment the owner will receive over the life of the bond. These cash flows may be known in advance (principal of a government bond) or uncertain (capital gains on the stock). Market participants may disagree in their estimates of the amounts. But the basic technique is always the same. Once you have determined the future cash flows, all you do is apply an appropriate interest rate to discount them to today. That rate reflects both the cost of money and the degree of uncertainty about the exact amount of the flows. The sum of all the discounted cash flows for a security (i.e., the present value) is what you should be willing to pay for that security (i.e., the price).

The main premise of discounting is the concept of the time value of money. Money can be *rented to* a bank to earn interest. Money can be *rented from* a bank by agreeing to pay interest. You would always pay less than $100 today for a promise of $100 in the future. This is not only because of a risk of the promise, but also because it would cost you less than $100 today to buy an investment that, with interest earned, would produce $100 in the future. Whether you use owned funds or borrowed funds to purchase an investment is not important. If you use borrowed funds you pay explicit interest. If you spend owned funds, you forgo the interest that you could have earned. This forgone interest is commonly referred to as an *opportunity cost* and it is as real a cost as the interest paid on borrowed funds.

College textbooks apply the notion of time value of money to single and multiple cash flow securities, like stocks and bonds, as well as capital-budgeting projects. We will devote a page to the review of that material; the reader is encouraged to study it more if necessary. Implicitly, many textbooks restrict themselves to using only one type of interest rate: the discount rate or a zero-coupon rate. That is, to compute the present value of each cash flow, they assume that interest compounds and accrues annually over the life of the cash flow and is due once at the end. This is just the tip of the iceberg. Interest can accrue and be paid according to many conventions. It may compound at one frequency (quarterly), but be paid at another (annually). The calendar for intra-year calculations may assume actual or even numbers of days per month or year. The rate of interest may be different for different future dates. Cash flows may not be due at even intervals. The complications abound.

To make sense of them, we review common compounding and day-count conventions and then we look at three main arrangements, dating back to Phoenician times, of how interest can be earned and paid:

- Zero-coupon (discount or add-on), with no intervening interest cash flows.
- Coupon, with periodic fixed or variable interest payments.
- Amortizing, with periodic interest payments and partial principal repayments.

Typically, textbooks dealing with capital budgeting cover the first arrangement, fixed-income books the second, and mortgage books the third, reflecting where the different forms of interest are most common. The rates quoted on these three different bases are not directly comparable with each other, even after conversion to the same day-count and periodicity. However, the three are mathematically related and can be computed from each other through arbitrage arguments.

2.1 INTEREST RATE BASICS

We start with present values (*PVs*), compounding rules, and day-count conventions.

Present value

Suppose you earn interest on $500 at 5%. How much will you have in 1 year? The answer is $500 plus 5% of $500, or $500(1 + 0.05) = \$525$. How much will you have if you invest $500 for 2 years? In year 1, your investment will accrue to $525, but, in year 2, you will earn interest on interest. You will get $525 plus 5% of $525, where each $525 is equal to $500(1.05)$. That is, after 2 years, you will have $500(1.05) + 0.05 \cdot 500(1.05) = 500(1.05)^2 = \$551.25$. Generally, if you invest PV_0 today at interest rate r for n years, your investment will have a *future value* of:

$$FV = PV_0(1 + r)^n$$

Let us reverse the question. How much would you have to invest today so that at an interest rate of 5% it would accrue to $500 2 years from today? Now, $500 is the future value and we need to solve for PV_0 in the above equation to get:

$$PV_0 = \frac{500}{(1 + 0.05)^2} = \$453.51$$

If you had easy access to borrowing and lending at 5%, you would be indifferent between $453.51 today and $500 2 years from today. You could convert one into the other at a known conversion ratio. In general, we can write an expression for the *present value (PV)* of a single future cash flow as:

$$PV_0 = FV \cdot \frac{1}{(1 + r)^n}$$

The expressions $(1 + r)^n$ and $\frac{1}{(1 + r)^n}$ are referred to as future value interest factors and present value interest factors, respectively, for a rate r and a number of periods n. Graphically, we can present our situation as:

PV_0 FV

```
0     1     2     3          n − 1    n
Today
```

Now suppose we ask a slightly more difficult question. How much would you have to invest today in an account paying 5% interest, so that you could withdraw from the account $500 every year for the next 4 years? The first withdrawal is 1 year from today and there is no money left in the account after the last withdrawal 4 years from today. Graphically, we can present this situation as:

$$PV_0 = ?\quad 500\qquad 500\qquad 500\qquad 500$$

$$\begin{array}{ccccc} \llcorner & \text{___} & \text{___} & \text{___} & \text{___} \\ 0 & 1 & 2 & 3 & 4 \end{array}$$

To solve, we can imagine that, if we had money today, we could divide it into four separate investments each generating a $500 cash flow at different times. That is, we could divide it into these amounts:

$$PV_0 = 500 \cdot \frac{1}{1+r} + 500 \cdot \frac{1}{(1+r)^2} + 500 \cdot \frac{1}{(1+r)^3} + 500 \cdot \frac{1}{(1+r)^4}$$

The total amount to be invested today is:

$$PV_0 = 500 \left[\frac{1}{1+r} + \frac{1}{(1+r)^2} + \frac{1}{(1+r)^3} + \frac{1}{(1+r)^4} \right] = \$1,772.98$$

A constant cash flow (CF) over n periods starting one period from today is referred to as an ordinary annuity. Its present value is:

$$PV_0 = CF \left[\frac{1}{1+r} + \frac{1}{(1+r)^2} + \cdots + \frac{1}{(1+r)^n} \right]$$

and the expression in brackets is referred to as a present value annuity factor at a rate r for a number of periods (years) n.

The present value of a stream of cash flows can be interpreted as today's value of the promise of the entire future stream. It is an amount that would make one indifferent between (1) receiving it in one lump sum of PV_0 today and (2) in the form of a cash flow stream in the future.

Compounding

When interest compounds intra-year instead of year to year, the calculations become a little more complicated.

Annual example

On June 1, we invest €1,000 in a 1-year certificate of deposit (CD) yielding 3.25%. On June 1 of next year, we will get $1,000(1 + 0.0325) = €1,032.500$.

Quarterly example

Suppose instead, on June 1, we invest €1,000 in a 3-month CD yielding 3.25%. How much will we get on the due date of September 1?

The first thing we need to keep in mind is that the rate of interest is always stated per annum. The rate of 3.25% (p.a.) as quoted, first has to be de-compounded to obtain the interest rate per quarter. This can be done by dividing the rate by the number of interest periods per year. Once we have done that, the answer becomes simply $1,000(1 + 0.0325/4) = €1,008.125$.

Quarterly rollover example

Suppose we invest €1,000 for a total of 1 year by first investing it in a 3-month CD. We assume that CD rates do not change over the next year and we roll over the principal plus interest every 3 months into new CDs yielding 3.25% (p.a.). Our reinvestment dates are: September 1, December 1, and March 1. The final maturity is June 1. How much will we get a year from today? The answer is a compound formula of $1,000(1 + 0.0325/4)^4 = €1,032.898$. We will get €1,000 principal and €32.898 in total interest.

Equivalent annual rate

We define the *equivalent annual rate* (EAR), in the CD example equal to 3.2898%, as the rate that would have had to be offered on an annual investment to generate the same amount of interest over 1 year as the compound investment at a quoted rate. If we denote the quoted rate by r in percent per annum, and the number of compounding periods per year as m, then the relationship between the quoted rate r and the EAR is:

$$(1 + r/m)^m = 1 + EAR$$

For example, for a semi-annual rate $m = 2$, while for a monthly compounded rate $m = 12$. When comparing yields on investments of different compounding frequency, we convert the stated rates to EARs. As we will see, even that is not enough.

Day-count conventions

Each fixed-income market has its own quote and day-count convention. Our examples were simplified so that for quarterly periods we divided the stated rates by 4. Implicitly, we were using what is called a *30/360* day-count convention. A *day-count convention* is a commonly accepted method of counting two things: the number of days within the interest calculation period and the number of days in a year. Under the 30/360 convention all months are assumed to have exactly *30* days and each year has *360* days, so that each 3-month period represents exactly one-quarter of a year. In the above calculations, the division by 4 and raising to the power of 4 were shortcuts for multiplying the quoted rates by *90/360* (i.e., computing the actual interest rate per 90-day period) and raising the gross de-compounded return (the one-plus-interest expression) to the power of *360/90* (i.e., compounding it as many times as there are periods). In the rollover example, we could have written $1,000(1 + 0.0325 \cdot 90/360)^{360/90} = €1,032.898$. We also should have amended the EAR definition to:

$$\left(1 + r \cdot \frac{days_{calc}}{days_{year}}\right)^{days_{year}/days_{calc}} = 1 + EAR$$

where $days_{calc}$ is the number of days in the interest calculation period and $days_{year}$ is the assumed number of days in a year.[1]

Many deposits, notably LIBOR (London interbank offered rate)-based Eurodollars, use an *Act/360* day-count convention. For our 3-month (June 1–September 1) CD, the Act/360 convention means that the numerator is the actual number of calendar days in the interest period, and in the denominator we assume that a year has exactly *360* days, and not *365* or *366* as it may be. On September 1, our 3-month CD would return the principal and interest worth $1,000(1 + 0.0325 \cdot 92/360) = €1,008.306$. The 1-year (June–June) rollover strategy would pay:

$$1,000\left(1 + 0.0325 \cdot \frac{92}{360}\right)\left(1 + 0.0325 \cdot \frac{91}{360}\right)\left(1 + 0.0325 \cdot \frac{90}{360}\right)\left(1 + 0.0325 \cdot \frac{92}{360}\right)$$

$$= €1,033.361$$

as there are 92, 91, 90, and 92 days, respectively, in each 3-month reinvestment period. The EAR is equal to 3.3361%. LIBOR-based sterling deposits use an *Act/365* basis, where we compute the actual number of days in the interest calculation period, but always assume 365 days per year even if it happens to be 366.

Let us consider one last "wrinkle". Suppose we deposit money on June 1 for the period ending December 15. How much will we get back on the due date if we are earning 3.38% quarterly compounded on an Act/360 basis? The following expression describes our accrual on a €1,000 investment:

$$1,000\left(1 + 0.0338 \cdot \frac{92}{360}\right)\left(1 + 0.0338 \cdot \frac{91}{360}\right)\left(1 + 0.0338 \cdot \frac{14}{360}\right) = €1,018.593$$

Most commonly used day-count conventions include *Act/365*, *Act/Act*, *Act/360* and *30/360*. Government bond markets typically follow one of the first two, money markets follow the third, and corporate bond markets use the last one. There are exceptions to these rules, and OTC derivatives markets can follow "wrong" conventions for different underlying securities. Many unsuspecting investors have been burnt in the past by ruthless dealers playing day-count tricks!

In this book, except when explicitly noted, we will assume the simple 30/360 convention. We will end up with more familiar divisions by 4, 2 or 1 for quarterly, semi-annual, and annual periods.

Rates vs. yields

Throughout the text, we use the word *rate* to denote the interest percentage that is typically explicitly stated and is used in a convention to compute the actual monetary amount of interest paid to the holder of a security. We will use the word *yield* to denote the interest percentage earned on the amount invested. The market sometimes uses the two interchangeably, but they should not be. A bond with a 5% coupon rate selling at par (price equal to 100% of the face value) *yields* 5%. A bond with a 5% coupon rate selling below par (price less than 100% of face) *yields* more than 5% as the buyer has to spend less than the principal value of the bond.

---

[1] Actually, even that formula is not general enough. The best reference on the subject is Marcia Stigum and Franklin L. Robinson, *Money Market and Bond Calculations*, 1996, Irwin, Chicago.

The definition of EAR has the word *rate* in it, even though it is more akin to a yield, because EAR is typically computed upfront, using a stated rate and assuming a purchase at par. In the above examples, if the 1-year €1,000 CD with a quarterly rate of 3.25% were purchased for €990, then the *quarterly equivalent yield* (QEY) could be defined implicitly by the equality $990(1 + QEY/4) = €1,032.50$.

The investor would be said to earn a yield of $QEY = 17.7\%$ on a €990 investment. A *bond-equivalent yield* (BEY) is the yield earned on buying an investment at its market price and collecting the cash flows as defined by the stated rate, but restated in a frequency convention of the bond market (e.g., semi-annual in the U.S. and the U.K. but annual in some continental European markets). That is, it is an annual equivalent yield (AEY) or semi-annual equivalent yield (SAEY), grossed up or down from a yield expressed in a natural frequency of the investment. The quarterly yield on the CD in our example could be grossed up to arrive at a semi-annual bond-equivalent yield by pretending that the CD is rolled over for another quarterly period; that is:

$$(1 + QEY/4)^2 = (1 + SAEY/2)$$

2.2   ZERO, COUPON, AND AMORTIZING RATES

Next we review the distinction between zero, coupon, and amortizing rates. Zeros are the purest form of discounting rates in the sense that they translate directly any future cash flow into its present value. A stream of cash flows is discounted by applying an appropriate zero rate to each cash flow to compute its present value and then by summing the individual present values to obtain the present value of the entire stream. This can be done using one of the blended rates: coupon or amortizing. In that case, however, while the present value of the stream may be correct, the present value of each individual cash flow is not, as it has the wrong rate applied to it. The blended rate is imaginary; there is no investment accruing interest at that rate to generate any one of the cash flows in the stream. Let us go into more detail.

Zero-coupon rates

All the examples so far involved zero-coupon rates[2] (commonly referred to as discount rates as they can be used directly in cash flow discounting). These are earned on investments for which the accrued interest is received only once with the principal repayment on the maturity date. The investment does not generate any intermediate coupon interest cash flows (i.e., it has a zero coupon). The 3-month CD investment was a zero-coupon investment over one quarter. The 1-year rollover strategy consisted of four consecutive quarterly zero-coupon investments. The investor received no cash flows during the entire year. All interest and principal were fully reinvested every quarter. Graphically, the simplest way to present a zero-coupon rate is as follows:

$$PV_0 \quad * \quad (1 + r/m)^{nm} \quad = \quad CF$$

0	1	2	3		$n-1$	n	Years
0	m	$2m$	$3m$			nm	Sub-annual periods, if any

---

[2] Zero-coupon rates are also referred to as spot rates. This is very misleading, since all rates (zero, coupon, and amortizing) can be spot (i.e., for an interest period starting now and ending in the future). They all can also be forward (i.e., for an interest period starting in the future and ending in the future).

Notice the absence of any intervening cash flows between today and the future date $t = nm$. The 1-year rollover strategy has zero net intervening cash flows as both the principal and interest are fully reinvested each quarter. This is shown in the following picture (+ denotes an inflow, − denotes an outflow):

$$
\begin{array}{ccccc}
 & +P_{3m} + I_{3m} & +P_{6m} + I_{6m} & +P_{9m} + I_{9m} & \\
-P_0 & -P_{3m} - I_{3m} & -P_{9m} - I_{9m} & -P_{9m} - I_{9m} & +P_{12m} + I_{12m} \\
\end{array}
$$

| 0 | 3 months | 6 months | 9 months | 12 months |

Zero-coupon interest can accrue on either an *add-on* or a *discount* basis. The distinction here is only of the form, not of substance. In the add-on case, the investment is purchased for a full face value, which is a multiple of some round number, and interest accrues based on the principal equal to the face value of the security. In our retail CD, the investor deposited €1,000 and received, 3 months later, the principal and interest worth of €1,008.306. In contrast, most short-term securities sell at a discount from face value, and the interest rate is only implied by the ratio of the round-numbered face value and the purchase price of the security. For example, the price of 99.05 for a 3-month U.S. Treasury Bill is expressed as percent of par. For a T-Bill promising to repay exactly $10,000 in 3 months, the investor pays $9,905. The implied yield on a 30/360 basis he earns can be obtained by solving the expression $9905(1 + r \cdot 90/360) = 9905(1 + r/4) = 10,000$ for $r = 3.8364\%$. Similarly, a buyer of a 6-month U.S. T-Bill paying 98.1179 would compute his implied yield by solving in the expression $98.1179(1 + r/2) = 100$ for $r = 3.8364\%$. Even though the two T-Bills have the same 3.8364% yield, they are not truly comparable: one matures in 3 months, the other in 6. Depending on at what rate we can reinvest the 3-month T-Bill, we could end up with more or less than the principal and interest on the six-month T-Bill in 6 months. Assuming no change in rates, we can use EAR as a comparison tool. To obtain EARs, we compute the yields each investment earns if it is rolled over at its original yield for a total holding period of 1 year.

$$EAR_{3m} = (1 + 0.038364/4)^4 - 1 = (100/99.05)^4 - 1 = 3.8920\%$$

$$EAR_{6m} = (1 + 0.038364/2)^2 - 1 = (100/98.1179)^2 - 1 = 3.8732\%$$

Alternatively, we could compute the semi-annual equivalent of the 3-month rate by following the logic behind EAR but only over a 6-month horizon. The equivalent semi-annual rate (ESR) of the stated 3-month rate, $r_{3m} = 3.8364\%$, would satisfy the equation $(1 + r_{3m}/4)^2 = 1 + ESR/2$. This is the essence of the *BEY* whose precise definition varies by market. Let us re-emphasize that, upfront, the realized yield on any rollover strategy is not known, as the reinvestment rate can change. The equivalent yield calculation relies on the unrealistic assumption that the reinvestment rate is known and will not change.

Coupon rates

The word *coupon* comes from a physical piece of paper bond investors used to clip off the bond to send to the bond issuer (borrower) to claim their periodic interest receipt. Today, only some Eurobonds come in bearer form with physical coupons. All U.S.

government and corporate bonds and all European government bonds are *registered* and often exist only "virtually" as computer entries of the owners' names and addresses. But the way interest is paid on bonds is the same as ever. Once or twice a year, depending on the coupon frequency stated on the bond, the owners receive a cash flow equal to the coupon rate times the face value of the bond they hold multiplied by the appropriate day-count fraction.

Let us consider an example. On June 30, 2004 an investor purchases a 10-year bond with a face value of £2,500 and a stated annual coupon rate of 4.5%. The maturity date is June 30, 2014 and coupons accrue from June 30 to June 30. On June 30 of each year between 2005 and 2014, the bond holder receives interest payments equal to $2,500 \cdot 0.045 = £112.50$. Additionally, on June 30, 2014 he receives his principal of £2,500 back. The actual CFs from the bond are portrayed in the following picture:

112.50	112.50	112.50	112.50	112.50	112.50	112.50	112.50	112.50	2,612.50
0	1	2	3	4	5	6	7	8	9	10

Most commonly, CFs are represented as percentages of par, as in the following normalized picture:

4.5	4.5	4.5	4.5	4.5	4.5	4.5	4.5	4.5	104.5
0	1	2	3	4	5	6	7	8	9	10

The main difference between a coupon bond and a zero-coupon bond is the stream of 4.5% or £112.50 cash flows in years 2005–2014. These are not simply accrued and rolled up until the final maturity date, but physically paid out. A zero holder would only receive one large payment at maturity, on June 30, 2014, which would consist of the face value repayment of £2,500 and a 10-year accumulation of interest.

Coupon yields and rates can be expressed on a variety of compounding and day-count bases, typically following a particular convention. The bond debenture contract (fine print) always states clearly how the interest is accrued and paid. But the legal language can be far from plain English. The stated rate is always annualized and needs to be de-compounded. For example, a 6% quarterly bond does not pay a coupon equal to 6% of the face value every 3 months; rather, it pays a coupon close to but not necessarily identical to 1.5% of the face value every 3 months. On a 30/360 day-count basis, it is exactly 1.5%. On any other basis, the numerator and the denominator of the day count may not result in an exact division by 4 for all periods. The only thing really "fixed" is the stated rate; the dollar interest payment may change each period. At least the language is consistent: the percentage rate is always expressed on a per annum basis and must be adjusted by the compounding frequency to get the periodic cash flow. A 3-year 4.5% semi-annual coupon bond would have the coupon cash flows of $4.5/2 = 2.25\%$ every 6 months and principal repayment flow of 100 in 36 months:

2.25	2.25	2.25	2.25	2.25	(100 + 2.25)
0	6m	12m	18m	24m	30m	36m

Notice that the 3-year 4.5% semi-annual coupon bond can be viewed as an ordinary annuity of 2.25 over six periods and a one-time cash flow of 100 six periods from the purchase date. When computing the present value of the bond, it is convenient to break it down into these two components. Suppose the interest rate with which to discount all the cash flows is 5% semi-annual. To get the value of the bond, we would set up the following equation:

$$PV_0 = \frac{2.25}{\left(1 + \frac{0.05}{2}\right)} + \frac{2.25}{\left(1 + \frac{0.05}{2}\right)^2} + \frac{2.25}{\left(1 + \frac{0.05}{2}\right)^3} + \frac{2.25}{\left(1 + \frac{0.05}{2}\right)^4}$$

$$+ \frac{2.25}{\left(1 + \frac{0.05}{2}\right)^5} + \frac{102.25}{\left(1 + \frac{0.05}{2}\right)^6}$$

which, collecting terms for the annuity component and the principal repayment component, looks like this:

$$PV_0 = 2.25 \left(\frac{1}{\left(1 + \frac{0.05}{2}\right)} + \frac{1}{\left(1 + \frac{0.05}{2}\right)^2} + \frac{1}{\left(1 + \frac{0.05}{2}\right)^3} + \frac{1}{\left(1 + \frac{0.05}{2}\right)^4} + \frac{1}{\left(1 + \frac{0.05}{2}\right)^5} \right.$$

$$\left. + \frac{1}{\left(1 + \frac{0.05}{2}\right)^6} \right) + \frac{100}{\left(1 + \frac{0.05}{2}\right)^6}$$

The value in this case is $PV_0 = 98.6230$ which is less than 100. We used a *yield* of 5.00% to discount the cash flows of a bond with a coupon *rate* of 4.5%. If the bond sells in the market for 98.6230, then the 5.00% is the bond's yield to maturity (see below).

Zero-coupon bonds are special cases of coupon bonds with the coupon rate equal to 0. However, they should be viewed as fundamentally different from their coupon cousins. Later in this chapter, we show how we can build a set of zero yields from coupon yields and vice versa, but before that let us attempt to define what a yield on a coupon instrument is.

Yield to maturity

A *holding period return* (HPR) is a theoretical single yield earned on purchasing an investment for a given price, receiving cash flows from it, if any, over some known *holding period* and selling it at some known price at the end of that period. That is, the knowns are:

- Purchase price.
- Intermediate cash flows.
- Sale price.

In computing a yield over a holding horizon, one could make an assumption that the cash flows obtained from the investment have been re-invested at different rates. For HPRs, the reinvestment rate is assumed to be constant and equal to the HPR, but the holding period may be different from the maturity of the instrument (e.g. a 2-year holding period for a 5-year bond or a 3-year holding period for a stock with infinite maturity). HPRs can be expressed on any compounding and day-count basis.

A *yield to maturity* (YTM) is a holding period return over a holding period equal to the maturity of the instrument. All the cash flows are assumed to have been received and reinvested at the rate equal to the holding period return. The assumption that the instrument is held to maturity also ensures that the sale price is equal to the face value. YTMs can be expressed on any compounding and day-count basis. Most dealers convert non-native YTMs to a *bond-equivalent* basis which, in the U.S., is defined as the SAEY on an *Act/Act* (governments) or *30/360* (corporates) basis, and, in most of Europe, as the AEY on an *Act/Act* basis. We illustrate the concepts of a holding period return and a YTM through some examples.[3]

Suppose 2 years ago you purchased a 2-year discount (zero-coupon) bond for 91.00. Today it matures and you receive 100.00 back. What semi-annual YTM have you earned? We solve for the implied zero rate r such that $91.00(1 + r/2)^4 = 100$. We get $r = 4.7716\%$. The YTM on a zero-coupon bond is equal to the zero rate itself as the zero, by definition, has no reinvestment. Now let us look at the coupon bond.

Suppose 2 years ago you purchased a 2-year 4% semi-annual coupon bond for 99.0538. Today it matures and you receive 100.00 back. What semi-annual YTM have you earned? Let us examine the cash flows promised by the bond. We had an outflow of \$99.0538 upfront, four inflows of $0.04 \cdot 100 \cdot \frac{1}{2} = \$2.00$ on each coupon date and an inflow of \$100 on the final date (today).

Textbooks offer the following definition of YTM: YTM is equal to an interest rate such that if we discount all the cash flows from the bond at that rate, then the obtained present value is equal to the price of the bond. This follows the logic of how we solve for the YTM. The cash flows can be portrayed as:

	2.00	2.00	2.00	(100 + 2.00)
0	6m	12m	18m	24m

To discount all the cash flows at some rate r to today, we would set up the following equation:

$$PV_0 = \frac{2.00}{\left(1 + \dfrac{r}{2}\right)} + \frac{2.00}{\left(1 + \dfrac{r}{2}\right)^2} + \frac{2.00}{\left(1 + \dfrac{r}{2}\right)^3} + \frac{102.00}{\left(1 + \dfrac{r}{2}\right)^4}$$

Then we would solve for r such that the present value is equal to the initial investment $PV_0 = 99.0538$. We could use a financial calculator (solving for the equivalent notion of the *internal rate of return*, or IRR), use a polynomial root finder, or solve by trial and error in a spreadsheet. (For example, we would try 4% and 5% as two possible solutions: the first would result in a $PV > 99$, the second in a $PV < 99$. We could then try a rate between 4% and 5% to get closer to the true value of 99.0538. And

---

[3] All of our examples assume that the investment is purchased a moment after a coupon has been paid. That is, we do not need to make here, and in fact throughout the entire book, a distinction between the *dirty price* and the *clean price*. When a coupon bond is purchased between coupon payment dates, the buyer pays the seller the so-called dirty price, which includes an allowance for the interest that has accrued between the last coupon date and the purchase date. The seller is entitled to that interest, but by surrendering the bond, he has no possibility to collect it. The buyer will receive it included in the whole coupon payment on the next coupon date. The so-called clean price is equal to the dirty price minus the accrued interest.

so on.) We can verify that the solution is $r = 4.5\%$ by substituting 4.5 for the rate and solving to get 99.0538 as the PV.

The calculation mechanics hide the true nature of YTM as a "blended", or "average", yield actually earned on the investment. Let us imagine that we have a money-market account that pays a semi-annually compounded rate $r = 4.5\%$ on any deposits into it. Suppose 2 years ago we deposited into that account $99.0538. On each coupon date, we withdrew $2.00 from the account. At maturity, we withdrew $100. We can show that if the interest rate the money-market account paid on any balances left in it was equal to the computed YTM of 4.5%, then we could make the withdrawals and end up with no balance in the account at the end.

We deposit $99.0538 into the account.   At 4.5% semi-annually, 6 months later we have at our disposal $99.0538\left(1 + \dfrac{0.045}{2}\right) = 101.2825$. Of that, we pay ourselves $2.00. We redeposit the remaining $99.2825 for another 6 months at 4.5% semi-annually to get $99.2825\left(1 + \dfrac{0.045}{2}\right) = 101.5164$ in 12 months. We pay ourselves $2.00 and redeposit the remaining $99.5164 for another 6 months at 4.5% semi-annually to get $99.5164\left(1 + \dfrac{0.045}{2}\right) = 101.7555$ in 18 months. We pay ourselves $2.00 and redeposit the remaining $99.7555 for another 6 months at 4.5% semi-annually to get $99.7555\left(1 + \dfrac{0.045}{2}\right) = 102.00$ in 24 months. We withdraw $102.00 and close the account with a balance of $0.00. We repeated the wording of "reinvesting for another 6 months at 4.5% semi-annually" to stress the following point:

Conclusion 1   YTM is the assumed constant reinvestment rate over the life of the bond.

There is another interpretation of YTM. Suppose we divide the original sum of $99.0538 into four separate investments:

- A 6-month CD of $1.9560 yielding 4.5% semi-annually compounded.
- A 12-month CD of $1.9129 yielding 4.5% semi-annually compounded.
- An 18-month CD of $1.8709 yielding 4.5% semi-annually compounded.
- A 24-month CD of $93.3140 yielding 4.5% semi-annually compounded.

The reader should convince himself that the CD investments will accrue to $2.00, $2.00, $2.00, and $102 at their respective maturity dates (i.e., their cash flows will match exactly those of the coupon bond). This leads us to the following point:

Conclusion 2   YTM is the single zero-coupon investment rate for the maturity dates corresponding to all the cash flows over the life of the bond.

That is if all the *term* zero rates to different dates are assumed equal! In reality, both the reinvestment rates and the term rates are not likely to be constant or equal to each other. If we were to divide our $99.0538 into four different amounts in order to replicate the cash flows of the coupon bond, these amounts would have to be invested using the actual zero-coupon rates (term lending rates) in the market. The investment amounts would all be different from the ones arrived at using the YTM for discounting. YTM is a fictitious rate. It is a mathematical construct. It is the average rate earned over the life of the bond held to maturity given the price paid. That is why we called it "blended" or "average".

Amortizing rates

Another way of earning interest, in addition to zero and coupon rates, is through amortizing interest rates. Some bonds and most mortgage loans follow this arrangement. Like the fixed coupon bond issuer, the amortizing rate borrower agrees to constant periodic cash flows over the life of the loan. But each cash flow consists of an interest portion and a principal repayment portion so that the borrower does not have to repay the entire principal at the maturity of the loan. Instead, he repays it piece by piece with each periodic payment. To distinguish the amortizing loan from a coupon loan, the latter is often referred to as a *balloon* loan and the principal repayment at maturity as the *balloon* payment.

The best example of an amortizing rate loan is a 30-year fixed-rate mortgage. It consists of 360 equal monthly payments (30 years × 12 months each). The mortgage borrower obtains the full amount of the loan upfront with which he pays for a piece of real estate. The monthly payments cover both the interest on the loan and the repayment of the principal. Financial calculators and computer spreadsheets offer built-in functions to compute the constant monthly payment. They can also help construct the so-called *amortization table* which breaks down each payment into its interest and principal components. What is immediately clear from such a table is that over time the interest portion of the level payment decreases while the principal portion increases as the loan is paid down. This is obvious as each month interest is paid on the decreasing outstanding principal (i.e., the yet-to-be-repaid part), not the original amount of the loan. Interest and principal portions balance each other in such a way that the total payment remains constant.

An amortization schedule for a mortgage looks quite complicated. We can easily lose sight of the simple nature of the amortizing loan. It is nothing but an ordinary textbook *annuity*. Let us illustrate this point on an example. Consider a 2-year, 4.5%, semi-annual interest amortizing loan of $100. The repayment consists of four equal payments in 6, 12, 18, and 24 months such that the PV of those payments is equal to the face value of the loan. These can be portrayed as:

$$
\begin{array}{ccccc}
& CF & CF & CF & CF \\
\vdash & \quad \vdash & \quad \vdash & \quad \vdash & \quad \dashv \\
0 & 6m & 12m & 18m & 24m
\end{array}
$$

To solve for the constant payment of *cash flow* (*CF*) we have to set up the following equation:

$$
100 = \frac{CF}{\left(1 + \dfrac{0.045}{2}\right)} + \frac{CF}{\left(1 + \dfrac{0.045}{2}\right)^2} + \frac{CF}{\left(1 + \dfrac{0.045}{2}\right)^3} + \frac{CF}{\left(1 + \dfrac{0.045}{2}\right)^4}
$$

and we can group the terms:

$$
100 = CF\left(\frac{1}{\left(1 + \dfrac{0.045}{2}\right)} + \frac{1}{\left(1 + \dfrac{0.045}{2}\right)^2} + \frac{1}{\left(1 + \dfrac{0.045}{2}\right)^3} + \frac{1}{\left(1 + \dfrac{0.045}{2}\right)^4}\right)
$$

to see that the expression in parentheses is a 4-period annuity factor with an interest rate 2.25% per period. The solution is: $CF = 26.4219$.

Let us also illustrate the logic of interest and principal component calculation. For the first 6 months the interest portion is $\frac{0.045}{2} \cdot 100.00 = 2.25$. The remainder $26.4219 - 2.2500 = 24.1719$ goes toward the principal reduction. Right after the first payment, the outstanding principal is equal to $100.0000 - 24.1719 = 75.8281$.

Interest for the period starting in 6 months and ending in 12 months is equal to $\frac{0.045}{2} \cdot 75.8281 = 1.7061$. The outstanding principal gets reduced by $26.4219 - 1.7061 = 24.7158$ to $75.8281 - 24.7158 = 51.1123$.

Interest for the period starting in 12 months and ending in 18 months is equal to $\frac{0.045}{2} \cdot 51.1123 = 1.1500$. The outstanding principal gets reduced by $26.4219 - 1.1500 = 25.2719$ to $51.1123 - 25.2719 = 25.8404$.

Interest for the period starting in 18 months and ending in 24 months is equal to $\frac{0.045}{2} \cdot 25.8404 = 0.5814$. The outstanding principal is reduced by $26.4219 - 0.5814 = 25.8405$ to $25.8404 - 25.8405 = 0.0001 \approx 0.0000$. The loan balances are summarized in Table 2.1.

Table 2.1 Amortization table, $100 loan, maturity 2 years, 4.5% semi-annual rate

Period	Start principal	Payment	Interest portion	Principal portion	End principle
1	100.0000	26.4219	2.2500	24.1719	75.8281
2	75.8281	26.4219	1.7061	24.7158	51.1123
3	51.1123	26.4219	1.1500	25.2719	25.8405
4	25.8405	26.4219	0.5814	25.8405	0.0000

Floating-rate bonds

So far, we have considered only bonds with interest rates that are known in advance. Zero, coupon, or amortizing rates uniquely determine the cash flows a bond will pay over its life to maturity. Many bonds, however, pay cash flows that are not known in advance, but are instead tied to some interest rate index. The cash flows of these bonds can be present-valued only by use of rollover arguments. As a way of introduction to valuation of securities with unknown cash flows, we consider a floating rate bond.

Suppose ABC Inc. issues a 5-year $100 annual coupon bond. The coupon for each annual interest period will be set equal to the 1-year interest rate in effect at the beginning of that interest period and will be paid at the end of the interest period. The first coupon to be paid in 1 year is set today, at the time of the issue. The second coupon rate will be set 1 year from today and paid 2 years from today. It will be set equal to the then prevailing 1-year interest rate. The third coupon will be set 2 years from today and paid 3 years from today, and so on. How much will investors pay for such a bond?

In order to answer that question, we make a few observations. The coupon for each interest period will be "fair". It will change every year and it will reflect the cost of "renting" money for that year. The timing of the coupon-setting process corresponds to a sequence of new 1-year loans. On such loans, the rate would be set at the beginning of the year and paid at the end (i.e., it would be known in advance). The floating rate bond is equivalent to a revolving loan. Each year, ABC can be viewed as paying off a 1-year bond issued a year earlier and refinancing with a new issue of a 1-year bond.

We can use these observations to recursively deduce the price of the floating rate bond. Consider owning the 5-year bond 4 years from today, just after a coupon payment. The bond has 1 year left and the rate set is equal to $\tilde{x}_{4\times5}$. The present value of your remaining cash flow 1 year hence is:

$$P_4 = \frac{100 + \tilde{x}_{4\times5} \cdot 100}{1 + \tilde{x}_{4\times5}} = 100$$

That is, on an investment of $100, you will be paid a rate $\tilde{x}_{4\times5}$, which is also the 1-year discount rate at that time. Knowing that the bond will be worth 100 in year 4, the value of the bond in year 3 will be equal to the discounted value of the coupon of $\tilde{x}_{3\times4} \cdot 100$ set then, to be paid 1 year hence, plus the $100 you will be able to sell the bond for 1 year hence. That is, the price 3 years from today will be:

$$P_3 = \frac{\tilde{x}_{3\times4} \cdot 100 + P_4}{1 + \tilde{x}_{3\times4}} = \frac{\tilde{x}_{3\times4} \cdot 100 + 100}{1 + \tilde{x}_{3\times4}} = 100$$

The recursive argument continues all the way to year 1 for which the interest rate is known and equal to the 1-year discount rate.

Today, the price of the floating rate bond is equal to 100. That price will stay close to par throughout the life of the bond deviating only slightly inside the interest periods and returning to par right after each coupon payment.[4]

2.3   THE TERM STRUCTURE OF INTEREST RATES

At any given moment, zero rates, coupon rates, and amortizing rates are not equal to each other. Within the same category, interest rates for different maturities are not equal to each other. Not only are the different rates not equal to each other, but they also change all the time!

A graph of market interest yields against their maturities is called the *term structure of interest rates*, or the *yield curve*. The graph is a snapshot of the market YTMs for a given moment in time. What is plotted on the y-axis is *yields* and not *rates* as the first definition may misleadingly imply. The x-axis contains maturities relative to the date of the graph (e.g., 6 months from today, 1 year from today, 5 years from today, etc.). The yields can be on any day-count/compounding basis, but this is most commonly dictated by convention.

As there are many types of interest rates, there are many term structures. Bonds for different issuers which represent the different credit quality of the issuers can be grouped into rating categories. In that sense, we can talk about the BB+ term structure

---

[4] This assumes that the credit quality of the issuer remains the same throughout the life of the bond.

or the A— term structure. Even for each issuer, we can have many term structures as each bond may be collateralized differently. For example, U.S. municipalities issue either general obligation bonds, guaranteed by the general credit of the municipality, or revenue bonds, guaranteed by the revenues of a particular project like highway tolls. The two categories may enjoy different credit spreads and overall interest rates even for the same maturity. Abstracting from all these credit issues, generally, we look at two types of term structures:

- The term structure of discount rates (i.e., zeros).
- The term structure of par rates (i.e., yields on coupon bonds that trade close to par).

In the U.S., the most commonly watched term structure is that of *on-the-run* T-Bills. These are newly issued T-Bills, notes, and bonds with a few standard maturities. Because they are newly issued, they trade very close to par as the coupon rate is set close to the market yield, and they are very liquid as there is great interest in them among investors. On September 18, 2002 the Treasury yields in Table 2.2 were reported.

Table 2.2   U.S. Treasury bonds

Maturity	Yield	Yesterday	Last week	Last month
3 Month	1.54	1.55	1.56	1.52
6 Month	1.56	1.57	1.60	1.57
2 Year	1.95	1.98	2.15	2.20
5 Year	2.88	2.88	3.12	3.37
10 Year	3.81	3.81	4.05	4.28
30 Year	4.71	4.72	4.87	5.04

Source: http://bonds.yahoo.com/rates.html on September 18, 2002.

From this information we can produce the term structures for the four dates on one graph as in Figure 2.1.

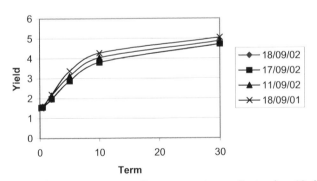

Figure 2.1   The term structure of treasury rates on September 18, 2002.

The graph illustrates how the par Treasury rates for different maturities had risen prior to September 18, 2002, but perhaps not equally; the greatest absolute increase being in the long end of the curve.

On any given date the slope of the curve can be smooth, jagged, humped, etc., as it reflects real market variables. A few shapes are of interest: upward sloping, downward sloping (inverted), or flat. These do not have precise definitions except as implied by the names. Market analysts and economists often aver that the shape of the yield curve predicts the economic cycle to follow. For example, upward sloping is purported to signal expansion; inverted, or downward, sloping a recession; and inverted with a high short rate perhaps a currency crisis. We show some examples in Figure 2.2.

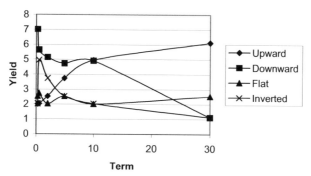

Figure 2.2   Yield curve shapes.

The Treasury yield curve blends discount (i.e., non-coupon-paying) T-Bills with coupon-paying Treasury notes and bonds. This is done for completeness as there are no 3-month coupon-paying Treasuries. For consistency, all rates are expressed as semi-annual bond equivalents.

Although most yield curves found in the press are those for coupon par instruments, the most useful one is the term structure of zero-coupon interest rates, commonly referred to as the *discount curve*, or the *zero curve*. Almost all trading desks compute the zero curve relevant for their market, because it allows them to simply read off the rates that must be used for discounting cash flows scheduled for different dates. When faced with valuing a new bond in the market, a quantitative analyst working for the desk determines each cash flow of the bond and discounts it using the zero rate corresponding to the date of the cash flow. We explain in the next few sections why that is the correct procedure. We also explain how to construct the discount curve from observed market yields.

Discounting coupon cash flows with zero rates

Let us consider the following:

Problem   We are considering buying €100 of a 4-year, 6%, annual coupon bond issued by a German company XYZ GmbH. The cash flows on the bond can be depicted as:

```
            6.00              6.00              6.00        6.00 + 100.00 = 106.00
|– – – – – – –|– – – – – – –|– – – – – – –+– – – – – – –|
0            1y              2y              3y              4y
```

Suppose we also observe that XYZ GmbH has four other zero-coupon bonds out-standing. Their maturities and yields are summarized in Table 2.3.

Table 2.3   XYZ GmbH's maturities and yields

Maturity	Zero yield
1	5.00
2	5.75
3	6.10
4	6.50

How much would we be willing to pay for the coupon bond?

Solution   Suppose, instead of buying the coupon bond, we bought four zero coupons issued by XYZ GmbH, each with the face value and maturity matching the cash flows of the coupon bond:

- For the 1-year zero with a face value of €6.00 we would pay $\dfrac{6}{(1+0.05)} = 5.7143$.

- For the 2-year zero with a face value of €6.00 we would pay $\dfrac{6}{(1+0.0575)^2} = 5.3653$.

- For the 3-year zero with a face value of €6.00 we would pay $\dfrac{6}{(1+0.061)^3} = 5.0235$.

- For the 4-year zero with a face value of €106.00 we would pay $\dfrac{6}{(1+0.065)^4} = 82.3963$.

The total we would spend would be €98.50. Since the cash flows from the four investments match exactly those of the coupon bond, we can argue that we would be willing to pay €98.50 for the coupon bond.

YTM relationship   The YTM on the coupon bond happens to be $ytm = 6.4374\%$. That is, if we discount each cash flow at 6.4374% instead of their respective discount rates we would get the following answers:

- For the 1-year zero $\dfrac{6}{(1+0.064374)} = 5.6371$.

- For the 2-year zero $\dfrac{6}{(1+0.064374)^2} = 5.2962$.

- For the 3-year zero $\dfrac{6}{(1+0.064374)^3} = 4.9759$.

- For the 4-year zero $\dfrac{6}{(1+0.064374)^4} = 82.5901$.

The sum equals €98.50. But the four "present values" obtained in this way are totally fictitious. That is, they do not represent the amounts we would have to pay for real securities. We had obtained those by discounting at the zero rates of the four real discount bonds.

Once we know the discount rates for any maturity, we know how to discount cash flows for any coupon or amortizing bond. This is because we can replicate the cash flows of that bond with real zero-coupon securities. The discounting is not a mathematical equation, but a reflection of a replicating strategy. Obtaining a zero curve greatly simplifies the analysis of any new security.

In reality, many issuers tend to only issue coupon securities (i.e., zero rates are not observed directly in the market). What can we do when this is the case?

Constructing the zero curve by bootstrapping

The discount curve can be obtained by a process known as a *zero bootstrap*. This takes as given the par coupon rates observed in the market and sequentially produces the zero rates one by one from the shortest to the longest maturity, just like lacing boots. A bootstrap looks messy on paper, but setting it up in a spreadsheet requires no skill. The only confusion usually has to do with day-count conventions. We will describe the process for annual rates.

Problem   We observe the following annual coupon bonds that XYZ GmbH has outstanding in the market. These are newly issued bonds and some old bonds that originally had much longer maturities.

Table 2.4   XYZ GmbH's annual coupon bonds

Maturity	Coupon	Price
1	5.10	100.0952
2	5.60	99.7618
3	6.10	100.0962
4	6.00	98.4993

Can we deduce what the zero curve for XYZ GmbH is given this market information?

Solving for the 1-year zero rate   Let us first look at the 1-year bond. There is only one cash flow from this bond equal to €105.10 at maturity. This can be depicted as:

$$105.10$$
$$|\text{-------}|$$
$$0 \qquad\quad 1y$$

Let us compare this with the 1-year €100 face value zero-coupon bond whose single cash flow can be depicted as:

$$100$$
$$|\text{-------}|$$
$$1 \qquad\quad 1y$$

Investors would be indifferent between the 1-year 5.1% coupon bond with a face value of €100 and a 1-year zero-coupon bond with a face value of €105.10. Both investments would have the same single cash flow of €105.10 in 1 year. Both are in fact pure discount bonds with a face value of €105.10. The coupon bond is just labeled "coupon" as that is presumably how it was originally issued. If the zero-coupon bond came in denominations of €0.10, investors could simply ask for 1,051 such "bondlets" to replicate the 1-year coupon bond. Given that the coupon bond and the zero-coupon bond are perfect substitutes for each other, they must have the same yield. We can easily compute the yield on the 1-year coupon bond implied in its market price by solving the following equation for z_1:

$$100.0952 = \frac{105.10}{(1 + z_1)}$$

The solution is $z_1 = 5\%$. Any cash flow payable by XYZ GmbH in 1 year should be discounted by 5%, because it could be replicated by holding the appropriate face value of the 1-year coupon bond. In other words, any 1-year discount bond issued by XYZ GmbH would have to yield 5%, because it could be replicated by holding the appropriate face value of the 1-year coupon bond.

The first step in the bootstrap is typically simple, because the shortest maturity coupon bond may not have any intervening coupons left.

Solving for the 2-year zero rate   Let us examine the 2-year coupon bond. It has a coupon rate of 5.60% and it sells for €99.7618. From that information, we can depict its cash flows as:

```
              5.60              105.60
|- - - - - - - -|- - - - - - - -|
0              1y              2y
```

From the first step of the bootstrap, we know that we can compute the PV of the 1-year cash flow by applying the discount rate $z_1 = 5\%$. That is, we can get:

$$PV(CF_1) = \frac{5.60}{(1 + 0.05)} = 5.3333$$

We also know that the total PV of the bond equal to its current price is €99.7618. So the present value of the second cash flow must be the difference:

$$PV(CF_2) = 99.7618 - 5.3333 = 94.4285$$

If the bond could be separated and sold as two separate *strips*, then the first one with the face value of €5.60 would sell for €5.3333 and the second one with the face value of €105.60 would sell for €94.4285. We can solve for the discount yield implied in the price of the 2-year strip by solving the following equation for z_2:

$$94.4285 = \frac{105.60}{(1 + z_2)^2}$$

to get $z_2 = 5.75\%$. If XYX GmbH had a 2-year zero outstanding, then it would have to yield 5.75%; otherwise, investors could replicate its cash flow of €100 in 2 years by buying the appropriate face value of the second strip.

The arbitrage argument   But suppose that the 2-year coupon bond cannot be separated and sold as two strips. Can we still claim that the 2-year discount rate should be 5.75%? This is actually the crux of the argument.

Suppose an investor wants to enter into a strategy in which a payment of €105.60 in 2 years is promised to her by XYZ GmbH (i.e., she wants to replicate the non-existent second strip or *synthetically* create a 2-year zero). She could do it by entering into the following two trades simultaneously:

- Buying €100 face value of the 2-year, 5.60% coupon bond for €99.7618.
- Shorting €5.60 face value of a 1-year zero for which she would receive €5.3333.

Her net investment is €94.4285. Her cash flows can be portrayed as:

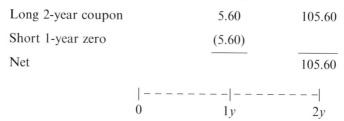

	1y	2y
Long 2-year coupon	5.60	105.60
Short 1-year zero	(5.60)	
Net		105.60

This matches exactly the 2-year strip. Thus, a 2-year zero investment can be synthetically replicated by going long a 2-year coupon bond and short a 1-year zero-coupon bond. Any 2-year zero-coupon bond issued by XYZ GmbH would have to yield at least 5.75%; otherwise, nobody would buy it. All investors would simply enter into synthetic replicating strategies.

Furthermore, if XYZ GmbH did issue a 2-year zero and it yielded more than 5.75%, all investors would buy that zero and simultaneously construct a *short* 2-year strip with offsetting cash flows, thereby locking in riskless profits. The strategy could be summarized as the following three trades:

- Buy the 2-year zero with a face value of €105.60 for less than €94.4285 (i.e., yielding more than 5.75%).
- Short €100 face value of the 2-year, 5.60% coupon bond to receive €99.7618.
- Buy €5.60 face value of a 1-year zero by paying €5.3333.

In the short coupon bond transaction, the investor would borrow the bond from a third party, sell it in the market for its current price, but would be obligated to replace the coupons and principal repayment cash flows to the bond lender. The last two trades—short coupon bond and long 1-year zero—would bring a cash inflow of €94.4285 today. If the first one—long 2-year zero—costs less than €94.4285 to enter into, then the arbitrageur would have a positive cash flow today. Her future obligations would be matched at every point in time as shown below:

	1y	2y
Long 2-year zero		105.60
Short 2-year coupon	(5.60)	(105.60)
Long 1-year zero	5.60	
Net	0	0

| 0 | 1y | 2y |

All she would have to do in the future is to collect the receipts on her 1-year and 2-year zero investments and use them to satisfy her coupon obligations to the lender of the bond. She would not be the only one pursuing this arbitrage strategy. *All* investors would immediately pursue strategies like this one, driving the price of the newly issued 2-year zero up and its rate down to the 5.75% level. It is also possible that the 2-year coupon rate might be driven up and the 1-year zero rate down at the same time. All three instruments would have to find a level at which arbitrage would be prevented and we could safely apply our bootstrap math.

One lesson from all of this is that the no-arbitrage principle requires that all instruments be freely traded and both longs and shorts allowed. Our example also presumes that the bid–ask spread (i.e., the difference in the prices at which the bonds are offered to be bought and sold) is very narrow (we assumed a spread of zero). Illiquid markets with wide bid–ask spreads also follow arbitrage rules, but the spread has to be explicitly taken into account to compute arbitrage bands around mid-market prices and rates. In liquid markets, the standard procedure is to use mid-market rates to compute the implied mid-market zero rate and then adjust it to bid or ask.

Solving for the 3-year zero rate   Let us examine the 3-year coupon bond. It has a coupon rate of 6.10% and it sells for €100.0962. From that information, we can depict its cash flows as:

$$\begin{array}{cccc} & 6.10 & 6.10 & 106.10 \\ |\,-\,-\,-\,-\,-\,-\,-\,-\,-|\,-\,-\,-\,-\,-\,-\,-\,-\,-|\,-\,-\,-\,-\,-\,-\,-\,-\vdash \\ 0 & 1y & 2y & 3y \end{array}$$

We have solved for $z_1 = 5\%$ and $z_2 = 5.75\%$, and we know how to discount the first two cash flows of the bond:

$$PV(CF_1) = \frac{6.10}{(1+0.05)} = 5.8095$$

$$PV(CF_2) = \frac{6.10}{(1+0.0575)^2} = 5.4547$$

We also know that the total present value of the bond equal to its current price is €100.0962. So the present value of the third cash flow must be the difference:

$$PV(CF_3) = 100.0962 - (5.8095 + 5.4547) = 88.8320$$

If the bond could be separated and sold as three separate strips, then:

- The 1-year strip with the face value of €6.10 would sell for €5.8095.
- The 2-year strip with the face value of €6.10 would sell for €5.4547.
- The 3-year strip with the face value of €106.10 would sell for €88.8320.

We can solve for the discount yield implied in the price of the 3-year strip by solving the following equation for z_3:

$$88.8320 = \frac{106.10}{(1+z_3)^3}$$

to get $z_3 = 6.10\%$. If XYX GmbH had a 3-year zero outstanding, then it would have to yield 6.10%. It is a pure coincidence that the 3-year zero rate, or the 3-year zero yield, is equal to the 3-year coupon rate of the particular bond we used. The 3-year coupon yield is not equal to 6.10% as the bond sells for a price higher than the par of 100. If XYX GmbH were to issue another 3-year coupon bond and wanted to sell it at par, then its coupon would have to be set below 6.10%. We will come back to this point after the completion of the bootstrap.

The arbitrage argument   Let us again show that the 3-year zero of 6.10% is not just a product of a mathematical procedure, but that market forces (i.e., real human behavior) will guarantee that level. We assume that the 1- and 2-year zero-coupon bonds issued by XYZ GmbH are actively traded in the market or they can be created *synthetically* by taking simultaneous positions in existing coupon bonds and zero bonds.

Suppose an investor wants to enter into a strategy in which a payment of €106.10 is promised to her by XYZ GmbH (i.e., she wants to *synthetically* create a 3-year zero with a face value of €106.10). She could do it by entering into the following three trades simultaneously:

- Buying €100 face value of the 3-year, 6.10% coupon bond for €100.0962.
- Shorting €6.10 face value of a 1-year zero for which she would receive €5.8095.
- Shorting €6.10 face value of a 2-year zero for which she would receive €5.4547.

Her net investment is €88.8320. Her cash flows can be portrayed as:

Long 3-year coupon	6.10	6.10	106.10
Short 1-year zero	(6.10)		
Short 2-year zero		(6.10)	
Net			106.10

$$|- - - - - - - -|- - - - - - - -|- - - - - - - -|$$
$$0 \qquad\qquad 1y \qquad\qquad 2y \qquad\qquad 3y$$

This matches exactly the 3-year strip. Any 3-year zero-coupon bond issued by XYZ GmbH would have to yield at least 6.10%; otherwise, nobody would buy it. All investors would simply enter into this synthetic replicating strategy with existing bonds.

Again, we can also argue the yield on a new 3-year zero could not be higher than 6.10%. Suppose that XYZ GmbH did issue a 3-year zero yielding more than 6.10%. All investors would buy that zero and at the same time construct a *synthetic short* 3-year zero with offsetting cash flows to lock in riskless profits. The strategy could be summarized as the following four trades:

- Buy the 3-year zero with a face value of €106.10 for less than €88.8320 (i.e., yielding more than 6.10%).
- Short €100 face value of the 3-year, 6.10% coupon bond to receive €100.0962.
- Buy €6.10 face value of a 2-year zero by paying €5.4547.
- Buy €6.10 face value of a 1-year zero by paying €5.8095.

In the short coupon bond transaction, the investor would borrow the bond from a third party, sell it in the market for its current price, but would be obligated to replace the coupons and principal repayment cash flows to the bond lender. The last three trades—

short coupon bond, long 2-year zero, and long 1-year zero—would bring a cash inflow of €88.8320 today. If the first one—long 3-year zero—costs less than €88.8320 to enter into, then the arbitrageur would have a positive cash flow today. Her future obligations would be matched at every point in time and can be depicted as:

Long 3-year zero			106.10
Short 3-year coupon	(6.10)	(6.10)	(106.10)
Long 2-year zero		6.10	
Long 1-year zero	6.10		
Net	0	0	0

$$|------|------|------|$$
$$0 \qquad\qquad 1y \qquad\qquad 2y \qquad\qquad 3y$$

In the future, she would simply collect the receipts from her 1-, 2-, and 3-year zero investments and use them to satisfy her coupon obligations to the lender of the 3-year coupon bond. Again, she would not be the only one pursuing this arbitrage strategy. All investors would immediately do the same, driving the price of the new 3-year zero up and its rate down to the 6.10% level. They might also force the yields on the other bonds to adjust to a level at which arbitrage would not be possible.

2.4 INTEREST RATE RISK

A vast majority of coupon bonds are issued at par or at a price close to par. Practically, what that implies is that at the time of issue the coupon rate is set close to the prevailing market yield. Zero-coupon bonds are sold at a discount from par, and the discounted price reflects the market yield. After the issue, all bond prices fluctuate with market yields. The coupon rate set at the time of issue does not change and the cash flows it defines do not change; neither do the dates of the cash flows. But as yields required by investors change, so do the discounted values of those cash flows. This phenomenon is normally portrayed as a downward-sloping concave relationship between the price of a bond and the YTM on the bond.

Consider a 12-year, 10%, semi-annual coupon bond yielding 10% semi-annually and let us assume a face value of $100. The bond pays $5 every 6 months for the next 12 years and returns the principal of $100 12 years from today. The price of the bond today, equal to the discounted value of its cash flows, is equal to:

$$P = \frac{10/2}{(1+0.10/2)} + \frac{10/2}{(1+0.10/2)^2} + \cdots + \frac{10/2}{(1+0.10/2)^{24}} + \frac{100}{(1+0.10/2)^{24}}$$

$$= \frac{5}{(1+0.05)} + \frac{5}{(1+0.05)^2} + \cdots + \frac{5}{(1+0.05)^{24}} + \frac{100}{(1+0.05)^{24}}$$

and, miraculously, to 100! If we set the denominator yield used to discount cash flows equal to the coupon rate, then the price will always come out equal to par. This can also be seen through a recursive argument. Six months prior to maturity (i.e., $11\frac{1}{2}$ years from now) the bond price is equal to the discounted value of the principal and last coupon received at maturity, or:

$$P_{11.5} = \frac{105}{1 + 0.05} = 100$$

Twelve months prior to maturity (i.e., 11 years from now) the bond price is equal to the discounted value of the next coupon and what the bond can be sold for the next period; that is:

$$P_{11} = \frac{5 + P_{11.5}}{1 + 0.05} = \frac{105}{1 + 0.05} = 100$$

and so on.

Now suppose that the market yield on a 12-year bond changes to 8% semi-annual. The new price of the 10% coupon bond is:

$$P = \frac{5}{(1 + 0.04)} + \frac{5}{(1 + 0.04)^2} + \cdots + \frac{5}{(1 + 0.04)^{24}} + \frac{100}{(1 + 0.04)^{24}} = 115.25$$

That is, in order to receive an above-market coupon of 10%, an investor would have to pay an above-par price. Conversely, if the market yield on a 12-year bond changes to 12% semi-annual, the price will drop to:

$$P = \frac{5}{(1 + 0.06)} + \frac{5}{(1 + 0.06)^2} + \cdots + \frac{5}{(1 + 0.06)^{24}} + \frac{100}{(1 + 0.06)^{24}} = 87.45$$

Plotting the relationship between the price of the bond and its yield, we would get Figure 2.3:

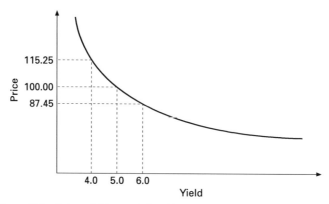

Figure 2.3 Price–yield graph for 12-year, 10%, semi-annual coupon bond.

Note that there is a maximum price for the bond. If the yield drops to 0, then the value of the bond will be equal to the sum of its cash flows, or:

$$P = \frac{5}{(1 + 0)} + \frac{5}{(1 + 0)^2} + \cdots + \frac{5}{(1 + 0)^{24}} + \frac{100}{(1 + 0)^{24}} = 220$$

The price for the bond approaches 0 asymptotically as the interest rate goes to infinity. Most of the time, we are somewhere in the middle. The graph is a convex (bowed to below) curve due to the nature of compound interest. This can also be seen from the fact that the change in price is not symmetric. When the yield went down by 2%, the price changed by 15.25; when the yield went up by 2%, the price changed by −12.55.

Observations   An increase in market yield lowers the price of the bond; a decrease in market yield raises the price of the bond; the price–yield relationship is convex; interest rate fluctuations are a source of price risk for bond holders.

What does the magnitude of that risk depend on? Three factors come to mind:

- Time to maturity—other things being equal, the longer the maturity of the bond, the larger the price swings are for the same change in interest rates. This can be seen by repeating our exercise for a 16-year, 10%, semi-annual coupon bond. At a yield of 10% semi-annual, the bond prices to par, at 8% to 117.87 and at 12% to 85.92. A change in the rate used for discounting the cash flows has a greater impact for a longer bond due to the compound interest effect on later cash flows.
- Coupon rate—other things being equal, the lower the coupon rate of the bond, the larger the price swings are for the same change in interest rates. The intuition is similar to the time to maturity argument. The principal repayment's weight in the overall present value is greater for a low coupon bond than for a high coupon bond. Therefore, a change in the discount rate affects a low coupon bond disproportionately more.
- Coupon frequency—other things being equal, the less frequently the coupons on the bond are paid, the larger the price swings are for the same change in interest rates. Monthly bonds bring the coupons closer to today than annual coupon bonds and, hence, are less sensitive to the discount rate change.

From the above, we can deduce that zero-coupon bonds have the greatest interest rate risk of all bonds with the same maturity, as there is only one cash flow at maturity.

Floating-rate bonds have virtually no interest rate sensitivity as their prices always return to par after coupon payments. Their price may deviate from par on a non-coupon date only to the extent that the first coupon rate that has been set is different from the discount rate for that first coupon. For example, today's 9-month (discount) rate may be different from a 12-month rate set 3 months ago for the current 1-year coupon period. All future coupons will be set at "fair" rates and have a present value of 100.

To compare the riskiness of bonds with different characteristics (maturities, coupon rates, and coupon frequencies), we require a metric of interest rate sensitivity. The most commonly used interest rate risk metrics are duration and convexity. Both of these measures are local in nature. They are summary statistics that describe the sensitivity of the bond's price to small changes in yields away from the current level. They are not appropriate for large market moves and they are not global in nature: the duration of the bond when yields are at 5% can be vastly different from the duration of the same bond when yields are at 8%. Fixed income portfolio managers dealing with hundreds or thousands of bonds with different maturities, coupons, or issuers routinely use duration and convexity measures to select bonds for their portfolios.

Duration

The universe of bonds, even for the same issuer, can be enormous. Imagine the bonds our XYZ GmbH might have outstanding on any given day: a 5-year, semi-annual, 4%

coupon bond; a $7\frac{1}{4}$-year, annual, 3% bond with next coupon due in 3 months; a 6-year zero-coupon; or a 4-year bond whose coupon starts at 3.5% but increases by 0.75% each year. How do we choose which bond to invest in or which one to sell out of a portfolio?

Investors compare bonds that have different characteristics by using the notion of *duration*. In its original form, as described by Macaulay,[5] duration D is defined as the present value-weighted average time to the bond's cash flows. The largest cash flow for a bond is the principal repayment at maturity. But the bond may also provide substantial coupons prior to maturity. The duration measure takes into account the final repayment and any interim flows of all cash flows in computing an average time of the cash flows, which is often much shorter than the maturity of the bond. In the averaging, the cash flows are weighted by their contribution to the total present value of the bond. Duration is defined by Macaulay in terms of time or years. We can say that a bond has, for example, a duration of 3.45 years or that another bond has a duration of 7.29 years, and we can compare bonds based on that number. As we will show, this is a very intuitive measure.

Duration has also another, more interesting interpretation: *modified duration* is the relative sensitivity of the bond price to a unit yield change. That unit can be 1%, but a preferred unit of yield change is 1 basis point, or 0.01%. For example, if a bond has a modified duration of 6.94 and the yield to maturity *increases* by 1 basis point, then the price of the bond will *decrease* approximately by 6.94 basis points. Modified duration is thus defined as the percentage change in the price divided by the change in yield, or:

$$ModD = -\frac{\Delta P/P}{\Delta y}$$

As it turns out, duration and modified duration are closely related through the following formula:

$$ModD = \frac{D}{1+\frac{y}{n}}$$

where n is the number of compounding periods per year for the yield y. Note that the denominator is close to one, and duration and modified duration are roughly the same. Often traders talk only of one duration, quoting exclusively the modified duration numbers as these reflect the local riskiness of bonds. But it is important to understand the intuitive Macaulay meaning of duration.

Let us consider an example of a 6-year, 7%, semi-annual coupon bond yielding 8%. That is, a $100 face value bond pays $3.50 at the end of each 6-month period and returns the principal of $100 in 6 years. Table 2.5 presents the logic of the Macaulay duration calculation. Columns 1 and 2 contain times and cash flows. Column 3 contains discount factors for each cash flow based on the yield of 8% semi-annual. Column 4 computes the present value of each cash flow with the sum of all present values at the bottom. The essence of the duration computation is columns 5 and 6. Column 5 presents the percentage that the present value of each cash flow represents in the total value of the bond. Each percentage can be construed as the weight of that cash flow in the total in today's dollars. Lastly, column 6 multiplies those weights by the times to the cash flows to arrive at a weighted-average time to cash flows.

---

[5] Frederick Macaulay, *Some Theoretical Problems Suggested by the Movement of Interest Rates, Bond Yields, and Stock Prices in the U.S. since 1856*, 1938, National Bureau of Economic Research, New York.

Table 2.5 Macaulay duration calculation logic

		Maturity in years:	6		
		Coupon:	7.00		
		Yield:	8.00		

Time	CF	DF	PV	%PV	$t \times$ %PV
0.5	3.5	0.961 538	3.365 385	3.53	0.017 7
1	3.5	0.924 556	3.235 947	3.40	0.034 0
1.5	3.5	0.888 996	3.111 487	3.26	0.049 0
2	3.5	0.854 804	2.991 815	3.14	0.062 8
2.5	3.5	0.821 927	2.876 745	3.02	0.075 5
3	3.5	0.790 315	2.766 101	2.90	0.087 1
3.5	3.5	0.759 918	2.659 712	2.79	0.097 7
4	3.5	0.730 690	2.557 416	2.68	0.107 3
4.5	3.5	0.702 587	2.459 054	2.58	0.116 1
5	3.5	0.675 564	2.364 475	2.48	0.124 0
5.5	3.5	0.649 581	2.273 533	2.39	0.131 2
6	103.5	0.624 597	64.645 79	67.83	4.069 7
Total			95.307 46	100.00	4.972 0

Figure 2.4 is yet another way to present the concept graphically. Each block represents the percentage of present value recovered through each cash flow. The height of the block is taken from the appropriate row of column 5.

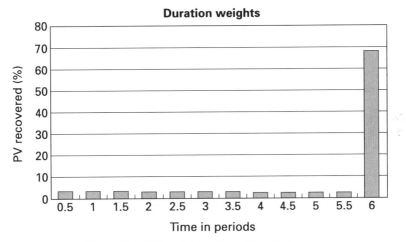

Figure 2.4 PV weights of bond's cash flows.

The weighted-average time to the cash flows, using the block heights as the weights, is equal to 4.968. That number is also the approximate percentage change of the price corresponding to a 1% change in yield.

The Macaulay concept is extremely intuitive. With a little experience, we can guess bond durations fairly accurately. Here are some heuristics:

- All other things being equal, the longer the maturity, the longer the duration (i.e., the blocks in our graph extend further out and so the weighted time to the repayment is longer).

- The larger the coupon, the shorter the duration (i.e., the higher the coupon blocks, the less weight is assigned to the principal repayment and the smaller the weighted average).
- The greater the frequency of the coupons, the shorter the duration (i.e., as more blocks are closer to today).

All three of these correspond closely to the heuristics behind the interest rate risk of bonds. Here are two more observations:

- The duration of a zero-coupon bond is equal to its maturity.
- Floating rate bonds have very short durations equal to the next coupon date.

Let us now examine the more practical meaning of duration, that of the interest rate sensitivity applied to our example bond. The 6-year, 7%, semi-annual coupon bond yielding 8% is valued at 95.3075. We computed the Macauley duration to be 4.9720. The modified duration is then:

$$ModD = \frac{4.9720}{1 + \dfrac{0.08}{2}} = 4.7807$$

If the yield on the bond were to increase from 8.00% to 8.15% (i.e., by 0.15%, or 15 basis points), then the price of the bond should decrease by 4.7807×0.15, or 0.7171%. Based on the starting value of 95.3075, this translates into a change to 94.6240. Mathematically, this can be expressed as:

$$P_{new} = P[1 + (-ModD)\Delta y]$$
$$= 95.3075[1 + (-4.7807)(0.15)] = 94.6240$$

An exact calculation of the value of the bond assuming an 8.15% yield produces the discounted value of the bond's cash flows equal to 94.6270. In the case of a small change in the yield, duration was a very good approximation to the change in the value of the bond. This would not be so if the yield change considered were large. In the extreme case of the yield going down to 0 (i.e., a yield change of 8%), multiplying that change by 4.7807 gives the predicted change in the bond price of 38.2456% of the current value, or $36.4509. Duration would predict that the bond price would increase to $131.7584. Yet we know that at a zero discount rate the value of the bond is equal to a simple sum of its cash flows or $142.

What went wrong? Duration is a local measure. It is the first derivative of the price with respect to the yield. Thus, it is a linear approximation based on a line that is tangent to a polynomial curve, the true price–yield relationship. This is represented in Figure 2.5.

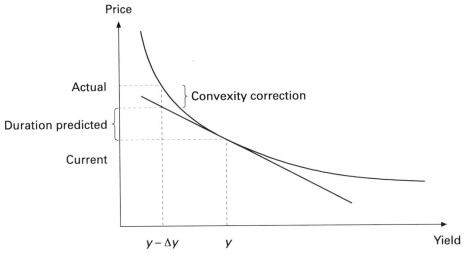

Figure 2.5 Price–yield relationship.

Later we show how the duration-based linear approximation can be improved with the use of convexity.

Most computer applications do not compute duration the way we presented it in Table 2.5. Rather, they revalue the bond using the yield a small number of basis points above and a small number of basis points below the current YTM, and then they divide the change in the bond's value by the combined size of the yield change "blip". That is, they compute the sensitivity of price to yield directly. Let us denote the value of the bond with a yield blipped up by dy basis points as P_{+dy} and the value of the bond with a yield blipped down by dy basis points as P_{-dy}. Then duration can be computed numerically by dividing the percentage price change by the total change in yield, or as:

$$ModD = -\frac{(P_{+dy} - P_{-dy})/P}{2dy}$$

In our case the two values can be easily arrived at using a financial calculator or a spreadsheet. For example, using the yield of 8.02 we get $P_{+2} = 95.216\,39$, and using the yield of 7.98 we get $P_{-2} = 95.39864$. The duration is thus computed as:

$$ModD = -\frac{(95.216\,39 - 95.398\,64)/95.307\,46}{2 \cdot 0.0002} = 4.7806$$

Of course, we could use a smaller yield change or adjust the centering in the numerator. Note that the estimate is off by 0.0001 due to the fact that we used a large blip of 2 basis points. The smaller the blip used, the smaller the error. We encourage the reader to repeat the calculation by using a 1 basis point or a 0.5 basis point yield change.

The numerical procedure of computing duration is very general and works also for the most complex bonds with embedded options, for which expected cash flows may change as we vary the yield.

Portfolio duration

Duration is very popular with managers of large bond portfolios. This is due to its one very attractive property: the duration of a portfolio is equal to the weighted average of the durations of individual bonds. The weight for each bond is simply the proportion of the portfolio invested in that bond. This property is a direct result of the fact that durations are first derivatives of the bond values with respect to yields and that first derivatives are additive. Let us look at an example.

Consider the following portfolio of bonds:

Investment ($ million)	Investment (%)	Coupon	Maturity	Duration
400	20	6.50	12	9.54
900	45	5.75	10	7.23
700	35	5.25	6	4.85
2,000	100			6.86

Duration $= 0.20 * 9.54 + 0.45 * 7.23 + 0.35 * 4.85 = 6.859$.

The interpretation of the portfolio duration is the same as that for individual bonds with the qualification that the duration of the portfolio is the sensitivity of the value of the portfolio with respect to a *parallel* shift in yield to maturities. In the case of the portfolio represented in the above table, this could translate into the following statement: if the YTM on each bond in the portfolio decreased by 7 basis points, then the value of the portfolio would increase by 6.859×7, or 48.013 basis points. In dollars, that is equal to an increase of $0.004\,801\,3 \times \$2$ billion, or $9,602,600. By knowing *one* statistic about the portfolio—its duration—the manager can predict the value change for the entire portfolio very accurately for small changes in yields!

Often, bond managers engage in what is called *duration matching*, or *portfolio immunization*. These terms refer to a conscious selection of bonds to be added to the portfolio in order to reduce the duration of the portfolio to 0 (i.e., to eliminate all interest rate risk). This is done by selecting the right amount of bonds to be shorted or by buying bonds with negative duration. Sometimes, managers do not attempt to eliminate risk completely, but rather to "shorten" (decrease) or "lengthen" (increase) the duration of a portfolio by reshuffling the allocations to various bonds. Many managers of corporate bond portfolios short government bonds with the same duration to eliminate exposure to interest rates, leaving themselves with pure credit spread exposure. Commercial banks engage in a form of portfolio immunization, by trying to decrease the duration of their assets (auto and home loan portfolios) and increase the duration of their liabilities (move depositors to long-term certificates of deposit, or CDs).

Note, in the above example, that if the YTMs do not change in parallel (e.g., some change by 8 basis points and others by 6 basis points), then the estimate based on portfolio duration will be somewhat inaccurate. However, an estimate obtained by summing the products of the changes in yields for all bond times will have individual durations that are still very accurate. This is still much easier than revaluing all bonds.

Convexity

Convexity is often used to improve the accuracy of the duration approximation to the change in value of the bond. It is important to include it in the approximation for:

- Large changes in YTM.
- Bonds whose price–yield relationship is highly non-linear (e.g., bonds with embedded options, some mortgage-backed securities).

Convexity is equal to half the second derivative of bond price with respect to the yield, and as such it measures the average rate of change in the slope of the tangent duration line. Numerically, it can be computed as the following difference formula:

$$C = \frac{1}{2} \cdot \frac{(P_{+dy} + P_{-dy} - 2P)/P}{(dy)^2}$$

We already have all the ingredients to compute convexity for our example bond. Let us plug the numbers into the formula to get:

$$C = \frac{1}{2} \cdot \frac{(95.216\,39 + 95.398\,64 - 2 \cdot 95.307\,46)/95.307\,46}{(0.0002)^2} = 14.4270$$

The convexity number measures the average change in the duration per dy basis points.[6] It tells us to what extent the true price–yield curve deviates from the linear approximation. What we are mostly interested in is in improving that approximation. In order to do that, we need to multiply the convexity by the relevant yield change Δy to obtain the change in the duration over that entire yield change. This may explain the logic behind the following duration-cum-convexity approximation formula for the bond price change:

$$P_{new} = P[1 + (ModD + C \cdot \Delta y)\Delta y]$$

The percentage price change in the bond value per unit of yield comes from two sources: the duration, which for most bonds will underestimate the magnitude of the change following a straight line, and the convexity that will correct for that underestimation by reducing the absolute value of the duration. Using the numbers for our example bond, we get:

$$P_{new} = 95.307\,46[1 + (-4.7806 + 14.4270 \cdot 0.0015) \cdot 0.0015] = 95.6271$$

We have improved our estimate considerably and are almost spot on! Recall the true value of the bond at a yield of 8.15% was 95.6270.

Convexity is widely used as a summary statistic to describe large bond portfolios. Typically, durations and convexities are computed for several possible yield increments relative to today's level (e.g., −50, −25, 0, +25, +50 basis points). It is important to remember, however, that convexities, unlike durations, are not additive and are computed by blipping entire portfolios and revaluing all the bonds in them. Just like with durations, managers engage in immunization strategies with respect to convexities by adding negatively convex bonds or reshuffling portfolio allocations to reduce or increase the convexity of the overall portfolio.

---

[6] Duration changes continuously between the original value P and the estimated value P_{new} corresponding to the yield change of Δy. The multiplication of the second derivative by $\frac{1}{2}$ averages the point estimates of convexity per unit of yield over the entire range of Δy.

Other risk measures

Duration and convexity calculations as described so far assume that the underlying cash flows of the bond do not change; only the YTM does. Yet the cash flows of bonds with embedded options often change as the yields change (e.g., a "blip" in the yield on a callable bond may trigger a call provision). In those cases, we can compute alternative measures of *effective* duration and convexity where the changed cash flows are explicitly taken into account when computing the blipped values P_{+dy} and P_{-dy}. We should, however, bear in mind that those values are not computed through simple discounting, but, rather, with the use of an option-pricing model. As such they take into account other inputs, the most important of which is the volatility of the yield.

The volatility of the yield enters into the analysis in a different way too. Imagine a portfolio of two corporate bonds both with the same maturity and both trading at par. But one of the bonds has a much higher coupon reflecting the lower credit quality of its issuer. Is it realistic to assume that the yields on the bonds will move in parallel or is it more realistic to assume that the riskier bond's yield will fluctuate proportionately more? The volatility of the yield refers precisely to that concept. Computing portfolio durations may be of little help in this case. Rather, we may prefer to compute individual durations and scale the assumed yield movements by the respective yield volatilities to arrive at portfolio value change approximations for more realistic yield movements.

Lastly, let us define the concept of the price value of a basis point, which is closely related to duration. Unlike duration, which is expressed in relative terms, the price value of a basis point (PVBP) measures the absolute value of the change in price of a bond per unit of yield change; that is, it is defined as:

$$PVBP = -\frac{\Delta P}{\Delta y}$$

and can be approximated by:

$$PVBP = -\frac{(P_{+dy} - P_{-dy})/10,000}{2dy}$$

In our bond example, it could be computed as:

$$PVBP = -\frac{(95.216\,39 - 95.398\,64)/10,000}{2 \cdot 0.0002} = 0.0456$$

and is defined in dollars. The interpretation of PVBP is that 1 basis point change in the yield causes \$0.0456 change in the value of the bond with a face value of \$100. For par bonds, modified durations and PVBPs scaled by 1/100 are identical since percentage changes and absolute value changes are the same if $P = 100$.

2.5 EQUITY MARKETS MATH

The main difference between the bond math and the stock math is the degree of uncertainty about the cash flows. For most bonds, coupons and principal repayments are guaranteed by the issuer. Unless the issuer defaults, the cash flows are known in advance. Because of that, we are able to construct very strict relationships between the different bonds of the same issuer and argue, using the arbitrage principle, that related yields must be certain numbers. We do not have to invoke any assumptions about the issuer's business, the company's management style, or the growth prospects for its portfolio of investments to compute what price we should pay for a bond or what yield we are earning given the price.

This is not the case with stocks. A company is under no obligation to pay dividends. If and when it returns cash to its shareholders, whether in the form of dividends or capital gains, is not known in advance. It is hard to discount cash flows if we do not know them. Even if we assume that we do, then what rate of discount should we apply? The principle of cash flow discounting requires that the rate used reflects the uncertainty of the cash flows. Equity holders get paid only after debt holders do. So the discount rate must be higher than that applied to bonds. What equity holders get paid depends on the company's success. Presumably, the greater the potential payoff in its investments, the greater the risk of these projects. Thus the value of the stock will depend on the subjective growth estimates for the company's projects. Given this uncertainty about both the cash flows and the discount rate, we will be able to compute the rate of return on the stock, knowing its price or the fair value of the stock assuming the discount rate, but not both. In addition, each relative valuation method will depend on the assumption about future profitability of the company's projects. Given all these uncertainties, the math applied will be much simpler than that for bonds, and, paradoxically, complicating it will not make things more accurate.

There is one more point of view to bear in mind. The value of the company's assets is equal to the value of its equity plus the value of its debt. So if we know the value of all the assets, why do we have to make profitability assumptions when valuing stocks and not when valuing bonds? Aren't the two supposed to add up to a known value?

There are two related ways to answer that question. The first, an option-theoretic point, is that we never really know the value of the assets until the company gets liquidated or acquired. The accounting book value is of very little help; rather, it is more realistic to view the value of the debt as known. After all, we can discount the value of all future debt obligations. The discount rates can be easily gleaned from bond yields and rates quoted on bank debt. In this way, the equity value can be looked on as equivalent to a call option on the company's assets after creditors have been paid off. That is, it can be written as a payoff for the call with a strike price equal to the value of the debt:

$$Equity = Max[Assets - Debt, 0]$$

The related second point is that perhaps the debt value is not so well known. After all, when the credit quality of the company declines and bonds get downgraded, the yield spreads over the risk-free rates can fluctuate and with them so can the value of the debt. Thus, although for risk-free government debt all the discounting machinery is well established, for risky corporate debt it is not so simple. Even if the value of assets is known, both equity and debt values can fluctuate with the prospects of the company. This point becomes very clear when we consider hybrid securities like convertible debt. It becomes even clearer when we consider companies close to bankruptcy, where the possibility that debt holders will soon become equity holders is very real. Add to that the uncertainty in the value of the assets (how much is the Starbucks brand worth?) and the point is made.

A dividend discount model

Let us start by assuming that we know the rate that we should apply to discount the company's future cash flows. Perhaps we examined the company's business plan and compared it with that of other similar ventures. Perhaps we used the standard capital asset-pricing model (CAPM)[7] which related the discount rate for the stock to the rate on risk-free government obligations and a market risk premium. In any case, we have determined the appropriate rate r, which we will assume to remain constant over time.

We want to buy one share of ABC Corp. ABC will pay a dividend of D_1 dollars a year from today and, at that point, we will be able to sell the stock for P_1 dollars. Then the present value of the cash flows today (i.e., the fair price for the stock, P_0) is equal to:

$$P_0 = \frac{D_1 + P_1}{1 + r}$$

D_1 could be 0 here. Also note that we may not know the value P_1 that we will be able to sell the share for 1 year from today. However, we can argue that tomorrow's purchaser will expect to earn a return of r percent on the stock over the following year. In other words, he will pay the discounted value of next year's dividend and sale price; that is:

$$P_1 = \frac{D_2 + P_2}{1 + r}$$

Today's fair value for the share is:

$$P_0 = \frac{D_1}{1 + r} + \frac{D_2 + P_2}{(1 + r)^2}$$

We can extend the argument to a potential purchaser at the end of year 2, and so on, to get a general formula:

$$P_0 = \frac{D_1}{1 + r} + \frac{D_2}{(1 + r)^2} + \frac{D_3}{(1 + r)^3} + \cdots + \frac{D_n + P_n}{(1 + r)^n}$$

We would have gotten the same result if we had assumed that we did not intend to sell the stock after 1 year, but that we were going to hold it for n years, collect all intervening dividends, if any, and then sell only at the end of year n. That is, the formula does not depend on our, or anyone else's, holding horizon n. It does not depend on who will hold the stock over the next n years. It also does not depend on whether the company pays any dividends at all (i.e., whether any of the D_i's are non-zero) or whether all potential gains come from price appreciation. We can also extend the argument to infinity to obtain the price as the sum of all future discounted cash flows:

$$P_0 = \frac{D_1}{1 + r} + \frac{D_2}{(1 + r)^2} + \frac{D_3}{(1 + r)^3} + \cdots + \frac{D_n}{(1 + r)^n} + \cdots$$

Note that if no one believed that the company would ever pay anything, then the price would be 0. That is, if everyone agrees that the company will never be profitable, then no one would invest in it. This is different from believing that the company would never pay any dividends. After all, value can come from price appreciation only, and we argue

---

[7] All college finance textbooks provide the exposition of the CAPM which relates the required return on the stock to the market risk premium through the stock's beta. For example, see Richard A. Brealey, Stewart C. Myers and Alan J. Marcus, *Fundamental of Corporate Finance* (4th edn), 2004, McGraw-Hill Irwin.

that price appreciation reflects all potential future cash flows from the company. The owners could always force liquidation after n years to get P_n.

ABC's sister company, ABC-NoGrowth Corp., pays a constant non-zero dividend $\overline{D}$ (i.e., $D_i = \overline{D}$ for all i). The dividend discount equation simplifies to the perpetuity formula:

$$P_0 = \frac{\overline{D}}{r}$$

A more attractive sister company, ABC-ConstGrowth Corp., expects its dividends to grow at a constant rate g. The dividend discount equation simplifies to the growing perpetuity formula:

$$P_0 = \frac{D_1}{r - g}$$

Lastly, ABC-NonConstGrowth Corp.'s dividends are uneven for the first n years and grow at rate g afterwards. We can discount the first n years of dividends individually and then apply the constant growth formula, correcting by the discount factor for n years, by writing:[8]

$$P_0 = \frac{D_1}{1+r} + \frac{D_2}{(1+r)^2} + \cdots + \frac{D_n}{(1+r)^n} + \frac{1}{(1+r)^n} \frac{D_n(1+g)}{r-g}$$

Let us look at some numerical examples. We assume that the discount rate investors apply to the ABC companies is 15%. If ABC-NoGrowth pays a $6 dividend per share every year, the fair value for its stock is:

$$P_0 = \frac{6}{0.15} = \$40$$

ABC-ConstGrowth is expected to pay a $6 dividend next year, but its dividends are expected to increase by 5% every year (i.e., the dividends are expected to be $D_1 = 6$, $D_2 = 6.30$, $D_3 = 6.615$, ... , $D_{10} = 9.308$, ... , and so on). The fair value for its stock will be:

$$P_0 = \frac{6}{0.15 - 0.05} = \$60$$

For ABC-NonConstGrowth, let us assume that it will pay a constant dividend of $6 for the first 3 years and then that dividend will grow by 5%. The price of its stock will be:

$$P_0 = \frac{6}{1.15} + \frac{6}{(1.15)^2} + \frac{6}{(1.15)^3} + \frac{1}{(1.15)^3} \frac{6 \cdot 1.05}{0.15 - 0.05} = \$55.12$$

Implicit in these price calculations is the assumption that each company will be able to maintain a particular stream of dividends. For example, ABC-NoGrowth will not have to grow its dividends, while ABC-ConstGrowth will have to be able to maintain the 5% growth in dividends for ever. Does this mean that ABC-ConstGrowth must necessarily be a "growth" company and ABC-NoGrowth has no growth?

So far all we have considered were cash flows distributed to investors in the form of dividends or capital gains, not company earnings.

---

[8] Analysts often assume a lower discount rate in the perpetuity stage of the model (last term), assuming steady-state growth in dividends or free cash flows from then on. The rate used is the average for the economy as a whole (i.e., return on the market portfolio).

Let us think of our ABC companies as manufacturing operations. Imagine both ABC-NoGrowth and ABC-ConstGrowth invest the same amount in plant and equipment. It is hard to imagine that ABC-NoGrowth would be able to maintain a steady dividend without replacing and modernizing its equipment. Its earnings before depreciation must grow just to keep the dividend constant. Its earnings net of depreciation can be constant as long as it pays out all of its earnings as dividends. In that case the dividend payout ratio d is 100% and the earnings retention (plowback) ratio is 0%. The stock price can also be calculated as:

$$P_0 = \frac{E_1}{r}$$

Suppose, instead of paying a dividend next year, ABC-NoGrowth decides that it will reinvest the dividend in existing operations. What must its return on investment (ROI) be just to keep investors equally happy? Supposing the dividend is skipped only once, we can write the discounted value of the company's cash flows as:

$$40 = \frac{1}{1+r} P_1 = \frac{1}{1+r} \frac{E_1(1+ROI)}{r}$$

We apply the perpetuity formula 1 year from today and then discount the fair value 1 year from today back to today. It is easy to see that the ROI must be equal to the discount rate investors apply to the company's cash flows (i.e., $ROI = r$). It can also be easily shown that it does not matter for how long the company decides to reinvest earnings, instead of paying them out as dividends. If the company decides to reinvest earnings for 2 years and then pay them out as dividends, then the fair value formula would simply reflect that:

$$40 = \frac{1}{(1+r)^2} P_2 = \frac{1}{(1+r)^2} \frac{E_1(1+ROI)^2}{r}$$

In particular, if the company decides never to pay any dividends, then it must ensure that the reinvested earnings always yield a return that is at least equal to the discount rate.

Next we show that the same logic applies to ABC-ConstGrowth, except that it must ensure that its reinvested earnings not only return the discount yield, but also that the return on that return grows at rate g! Recall that, even before the company decides to skip dividends, investors expect growth in the distributed cash flows.

Let us consider a scenario where ABC-ConstGrowth decides that it will not pay out its earnings E_1 in the form of dividends D_1 1 year from now. Instead, it will reinvest those earnings in projects yielding the return on investment equal to ROI. We would like to use the same valuation trick as before by applying a growing perpetuity formula 1 year from today and then discount it by one period back to today. That is, we would like to write:

$$P_0 = \frac{1}{1+r} P_1 = \frac{1}{1+r} \frac{E_1(1+ROI)}{r-g}$$

In order for investors to continue to be willing to pay $60 for the stock, we need $ROI = r$ *and* for the year 2 earnings $E_2 = E_1(1+ROI)$ to continue to grow at rate g. This implies that the production base that yielded year 1 earnings E_1 must grow at rate r and it must sustain the growth of those earnings E_1 at the rate g. But it must also sustain the growth in the earnings on earnings $E_1 \cdot ROI$ at the rate g. The growing perpetuity formula assumes that the entire numerator grows at the rate g for ever.

If ABC-ConstGrowth decides to reinvest next year's earnings of $6, then that re-investment must be in projects at least as good as the current ones. That is, they must guarantee not just a return of future value of $6, but also generate future growth in the earnings on those reinvestments at the rate of 5% per year. So, in year 2 the payout must be $6(1 + 0.15)$, or $D_2 = \$6.90$, and then, growing at 5%, it must be $D_3 = \$7.245$, $D_4 = \$7.607$, and so on.

In general, if a company decides not to distribute earnings in the form of dividends, the projects that it invests these retained earnings in (i.e., new businesses it goes into) must be at least as good as the current base investment (i.e., they must guarantee additional perpetual growth at the rate g). If the company always reinvests its earnings, then all future reinvestments must guarantee that growth rate. This argument also applies to partial reinvestments where a fraction equal to the dividend payout ratio d is paid out in the form of dividends and the remainder $1 - d$ is "plowed back".

Observation   A *growth* company is not simply one whose earnings grow, but one for which any new investment, whether in the form of retained earnings or additional capital, is expected to produce new earnings that will grow at a rate at least equal to the return on its current earnings.

That is a tall order especially if the current market price already assumes that the growth will continue for ever.

Beware of P/E ratios

Price/Earnings (P/E) ratios are a popular metric for valuing stocks. They are intuitive as they indicate how much per $1 of earnings investors pay in a stock price. Consider two more ABC sisters. ABC-Value Corp.'s shares trade at $40 and the company is expected to earn $6 per share. ABC-Growth Corp.'s shares trade at $60 and the company is expected to earn $6 per share. A P/E enthusiast would compute a P/E ratio for ABC-Value Corp. to be 6.67 (40 divided by 6) and for ABC-Growth Corp. to be 10 (60 divided by 6). These could be interpreted to mean that investors pay a lot more per dollar of earnings for the ABC-Growth shares. Should they then sell ABC-Growth and buy ABC-Value?

Simply computing the P/E ratio does not offer any clues as to what is expected to happen to those earnings. It may be that ABC-Value is simply our ABC-NoGrowth company, which replaces its production base only to return a level stream of dividends, while ABC-Growth is our ABC-ConstGrowth company, which, in addition to depre-ciation replacement, offers sustained growth in earnings. It is easy to imagine ABC-Value to be a mature company with stable earnings, but no growth prospects, and ABC-Growth as a young entrant into a new, rapidly expanding industry. Why would one not invest in the latter? After all, its growth rate may even exceed that imputed in its share price, while ABC-Value may fail to deliver the steady earnings it has produced so far. The situation could easily be reversed: ABC-Growth's assumed growth may not live up to its expectations, while ABC-Value may enter growth businesses. What determines the value of a stock is not only its current earnings, but also the earnings growth prospects and the riskiness of the overall business as summarized by its capitalization (discount) rate. None of these factors remain constant and there are many less tangible ones (management, state of industry, economy, etc.).

It is even harder to defend the use of more complicated ratios, like price/earnings/ growth (PEG), popularized in the late 1990s during the technology boom. These purported to allow comparisons among companies with tiny current earnings, but enormous "growth" prospects. For these companies, P/E ratios are unappetizingly large, but if divided by large growth rates they become supposedly manageable and meaningful. Let us simply offer an extreme example: How much would you be willing to pay for a brilliant idea of a brilliant product in someone's head?: no earnings, but high potential growth?

2.6   CURRENCY MARKETS

Currencies are commodities like gold, oil, or wheat. A €20 note can be, without any loss of value, replaced by 20 €1 coins. Normally, the price of commodities is quoted in terms of a monetary unit per a commonly used quantity of commodity, like bushel, barrel, or metric ton. We rarely ask the question in reverse: for example, how many barrels of oil can $1 buy? Foreign exchange (FX) or currency rates are special in that they are often quoted both ways: £1 sterling may cost U.S.$1.5 or U.S.$1 may cost £0.6667. Expressing the price in pounds per dollar is equivalent to fixing it to the reciprocal in dollars per pound. The other feature distinguishing currencies from other commodities is that we often want to know the cross-ratio. We are rarely interested in how many barrels of oil 20 bushels of wheat can buy. However, when returning to the U.K. from a vacation in Mexico, we may want to know how many pounds the leftover 300 pesos will get even though the exchange rate may be quoted in pesos per dollar.

Let us review quote conventions and some potential issues. In what follows, we use the easily recognizable three-letter currency codes as adopted by the payment clearing system SWIFT. Most currencies around the world are quoted with respect to a *vehicle* currency, which is one of the major hard currencies (e.g., USD, GBP, or EUR). A currency can be quoted in European terms (i.e., in currency per dollar) or in American terms (i.e., dollars per currency). Most former Commonwealth currencies (AUD, NZD, etc.) and the euro follow the latter convention. Most others (e.g., CHF, JPY, HKD) follow the former. Remembering this is only important when observing quotes or percentage appreciation rates that are not labeled; this text follows the notation in which a spot foreign exchange rate X is labeled with the terms in square brackets or as a superscript. The terms describe the "pricing currency" in the numerator and the "priced currency" in the denominator. This is analogous to everyday supermarket pricing where £1.50 per 1 loaf of bread can be written as £1.50/loaf. That is, the price in £/loaf is 1.50. In the same way, the price of 1.5 dollars per pound sterling is written as:

$$X^{USD/GBP} = X\left[\frac{USD}{GBP}\right] = 1.50$$

The readers should be aware that confusing notations abound in the market, where a cable rate may be written as GBP/USD (i.e., with the base currency coming first) followed by a number like 1.65 which obviously means 1.65 USD/GBP and not the other way around.

For any two currencies, the FX rate in currency 1 per unit of currency 2 uniquely determines the FX rate in currency 2 per unit of currency 1 (i.e., $X[Curr1/Curr2] = 1/X[Curr2/Curr1]$). In our example:

$$X\left[\frac{GBP}{USD}\right] = \frac{1}{X\left[\dfrac{USD}{GBP}\right]} = 0.6667$$

Most FX rates are quoted to four decimal places, except when the whole number is large, then they are quoted to two decimal places (e.g., a JPY/USD quote may be 119.23). Often, the quotation units follow a convention and are dropped. This may lead to misinterpretation of appreciation statistics. Consider the following table which is similar to many you see in the press:

Currency changes against the USD as of XX/XX/2003

	Last	Change	%Change
AUD	0.5457	−0.0014	−0.3
EUR	1.0205	−0.0020	−0.2
CHF	1.6844	−0.0030	−0.2

Does this mean that all the listed currencies depreciated against the dollar? On the contrary, the CHF, quoted as CHF/USD, has actually appreciated as it takes 0.0030 fewer Swiss francs to buy $1 than it did yesterday, while the other two currencies, AUD and EUR, may have in fact depreciated.

Another confusion comes with the percentage change statistic. If the AUD costs USD 0.5457 today and it cost 0.5471 yesterday, then we can compute the percentage depreciation as:

$$\%\Delta X^{USD/AUD} = -0.0014/0.5471 = -0.002\,559 = -0.2559\%$$

as shown in the table. Does this mean that the USD has appreciated by 0.2559%? Absolutely not. Today the USD costs:

$$X^{AUD/USD} = 1/X^{AUD/USD} = 1/0.5457 = 1.832\,509$$

Yesterday it cost:

$$X^{AUD/USD} = 1/X^{AUD/USD} = 1/0.5471 = 1.827\,819$$

or AUD 0.004689 more. The percentage change in the value of the USD expressed in AUD is then:

$$\%\Delta X^{AUD/USD} = 0.004\,689/1.827\,819 = 0.002\,566 = 0.2566\%$$

The simple explanation is that the percentage change is not equal to the negative of the percentage change in the reciprocals. Over longer periods of time the differences can be greater.

Additional complications arise when looking at analysts' mean forecasts of currency rates. Suppose that currently:

$$X^{USD/AUD} = 0.75, \qquad \text{or, equivalently,} \qquad X^{AUD/USD} = 1\tfrac{1}{3}$$

Suppose half the analysts polled predict the rate to go to $X^{USD/AUD} = 0.50$ (i.e., $X^{AUD/USD} = 2$) and the other half to $X^{USD/AUD} = 1.00$ (i.e., $X^{AUD/USD} = 1$). On average, in USD/AUD terms, they predict the rate to be 0.75 (i.e., no appreciation). At the same time, using reciprocals, on average they predict the rate in AUD/USD terms to be 1.5 (i.e., a USD appreciation from $1\tfrac{1}{3}$). We can come up with examples where, on average, both currencies may be expected to appreciate at the same time! The main lesson from these examples is that we always need to be aware of what quotation terms are assumed when interpreting statements about appreciation or depreciation.

The main law governing spot currency trading is the law of one price. In the inter-dealer market, all spot FX rates have to be in line with each other in such a way that buying one currency through a vehicle is no cheaper/more expensive than buying it directly. The rule, of course, does not apply to retail markets. If we observe in New York $X^{JPY/USD} = 118.50$ and $X^{HKD/USD} = 7.80$, and at the same moment a dealer in Tokyo quotes $X^{JPY/HKD} = 15.02$, we can profit because in New York 1 HKD costs JPY 15.192. The law of one price is violated, as the same commodity, the HKD, trades at two different prices at the same time. We can buy it where it is cheaper and sell it where it is more expensive.

If we had JPY 1,000,000 and used it to purchase HKD 66,577.8961 in Tokyo, then in New York sold the HKD 66,577.8961 for USD 8,535.6277 and sold the USD 8,535.6277 for JPY 1,011,471.88, we would make an instant profit of JPY 11,471.88. This *triangular arbitrage* would be possible because HKD is cheap in the direct (cross) market in Tokyo relative to the indirect market in New York. Dealers in New York would sell dollars for yen, convert the yen into HK dollars in Tokyo, and, with HK dollars, buy back US dollars in New York. All dealers would transact in the same direction. The USD-into-JPY trade would drive up the yen, the JPY-into-HKD trade would drive up HKD relative to JPY, and the HKD-into-USD trade would drive the USD up against the HKD. Most likely all three quotes would change until the yen price of HK dollars is the same in New York and Tokyo. More discussion of triangular arbitrage is provided in Chapter 5.

In all of the above, we ignore the transaction costs in the form of a bid–ask spread. In reality, we need to modify the computed amounts by considering that we would sell at the bid and buy at the ask. Instead of simply one FX cross-rate, we need to compute its bid and ask. The principle remains the same.

The law of one price binds hundreds of possible currency combinations together. As soon as one FX quote changes in the market, many others follow.

3

Fixed Income Securities

To finance their activities, governments, financial, and non-financial corporations raise debt funds by borrowing from financial institutions, like banks, or by issuing securities in the financial markets. Securities are distributed in the primary markets, where they are sold directly from borrowers to investors, sometimes with the help of an investment bank. They are traded among investors in the secondary markets. Securities markets can be, in general, divided into money and capital markets. Money market instruments are those whose maturities are less than 1 year. Capital market instruments are those whose maturities are more than 1 year; they include preferred and common stocks whose maturities are infinite. This division is largely artificial and due to different legal requirements.

In this chapter, we review the spot markets for debt securities, also called fixed income securities. Debt contracts typically have a stated maturity date and pay interest defined through a coupon rate or a coupon formula. They include a variety of money market instruments and long-maturity securities, like straight bonds, asset-backed debt, and mortgage-backed securities. They also include spot-starting swaps and other non-securities (Chapter 8 covers swaps in detail). These may be private derivative contracts, but because of their fungible nature are frequently created simultaneously with bonds in order to change the nature of the issuer's liabilities.

The review of each product is brief. We outline the main features of each instrument and the structure of the market. We provide recent growth statistics with breakdowns by types, currencies, etc., to provide a feel for the richness of the markets. For product details, readers are referred to the many voluminous "handbooks" available in bookstores. For market statistics, readers are referred to the publications of the U.S. Federal Reserve, Bank for International Settlements, International Swaps Dealers Association, rating agencies, and other industry sources.

3.1 MONEY MARKETS

Money market securities are debt instruments of high credit quality issuers with maturities up to 1 year. They have short durations, low convexities, and very low default probabilities. Most are issued by governments, and prominent financial and non-financial corporations. They are very liquid. They trade in large denominations in the over-the-counter (OTC) markets with many buyers and sellers present at all times. We describe the markets for the following instruments: U.S. Treasury Bills (T-Bills) and U.S. federal agency discount notes, short-term municipal securities, Fed Funds (U.S.), bank overnight refinancing (Europe), repurchase agreements (repos), Eurocurrency deposits, commercial paper, and other (negotiable certificates of deposit, or CDs, banker's acceptances).

U.S. Treasury Bills

About one-fifth of all U.S. government marketable debt is in the form of T-Bills, which are book-entry (no paper security) discount (zero-coupon, issued at a discount from par) securities issued by the U.S. Treasury and initially distributed by a handful of primary dealers who participate in auctions conducted by the New York Federal Reserve Bank, similar in format to those for Treasury notes and bonds. They trade in the most active and liquid market (i.e., they can be easily sold and bought prior to maturity).

In the secondary market, T-Bills are not quoted in terms of prices, nor are they quoted in terms of meaningful yields. The quoting convention they follow, the *Act/ 360 discount yield* basis, derives its logic from percentage rebates of list prices and is most unappealing. We review this bizarre code.

On April 23, 2003 some T-Bill prices were quoted in the *Wall Street Journal* as follows:

MATURITY	DAYS TO MAT	BID	ASKED	CHG	ASK YLD
May 15 03	22	1.12	1.11	. . .	1.13
Jun 19 03	57	1.13	1.12	−0.01	1.14

The bid/asked discount yields of 1.13/1.12 quoted on the June 19 T-Bill are not real yields, but strange shorthand for prices. Normally, we would want to compute a raw yield earned on a security as $(P_{end} - P_{begin})/P_{begin}$, where P_{begin} is the purchase price and P_{end} is a redemption price. Unfortunately, the T-Bill convention assumes something more akin to: $(P_{end} - P_{begin})/P_{end}$. T-Bills are sold at a discount from par, and so $P_{end} = 100$. The annualized *discount yield* is defined as:

$$y_{disc} = \frac{(100 - P)}{100} \cdot \frac{360}{Act}$$

where *Act* represents the actual number of days to maturity. So, if we know the maturity of the T-Bill and the quoted discount yield y_{disc}, we can figure out the price by solving for:

$$P = 100 - 100 \cdot y_{disc} \cdot \frac{Act}{360}$$

Using the asked discount yield for the June 19 T-Bill, this translates into:

$$P = 100 - 100 \cdot 0.0112 \cdot 57/360 = 99.8227$$

The T-Bill is offered for a price of 99.8227% of the face value. Once we have the price, we can compute the real yield (on an *Act/365* basis) on a purchase of the T-Bill. We divide the numerator by the purchase price P_{begin} instead of the sale price P_{end}:

$$y = \frac{100 - P}{P} \cdot \frac{365}{Act} = \frac{100 - 99.8227}{99.8227} \cdot \frac{365}{57} = 0.0114 = 1.14\%$$

The result (1.14%) is what is reported in the last column as the ask yield.

Many money market instruments, which we review next, follow the same discount yield-based rather than price-based quotation convention.

Federal agency discount notes

The U.S. government has sponsored several agencies whose job is to pursue public policy goals that include housing, education, or farming support. The agencies are set up as governmental units or public corporations. A few enjoy full, and most enjoy implicit credit guarantee of the U.S. government.[1] The mortgage support agencies, like Federal Home Loan Banks, the Federal Home Loan Mortgage Corporation (Freddie Mac), the Federal National Mortgage Association (Fannie Mae), or the Government National Mortgage Association (Ginnie Mae), issue their own short- and long-term debt obligations and buy, from commercial banks, mortgage loans that conform to certain standardized norms. This replenishes the banks' funds and allows them to issue new loans. The agencies also sell to investors mortgage-backed bonds in various forms in order to reduce their balance sheets. The Student Loan Marketing Association (Sallie Mae) and the Farm Credit Banks perform similar useful functions for the student loan and farming markets.

The agencies often seek short-term funding by issuing *agency discount notes* (discos). These notes resemble T-Bills: they are quoted the same way using discount yields, they have similar maturities, and they are sold at a discount from par. Today, there are over $100 billion of these notes sold through a small circle of U.S. broker-dealers. Most investors hold them to maturity ensuring nearly risk-free return. The trading in them is thin with the spreads above T-Bill yields reflecting both the relative lack of liquidity and minimal credit risk. The main buyers are money market mutual funds and commercial banks.

Short-term munis

State and local governments in the U.S. issue short-term securities of two kinds: interest-bearing and discount notes. The interest-bearing notes typically have variable rates tied to T-Bills. The spreads over T-Bills on both types are *negative* to reflect their tax-exempt status. Like their long-term counterparts, both can be unsecured *general obligation* securities (GOs are backed by the credit of the municipality) or *revenue* securities (backed by revenue from specific projects). Revenue paper is generally riskier. Trading is thin (most are held to maturity) and credit varies greatly.

[1] Investors perceive the U.S. government unlikely to let such large and important institutions fail. Thus they enjoy a lower cost of funding than comparable private banking conglomerates. Recently (e.g., see the *Wall Street Journal* of February 25, 2004), some members of Congress as well as the Chairman of the U.S. Fed, Alan Greenspan, have recognized that the largest agencies pose serious financial risks to the system and urged curbs on their growth and separation from the credit backing of the government.

In Europe, regional authorities, state-run organizations, and sometimes cities issue short- and long-term bonds. They do rely, to a greater extent than their U.S. counterparts, on intermediaries and typically negotiate loans directly from banks.

Fed Funds (U.S.) and bank overnight refinancing (Europe)

Despite its name, the Fed Funds (FFs) market is administered solely by private financial institutions and is largely unregulated by the U.S. government. The core of the market has been the trading of excess reserves by commercial banks that must satisfy reserve requirements set by the central bank against their deposits. Banks with excess reserves lend them as overnight funds to banks short of cash reserves. The market comprises any funds in reserve accounts at the Federal Reserve Bank. These are used not only to satisfy the stated reserve ratio, but also to clear securities and wire transactions in the U.S. These include purchases and sales of commercial paper, banker's acceptances, T-Bills, etc., as well as U.S. Treasury bonds and notes. Settlement occurs through an immediate transfer of funds that can be used to effect other transactions the same day.

Trading in FFs involves overnight borrowing and lending of claims on cash deposited at the Federal Reserve. A borrower of cash is called an FF buyer, a lender is an FF seller. It is an interbank market; only commercial banks are permitted to hold balances at the Fed. Over 10% of the daily volume is attributed to banks acting on behalf of non-banks. Banks act as dealers and trade FFs either directly ($\sim 60\%$) or through brokers ($\sim 40\%$), like Prebon, Garvin, or Noonan. FF loans are unsecured; there is no protection against default. About 75% of transactions are overnight, the rest are *term FFs* of up to 6 months.

The FF rate is set by the transacting banks. However, it is also the main tool used by the central bank to control the money supply. Cash owned by banks is subject to a money multiplier in the process of credit creation. The Federal Reserve, not being a party to any of the FF transactions, attempts to affect the FF rate through Federal Open Market Committee (FOMC) announcements, followed by *open market operations*. In their eight meetings throughout the year, the Fed governors state their preferred level for the FF rate, and on the next day back their words with actions by directing the manager of the open market operations desk in New York to buy or sell securities for cash, thereby injecting or removing cash from the economy. These securities transactions are done outright (permanent) or as *system repos* (temporary). Most of the time, the mere statement from the Fed alters the rate banks charge each other. But it is worthwhile remembering that the real influence is indirect through open market securities transactions. On rare occasions, like in the days after September 11, 2001, in order to ensure liquidity the Fed flooded the market with cash (in effect causing the FF rate to drop dramatically) by buying securities.

In Europe, the European System of Central Banks (ESCB) conducts refinancing operations. Banks trade funds to satisfy reserve requirements, charging each other an overnight rate. The volume-weighted average of all overnight unsecured lending transactions initiated within the Eurozone by a particular panel of banks (with the highest volume) is known as Eonia.

Repos (RPs)

Legally, *repos*, or repurchase agreements (RPs), are simultaneous spot sales of market-able securities and (forward) repurchases of the same securities at a pre-specified (higher) price at a later date. Economically, they are borrowings: a sale results in a cash inflow and the subsequent repurchase in a larger cash outflow. The difference is the interest on this collateralized loan. The arrangement is typically over-collateralized through an upfront haircut. That is, the amount borrowed is less than the market value of the collateral. The borrower (i.e., the seller/repurchaser) is said to enter a repo; the party to the other side of the transaction (i.e., the buyer/forward reseller or the lender) is said to be enter a *reverse repo*. The interest rate is quoted as simple interest on an Act/360 basis. Since the collateral is composed of marketable securities (Treasuries in the U.S., government bonds in Europe), the biggest users of the repo market, on both sides, are broker-dealers (followed by banks) as they have access to the collateral. For broker-dealers, the repo market is the primary source of funds (just like FFs for banks). Central banks use repo markets to conduct monetary policy through open market operation. Municipal governments with seasonal cash flows use repo markets to temporarily invest their cash balances in credit risk-free assets. Repos can be *overnight* or *term* with the longest reverse maturity dates up to 1 year. Sometimes the repo is *open*, which means it is automatically renewed every day until one party decides to close it down.

For broker-dealer firms, repos are the primary means of financing the inventory and covering short positions. But almost every dealer firm also uses the repo market to run a *matched book*, by taking on repos and reverse repos with the same maturity, and capturing the spread between the funds lent (reverse repos with non-dealers) and borrowed (repos with dealers and non-dealers). The principle at work here is simple arbitrage of lending at a higher rate than borrowing. Theoretically, the collateral in a matched book should be of the same quality on both sides; practically, part of the spread may come from mismatched collateral. Dealers often use *repo brokers* to identify parties willing to enter reverse repos (from the dealer's perspective).

The biggest repo market by far is in the U.S, but the European repo market has grown considerably. It is close to EUR 3.4 billion, with 88.8% collateralized by government bonds and over 50% being cross-border transactions, as of the end of 2002, according to the International Securities Market Association (ISMA).

Table 3.1   European RPs

By area (%)		By currency (%)		By collateral (%)	
Domestic	42.9	EUR	77.2	Germany	28.9
Eurozone	24.0	GBP	10.0	Italy	18.5
Non-Eurozone	26.4	USD	7.7	France	10.7
Anonymous ATS	6.7	DDK, SEK	2.0	Spain	6.9
		JPY	2.2	Belgium	5.3
		Other	0.8	Other Eurozone	5.3
				U.K.	10.8
				DKK, SEK	2.3
				U.S.	2.6
				Other	7.7
				Unknown	0.9

Source: ISMA, *European Repo Market Survey*, December, 2002.

More than 75% of the Euro RPs are denominated in euros, with close to 30% of the collateral coming from Germany. Close to 40% of repos are arranged directly between two parties and slightly less brokered by repo brokers. Legally, more than 75% of the Euro market are standard repos and close to 90% of them have a fixed rate.

Table 3.2   European RPs

By arrangement (%)		By contract type (%)		By collateral (%)	
Direct bilateral	39.5	Classic repo	79.5	Fixed rate	89.7
Voice-brokered	36.5	Documented sell/buyback	10.8	Floating rate	7.0
ATS	16.8	Undocumented sell/buyback	9.7	Open	3.3
Direct tri-party	7.3				

Source: ISMA, *European Repo Market Survey*, December, 2002.

Historically, most repos have been overnight. Recently, *term repos* with maturitites up to 1 month have gained prominence, accounting for around 50% of the market. Of the overall lending activities collateralized by financial assets, RPs represent over 85% of volume. The market is moderately concentrated with the top 10 dealers accounting for about 50% of transactions and the top 30 dealers accounting for close to 90% of transactions.

Table 3.3   European RPs

Lending collateralized by financial assets (%)		RP Concetration (%)	
Repo	86.4	Top ten dealers	50.9
Securities lending	13.6	Top 11–20	22.1
		Top 21–30	14.6
		Rest	12.4

Source: ISMA, *European Repo Market Survey*, December, 2002.

Eurodollars and Eurocurrencies

A Eurocurrency is a currency deposited to earn interest outside its country of origin. U.S. dollars held in banks outside of the U.S. (not necessarily in Europe) are called Eurodollars (EDs). Euroeuros are euro deposits outside the Eurozone (say, in Japan). The main center of activity is London. The size of the market is largely unknown, but estimated at over $2 trillion outstanding (known to be greater than any other money market), and dominated by EDs. Based on the volume of futures trading, the ED represents close to 90% of the daily transaction activity of the entire money market.

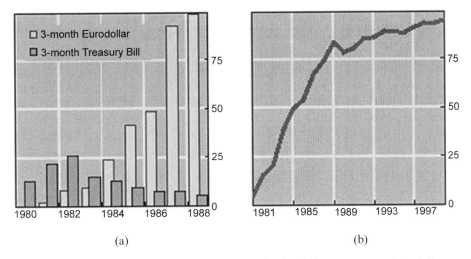

Figure 3.1   U.S. Treasury and private instruments in the dollar money market, daily average transactions (in billions of U.S. dollars and percentages): (a) T-Bill and Eurodollar futures transactions; (b) Eurodollar turnover as a percentage of money market activity (including cash market transactions in T-Bills).
Data from Federal Reserve Bank of New York (FRBNY), FOW TRADE, and BIS calculations. *Source*: R. N. McCauley, Benchmark tipping in the money and bond markets, *BIS Quarterly Review*, March, 2001. Reproduced with permission from Bank for International Settlements.

Since Eurocurrency transactions exist outside the authority of any national government, they are free from regulation and intervention.[2] The origin of the market dates back to the Soviet deposits of U.S. dollars in Paris and London (rather than in the U.S.) in the 1950s, Arab deposits of dollars in Europe after the Suez War of 1956 and the recycling of "petrodollars" in the 1970s. The U.S. and Japan allowed their domestic banks to participate in the ED and Euroyen markets through International Banking Facilities (IBFs) and Japanese offshore markets, respectively. Today, the Eurocurrency market is the foundation of all swap and all Eurobond activity, the scene of the greatest innovations in finance. Free of regulation, deposits are traded actively around the clock with ED and other Eurocurrency futures markets alternating between London, Chicago, and Singapore. The spot deposit rate, quoted on an Act/360 basis for dollar deposits, is determined daily by a rate fixing of the most active London banks at 11 a.m. GMT.[3] The settlement is same-day through a clearing system called CHIPS which competes with the same-day settlement procedure of the Fedwire. Swaps based on EDs commonly take two London business days to settle (e.g., a 90-day deposit of today would start earning interest 2 days from today and end earning interest 92 days from today). For spot deposits (i.e., placed today), the maximum maturity tends to be 12 months with the most common one being 3 months, for all currencies. Many broker-dealers, money center banks, and large institutional investors participate in both the spot and forwards market on both sides (i.e., as lenders and borrowers). In the

---

[2] Strictly speaking, governments do regulate the banking facilities engaged in Eurocurrencies. However, at a minimum, Eurocurrency deposits are not subject to reserve requirements and deposit insurance fees.
[3] It is officially calculated by the British Bankers Association (BBA).

institutional market, deposits can be arranged as time (fixed maturity), placements (overnight), or as call money (no maturity, withdrawn at will).

The spread between the 3-month ED deposit rate and the T-Bill rate is known as the *TED spread*. It reflects the difference in the default probability of the average credit quality of ED market participants and the risk-free rate (the same way the swap spread does). Presumably, it also reflects the supply and demand for unrestricted deposits (i.e., the relative demand for borrowing vs. lending). The TED spread varies over time and spikes up in times of economic uncertainty.

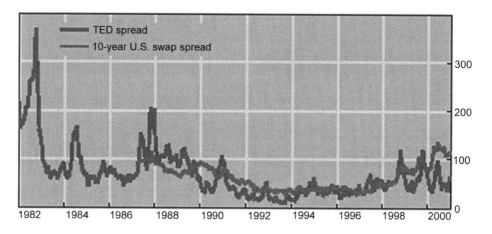

Figure 3.2   Spread between U.S. Treasury and private yields (in basis points). The TED spread is measured as the monthly average of the spread between the 3-month T-Bill and ED rates. Data from Datastream and BIS calculations. *Source*: R. N. McCauley, Benchmark tipping in the money and bond markets, *BIS Quarterly Review*, March, 2001. Reproduced with permission from Bank for International Settlements.

Negotiable CDs

Certificates of deposit (CDs) similar to those offered to retail customers are traded among institutional investors in most major currencies. Banks post daily current rates on an Act/360 basis for denominations larger than the equivalent of $100,000. Institutional investors typically buy them at a discount from par and can trade them prior to maturity, though they rarely do.

Bankers' acceptances (BAs)

BAs are a popular form of export and import finance. They originate when banks guarantee time drafts open on behalf of importers who promise to pay for goods on their receipt. Exporters often sell them at a discount prior to their due date and they become de facto obligations of the guaranteeing bank.

Commercial paper (CP)

CP represents unsecured promissory notes issued in large denominations by large, well-known corporations, with maturities ranging from a few days to 9 months. These are sold directly to investors (direct placement paper) or through dealers (dealer-directed paper). Issuers must be sufficiently known to the investing public to access the market directly. Direct paper is typically sold by the salesforce of financing arms or finance subsidiaries of large corporations, like GE Capital or GMAC in the U.S. The 9-month maturity limit is an artifact of a U.S. registration exemption. CP represents about 25% of all commercial and industrial lending in the developed world. Significantly more than half of the CP is issued in the U.S. where the secondary market is not active. The Euro CP market maturities are shorter (up to 180 days), but more active in secondary trading. Foreign issuers favor the U.S. domestic market where they constitute about 50% over the ED markets where the interest rates are slightly higher. Financial regulations in parts of Europe make it less attractive or impossible for foreign borrowers to issue paper. The volume of offerings tends to be cyclical. The largest holders of CP are retail money market mutual funds. CP is quoted on a discount yield basis (360-day year) similar to U.S. T-Bills.

Until the 1980s, there were only three CP markets: the U.S., Canada, and Australia. The U.S. CP still accounts for nearly 77% of the global CP outstanding, with 50–75% of new issuance. Net issuance fluctuates dramatically year to year.

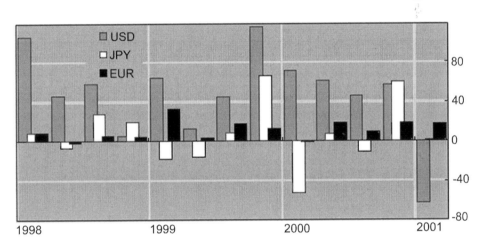

Figure 3.3 Domestic and international net issuance of commercial paper (in billions of U.S. dollars). Data on domestic issuance for the first quarter of 2001 are preliminary.
Data from Euroclear and national authorities. *Source*: B. H. Cohen and E. M. Remolona, Overview: Are markets looking beyond the slowdown? *BIS Quarterly Review*, June, 2001. Reproduced with permission from Bank for International Settlements.

According to the U.S. Federal Reserve, as of August, 2000 the global outstandings totaled $1,538 billion, around 40% of that being asset-backed CP. The dynamic growth in the issuance of asset-backed CP (collateralized by revenue from specific assets) is a relatively recent phenomenon which has been brought about by the thirst for low-cost, short-term capital and the entry into the CP market of lower credit quality issuers.

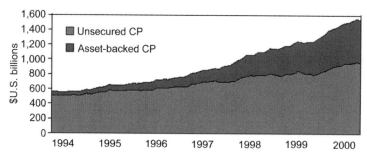

Figure 3.4   Exhibit 1—monthly global CP outstandings, January, 1994–August, 2000, outstandings double in 5 years amid rising interest rates.
Data from Board of Governors of the Federal Reserve System. *Source*: *Global Credit Research*, October, 2000 and *Commercial Paper Defaults and Rating Transitions*, 1972–2000. Copyright Moody's Investors Service, Inc. and/or its affiliates. Reprinted with permission. All rights reserved.

The Euro CP market nearly tripled in the latter part of the 1990s to about $268 billion by 2000. It continues to enjoy extraordinary growth. The third largest, the Japanese CP market, stagnated by the end of the 1990s to the equivalent of about $152 billion. Figures 3.5–3.7 show the growth of CP in Europe, non-U.S., and nascent markets.

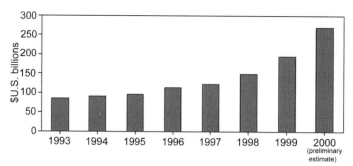

Figure 3.5   Exhibit 2—Euro CP outstandings, market nearly triples in 5 years.
Data from Bank for International Settlements. *Source*: *Global Credit Research*, October, 2000 and *Commercial Paper Defaults and Rating Transitions*, 1972–2000. Copyright Moody's Investors Service, Inc. and/or its affiliates. Reprinted with permission. All rights reserved.

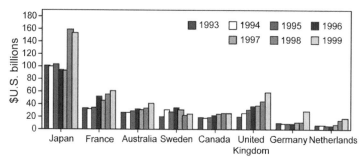

Figure 3.6   Exhibit 3—CP outstandings by country in major non-U.S. markets, worldwide CP markets generally enjoy steady growth.
Source: *Global Credit Research*, October, 2000 and *Commercial Paper Defaults and Rating Transitions*, 1972–2000.

Fixed Income Securities

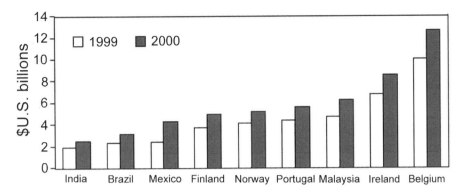

Figure 3.7   Exhibit 4—CP outstandings by country in Nascent markets, European and Latin American entrants spur growth. Outstandings for 2000 are preliminary estimates.
Source: Global Credit Research, October, 2000 and *Commercial Paper Defaults and Rating Transitions*, 1972–2000. Copyright Moody's Investors Service, Inc. and/or its affiliates. Reprinted with permission. All rights reserved.

About 35% of the CP is issued by non-bank financial institutions. They are followed by industrial corporations (17%) and banks (12%)

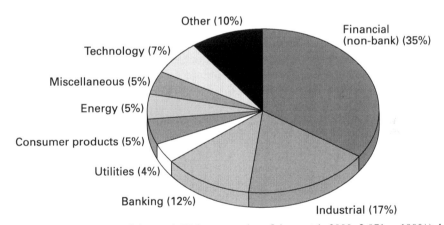

Figure 3.8   Exhibit 5—Moody's rated CP by sector (as of August 1, 2000; 2,071 = 100%), bank and non-bank financial institutions dominate market. "Other" segment includes retail, media, sovereign, transportation and hotel, gaming and leisure.
Source: Global Credit Research, October, 2000 and *Commercial Paper Defaults and Rating Transitions*, 1972–2000. Copyright Moody's Investors Service, Inc. and/or its affiliates. Reprinted with permission. All rights reserved.

Close to half of Euro CP is unrated, whereas most issues in the U.S. are rated either by S&P or Moody's. In Europe there are fewer rating categories, ranging from prime 1 to prime 3 for investment grade issues and non-prime for non-investment grade. The correspondence to Moody's bond ratings is shown in Figure 3.9.

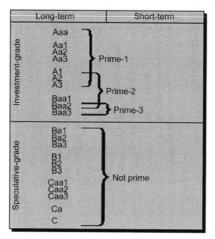

Figure 3.9   Exhibit 6—Moody's short-term vs. long-term ratings.
Source: Global Credit Research, October, 2000 and *Commercial Paper Defaults and Rating Transitions*, 1972–2000.
Reproduced with permission from Bank for International Settlements.

At the time of issuance, 80% of CP is rated prime 1 and 17% is rated prime 2. As issues age (i.e., approach maturity) the probability of default decreases, resulting in the fact that the vast majority (88.9%) of outstanding CP is rated prime 1. No more than 11 issuers per year have ever defaulted prior to the year 2000. The frequency of defaults by country and industry reflects the composition of the CP market. The U.S., Sweden, and Mexico-domiciled issuers lead the country default table, while financials, industry, and utility issuers lead the sector default category.

   The spread between prime 1- and prime 2-rated issues has remained relatively stable over time. In general, it has followed the economic business cycle, spiking up dramatically during economic downturns. The frequency of downgrades has been an excellent leading indicator of increases in CP defaults.

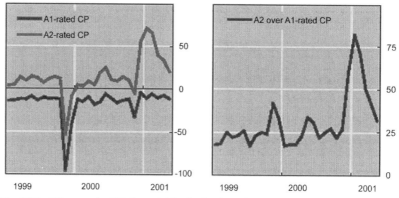

Figure 3.10   U.S. CP spreads (30-day yields, in basis points, at month-end): (a) spreads over LIBOR; (b) relative spread.
Data from Bloomberg, Datastream, and BIS calculations. *Source*: B. H. Cohen and E. M. Remolona, Overview: Are markets looking beyond the slowdown? *BIS Quarterly Review*, June, 2001. Reproduced with permission from Bank for International Settlements.

The credit quality of CP relative to EDs depends on the ratings of the CP issues or issuers relative to the average credit quality of the interbank participants of the ED market, believed to be approximately AA. The spread over LIBOR (London interbank offered rate) of prime 1 issuers is normally negative, reflecting their high quality. The spread of prime 2 issuers is positive. Both spreads are somewhat volatile over time, reflecting changes in the overall economic conditions relative to those of money center banks. In the early 2000s, spreads on lower quality CP shot up as many issuers faced a difficult short-term financing environment that forced them to resort to bank financing. This caused the divergence of the perceived default probabilities between the A1 and A2 categories.

3.2 CAPITAL MARKETS: BONDS

The global bond market is enormous. The total amount outstanding is close to $40 trillion with three-quarters of that amount in domestic and one-quarter in international bond markets. U.S. and European financial institutions are the biggest issuers in both segments. In recent years, the net issuance (i.e., the excess of the amount issued over the amount retired) has reached close to $3 trillion. Two-thirds of that amount is issued in domestic bond markets and one-third in international bond markets. Governments are the biggest issuers in both domestic and international markets, representing over one-half of all the new issues.

The U.S. and Japanese governments issue almost exclusively in domestic markets, while emerging markets governments and international organizations issue pre-dominantly in international markets. European governments issue in both. The total indebtedness (public and private) of U.S. and European residents continues to grow. The U.S. experienced a brief reduction in debt in the late 1990s, but with new government deficits in the early 2000s debt issuance returned to its previous levels. Domestic private debt issuance exploded in the U.S. in the late 1990s, with non-bank financial institutions and corporations leading the charge and more than twice offsetting any reductions in government debt. In Europe, banks and telecom corporations did most of the borrowing. In the 1990s, Europeans became the keenest to issue international private debt, overtaking the U.S. in the market for international bonds. This was the result of further integration of European capital markets and an explosion of cross-border issuance. The issuance of international bonds by U.S. residents also increased dramatically.

Japan's net issuance has been almost flat in recent years. Banks retired debts and corporations added little domestic bond financing to their balance sheets. The pace of issuance by the government of Japan has, however, accelerated, overtaking the U.S. and Europe to become the largest government issuer in the world.

During the same time, emerging economies experienced continued development of their securities markets. East Asian countries worked through their debt burdens. Bank financing in Asia declined, while debt securities issuance remained flat. Latin America increased its indebtedness to the rest of the world, mostly through restructuring of old and the issuance of new debt securities. The emerging economies of Europe continued to experience capital inflows. Government and private debt markets continued to absorb a portion of that inflow.

Figures 3.11–3.14 contain statistics for domestic and international bond markets.

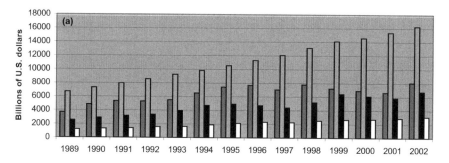

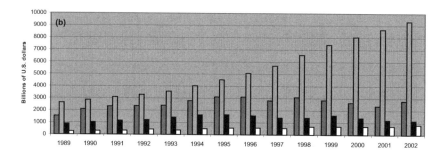

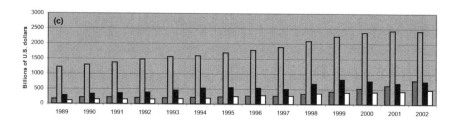

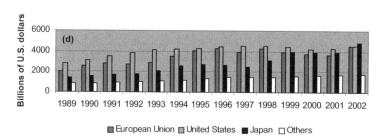

Figure 3.11 Domestic debt securities—amounts outstanding: (a) all issuers; (b) financial institutions; (c) corporate issuers; (d) governments.
Source: BIS securities statistics (see http://www.bis.org/publ/qcsv0306/anx....csv with file numbers 12 through 16). Reproduced with permission from Bank for International Settlements.

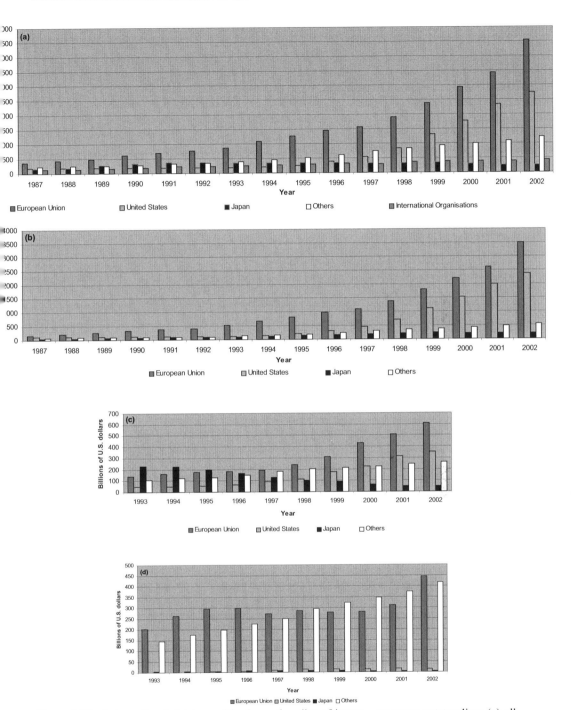

Figure 3.12 International debt securities by nationality of issuer—amounts outstanding; (a) all issuers; (b) financial institutions; (c) corporate issuers; (d) governments.
Source: BIS securities statistics (see http://www.bis.org/publ/qcsv0306/anx....csv with file numbers 12 through 16. Reproduced with permission from Bank for International Settlements).

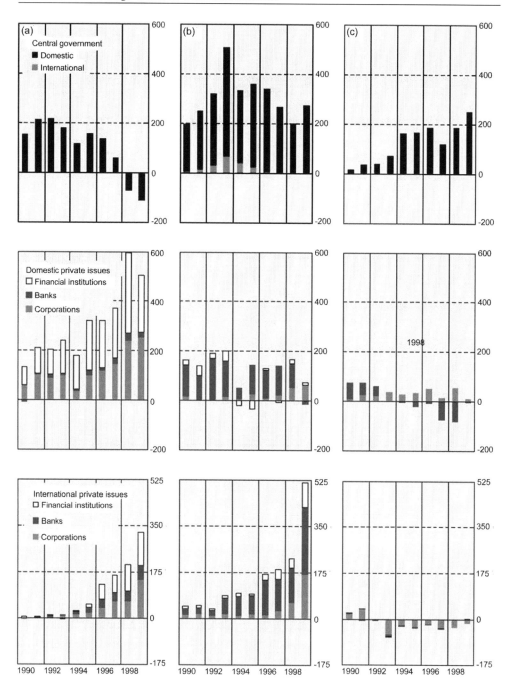

Figure 3.13 Net issuance of domestic and international bonds and notes (in billions of U.S. dollars), by country of residence: (a) U.S.; (b) Europe (EU 15 countries, Norway, Switzerland, and Turkey); (c) Japan.

Source: R. McCauley and E. Remolona, Special feature: Size and liquidity of government bond markets, *BIS Quarterly Review*, November, 2000. Reproduced with permission from Bank for International Settlements.

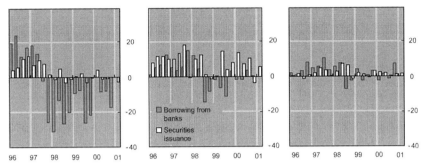

Figure 3.14 International bank and securities financing in emerging economies (in billions of U.S. dollars): (a) Asia and Pacific; (b) Latin America and Caribbean; (c) Europe. Data from Bank of England, Capital DATA, Euroclear, ISMA, Thomson financial securities data, national data, BIS locational banking statistics.

Source: B. H. Cohen and E. M. Remolona, Overview: Are markets looking beyond the slowdown? *BIS Quarterly Review*, June, 2001. Reproduced with permission from Bank for International Settlements.

U.S. government and agency bonds

The U.S. Treasury has over $4 trillion in total debt outstanding, of which $2.3 is marketable and actively traded in an OTC market. The securities are considered default-free (the government can print money to pay off debt). The only entity that can jeopardize that status is the U.S. Congress itself, which it did in 1995 when it refused to issue new debt to retire the old. More than two-thirds of the newly issued Treasuries are bought by non-U.S. residents. The Treasury market serves as the risk-free benchmark to other markets (corporate bonds, swaps, etc.). Unlike T-Bills, Treasury notes, with maturities of 2–7 years, and bonds, with maturities of 10–30 years, are quoted in terms of prices with 1/32 as the tick (supplemented with a "+" as the half-tick 1/64). The whole number is separated from the /32 fraction by a colon or a dash (e.g., 100:27, or 100-27), but sometimes misleadingly by a decimal (100.27). Prices are commonly converted to semi-annual bond equivalent yields on an Act/356 basis. Current benchmark issues, closest to the 2-, 5-, 10- and 30-year maturities that are most actively traded, are called *on-the-run* Treasuries and are normally boldfaced. Treasury notes and bonds pay semi-annual coupon interest. Treasury STRIPs (separated coupons or principals off original Treasuries sold as individual securities, or separate trading of registered interest and principal of securities) trade as zero-coupon instruments sold at a discount from par. On April 23, 2003 some U.S. Treasuries and STRIPs were quoted in the *Wall Street Journal* as follows:

Government Bonds & Notes					
	MATURITY				ASK
RATE	MO/YR	BID	ASKED	CHG	YLD
4.250	Nov 03n	101:21	101:22	−1	1.19
5.375	Feb 31	107:04	107:05	−3	4.90

U.S. Treasury STRIPS					ASK
MATURITY	TYPE	BID	ASKED	CHG	YLD
Feb 09	ci	82:11	82:14	−1	3.35

The T-Bond paying 5.375% coupon semi-annually (i.e., 2.6875% every 6 months) and maturing in February of 2031 is offered at a price equal to $107\frac{5}{32}$ percent of par to yield 4.90% semi-annual Act/365 equivalent.

At any given time there may be well over a hundred different old and new issues being quoted and traded. The on-the-run issues comprise the bulk of the trading and are referred to simply by maturity (e.g., the 2-year or the 10-year). Off-the-runs are referred to by stating the month and year of maturity and the coupon rate. The issues considered current (on-the-run) change as new notes and bonds are sold by the U.S. Treasury following an auction calendar published well in advance. In fact, new on-the-runs start trading even a few days before they are auctioned for the first time (i.e., even before the coupon rate is known). They trade on a yield basis and appear on dealer screens as *when issued* (WI) securities. As soon as they are auctioned (and the coupon rate is known) and dealers have them in their inventory, the yield is converted to price. This process allows a smooth repositioning by hedgers (e.g., swap traders) from old issues into new ones. Hedgers are often balanced. Some buy new issues; some short them. Long-term investors (e.g., insurance companies or bond funds) typically buy up old issues to hold to maturity. The comparison of the yields on the WIs and old on-the-runs is the first indication of whether the auction may be over- or undersubscribed. A WI is said to trade rich if the yield on it is lower (future price higher) than that on the relevant current on-the-run.

The U.S. Treasury publishes a schedule (calendar and amounts) of auctions for all new notes and bonds. Two types of bids are accepted: competitive (large, based on price/yield) and non-competitive (based on quantity limited to $1 million). At each auction, winning competitive bidders do not pay the price they bid, but the cutoff *stop price* arrived at by subtracting from the total the amount of non-competitive bids and competitive bids arranged from the lowest to the highest yield until all bonds are sold. This is called a single-price Dutch auction.

As described in Chapter 2, coupon securities are packages of zero-coupon securities. U.S. Treasuries are packages of STRIPs. Mechanically, STRIPs are created by separating all coupon payments from notes and bonds. For example, 21 STRIPs can be created from a 10-year semi-annual bond: 20 coupon payments and principal. They are then traded as separate securities with their own CUSIP (identification) numbers. Yields on coupon bonds and STRIPs are bound by a strict arbitrage relationship.

Let us review these on a simplified example with perfectly even semi-annual periods. Suppose you observe that the 3-year 5% note has a yield to maturity (YTM) of 5.3653% (i.e., its price is 99.00). Suppose also that the 6-, 12-, and 18-month STRIPs yield 5.25%, and the 30- and 36-month STRIPs yield 5.37%. Can the 24-month STRIPs yield 5.5%? No, its yield will be given by the equation for the price of the coupon bond with coupons discounted at the zero rates; that is:

$$99 = \frac{2.50}{\left(1 + \frac{0.0525}{2}\right)} + \frac{2.50}{\left(1 + \frac{0.0525}{2}\right)^2} + \frac{2.50}{\left(1 + \frac{0.0525}{2}\right)^3} + \frac{2.50}{\left(1 + \frac{x}{2}\right)^4} + \frac{2.50}{\left(1 + \frac{0.0537}{2}\right)^5}$$

$$+ \frac{2.50}{\left(1 + \frac{0.0537}{2}\right)^6} + \frac{100}{\left(1 + \frac{0.0537}{2}\right)^6}$$

and so it will be equal to $x = 5.2665\%$. This must be so; otherwise, arbitrage profits could be made. If, for example, it were to yield 5.5%, all traders would buy all the seven STRIPs with face values of 2.50 and 100, in effect *reconstituting* the purchase of a coupon bond, and short the 5% coupon. This would yield a riskless profit, as the sum of the prices paid for the STRIPs would be less than 99.00.

Synthetic Treasuries with any maturity and any coupon can be created through a similar process. Suppose there were no 12% Treasury notes with $7\frac{1}{2}$-year maturity. A dealer can create one by putting together a portfolio of STRIPs and coupons. The yield on the combined synthetic security would be governed by the same arbitrage principle. Synthetic forwards can also be created by combining bought long-term Treasuries with shorted short-term ones. For example, buying a \$100 million 12-year 6% coupon, shorting a \$100 million 3-year 6% coupon, and buying a 3-year \$100 million STRIP is equivalent to buying a security that starts paying 3% coupons $3\frac{1}{2}$ years from today and ends with the last coupon and principal 12 years from today (i.e., is a 3-year-by-12-year forward).

Arbitrage is the principle behind building a *Treasury curve*. The Treasury zero curve is a schedule of zero-coupon rates (or discount factors) paid by the U.S. government for any maturity between now and the maturity of the longest Treasury in existence. These rates are used to discount cash flows and to compute a price on any other bond issued by or collateralized by U.S. Treasuries. Any such bond can be synthesized by a portfolio of coupons and STRIPs. Similar to the Treasury zero curve, we can build a Treasury par curve (i.e., a schedule of YTMs on par coupon Treasuries). The curve is used as a benchmark for quoting bonds (munis, mortgages, or corporates).

Treasuries are the most common security underlying a repo contract. To the lender, often it does not matter whether the collateral is the 2-year or the 5-year on-the-run. That is why most repos yield the same *general* repo yield. Sometimes, they go *special*, which means, because the underlying Treasuries are in demand (to own), the repo lender (buying securities to resell tomorrow) will lend funds at a rate much lower than on other repos. That rate may even be zero. Dealers vie to own liquidity-squeezed Treasuries in order to be able to lower their cost of (borrowing) funds by repoing them. The special nature of some notes and bonds enters into the arbitrage equations when constructing synthetic spot or forward Treasuries.

In the mid-1990s the U.S. government started issuing Treasury inflation-protected securities (TIPS). The TIPS coupon is set to reflect a real rate of return. The principal accrues based on the annual measure of inflation. TIPS are designed to provide a perfect purchasing power hedge. Curiously, their volume of trading is rather low.

In addition to the U.S. Treasury, federally sponsored agencies issue bonds to finance activities in a few politically preferred sectors. These *government-sponsored enterprises* (GSEs) were described in the money market review. They issue uncollateralized debentures as well as mortgage-backed securities (collateralized by mortgage pools with common characteristics). Some agencies, like Fannie Mae, in addition to bullet bonds, also issue callable bonds. Several agencies follow a calendar of issuance (or reopening of old issues) of large bullet bonds with 2-, 5-, 10-, and 30-year maturities, similar to that of U.S. Treasury on-the-runs. These are called benchmark bonds for Fannie Mae and the Federal Home Loan Banks or reference bonds for Freddie Mac. Today, the volume of the agency bonds traded rivals that of the U.S. Treasuries.

Government bonds in Europe and Asia

National government bond markets in Europe and Japan follow a structure similar to that of the U.S. Primary dealers participate in auctions and then distribute bonds to institutional and retail investors. The auction procedures vary a little. While France and Germany follow the single-price Dutch auction based on a published calendar, the Bank of England uses an *ad hoc* auction system, where the maturity and the total amounts of the securities are announced only at the time of the auction. This allows greater borrowing flexibility and leads to less yield volatility in the markets, as old issues are not dumped in favor of new known ones prior to an auction. Some governments use a multiple-price Dutch auction similar to that used in the U.S. prior to the 1990s where competitive bids are awarded at the actual bid yield. Several governments, like the U.K., the Netherlands, and the U.S. have also used a *tap system* by reopening old issues at auctions. Many governments do not issue a great variety of maturities of bonds. In Germany and Japan, the longest benchmarks are 10-year bonds with no intervening, liquid on-the-runs. Several governments issue inflation-linked securities. In the U.K., index-linked gilts have coupons and final redemption amounts linked to the retail price index (RPI); Canadian and Australian governments have issued bonds linked to national inflation indices. The U.K. government also issues short-term bonds called convertibles which give the holder the right to convert to longer maturity bonds.

Government bonds around the world have easily recognizable nicknames. Among the major ones, U.K. bonds are called *gilts* and German bonds are referred to as *bunds*. These serve as benchmarks for pricing corporate bonds and swaps in the national markets and nearby (Swiss swaps are priced off bunds).

Secondary government bond markets around the world differ substantially in terms of their liquidity. The turnover ratio is the greatest in the U.S. where more bonds are traded every day than the total amount outstanding. The U.S. also enjoys the smallest bid–ask spreads (less than 3 basis points). By contrast, the Swedish, Swiss, and French markets trade with spreads of 10 or more basis points.

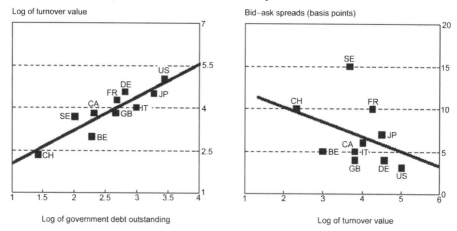

Figure 3.15   Size and liquidity.

Data from Salomon Smith Barney; H Inouc. The structure of government securities markets in G10 countries: Summary of questionnaire results. *Market Liquidity: Research Findings and Selected Policy Implications*, May, 1999, Committee on the Global Financial System, Basel; R. McCauley and E. Remolona, Special feature: Size and liquidity of government bond markets, *BIS Quarterly Review*, November, 2000. Reproduced with permission from Bank for International Settlements.

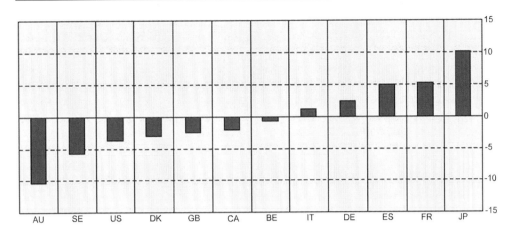

Figure 3.16 Estimated net issuance of government bonds in 2000 as a proportion of outstanding debt.
Data from Salomon Smith Barney; JP Morgan; and R. McCauley and E. Remolona, Special feature: Size and liquidity of government bond markets, *BIS Quarterly Review*, November, 2000. Reproduced with permission from Bank for International Settlements.

In any given year, the policies of central governments as to the overall new issuance and its composition differ across countries. For example, in the early 2000s, while the governments of Australia, Sweden and the U.S. were paying off their debts and shortening the maturity of their overall debt, Japan, France, and Spain were stepping up new issuance.

Corporates

Most corporate bonds are *term* or *bullet* bonds (i.e., they pay interest for a term of years and repay the principal at maturity). Most have final maturity dates of up to 30 years. The bond indenture may specify early redemption provisions serially, through a refunding, or a call. Bonds not collateralized by property, equipment, or specific revenue are called debentures. In case of default, they enjoy seniority over bank debt. They can also be *subordinated* (i.e., offer the least creditor protection relative to bank debt or senior bonds). Bond information services generally classify bonds into four categories: utilities, transportations, industrials, and financials. Prior to issue, most U.S. bonds and more than 50% of European bonds are rated by rating agencies like S&P's and Moody's with the familiar letter codes starting from AAA or Aaa, respectively, all the way down to C and D. The top four grades: prime, upper medium, medium, and lower medium, spanning S&P ratings above BB, are referred to as *investment-grade* bonds, the rest as *noninvestment-grade*, *high-yield*, or *junk* bonds (all synonyms). Rating agencies publish *credit watch* lists with bonds reviewed for potential upgrades or downgrades.

The origin of the modern junk bond market goes back to the 1980s which ushered in original-issue high-yield bonds. These were rated junk from the beginning and for issuers they represented convenient longer term alternatives to private bank loans or being shut off from credit. To alleviate the cash flow problems of junk or leverage buyout issuers, these bonds have often been issued with deferred or step-up coupons.

Traditionally, the largest corporate bond market has been the *domestic* bond sector, particularly in the U.S., where the domicile of the issuer, the currency, and the country of issue are the same. Rapidly growing is the *Eurobond* sector, where investors simultaneously come from several countries, the currency of issue is outside its home jurisdiction and bonds may be issued in unregistered form. Like domestic bonds, they are sometimes listed on an exchange, but most trade OTC. Borrowers are often non-financials, banks, and sovereign states. The currency of choice has traditionally been the U.S. dollar, but its share has steadily declined. Only some Eurobonds are Euro straights with normal fixed coupons: many have innovative coupon structures, like zeros, deferreds, or step-ups; many are dual-currency (coupon and principal currencies are not the same); some are convertible or exchangeable, and some have detachable stock and debt or currency warrants. Non-U.S. banks often issue dollar floating-rate Eurobonds, sometimes capped or collared, and sometimes with drop-locks (i.e., automatic conversions to fixed).

Medium-term notes (MTNs) are corporate debt instruments, both in the U.S. and Eurobond markets, offered continuously to investors by a program agent with maturities anywhere from 9 months to 30 years. Most MTNs are not underwritten, but distributed on a best efforts basis. Coupon structures are very innovative, both with fixed and floating-rate features. Many MTNs are structured (i.e., they are coupled with derivatives to provide the most appealing payoff structures, like inverse floating coupons). With an MTN, the borrower has the flexibility to issue highly customized debt and can do so as needed, under a previously announced and shelf-registered program. The only drawback may be the cost of registration and distribution.

Corporate bonds for different maturities trade at different rates. A corporate bond rate for a given maturity reflects the cost of borrowing/lending funds risklessly (government rate) plus an allowance for issuer default and other demand and supply issues (spread). Corporate spreads have their own term structure and are quoted relative to the same maturity government security or swap rate. The shape of the par coupon curve typically follows, but is not necessarily similar to the shape of the government bond curve. Corporate spreads in the late 1990s and early 2000s reached their historical highs, reflecting the deteriorating credit quality and exploding leverage ratios of private issuers. This has been true for all investment-grade rating categories. During the same period, the spreads between the highest and lowest rating increased. The spreads relative to benchmark swap rates also increased.

Munis

In the U.S., the primary driver behind the popularity of municipal bond (*muni*) finance is the exemption of the interest received from federal income taxes. The exemption applies to interest income (not capital gains) on obligations of all municipalities below the federal level (i.e., states, cities, utility and highway authorities, counties, etc.). From an individual investor's perspective, the yield on a muni can remain attractive at a level substantially lower than that of a corporate or a Treasury. Muni yields are frequently converted to taxable equivalent using the following formula:

$$y_{tax-equiv} = \frac{y_{muni}}{1 - \tau_m}$$

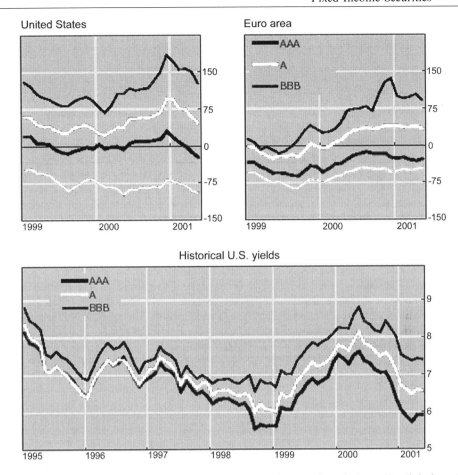

Figure 3.17 Corporate and government bond spreads, month-end data. Bond index yields against 10-year swap rates (in basis points), except for historical U.S. yields (in %).
Data from Bloomberg, Merrill Lynch, and national data. *Source*: B. H. Cohen and E. M. Remolona, Overview: Are markets looking beyond the slowdown? *BIS Quarterly Review*, June, 2001. Reproduced with permission from Bank for International Settlements.

where τ_m is an individual's marginal tax bracket. Municipal bonds are most popular with high-net-worth individuals.

In the U.S., the financing of schools, police, and infrastructure projects is highly decentralized and often obtained at a local level. Governments at low levels are forced to finance their own activities, expecting little help from state or federal institutions. This contributes to the great proliferation of issuers. For example, Bloomberg's database lists close to 60,000 active issuers.

Municipalities finance periodic funding imbalances and long-term projects using two main kinds of bonds: *general obligation* (GOs) and *revenue*. GOs are backed by the issuer's unlimited taxing power. Revenue bonds are backed by revenues from specific projects (highway tolls, water authority fees).

All municipal bonds are exempt from registration requirements. Munis can be issued as serial bonds, with pre-specified redemptions prior to final maturity, or as term bonds, but often with sinking bond provisions. Many are callable. Shorter term notes up to 3 years, issued in anticipation of tax, grant, revenue, or bond fund inflows, are respectively labeled tax-, grant-, revenue-, and bond-anticipation notes (TANs, GANs, RANs, and BANs). Like corporates, munis are rated on their default likelihood by S&P and Moody's using the same letter codes. It is worth noting however that many newer hybrid bonds' default provisions have not been tested in court and there may be no prior precedents of investors' recovery claims.

Primary market issuance procedures parallel those of the corporate bonds. Typically, large and small issues are underwritten by large and small investment banks, or privately placed with small groups of institutional investors. Their sales are announced in *The Bond Buyer*. The secondary market is widespread but not deep. Large brokerage firms trade in general names (nationally recognized municipal issuers), while smaller ones trade in local credits, both posting their inventory offerings over the Internet. Given the variety of issuers and bond types, most munis are quoted on a yield-to-call (YTC) or yield-to-maturity (YTM) basis, rather than price. This allows comparisons across all bonds of the same issuer and across issuers.

Occasionally, muni yields exceed Treasury yield, despite their tax advantage. This happens during periods when many large issues hit the market simultaneously. This sharply increases the supply of bonds and causes muni spreads to widen. In the summer of 2004, $15 billion of California bonds hit the market at the same time as other states and cities issued their own bonds in order to deal with their own budget deficits.

3.3 INTEREST-RATE SWAPS

Unlike securities markets where a piece of paper originally sold by an issuer changes hands between unrelated third parties, swaps are customized private contracts with each party exposed to the default risk of the other. Every time a swap is entered into, a new contract between two new *counterparties* is initiated. However, because swap conventions are so well established and because they are priced in the dealer market to reflect the average credit quality of the counterparty (i.e., uniformly), they are highly fungible (substitutable). Institutional counterparties willing to get out of previously established swaps can *unwind* the transactions not only with the original dealer, but frequently by auctioning off their side to other dealers as well. This involves a payment or receipt of the current mark-to-market, easily established by polling dealers, and an *assignment* of the swap. An unwind or assignment are not quite as simple as a purchase or sale of a security, but nowhere near as difficult as a break-up of a non-standard private contract. The main feature stopping the swaps from enjoying the liquidity of government bonds is their degree of customization and legal credit issues. At the same time, their volume has increased so dramatically in recent years as to rival the amount outstanding of the government bonds (summarized in Figures 3.18 and 3.19). This is true in terms of total swaps outstanding as well as daily cash and futures turnover, where swap-related transactions represent nearly half of the dollar market.

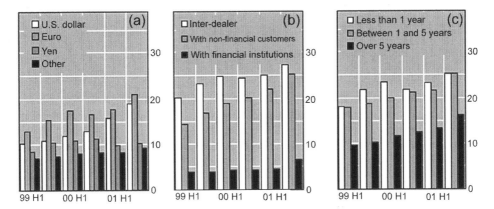

Figure 3.18 Interest rate swaps, notional amounts outstanding (in trillions of U.S. dollars): (a) by currency; (b) by counterplay; (c) by maturity (includes forward rate agreements, which account for approximately 15% of the total notional amount outstanding).
Reproduced with permission from Bank for International Settlements.

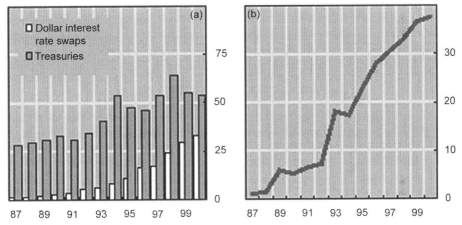

Figure 3.19 U.S. treasury and other instruments in the dollar bond market, daily average transactions (in billions of U.S. dollars and percentages): (a) treasury futures and swap transactions; (b) swap and non-Treasury transactions as a percentage of bond market activity (bond market activity includes swap transactions. Treasury cash and futures turnover, and turnover of U.S. dollar-denominated agencies, Eurobonds and global bonds).
Data from Cedel, FRBNY, national central banks, Euroclear, FOW TRACE, ISDA, BIS estimates. *Source*: R. N. McCauley, Benchmark tipping in the money and bond markets, *BIS Quarterly Review*, March, 2001. Reproduced with permission from Bank for International Settlements.

When governments were paying off national debts in the early 2000s, swaps replaced government bonds as de facto benchmarks for pricing other securities. This was particularly true for maturities where government bond markets were thin or did not exist, like the 11-year to 25-year maturity segment of the U.S. market, and is still true in some segments, like the Japanese market past the 10-year maturity point.

An interest-rate swap is an exchange between two counterparties of streams of cash-flows, typically resembling coupon streams of bonds. In a *plain vanilla swap*, one side is fixed, the other floating. The two parties agree on the final maturity of the swap (e.g., 10 years), the *notional principal* (e.g., $100 million), the interest rate for the *fixed leg* of the swap (e.g., 6%) to be paid on that notional principal, the floating rate index (e.g., 3-month LIBOR), the spread on top of it (e.g., +25 basis points) to be received on the notional principal, and the frequency and the day-count convention of both sides of the payments. The language of buying or selling a swap, like in securities, is never used. Instead, one party, called *a fixed rate payer* or simply a payer, pays fixed and receives floating interest amounts, while the other, called the *receiver*, does the opposite. The principal amount is referred to as the *notional*, as it can be thought of as a face value of two exchanged notional (i.e., fictitious) bonds. The notional in interest rate swaps is never exchanged as it is a wash (the same principal is paid and received). No spread over the floating side is called index *flat*. Paying fixed on a swap is economically equivalent to shorting a fixed coupon bond, reimbursing the lender of the shorted bond for missed coupons and principal, and with the proceeds buying a floating rate bond and receiving coupons and the principal on it. As the principals of both sides of the swap are the same, exchanging them at the end is not necessary. Swap settlement convention is 2 business days, and LIBOR fixings for the floating interest payments are 2 days, prior to the start of the accrual period, paid at the end of the accrual period.

Swaps are often done on the back of bond issues. In a low interest rate period like the early 2000s, investors tend to prefer floating rate bonds in the hope that as interest rates go up they can benefit. Imagine Coca-Cola issuing a $1 billion floating coupon bond, but the company really wants a fixed rate liability to focus on making syrup(!) and not on market speculation. Coca-Cola can issue a floating rate bond and enter into an interest rate swap with a dealer like Citibank paying fixed and receiving floating, with dates of payments exactly matching the coupon dates on its bond. The floating receipts from the swap would then exactly offset its payments of the bond coupons, leaving Coca-Cola with a fixed-rate liability. Often, swaps are done well into a life of a bond to lock in a gain or hedge against (read: speculate on) future rate movements. Suppose several years after issuing the floating rate bond, rates have actually declined. Coca-Cola can swap into fixed and pay a fixed rate lower than it would have had it swapped immediately. Many swaps are unrelated to bond issuance.

Normally, *on-market* swaps are entered into with no money changing hands upfront. The fixed rate (or the floating rate spread) is adjusted such that the present value of the payments is equal to the present value of the receipts. Market-making dealers compete on the spread they quote over a benchmark for the fixed rate of the swap against LIBOR flat. In the final negotiations, that translates into a specific fixed rate written into the swap's documentation. But swaps can also be customized to match specific rate targets. In that case, depending on whether the agreed-on fixed rate is higher or lower than the currently quoted swap rate for a given maturity, there may be a payment or receipt of the present value of the swap by the dealer. Such swaps are called *off-market* swaps.

Many swaps are not plain vanilla. The simplest example is when a rate paid on either side of the swap does not conform to its standard, like semi-rate paid annually. Other examples involve *floating-for-floating swaps*, where both sides are floating but off different indices (LIBOR vs. FF rate), or *zero-coupon* swaps, where one side only accrues but does not pay until a certain date. Chapter 4 also describes *currency swaps*, sometimes called *cross-currency swaps*, where the pay side of the swap is in one currency and the receive side in another. These can be fixed-for-floating, fixed-for-fixed, floating-for-floating or even multicurrency, referring to the types of payments and receipts.

We will defer the discussion of swap valuation to Chapters 6 and 8. Here we go through a simple example of the cash flows of a plain vanilla swap in U.S. dollars. Let us pretend that we are Citibank and, on August 19, 2003, we are entering into a 2-year $100 million swap to pay 6% semi-annually on a 30/360 basis and receive 3-month LIBOR quarterly on an Act/360 basis. Dollar swap settlement is 2 business days, so the fixed payments will *roll* on May 21 and August 21, and the floating receipts will roll on November 21, February 21, May 21 and August 21, based on LIBOR fixings 2 business days prior to those dates.[4] Consider Table 3.4 which is full of relevant information. In columns 1 and 2, we have the set dates and LIBORs we observe over the life of the swap, columns 3 and 4 contain the start and end dates for the quarterly interest accrual period of the floating side of the swap. For simplicity, we assume in column 5 that, in each quarterly interest accrual periods running from August 21 to November 21 and from May 21 to August 21, there are exactly 93 days and, in each of the other accrual periods, there are exactly 92 days. In real life, we would have to count the actual days. Also, if any of the LIBOR set dates were not a business day, we would have to take LIBOR from 1 day prior or refer to the swap documentation. The semi-annual accrual periods for the fixed leg of the swap are not shown, as each simply includes two quarterly periods of the floating side (i.e., they run from 21 August to 21 February and from 21 February to 21 August).

Table 3.4 A 2-year $100 million interest-rate swap on August 19, 2003. Pay 6% semi *30/360*, receive 3-month LIBOR *Act/360*

Set date	LIBOR	Accrual period		No. days	Floating cash flows		Fixed cash flows	
		Start date	End date		Pay date	Amount	Pay date	Amount
19-Aug-03	5.00	21-Aug-03	21-Nov-03	93	21-Nov-03	1,291,667		
19-Nov-03	*5.10*	21-Nov-03	21-Feb-04	92	21-Feb-04	1,303,333	21-Feb-04	3,000,000
19-Feb-04	*5.50*	21-Feb-04	21-May-04	92	21-May-04	1,405,556		
19-May-04	*5.60*	21-May-04	21-Aug-04	93	21-Aug-04	1,446,667	21-Aug-04	3,000,000
19-Aug-04	*6.00*	21-Aug-04	21-Nov-04	93	21-Nov-04	1,550,000		
19-Nov-04	*6.20*	21-Nov-04	21-Feb-05	92	21-Feb-05	1,584,444	21-Feb-05	3,000,000
19-Feb-05	*6.10*	21-Feb-05	21-May-05	92	21-May-05	1,558,889		
19-May-05	*5.90*	21-May-05	21-Aug-05	93	21-Aug-05	1,524,167	21-Aug-05	3,000,000

Floating leg cash flows (columns 6 and 7) are based on LIBOR sets *2 days prior* to the start of the interest accrual period and are received on the end date of the accrual period (i.e., in arrears), the same way a floating rate bond would pay. Note that the first LIBOR is known at the time of the swap; the rest, shown in italics, are not known until the actual set dates. For the first interest period, we take:

$$100,000,000 \cdot 0.0500 \cdot 93/360 = 1,291,667$$

---

[4] Settlement day conventions vary somewhat across currencies: USD swaps use LIBOR sets from 2 business days prior, while GBP swaps use same day sterling LIBOR sets and the effective date is the trade date.

Fixed rate leg cash flows are all based on the same quoted 6% rate and are paid on the end dates of the semi-annual interest period, the same way a fixed coupon bond would pay. For each period, we take:

$$100,000,000 \cdot 0.0600 \cdot 180/360 = 3,000,000$$

For an on-market swap, the present value of the fixed cash flows is equal to the present value of the floating cash flows, where we substitute today's forward 3-month rates for the unknown future LIBOR sets. We explain the logic of that arbitrage condition in Chapters 6 and 8.

Like bonds, swaps for different maturities trade at different rates and reflect the cost of borrowing/lending funds risklessly (government rate) plus an allowance for counterparty default and other transaction-related issues (spread). Swap spreads have their own term structure and are quoted relative to the same maturity government security. The shape of the swap (par coupon) curve typically follows, but is not necessarily similar to, the shape of the government bond curve. Swap spreads in the late 1990s and early 2000s reached their historical highs, reflecting the deteriorating credit quality of an average counterparty.

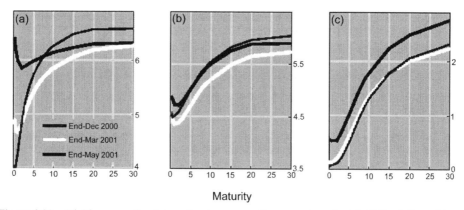

Maturity

Figure 3.20   Yield curves for interest rate swaps (in percentages): (a) U.S. dollar; (b) euro; (c) yen.

Data from Bloomberg. *Source*: B. H. Cohen and E. M. Remolona, Overview: Are markets looking beyond the slowdown? *BIS Quarterly Review*, June, 2001.

3.4   MORTGAGE SECURITIES

Mortgage-backed securities (MBSs) are obligations of an issuing agency or a financial institution fully collateralized by the stream of interest and principal payments of the underlying mortgage pool. Traditional mortgages in the U.S. have been fixed interest fully amortized loans with level monthly payments. These give borrowers the right and incentives to prepay the loan prior to its maturity which is typically 30 years (less often 15). To understand the mechanics and risks of this segment of fixed income markets, it is useful to review the basics of real estate financing.

A purchaser of a house, after supplying a down payment from his own funds (typically 20% but often less) obtains a significant portion of the funds (the loan-to-value ratio) needed from the original lender of funds, the mortgage originator. The originator makes money by charging an origination fee and other fees and by selling the mortgage in the secondary market to a larger financial institution for a higher price. This allows the originator to replenish his funds to make new loans. The new owner of the mortgage loan may outsource the collection of the monthly payments to the originator or a third party by paying a servicing fee. The mortgage investor buys many similar loans. He has an incentive to further sell the collected pool of mortgages in order to be able to acquire new loans (otherwise, he would quickly run out of funds to invest). He assembles pools of mortgages according to government agency guidelines and sells them to agencies for the purposes of securitization or issues collateralized securities directly to investors. The only spoiler in this process can be the homeowner himself who has the right to prepay the mortgage partially (by sending more money each month) or completely (e.g., by selling the property). He does so especially when interest rates drop and he can re-finance at a lower rate. But the homeowner is not an efficient refinancer and he prepays for unique reasons too (e.g., inheritance); in a pool of mortgages there will be some that pay off fast, some that pay off slowly. In general, *the prepayment speed* will increase as interest rates go down. The prepayment speed is measured by a standard unit called a PSA (public securities association): 100% PSA means that a pool prepays at a rate of 6% per year if the mortgages are over 30 months old or by a percentage, starting at 0% all the way to 6%, increasing by 0.2% for the first 30 months, that percentage reflecting the fact that newly issued mortgages rarely prepay.

The securitization of mortgages takes two basic forms. The first stage is to issue *pass-through certificates*. Pools of similar mortgages (by geography, size, type of dwelling, etc.) are placed in a trust entity and certificates entitling holders to a proportional share of monthly receipts are sold (98% of pass-throughs are created by the agencies, the rest by financial institutions). As homeowners prepay their loans, particularly in a low interest rate environment, the effective duration of mortgages shrinks with investors receiving larger amounts in the early years of the pass-through and next to nothing toward the end. The greatest risk of a mortgage security is this implicit call option sold to homeowners. This entails contraction risk if prepayments speed up or extension risk if they slow down relative to baseline PSA. The default risk is minimal as all underlying loans are mortgages with full recourse rights of the lender to foreclose and sell the property.

In order to create securities that enjoy the default protection of mortgages but are relatively immune to prepayment risks, the second stage of securitization involves the issuance of *collateralized mortgage obligations* (CMOs). Pass-throughs are put in a trust, and several distinct tranches of bonds with fixed coupons are issued. The sum of the face values of all the tranches is equal to the face value of the collateral pass-through. However, monthly payments received from the collateral are sliced and allocated to the tranches in the order of pre-assigned priority. For example, in a *sequential-pay CMO*, all interest payments are allocated equally to all tranches based on the assigned principal, but all the principal payments go first to paying off tranche A, then B, etc. Tranches C and D may not receive principal payments until later years. The effective duration of the tranches depends greatly on the speed of prepayments. Early tranches enjoy extension risk protection. Later tranches enjoy prepayment risk protec-tion, but also face the most uncertainty as to the timing of principal retirement.

A common variation on the sequential pay CMO structure is one with an added residual accrual tranche called a Z bond. The accrual tranche initially does not receive current coupon interest. Instead, interest is accrued and added to the principal to be paid when the tranche starts receiving distributions. Another variation ensuring a greater stability of the average life of a bond is a CMO that includes a planned amortization class (PAC) bond as the first tranche and the support of companion classes as the other tranches. In this CMO, payments are diverted from the companion classes to ensure that the PAC class follows a pre-specified principal repayment schedule based on a stated PSA percentage. This protects against both contraction and extension risk of the PAC class, with most of the risk shifted to the companion classes.

MBSs also trade in stripped forms, most often as interest-only (IOs) and principal-only (POs). Similarly to the sequential and PAC CMOs, pass-throughs are put in a trust that issues certificates entitling holders to the portions of the monthly payments separately relating to interest and principal. Thus an IO holder receives the coupon interest portion only, calculated on an ever-declining principal, and, if prepayments speed up, the total sum of receipts may be lower than the original amount paid for the IO. On the other hand, if prepayments are slow, the IO holder may receive payments for the full maturity of the mortgages. The unique feature of an IO is that its value rises as interest rates rise, which slows the prepayments. POs are sold at a discount from face value and benefit from interest rate declines that speed up prepayments. Their values are highly interest rate-sensitive.

The valuation of MBSs is a mix of PV calculations and statistics. The statistics part relates to prepayment modeling, which involves estimation from past history of homeowner responses to financial and non-financial variables. As we mentioned before, the homeowner has the right to prepay equivalent to the right to call the loan at par (like an issuer of a callable bond). In most models, it is assumed that the homeowner compares the rate on his mortgage to the 7- or 10-year rate on U.S. Treasury, which is the benchmark for 30-year fixed rate mortgages. However, more often than not the homeowner does not exercise this option as soon as it is optimal to do so. He may have just refinanced, refinancing may be costly, or the homeowner may have other family issues. Sometimes, the homeowner exercises early (e.g., when his family relocates and the property is sold). Even if the mortgagee is interest rate-sensitive and tends to exercise as rates decline, he may take other factors into account, like the last date of refinance, the rate change not the level, rates on alternative mortgage structures, etc. Homeowners also vary in some individual characteristics, like age, income, location, type of property, etc. Even when a statistical model of prepayments is constructed, the valuation of an MBS typically involves more than present value discounting of cash flows based on estimated principal. Because the principal itself is not interest rate-level but path-dependent, the valuation involves a Monte Carlo or tree simulation, or some other valuation technique similar to option pricing. The excess yield spread over a static present valuing is referred to as an *option-adjusted spread* of an MBS. It is at best an estimate value of the implicit options held by the homeowner.

3.5 ASSET-BACKED SECURITIES

Similar to MBSs, asset-backed securities (ABSs) are securities collateralized by receipts from other underlying assets. The most popular are home equity loans, student loans, auto loans, credit card debt, and, lately, other bonds, like high-yield, distressed debt, and emerging market bonds. The underlying securities or loans, which can be amortizing or not, are placed in a trust or a special purpose vehicle (SPV). Often the SPV is over-collateralized as a form of internal credit enhancement. Interest rate paid on ABSs can be fixed or floating, reflecting the nature of collateral. The structure can be *pay-through*, analogous to MBS pass-throughs, where each ABS represents a fractional interest in the cash flows of the collateral, or tranched with one senior and several subordinated tranches. Almost all ABSs are subject to prepayment risks. Home-equity ABSs have published prospectus prepayment curves (PPCs) similar to PSA schedules. Auto loan ABSs are measured in terms of absolute prepayment speed (ABS). Auto loan-backed ABSs are issued by subsidiaries of auto manufacturers, banks, and finance companies. Many student loan ABSs enjoy at least fractional government default protection. Credit card receivable-backed ABSs, sold by banks, retailers, and travel companies, are structured as master trusts of principal and finance charge receivables. The issuer sells several series from the same trust, often by randomly selecting accounts. Credit card ABSs are non-amortizing due to a lock-out period provision. During the lock-out the principal repayments are reinvested in additional receivables.

The U.S. has the largest ABS market, but the last 5 years have seen an explosive growth of the market in Europe. A new but growing segment is the corporate asset-backed market, originating mainly in the U.K. The largest asset used for backing, reflecting its large market value, is commercial real estate, accounting for 32% of the total. But the market enjoys a wide variety of assets used for backing, including equipment and auto leases, aircraft leases, trade receivables, and others.

Short-term ABS spreads have historically exceeded long-term spreads, reflecting the expected relative price stability of the longer term assets backing the bonds. While unsecured borrowing spreads for European corporates have increased and become increasingly variable, due to the credit problems of the issuers, ABS spread averages have remained relatively stable.

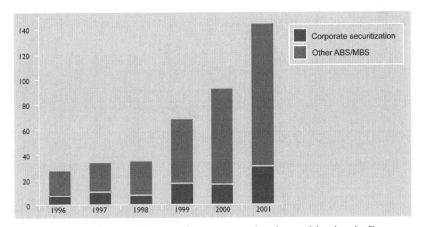

Figure 3.21   The increasing prominence of corporate-related securitization in Europe.
Reproduced with permission from Ganesh Rajendra (Managing Director, Global Markets Research, Deutsche Bank AG) and White Page, author and publisher, respectively, of *The Use of Securitization as an Alternative Funding Tool for European Corporates*.

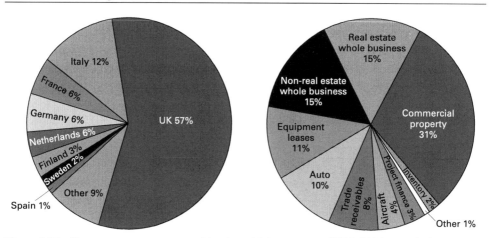

Figure 3.22 European corporate securitization: (a) by country (1999–2001 cumulative); (b) by asset type (1999–2001 cumulative).

Reproduced with permission from Ganesh Rajendra (Managing Director, Global Markets Research, Deutsche Bank AG) and White Page, author and publisher, respectively, of *The Use of Securitization as an Alternative Funding Tool for European Corporates.*

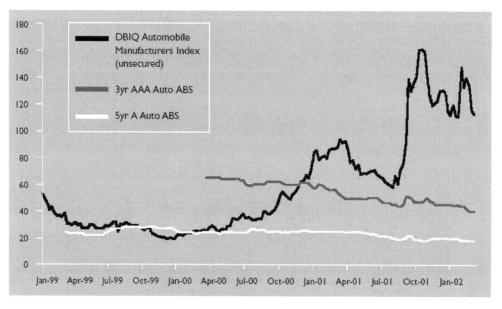

Figure 3.23 Spreads in the unsecured bond market and ABS market compared.

Rproduced with permission from Ganesh Rajendra (Managing Director, Global Markets Research, Deutsche Bank AG) and White Page, author and publisher, respectively, of *The Use of Securitization as an Alternative Funding Tool for European Corporates.*

One category of ABS that has emerged only in the last 10 years is the collateralized debt obligation (CDO), known in its two guises: a collateralized bond obligation (CBO) and collateralized loan obligation (CLO). A CBO is backed by a diversified pool of high-yield or emerging market bonds; a CLO is backed by a pool of bank loans or distressed debt. An asset manager sponsoring the CDO for arbitrage or balance sheet reasons typically sells three tranches of certificates in the order of cash flow claim: senior, mezzanine, and subordinate equity. The funds obtained from the sale of certificates are used during the ramp-up period to acquire collateral. The division allows the senior tranche to obtain a rating that is higher than the average of the underlying collateral. The pool is managed to generate the requisite cash flows during the life of the CDO.

4
Equities, Currencies, and Commodities

Spot markets in securities other than fixed income are simpler and more complex at the same time. The underlying mathematics are much simpler because these securities do not normally involve multiple cash flows (a currency does not pay coupons like a bond) and there are few or no close substitutes that can be repackaged to create a stock, a currency, or a commodity (like coupon bonds with zeros). Each spot currency or stock is unique and its value cannot be mathematically related to that of another currency or stock. There is no stated maturity value, and thus there is much greater uncertainty about the future redemption price. Because they rely on estimates of future economic variables, cash flow-discounting techniques for valuing stocks or commodities are at best good approximations of the fundamental value. Current market prices are not strict functions of those cash flows the way bond prices are of coupon streams. At best, they are educated guesses based on economic analyses of supply and demand, growth assumptions, and a lot of other subjective measures. The upshot is that the discounting techniques are relatively simple, but imprecise, as they rely on a lot of uncertain economic variables.

4.1 EQUITY MARKETS

Secondary stock trading around the world is arranged to force buyers and sellers of each stock into one marketplace in order to discover the best price for the stock. The bottleneck design ensures that all relevant information about the stocks reflected in the bid and offered prices flows into one place. This helps establish the price that reflects the balance of all demand and supply for the stock. It also guarantees maximum liquidity of trading, allowing traders and investors to buy and sell nearly instantaneously and with minimal transaction costs. The bottleneck can be designed in two ways: one is through a physical exchange; the other is through a virtual exchange which is really a network of dealers linked by phones and computers. The first typically creates a greater concentration of supply and demand, while the second offers more competition.

Primary equity sale works roughly the same around the world. New issuers of stock contact investment bankers who help them navigate through the regulatory process and help them sell the stock certificates to investors. In most countries new shares have to be registered with a national government regulator to ensure a minimal level of information disclosure. The stock is then offered to investors as a fully underwritten issue or on a best efforts basis. In the former, the investment banking firm buys the entire issue and then sells it to investors out of its own inventory. In the latter, the investment-banking firm does not take all the resale risk. Instead, it only sells as much of the issue as it can.

The process is the same whether the issues are offered in an initial public offering (IPO), where new companies sell stock for the first time, or in a seasoned equity offering (SEO), where well-established firms distribute additional shares to new investors. The flip side of the primary market is the repurchase of shares by the original issuers, or a buyback. This is done in the secondary market, but is normally preceded by an announcement of a buyback program. Buybacks permanently reduce the number of shares circulated among investors.

Compared with markets for bonds, commodities, or derivatives, equity markets are well understood by novice investors. We focus on some interesting recent developments.

Secondary markets for individual equities in the U.S.

The largest and most important secondary market for individual equities is the New York Stock Exchange (NYSE). The NYSE processes about 1.4 billion shares every day and derives its strength from a unique setup based on specialist trading posts. The floor of the NYSE consists of trading booths, each trading in a handful of stocks assigned to them. In order to provide the maximum liquidity of trading (force buyers and sellers to meet at one bottleneck spot), each stock is assigned to only one booth and one author-ized dealer for that stock—the specialist sitting in the booth. Most orders arrive through and are electronically matched by a SuperDot computer system. The rest come from the crowd of brokers gathered around each post. Unmatched limit and stop orders are entered into the limit order book maintained by the specialist. They are prioritized based on their size and best execution price. The specialist is in a unique position to see who wants to buy and sell and at what prices. Since 2002, the crowd has been allowed to see the total size and price for each bid and offer. The specialist enjoys a monopoly power to trade for his own account by observing the flow of trading in the limit order book. For the privilege of being able to profit from knowing the flow of buy and sell orders for his stock, the monopolist is obligated to "maintain fair and orderly market" (i.e., sometimes lose money when trading imbalances occur). He is a market maker and must post bid and offer prices at all times. He is forced to trade when he may not want to. This ensures the continuity of the price and reasonable depth of quotes. It may seem unfair to allow the specialist to profit at the expense of public investors, and recent scandals over the abuse of monopoly power by specialists may force the NYSE to re-examine its reluctance to adopt a dealer model. The specialist's monopoly profit is the price for continuous price discovery. The Tokyo Stock Exchange is the best example of where machines sometimes fail to deliver. All buyers and sellers are forced to submit orders into the same limit order book. Market participants have electronic access to it (they can see the size and the identity of the bidders and sellers), but if at any given time there are no market orders and no seller wishes to trade at a price equal to the highest bid, then no trading occurs. At the NYSE, the specialist must step in to trade.

There are disadvantages to this arrangement. With the advent of decimal trading (quoting prices in dollars and cents as opposed to eighths and sixteenths of dollars) and more importantly the reduction of the tick size (minimum price increment) to 1 cent, specialists have had incentives to front-run investors by showing prices only 1 cent better than the best bid or offer. Front-running tips the balance of fairness away from the investor and in favor of the specialist. The NYSE has had to police the specialists more to ensure that the tradeoff of monopoly profits for continuous price making is balanced.

NYSE, also called the "Big Board", lists over 2,000 U.S. and foreign stocks. The American Stock Exchange, the AMEX or the "Curb", lists about 700 mostly smaller companies (in terms of market cap), but has become known for its innovation in warrants and a variety of standardized stock baskets. Both the NYSE and the AMEX are physical exchanges based on a single market-maker auction. In contrast, the U.S. over-the-counter (OTC) market called NASDAQ, owned and operated by the National Association of Securities Dealers (NASD), has no single physical location and is based on multiple market-makers who quote and trade shares through a computerized automatic quotation system ($-AQ$). There are well over 4,000 stocks listed on the two tiers of the NASDAQ (national and small-cap). Just like the physical exchanges, the NASD maintains listing requirements (albeit less stringent and costly), yet the NASDAQ stocks are referred to as "unlisted". All NASDAQ members are dealers (i.e., they trade for their own account, and many trade the same stocks). They are obligated to continuously display firm bids and offers good for 1,000 shares and, when hit, trade at those quotes with other members. The practice common on NASDAQ, but not permitted on the exchanges, is the internalization of many customer trades. The dealer may execute customer orders acting as a principal and not show the order to other dealers. This takes liquidity away from the central market which is already, by design, fragmented. The positive of this setup over the single auction specialist is the competition multiple dealers provide. This may not be enough to compensate for the shortcomings of diminished liquidity as evidenced in NASDAQ's wider bid–ask spreads relative to NYSE.

The vast majority of OTC issues (about 8,000) not listed on NYSE, AMEX, or NASDAQ trade on the OTC Bulletin Board (most) or on the electronic version of old "Pink Sheets" (penny stocks). Both of these are reported by the NASD. In addition, in the so-called "third market", exchange-listed stocks trade OTC via a system similar in functionality to and operated by the NASD.

Since the 1990s, a fourth market has emerged in the form of for-profit brokers' networks. To avoid exchange commissions, customers can meet directly in fully electronic markets maintained by third parties. These can be either electronic communications networks (ECNs) or crossing networks. ECNs operate within the NASDAQ system (representing 30% of volume) as widely disseminated electronic limit order books. Subscribers link to them to anonymously post quotes and execute trades. The largest ECNs include Instinet, Island, and Archipelago. ECNs are economical ways to handle small retail orders. Crossing networks are designed for institutional investors. They match buyers and sellers directly by aggregating orders for execution as a batch at a specified time. They are popular with mutual funds.

Secondary markets for individual equities in Europe and Asia

Lacking a single, integrated market for equity capital, European companies list on national exchanges or cross-list on several European exchanges. The London Stock Exchange (LSE) has struggled to maintain its lead in having the most international equities traded on its floor (about 20% of issues). The trading mechanism includes both an order book and multiple market makers. Dealers are linked through a screen quotation system, but matched bids and offers in FTSE 100 shares are executed automatically. Any appropriately capitalized firm can compete as a dealer in multiple stocks on the LSE. The order-matching book of the LSE is known as the SETS and the dealer quotation system as the SEAQ. In Germany, stock trading is concentrated on the Deutsche Börse which combines floor and electronic transacting. Buyers and sellers must submit their trades through a bank represented on the Börse. Stock trades are considered banking transactions according to the German universal bank tradition. The exchange operates three segments: the official market, the regulated market, and the Neuer Markt for smaller companies. Xetra is the electronic order-matching system operated as the central limit order book. All European countries operate national exchanges. Recently, competition among them has forced many to seek alliances as each tries to become the continent's dominant one. Euronext combines the Amsterdam, Brussels, Lisbon, and Paris exchanges and is second to LSE in the number of international stocks listed. Spain's exchange lists most companies in Europe, mostly domestic. Not a single European exchange is based on the specialist posts. Only Amsterdam affords that status to some dealers (Montreal and Toronto also have single-auction market-makers). Most are based on a competitive dealer principle. This means, for example, that London dealers may take larger positions in stocks than dealers in New York. This is not so in Paris because the automated trade systems do not afford enough anonymity to block trading firms. Clearing of trades in Europe is fragmented along national lines and contributes to the high cost of executing transactions.

The Japanese stock market, over 120 years old, consists of six exchanges, the dominant one being the Tokyo Stock Exchange (TSE). Over 1,800 domestic TSE shares are classified, based primarily on size, into two sections, the majority being traded in the first section. In the continuous-auction TSE market, the "Saitori" intermediaries, who are not allowed to trade for their own account, maintain the computerized central book. They match orders based on price priority and time precedence and rely on an open outcry to solicit new orders. All securities must be traded by an authorized dealer. The three major dealing firms are Nomura, Nikko, and Daiwa.

In China, the principal exchanges exist in Shanghai and Shenzen. They trade class A shares denominated in the nonconvertible yuan and class B shares denominated in U.S. dollars and HK dollars, respectively. In 2001, the government permitted the ownership of B shares by Chinese nationals via hard currency accounts and allowed state-owned companies to sell B shares. However, property rights and accounting rules have continued to hamper trading in B shares. In addition, companies are tied strongly to the Chinese economy trade on the Hong Kong exchange. They are often referred to as H shares.

Depositary receipts and cross-listing

As of 2001, there were more than 1,800 sponsored depositary receipts (DRs) from almost 80 countries[1] traded around the world. Depositary receipts are claims to shares of foreign companies. In the U.S., *American depositary receipts* (ADRs) are created by a bank, like the Bank of New York, by accumulating shares of foreign companies. The claims on those shares, one for one, are then traded on the stock

---

[1] See the Bank of New York's site at www.adrbny.com

exchanges as if they were shares of domestic stocks. They are convenient for investors; they trade in U.S. dollars, their dividends are paid in dollars, and they can be bought and sold in the U.S. market lowering the legal risk and cost. DRs can be *sponsored* by a foreign company actively seeking listing and selecting one authorized depositary bank or *non-sponsored* (i.e., created by any bank). Legally, a DR holder may give up voting and pre-emptive rights. Creation of DRs allows companies around the world to cross-list on several national exchanges in order to tap new sources of capital. For example, large Swiss or Dutch multinationals choose to have their shares traded simultaneously on their small domestic exchanges, as well as in London and in New York.

Stock market trading mechanics

In most markets around the world, investors can enter several types of orders. The most important are market orders and limit orders. *Market orders* are orders to buy at the current offer price and to sell at the current bid price a given number of shares of stock. The number of shares is normally specified in terms of whole lots (normally 100 or 1,000 shares). The customer specifies just the ticker symbol of the security and the quantity to be bought or sold. The price at which he will buy/sell is that currently quoted when the order arrives on the floor of the exchange or is posted on an ECN. The market order is executed immediately against existing limit and market orders. *Limit orders* are orders to buy or sell a specified quantity of a stock at a price equal to or better than a specified limit. Thus, in a limit order, the customer must specify the price at which he is willing to trade.

For example, a limit order may read "Buy 200 shares of IBM at 76.75." If there are other customers' orders in the book to buy IBM at 77, they will be executed ahead of the limit order at 76.75 as they enjoy a price priority. If there are no better bids and the lowest offer is to sell at 77.25, then the limit order at 76.75 will not be executed until a market sell order or another limit sell order at 76.75 or lower are entered into the order book.

All orders can have additional instructions like "good for the day", "good till canceled", all or nothing, etc. In most markets, orders are entered into a central book and prioritized based on price. The highest bid is waiting to be executed first, then the second highest bid, etc. The lowest offer is waiting to be executed first, then the second lowest offer, etc. The time of the order arrival has only secondary precedence (i.e., only for orders at the same price). This priority arrangement contributes to achieving the smallest spread between the lowest offer and the highest bid. The size of the spread is a measure of market liquidity, and the cost of trading is as real as any explicit commission, fee, or duty. For large institutions, anonymity is of paramount importance in minimizing impact costs. A large block for sale by a well-known dealer may cause the selling price to drop and thus lead to lower total proceeds. The *upstairs market* in New York attempts to alleviate the impact of block trades that constitute about 50% of all volume on the NYSE. There, block traders (minimum 10,000 shares) arrange transactions directly with each other, with only the unmatched balance executed through the floor crowd.

There are also explicit costs of trading stocks, like commissions and clearing fees. Often these cover "free" services customers get from brokers, like access to research reports and trade data. These are commonly referred to as "soft dollar" payments as they are hidden in trading fees. Regulators, like the Securities and Exchange Commission (SEC) in the U.S. or the Financial Services Authority (FSA) in the U.K., limit the types of implicit perquisites investors can obtain in this manner. In the OTC markets, market makers offer cash payments to brokerages with access to customer trades. This entices brokerages to send all their orders to a select few market makers in order to accumulate commission rebates. This practice is commonly referred to as *payment for order flow*. It continues to be controversial as it provides perverse incentives for brokers to send orders to markets with the highest level of these "kick-backs" as opposed to those with the best execution price. It can be argued that they contribute to unjustifiably high bid–ask spreads. It can also be argued that they represent a fair payment for access to information flow. It is doubtful that cost benefits are passed on to retail customers.

Stock indexes

Investors around the globe follow stock markets with the help of stock indexes. Today, some of them are household names: Dow Jones, S&P 500, and NASDAQ in the U.S., FTSE 100 in the U.K., CAC-40 in France, DAX in Germany, Nikkei 225 in Japan, Hang Seng in Hong Kong, All Ords in Australia, to name a few. Stock indexes reflect the price movement of diversified baskets of stocks in each national market. Most are capitalization weighted (notable exceptions are the Dow Jones in the U.S. and the Nikkei 225 in Japan which are price-weighted) to ensure proper weighting (by size) of all companies in the basket. Sometimes the baskets are not as diversified as most believe. The Dow Jones and DAX reflect only 30 stocks. The Nikkei has 225 stocks. The CAC-40 has only 40. In most markets, better alternatives exist, but are less popular. In the U.S., the Wilshire 5000, Russell 1000 and 2000 indexes are broader indexes. In Japan, TOPIX includes all first-section TSE stocks. There is also a variety of index indicators covering major world regions. The most widely used of those are the Morgan Stanley Capital International and Financial Times World Indexes that divide the world into logical economic regions roughly based on continental boundaries. These are calculated in local as well as major currencies.

The publishing of indexes is a business run by private companies or exchanges. Often companies vie to be included in some indexes in a belief that doing so increases the liquidity of their stocks. Index companies charge fees to bond and warrant issuers and derivatives dealers for referencing the index names in settlement documents of contracts. Indexes are a basis for many futures and options contracts, both exchange and OTC-traded. There have been hundreds of principal-protected bond issues whose coupons are linked to stock indexes that have been sold to retail investors in Europe and the U.S. in the last 10 years. There are hundreds of mutual funds that compete on passively replicating the indexes at the lowest cost.

A capitalization-weighted, or cap-weighted, index is created by computing a weighted average price of a basket of stocks with all stocks included in the index taken in proportion to their total market value (stock price × the number of shares outstanding), initially divided by some constant number to normalize the index. Every day as the price of each stock changes the index value will change as a result of the price change itself and indirectly of the total market capitalization change. Funds, attempting to replicate indexes, continuously monitor the proportions of their holdings, even though they are largely self-adjusting. It is important to note that even though the S&P 500 is a cap-weighted index of the 500 largest U.S. companies, their inclusion in the index is not automatic: rather, it is decided by a selection committee run by Standard and Poor's.

Exchange-traded funds (ETFs)

Until a few years ago, small investors hoping to replicate the performance of a stock index could only buy index mutual funds. The largest one of these in the U.S. is the Vanguard Equity Index 500 (ticker: VFINX). The fund itself could be bought and sold directly from Vanguard at the end-of-the-day net asset value (NAV). The NAV of a fund is calculated by taking the total value of all the holdings using the market prices at the close of a business day (4 p.m. New York time) and dividing it by the number of shares issued by the fund. The portfolio manager for VFINX would try to replicate the performance of the S&P 500 index, charging only minimal running costs subtracted from the value of the holdings in the calculation of the NAV. Recently, funds similar in objective to index mutual funds started trading directly on the exchanges. The AMEX lists over 100 such funds. These ETFs can be bought and sold like ordinary stocks throughout the day in the secondary market (investor-to-investor). Each share represents a mini closed-end (trust) fund representing a claim to a basket of stocks resembling the targeted index. The funds are run by depositary banks (the State Street Bank sponsors S&P 500 Depositary Receipts, or SPDRs) or asset management companies (Barclays Capital sponsors iShares), including those managing traditional open-end mutual funds (Vanguard). The institutions charge stated management fees reflected in the current prices of the funds. The most popular ETFs are "Cubes" (ticker: QQQ), "Spyders" or SPDRs (SPY), and "Diamonds" (DIA) replicating the performance of NASDAQ 100, S&P 500, and the Dow, respectively. There are other index ETFs, like iShares-Russell 2000 (IWM), and foreign stock and sector ETFs, like iShares-MSCI Japan (EWJ) or Select Sector SPDR-Financial (XLF).

In Europe, after an initial run by investment banks to create a variety of ETFs, the industry underwent a consolidation, reflecting the low-cost nature of the business.

Custom baskets

The most widely popular custom baskets in the U.S. are HOLDRS (pronounced "Holders", short for holding company depositary receipts) traded on the AMEX. A HOLDR is a depositary receipt issued by a trust representing ownership interests in the common stock or ADRs of companies involved in a particular industry, sector, or group. HOLDRs allow investors to own a diversified group of stocks in one investment (like mutual funds or ETFs). The composition of a HOLDR is specified in a prospectus and typically consists of 20–50 stocks. As of May 2003, the following HOLDRs were traded on the AMEX:

Table 4.1 AMEX-listed HOLDRs

Name	Symbol
B2B Internet	BHH
Biotech	BBH
Broadband	BDH
Europe 2001	EKH
Internet architecture	IAH
Internet	HHH
Internet infrastructure	IIH
Market 2000+	MKH
Oil service	OIH
Pharmaceutical	PPH
Regional bank	RKH
Retail	RTH
Semiconductor	SMH
Software	SWH
Telecom	TTH
Utilities	UTH
Wireless	WMH

Source: The AMEX website: www.amex.com/holdrs/prodInf

HOLDRs can be disassembled by their owners. For a small fee, investors can turn them in and obtain individual shares underlying each "mini-trust".

In addition to exchange-traded baskets designed for retail investors, brokers execute buy and sell orders from large investment companies on very customized, one-off baskets. Institutions transmit the composition of the basket to be traded. The basket may contain stocks from different exchanges. Brokers then execute *program trades* (buy or sell orders for a group of at least 15 stocks with a total market value of at least $1 million, sent electronically to the SuperDot computer of the NYSE) or "work the orders" according to customer instructions (e.g., trade the order throughout the day on the NASDAQ in an attempt to get the best price or to find buyers). The competition is based on speed and execution costs which often run at less than 3 cents per share in the U.S. Program trading is also used for an index arbitrage strategy involving index futures contracts (see Chapter 7).

The role of secondary equity markets in the economy

One of the main reasons regulators around the globe endeavor to establish and maintain orderly stock exchanges is their role in facilitating the flow of capital from savers to new productive ventures (businesses), even though exchanges do not participate in that process directly. Most stock market regulation is aimed at investor protection which includes financial disclosure, fraud prevention, and protection of the property rights of small investors. Exchanges are "used merchandise" markets in that capital flows from investor to investor. None of it goes to companies that issue shares to finance manufacturing or service businesses. That initial transfer of capital takes place in the IPO or SEO market. There, newly issued shares are sold to investors. Stock exchanges indirectly play three paramount roles in this process. First, the original IPO or SEO investors know that they will not be stuck with their investments for ever. They can share their risk by selling their stakes to others. By going to a broad market with many buyers and sellers, they are reasonably assured to get a fair price for their shares. Second, the exchanges provide fair price discovery not only for investors, but also for the issuers. Companies often contemplate share buybacks or seasoned offerings as ways of shrinking or expanding the equity capital invested in their businesses. The secondary equity markets provide a way of estimating the cost of that capital in the same way that bond markets offer a way of discovering the interest rate on the company's debt. The third role for exchanges is as a risk-sharing mechanism for venture capital firms who use IPOs as their exit strategies. Their incentives to invest would be much reduced if the only exit available were to find other private investors.

4.2   CURRENCY MARKETS

The currency or foreign exchange (FX) markets are borderless. Spot and forwards trading takes place around the globe 24 hours a day. FX trades OTC (i.e., via a phone and computer network of dealers scattered in various locations around the world). As of 2001, the global turnover amounted to over $1 billion per day, of which 33% occurred in the U.K., 17% in the U.S., 10% in Japan, 7% in Singapore, 6% in Germany, 5% in Switzerland, and most of the rest in the developed nations of Europe and Australasia. About one-third of the daily turnover is spot trading, the rest is short-term currency swaps and outright forwards. During the day, trading volume shifts slowly westward through three zones: Australasia, Europe, and North America. The market has two segments: the wholesale or interbank market, dominated by over 100 international banks and some of the largest investment banks, and the retail market in which international banks trade with their customers. Two vendors, Reuters and EBS, are leaders in currency quote systems for the wholesale market. Most of daily volume of trading in the interbank market can be attributed to speculation and arbitrage. Inventory adjustments and central bank interventions represent only a small part. Clearing takes place via a private Brussels-based SWIFT (Society for Worldwide Interbank Financial Telecommunications) system or a combination of the CHIPS (Clearing House Interbank Payments System) network and Fedwire for U.S. dollar payments. Spot settlement in FX markets is 2 days hence, except for USD/CAD which is 1 day.

The U.S. dollar continues to be the dominant currency in the world. As of 2001, 90% of all FX transactions involved the U.S. dollar on one side, 38% involved the euro, and 23% the Japanese yen. Most currencies are quoted in European terms (i.e., in foreign currency per dollar). British Commonwealth currencies and the euro are quoted in American terms (i.e., in dollars per currency). With some exceptions, currencies are quoted to four decimal places except for larger numbers which are quoted to two. The first widely known significant digits, called the big figure, are often skipped. Only the small figure or points are quoted. For example, an FX rate of [USD/GBP] 1.4556, would be quoted on the phone as 56, with both parties knowing the implicit 1.45. The standard quote size for major hard currencies in the interbank market is $10 million referred to as "10 dollars".

Currency quotes are prices. Normally, the price of a good is expressed in terms of currency per unit of the good. Potatoes may be priced in dollars per pound or euros per kilo. Rarely does one see potato prices expressed in terms of how many kilos 1 euro buys. With currencies, the pricing good and the priced good are both currencies, and the price can be expressed both ways. In Chapter 2, we introduced the notation of spot quotes as X's followed by the quotation terms in square brackets (e.g., euros per U.S. dollar as [EUR/USD]) or as superscripts. Currencies can be easily converted from American terms into European terms and vice versa by taking reciprocals. For example, if one day the British pound (GBP) is quoted as: $X[USD/GBP] = X^{USD/GBP} = 1.5000$, which means that one pound buys 1.50 dollars, then that necessarily means that $X[GBP/USD] = X^{GBP/USD} = 1/1.50 = 0.6667$ (i.e., 1 dollar buys 0.6667 pounds sterling). In general:

$$X[CURR1/CURR2] = 1/X[CURR2/CURR1]$$

The conversions are easy, but can be confusing. Suppose $X[CHF/USD] = 1.7200$. How many dollars will 300 francs buy? Since we want the quote in dollars per franc, we need to invert the quote and multiply by the number of francs:

$$300 \cdot X[USD/CHF] = 300 \cdot \frac{1}{X[CHF/USD]} = 300 \cdot \frac{1}{1.7200} = 174.42$$

300 francs buys 174.42 dollars.

Like any market, FX trading is subject to a bid–ask spread. We are all familiar with the most egregious example of that from the airport currency counters. Suppose for the USD/GBP you observe: 1.4556/1.4782. But, which is the bid and which is the offer? Ignoring commissions, the counter will buy pounds for 1.4556 dollars apiece and sell pounds for 1.4782 dollars apiece. So 1.4556 is a bid for pounds and 1.4782 is the ask or offer for pounds. But, 1.4556 is also an offer for dollars: when the counter buys pounds, it automatically sells dollars. Similarly, the 1.4782 is also a bid for dollars.

Bank trading rooms are organized into *major currency desks* and *cross-desks*. The former deal in yen, euros, etc. against the dollar. The latter quote *cross rates*, which are FX rates directly of non-dollars against non-dollars (e.g., CHF against JPY). Emerging economies' currencies are normally traded against the dollar, but cross-trading against the euro can be just as significant, depending on the region (e.g., PLZ/EUR). *Triangular arbitrage* (described in Chapter 5) ensures that cross rates stay in line with FX rates against the dollar or another major. Apart from triangular arbitrage performed by cross traders and currency arbitrage desks and inventory adjustment trading due to customer flows through the major currency desks, the rest of trading is dominated by speculation. Dealers interpret macroeconomic data and take positions on future FX rate changes. This is quite different from bond market dealers making profits off the bid–ask spread on customer flows. Cash bond markets are characterized by *flow trading*; currency markets are distinctly speculative with less customer flow. Occasionally, central banks attempt to manipulate FX markets through two types of interventions: sterilized, where currency-for-bonds transactions offset currency-for-currency flows, or unsterilized, with only the latter. In recent years, the central banks of developed economies have engaged in very little intervention, as the predominant macroeconomic orthodoxy has been to allow free-floating and only to use moral suasion (i.e., issuing deliberate public statements to be widely (mis-?) interpreted by the markets). The central banks of non-major currencies, on the other hand, have tried a variety of other tools aimed at stabilizing their FX rates, mostly falling into the categories of pegging or exchange controls. The most common exchange control arrangement is to limit the amount of FX that can be exchanged at the official rate to a specified amount, sometimes tied to the level of export earnings of the owner. Often, weaker currencies are pegged to a major or a basket of major currencies with the central bank intervening if the market rate deviates too much from the desired target rate. A popular arrangement in the emerging economies in the 1990s was a currency board (Hong Kong, Argentina, Brazil) where local currency notes were issued at a fixed ratio against a pool of foreign exchange held by a monetary authority and are freely exchangeable into it. Currency traders watch closely the performance of these and other arrangements against the real flows of FX and take speculative positions through spot and forwards currency and money markets.

4.3 COMMODITY MARKETS

Spot commodity markets are comprised of networks of dealers who buy, store, and sell commodities and their derivatives. Many commodities come in a variety of quality grades. Some are integrated with futures markets and have financial speculators in them; some are not integrated with futures and have mostly industrial buyers and sellers. All are governed by the specifics of the production process involved in delivering the commodity to the market. Let us review spot trading in commodities with a view toward its relationship to futures markets.

Metals range from precious (gold, silver, platinum) to industrial (copper, aluminum). Some have both uses (palladium, platinum). Metals are relatively homogeneous. As a consequence, the metals markets are liquid. They trade through a network of OTC dealers, similar to the FX market, or on some exchanges (London Metal Exchange).

Petroleum product markets are dominated by producers, not dealers, and are very complex. Products trade at many stages of the production cycle. There is an active market for oil and gas reserves in the ground. Participants are diversified petroleum companies as well as companies purely owning reserves. There is an active market for crude oil and gas extracted from the ground. Participants are oil companies, refiners, and end-users, as well as some investment banks for speculative purposes. There are very active markets in final products, such as gasoline, propane, and heating oil. The pricing power for crude oil rests with the Organization of Petroleum Exporting Countries (OPEC), with Saudi Arabia playing the role of a swing producer because it holds 50% of world's proven reserves and has large production overcapacity. Oil production and refined product delivery can be subject to frequent supply shocks. Futures markets in petroleum products can be seasonal and do reflect the convenience value of owning the spot commodity.

Grain markets are dominated by grain elevators who act as dealers and buy, sell, and store grains. The futures markets serve as the benchmarks for spot prices, quoted at a premium or discount to futures, depending on the season and production conditions. Soybeans are crushed to obtain soybean oil for use as fats in human food and soybean meal for use as a protein supplement in animal feeds. Prices are quoted directly by the producers of the two products.

Cattle and pork trade both as livestock and livestock products. Livestock can be traded in different stages of production. Cattle is traded at feeder weight (up to 800 pounds, roughly 1-year-old below optimal slaughter weight) or as fat cattle (~1,200 pounds). Similarly, hogs trade as feeder hogs or later as market hogs. Relative prices at different stages vary dependent on the cost of feeds and other factors. Both cattle and hogs are slaughtered evenly throughout the year. This renders the futures contract to trade at no convenience value.

In recent years, an active spot and futures market has developed in electricity, as governments throughout the world started deregulating electricity markets (Scandinavia, North America, the U.K. and continental Europe). The deregulation consisted of separating electricity generators from electricity transmitters and relaxing the previously tight price controls. Often, governments have been unwilling to give up some price controls. The result has been a lively and sometimes chaotic market for spot electricity. The product itself is uniform (there are no quality grades), but it is not storable. This automatically means that the generators must maintain an overcapacity to be able to deliver during peak times. This also means that demand and supply conditions during peak and off-peak times are completely different. Buyers and sellers must engage in what is called *load-matching*. Any delivery contract is extremely specific in terms of the quantities to be delivered at different times of the day, different times of the week, and the number of days per month guaranteed for on- and off-peak. In many cases, the arrangements are complicated by obsolete and overly regulated delivery networks. Most electrical grids suffer from natural bottlenecks (California–Oregon Border, or COB and Palo Verde, Arizona, or PV) and man-made bottlenecks (New Jersey–Pennsylvania separated from the Midwest by regulation and national grids in Europe). All of these factors contribute to the very high volatility of electricity prices (and recently a few, large blackouts in the U.S. and Europe). While the long-term cost of generation depends greatly on the price of fossil fuels (for the most part oil and gas), the short-term supply conditions often lead to great deviations from that.

In later chapters, we show how the spot prices of commodities are linked to futures prices through the cost of carry and convenience yields. We also cover more interesting aspects of electricity futures trading.

5
Spot Relative Value Trades

Relative value trades in spot markets are relatively simple in concept. They rely on speed of execution as they often take advantage of temporary mispricing of assets relative to each other. They are self-correcting in that the very transactions that exploit mispricings also eliminate them by pushing prices in line with each other. In many instances, their success depends on the existence of lesser informed traders or institutional and retail customers who are less price-sensitive. Some are pure arbitrages, but more often than not they rely on relative value principle and result in small secondary risks, like yield curve (YC) exposure, commodity basis risk, or market-neutral sector risk. We review them not in the order of simplicity, but rather in the sequence of the last two chapters.

5.1 FIXED INCOME STRATEGIES

We start with relative value trades which exploit the fact that coupon securities can be viewed as packages of zero-coupon securities and the whole must be equal to the sum of the parts (in terms of the present value, or PV, of the components).

Zero-coupon stripping and coupon replication

Zero-coupon stripping and coupon replication are most widely used in government bond markets around the world. Corporate bond traders with access to security lending may also engage in coupon replication, but limit the application of this strategy to the highest rated bonds of very large issuers because they may be additionally exposed to default or corporate spread risk.

The most basic zero-vs.-coupon arbitrage is executed in the U.S. Treasuries and STRIPs (separated coupons or principals off original Treasuries sold as individual securities) markets. The issuer of all securities is the same, the U.S. government. All securities are default-free and easily marginable (i.e., both coupons and zero-coupons can be shorted). Let us examine how we would screen for the possibility of arbitrage and how we would execute riskless trades to earn sure profit. We assume none of the securities is *on special* (i.e., no rebate is charged for borrowing and shorting through a repo; in other words, repoing). Consider the following set of quotes (semi-annual bond equivalents on a *30/360* basis, prices in decimals) for STRIP (zero) yields and coupon bond prices:

Table 5.1   Zero-coupon and coupon bond rates and prices

Maturity (years)	Zero (yield)	Coupon rate	Coupon price
0.5	3.5000	3.50	100.0000
1	3.5931	3.60	100.0073
1.5	3.7281	3.75	100.0362
2	3.7903	3.80	100.0263
2.5	3.8817	3.85	99.7642
3	4.1386	4.00	99.6646

From the coupon bond prices and given the coupon rates, we can compute the yields-to-maturity (YTMs) implied for the six coupon bonds following the formulae of Chapter 2. YTMs are defined as the single yields used to discount the cash flows of each bond to get the price (zero yields are not used in these calculations). We add the yield column to the table of quotes:

Table 5.2   Zero-coupon and coupon bond rates, prices, and yields

Maturity (years)	Zero (yield)	Coupon		
		Rate	Price	Yield
0.5	3.5000	3.50	100.0000	3.5000
1	3.5931	3.60	100.0073	3.5925
1.5	3.7281	3.75	100.0362	3.7250
2	3.7903	3.80	100.0263	3.7863
2.5	3.8817	3.85	99.7642	3.9500
3	4.1386	4.00	99.6646	4.1200

We can also discount the cash flows of each coupon bond by applying the appropriate zero yields to the coupon cash flows and principal cash flows to compute the theoretical price and then the theoretical YTM of each coupon bond, assuming the zeros are priced correctly (zero yields used). We replace the "Price" and "Yield" columns in the table with their theoretical equivalents:

Table 5.3   Theoretical prices and yields of coupon bonds computed by discounting cash flows with zero-coupon rates

Maturity (years)	Zero (yield)	Coupon		
		Rate	Price	Yield
0.5	3.5000	3.50	100.0000	3.5000
1	3.5931	3.60	100.0073	3.5925
1.5	3.7281	3.75	100.0362	3.7250
2	3.7903	3.80	100.0263	3.7863
2.5	3.8817	3.85	99.9410	3.8750
3	4.1386	4.00	99.6646	4.1200

We notice that the theoretical price and yield of the 2.5-year 3.85% coupon note is different from that actually quoted in the market. The 2.5-year trades *cheap*. Its price is lower than what it should be relative to the zeros; or, it may be that one of the zeros, specifically the 2.5-year one, trades *rich* relative to the coupon. We are not making a statement as to which is overpriced and which is underpriced by some absolute standard. The theoretical prices we computed were strictly for the purpose of discovering arbitrage.

One correct strategy in this case will involve buying the 2.5-year coupon and shorting five different STRIPs (zeros) ranging in maturity from 0.5 to 2.5 years. The face value of each zero shorted would be equal to 1.925 (semi-annual coupon of 3.85/2), except for the last one whose face value would be 101.925 per 100 face value of the coupon bought. The amounts are summarized in Table 5.4:

Table 5.4 Proceeds from shorting five STRIPs with face values matching the cash flows of the 2.5-year coupon bond

Maturity (years)	Zero (yield)	Face value	Price received
0.5	3.5000	1.925	1.8919
1	3.5931	1.925	1.8777
1.5	3.7281	1.925	1.8212
2	3.7903	1.925	1.7857
2.5	3.8817	101.925	92.5847
Total			99.9412

The total amount received from the shorts is greater than the price paid for the 2.5-year maturity 3.85% coupon, by $99.9412 - 99.7642 = 0.1770$, or 17.7 basis points. On a $100 million face value trade, this amounts to $177,000. There is no risk to the trade as the received coupon payments will cover exactly the return of the zero principals to the lenders of the securities. The only risk may be call risk if one of the STRIP shorts cannot be rolled over in an overnight repo market.

This is not the only arbitrage strategy that can be executed based on the quotes: another may be to buy the 2.5-year, 3.85 coupon, sell a shorter coupon, and buy and sell some zeros. For example, we can short the 2-year 3.80 coupon, combined with small shorted strips of 0.5- to 2-year zeros (with principal equal to $3.85 million minus $3.80 million divided by 2, i.e., $25,000), short a $101.925 million 2.5-year STRIP, and buy a 2-year $100 million STRIP to offset the principal of the 2-year coupon note. This will work because all zeros and coupons with maturities equal to or less than 2 years in our example are fairly priced relative to each other. So, they are costless substitutes. The only consideration for the trader is the availability of the components and the total bid–ask spread paid to execute all the transactions.

The coupon-stripping strategy is an example of a static strategy. Once all the initial transactions are executed, the trader simply collects the coupons and principals from the longs when they come due and allocates them to the shorts. All future cash flows match up exactly. There are no additional trades to be done. The profit is made upfront from the difference between monies received from the shorts and monies paid on the longs. We can simply wait for the last cash flow to consider the profit fully realized. The only time we may consider unwinding the entire trade would be if, during the life of the strategy, the total mark-to-market on the strategy, net of additional transaction costs, becomes positive, due to new relative mispricing of the components. That can be a source of additional profit.

Duration-matched trades

Another way of arbitraging spot bond markets is through dynamic strategies of duration matching. In some cases, the secondary speculative component is the difference in bond convexities if one intends to profit from parallel yield curve movements. More often, convexities may also be matched and profit is earned as duration- and convexity-matched bond positions adjust differently to non-parallel yield curve movements. (Chapter 2 offers definitions and explains the economic meaning of duration and convexity.) Typically, the relative arbitrageur selects a primary bond (or bonds) which is bought/shorted and hedges it by shorting/buying other bonds with the duration of the hedges equal in absolute value to that of the primary bond. This ensures that the speculation is not directly on the level of interest rates. The trader profits or loses due to parallel movements through a convexity mismatch (second-order variable) and/ or due to non-parallel yield curve movements even if the convexities are matched. The strategy is dynamic. The cash flows on the trade positions do not match. The trader does not intend to hold the positions to maturity, but only until he realizes a desired level of profit. He dynamically adjusts the duration match as interest changes.

Example: Bullet–barbell

Let us illustrate with a bullet–barbell combination, originally designed as a hedge strategy aimed at immunizing against parallel yield curve movements. Here we show how a duration- and convexity-matched bullet–barbell strategy profits from non-parallel movements.

Suppose we buy $116.460 million of a 5-year note with the modified duration of 3.22 and convexity of 0.33. That is, a 1 bp (basis point) increase in yield will cause a 3.22 bp decrease in value using the straight-line approximation minus a 0.33 bp correction for a curvilinear quadratic approximation term. At the same time, we short a barbell (two bonds, short-maturity and long-maturity): a $48.885 million 2-year note with the duration of 1.68 and convexity of 0.12, and a $42.507 million 10-year note with the duration of 6.89 and convexity of 0.76. As can be seen from Table 5.5, the face value amounts have been chosen so that the portfolio is duration-neutral and close to convexity-neutral.

Table 5.5   Long 5-year bullet, short 2–10 barbell

Bond	Face value	Duration	Convex	$ Duration per bp	$ Convexity per bp
2-year	(48,885,000)	1.68	0.12	8,213	(587)
5-year	116,460,000	3.22	0.33	(37,500)	3,843
10-year	(42,507,000)	6.89	0.76	29,287	(3,231)
Total				*(0)*	*26*

The 2-year bond position will gain (lose) $8,213 per 1 bp increase (decrease) in the

YTM, the 5-year will lose (gain) $37,500 per 1 bp increase (decrease) in the YTM, and the 10-year will gain (lose) $29,287 per 1 bp increase (decrease) in the YTM. Overall, if all three YTMs move (up or down) in parallel by 1 bp, or a few bp, the portfolio will not make or lose money. (Over a larger movement in yields, the portfolio will make a tiny amount of money as it is lightly convex.)

The portfolio will profit/lose from non-parallel yield curve movements. If the yield curve steepens (i.e., the 2–10-year yield curve differential increases by 10 bp), the portfolio will gain over $105,000. If the yield curve flattens by 10 bp, the portfolio will lose roughly the same amount. The portfolio will also profit or lose, if the yield curve twists. For example, if the 2-year and 10-year yields decline by 5 bp, but the 5-year yields decline by 10 bp, the portfolio will gain $187,501. The two scenarios are summarized in Table 5.6 which shows the sources of profits in each case.

Table 5.6 Long 5-year bullet, short 2–10 barbell—profit from yield curve (YC)

Bond	Duration	YC steepens		YC twists	
		Move (bp)	$ Profit	Move (bp)	$ Profit
2-year	1.68	5	41,063	−5	(41,063)
5-year	3.75	10	(375,001)	−10	375,001
10-year	6.89	15	439,310	−5	(146,437)
Total			105,372		187,501

Example: Twos vs. tens

One of the simplest and most common strategies to benefit from non-parallel yield curve movements is a duration-matched twos–tens trade in which the arbitrageur goes long 2-year notes and short 10-year notes, if he intends to profit from a steepening of the yield curve, or vice versa (i.e., short 2 years and long 10 years) if he intends to profit from a flattening. In this strategy, it is much more difficult to eliminate convexion risk, so there is normally some residual primary interest rate risk.

Suppose we want to profit from a yield curve flattening. We short $61.3 million of 2-year notes and we buy $14.947 of 10-year notes. We choose the amounts to eliminate interest rate risk (i.e., we match the duration of the short and the long).

Table 5.7 Short twos–long tens

Bond	Face value	Duration	Convex	$ Duration per bp	$ Convexity per bp
2-year	(61,300,000)	1.68	0.12	10,298	(736)
10-year	14,947,000	6.89	0.76	(10,298)	1,136
Total				(0)	400

If all yields (2-year and 10-year) rise in parallel by 10 bp, then the 2-year position will gain close to $103,000 and the 10-year position will lose the same amount. However, if the yield curve flattens (i.e., 2-year yields rise by more, or drop by less, than 10-year yields), then the strategy will make a profit. In Table 5.8, 2-year yields rise by 10 bp, while 10-year yields rise only by 5 bp, resulting in a 5 bp flattening. The strategy gains $51,492. At this point, the trader may choose to close out both positions. If an even greater flattening is anticipated, the trader may choose to rematch the durations or leave them slightly mismatched to ride the strategy longer.

Table 5.8 Short twos–long tens

Bond	Duration	YC moves parallel		YC flattens	
		Move (bp)	$ Profit	Move (bp)	$ Profit
2-year	1.68	10	10,984	10	102,984
10-year	6.89	10	(102,985)	5	(3,51,492)
Total			*(1)*		*51,492*

If both yields have risen, then the durations of both bonds have decreased. Given the original convexity numbers, the duration of the 2-year notes will have changed to 1.662 and that of the 10-year to 6.852. Duration rematching can be accomplished, for example, by shorting additional $0.101 million 2-year notes and leaving the 10-year position unchanged.

Table 5.9 Short twos–long tens—duration rematch

Bond	Face value	Duration	$ Duration per bp
2-year	(61,401,000)	1.668	10,242
10-year	14,947,000	6.852	(10,242)
Total			*0*

Another yield curve flattening of 5 bp will now result in a profit of $51,208, while a parallel move will result in no value change.

Negative convexity in mortgages

Because of the prepayment risk, the management of fixed-rate mortgages and mort-gage-backed securities (MBSs) is particularly risky. A duration-matched portfolio makes or loses money not only for large movements in yields, but sometimes for small parallel movements when yield curve movement leads to an acceleration or deceleration or prepayments. The change in the speed of prepayments causes the durations to become mismatched and the interest rate sensitivities of the various bonds in the portfolio to diverge. Mortgage bond durations are calculated for a given speed of prepayments. The latter is measured in PSAs. (PSA stands for the Public Securities Association, but it is commonly used as a unit of prepayment speed, as defined by the Association.). As current PSAs change, so do the durations and interest rate sensitivities. In addition, the changes are not symmetric. Downward movements in the yield curve may accelerate prepayments by more than upward movements will slow them down. There are many reasons for such a situation. One commonly considered factor is the past history of curve movements. If interest rates have not changed much in the past and started coming down only recently, a large wave of refinancings (and thus prepayments) may be unleashed. On the other hand, if interest rates have been coming down rather steadily in the past, a further drop may actually lead to a slowdown in prepayments as there may now be fewer mortgages to be refinanced. These issues are most acute with highly structured MBSs (like IOs, or interest-onlys, and POs, or principal-onlys) and are the main focus of statistical prepayment modeling done by most mortgage-dealing firms.

The crux of the matter is the potential *negative convexity* of fixed-rate mortgages. For a non-mortgage bullet bond, as interest rates come down the price and the duration of the bond increase. For a mortgage bond, the price may increase but the duration may decrease. To understand that recall from Chapter 2 that one interpretation of duration is the present value-weighted average time to the bond's cash flows. For bullet bonds, as rates decrease, the present value of far cash flows increases relative to near ones. The PV-weighted average time to the repayment of the bond (i.e., the duration) increases. In the extreme, when rates are zero, the duration is at a maximum and it is a cash flow- and not PV-weighted average time measure. Conversely, as interest rates rise, the PV of far cash flows including the principal, if any, declines more relative to the near cash flows and duration contracts. In the extreme, when rates go infinite, duration is zero.

The same intuitions apply to mortgages to the extent that they are coupon-paying, fixed-income instruments and prepayment speeds do not change. As interest rates decline, the PV of a given far cash flow from a mortgage increases more than that of a near one. But, if the prepayment speed increases, there may be fewer far cash flows and more near cash flows. The overall duration of the bond, instead of increasing, may actually decline. Consider a bond backed by a "pool" of two identical 15-year mortgages. As interest rates decline, the PV of the cash flows scheduled for years 10–15 increases more than that of the cash flows scheduled for years 1–5 (due to the power of compound interest). The PV-weighted average time to the repayment of the mortgage bond increases. But now suppose that the owner of the second mortgage decides to pay down her principal in order to avoid paying a now high interest rate. This moves the far cash flows to today. The PV-weighted average time for the entire pool declines; so does the sensitivity of the price of the pool-backed bond to interest-rate changes. The opposite is true for an interest rate increase. In that case, prepayments slow down, extending the bond's duration even though the PVs of far cash flows decline. The extreme case of this negative convexity is found in PO STRIPs of MBSs where the owner is entitled to the principal portion of monthly mortgage payments coming from the pool. As rates decline, a PO holder may be swamped with principal prepayments, practically extinguishing his bond and exposing him to the reinvestment risk at the now lower interest rates.

Some structured MBSs exhibit negative duration. The owner of the IO STRIP is entitled to the interest portion of mortgage payments. As rates decline and prepayment speeds increase, promised future interest never materializes and the PV of the cash flows decreases.

Mortgage bond portfolio managers are normally long on mortgage bonds and short on hedges. The hedges include government or agency bonds. The two sides can be duration-matched in an attempt to immunize against explicit interest rate risk. But duration matching is quite tricky in this case. At a given assumed prepayment speed, the portfolio may appear duration-neutral. But long mortgage bonds (negatively convex) combined with short governments (positively convex when owned, but here shorted, hence negatively convex) may lead to particularly short-convexity portfolios. These make money if PSAs do not change, but lose a lot of money when they do. Mortgage traders may resort to callable bonds or swaptions as hedges. Buying call swap options offsets the options implicitly sold to the homeowners in the pool. The hedge may be the best we can do, but may be highly imperfect as it depends on future rate levels, and not their histories or other macroeconomic and personal factors leading to mortgage refinancings.

The negative convexity of mortgages can be used to our advantage in a variety of yield curve strategies. Consider a twos–tens curve-flattening strategy. Suppose in addition to the 2-year and 10-year government notes we include in the portfolio some mortgage bonds backed by a pool of 30-year mortgages that are currently prepaying at some PSA rate such that the duration of these bonds is close to that of the 10-year government note. Their convexities, instead of being very similar to those of the 10-year notes, are actually negative because of the negative prepayment effect. Instead of shorting 2-years and buying 10-years, we short 2-years, buy 10-years, and buy mortgage bonds with face amounts chosen to zero out the overall convexity, as in Table 5.10.

Table 5.10   Short twos–long tens and mortgages

Bond	Face value	Duration	Convex	$ Duration per bp	$ Convexity per bp
2-year	(61,300,000)	1.68	0.12	10,298	(736)
10-year	10,600,000	6.89	0.76	(7,303)	806
Mortgages	4,524,000	6.62	−0.15	(2,995)	(68)
Total				—	*2*

We are still immunized to parallel yield curve movements, and we still make the same amount of $51,493 on a 5-bp yield curve flattening, but we have no exposure to non-parallel movements.

Table 5.11   Short twos–long tens and mortgages: Hedge performance

Bond	Duration	YC moves parallel		YC flattens	
		Move (bp)	$ Profit	Move (bp)	$ Profit
2-year	1.68	10	102,984	10	102,984
10-year	6.89	10	(73,034)	5	(36,517)
Mortgages	6.62	10	(19,949)	5	(14,974)
Total			*1*		*51,493*

We do have rebalancing to do if we want to continue the flattening strategy with a duration match. Convexity will continue to be close to 0. The summary of the rebalancing statistics is shown in Table 5.12.

Table 5.12 Short twos–long tens and mortgages—duration rematch

Bond		Duration	$ Duration per bp	$ Convexity per bp
2-year	(61,520,000)	1.668	10,262	(738)
10-year	10,600,000	6.852	(7,263)	806
Mortgages	4,524,000	6.6275	(2,998)	(68)
Total			*0*	*(0)*

Spread strategies in corporate bonds

Corporate bond trading at broker-dealer firms has two components: inventory trading due to customer flows and spread arbitrage. The first is similar to government bond trading and focuses on the bid–ask spread for the more liquid issues. As customers call with buy and sell orders, dealers trade out of their inventory, earning profit simply by charging more than paying for the same bonds, or their close substitutes (e.g., same issuer, different maturity, and coupon). The line between flow trading and spread arbitrage gets blurred as the definition of a substitute is expanded to include bonds of other issuers, but of the same credit quality. Dealers then accumulate bonds of one type and are short of another, staying neutral with respect to interest rate risk. This either happens naturally as flows become unbalanced or it is by design in order to benefit from spread movements. Let us give some examples of the latter.

Example: Corporate spread widening/narrowing trade

Suppose we are a corporate bond dealer and we believe that the spread between A-rated bonds and government securities is going to narrow. We believe that this will be a consequence of the sparsity of new corporate issuance which will limit the supply of the bonds. Our view on interest rates overall is neutral.

In order to benefit from the anticipated narrowing of the spread, we can buy A-rated corporate bonds and short governments with the same maturity. We match the durations of the long and the short by choosing the face amounts appropriately. This is summarized in Table 5.13.

Table 5.13 Long corporate, short government

Bond	Face value	Duration	Convex	$ Duration per bp	$ Convexity per bp
10-year government	(45,210,000)	6.89	0.76	31,150	(3,436)
10-year A-rated corporate	50,000,000	6.23	0.56	(31,150)	2,800
Total				*(0)*	*(636)*

Let us consider what will happen to the position as the spread between the yield on the A-rated bond and the government bond narrows. This can occur in a variety of ways. One scenario is that both yields rise, but the A yield rises by less than that of the government bond. Suppose the respective yield changes are 30 bp and 50 bp, resulting in a narrowing of 20 bp.

Table 5.14 Long corporate, short government—rates rise by 30 bp (corporate) and 50 bp (government)

Bond	Duration	Yield move (50 bp)		Spread move (−20 bp)	
		Move (bp)	$ Profit	Move (bp)	$ Profit
10-year government	6.89	50	1,557,485	0	—
10-year A-rated corporate	6.23	50	(1,557,500)	−20	623,000
Total			*(16)*		*623,000*

The change in the value of the portfolio due to the overall interest rate increase is nil. This result is ensured by the duration match. There is, however, a substantial profit of $623,000 which is due to the narrowing of the spread.

This strategy can be combined with a small outright bet on rates to form a speculative position. Spread widening often occurs during broad rate increases, and narrowing during rate declines. Suppose we want to bet on the scenario that the spread narrowing is going to follow a general rate decline. We can mismatch the durations slightly to leave ourselves net long. We can short fewer government bonds.

Table 5.15 Long corporate, short government—mismatch

Bond	Face value	Duration	Convex	$ Duration per bp	$ Convexity per bp
10-year government	(40,000,000)	6.89	0.76	27,560	(3,040)
10-year A-rated corporate	50,000,000	6.23	0.56	(31,150)	2,800
Total				*(3,590)*	*(240)*

This will earn additional profit if rates overall decline, but will hurt our profit if rates increase. We still benefit from the narrowing of the spread.

Table 5.16 Long corporate, short government—spread narrows

Bond	Duration	Yield move (50 bp, 30 bp)		Yield move (−30 bp, −50 bp)	
		Move (bp)	$ Profit	Move (bp)	$ Profit
10-year government	6.89	50	1,378,000	−30	(826,800)
10-year A-rated corporate	6.23	30	(934,500)	−50	1,557,500
Total			*443,500*		*730,700*

If the spread narrows by 20 bp while yields rise, our profit will shrink from $623,000 to $443,500. If the spread narrows while yields decline, our profit will increase to $730,700. The difference between the new profit levels and the original matched strategy is all due to net duration exposure to interest rates.

Example: Corporate yield curve trades

The duration-matched spread widening/narrowing strategy can be considered speculative. The bet is not outright on interest rates, but on the corporate spread which can be highly volatile at times, resulting in large profits or losses on the government-hedged corporate portfolio.

A finer trade is a bet on the spread between different maturity points of the corporate spread for a given category of issuers. In this case, the dealer is interest rate-neutral *and* corporate spread-neutral, but speculates that the difference between the corporate spread for 10-year maturities and 2-year maturities will change.

Suppose that currently the spread between A-rated issues and governments is 30 bp for 2-year maturities and 70 bp for 10-year maturities. We believe the 40-bp difference is going to increase, reflecting improved default prospects in the short run relative to the longer run. We do not have a view on interest rates in general or corporate spreads in general. This time we will match durations of corporates and governments for each maturity segment and across the segments. This is accomplished in the following way.

Table 5.17   Corporate spread steepening trade

Bond	Face value	Duration	Convex	$ Duration per bp	$ Convexity per bp
2-year government	(166,875,000)	1.68	0.12	28,035	(2,003)
2-year A-rated corporate	183,235,000	1.53	0.13	(28,035)	2,382
10-year government	40,700,000	6.89	0.76	(28,042)	3,093
10-year A-rated corporate	(45,000,000)	6.23	0.56	28,035	(2,520)
Total				*(7)*	*953*

The strategy is immune to parallel and non-parallel yield curve movements. It is also immune to parallel corporate spread movements. It only makes money if the difference between the 10-year and 2-year spread increases (i.e., the corporate spread curve steepens). It loses the same amount if the difference decreases.

Table 5.18   Corporate spread steepening trade

Bond	Duration	0 bp steepening		20 bp steepening	
		Move (bp)	$ Profit	Move (bp)	$ Profit
2-year government	1.68	10	280,350	10	280,350
2-year A-rated corporate	1.53	10	(280,350)	10	(280,350)
10-year government	6.89	20	(560,846)	20	(560,846)
10-year A-rated corporate	6.23	20	560,700	40	1,121,400
Total			*(146)*		*560,554*

In Table 5.18, a yield curve steepening of 10 bp results in no profit, but the same yield curve steepening combined with a steepening of the corporate spread curve of 20 bp results in a profit of $560,554.

Example: Relative spread trade for high and low grades

The spread between low investment grade and high investment grade issues can be quite variable. In order to benefit from the relative value trades between these two categories we can design trades similar to the strategies described in the previous two subsections, where the role of the government bond is played by the high-grade category. The philosophy of the trade is the same. We show one example of such a trade.

Suppose we believe that the spreads between low-grade and high-grade issues will narrow and that the spread for the 10-year maturity point is going to narrow more than that for the 2-year point. We have no view on government yields, the spreads between high grade issues and governments, or the 10-year–2-year spread for each category alone.

Table 5.19   Low-grade–high-grade spread trade

Bond	Face value	Duration	Convex	$ Duration per bp	$ Convexity per bp
2-year AAA-rated corporate	149,196,000	1.68	0.12	(25,065)	1,790
2-year A-rated corporate	(183,235,000)	1.53	0.13	28,035	(2,382)
10-year AAA-rated corporate	(45,000,000)	6.89	0.76	31,005	(3,420)
10-year A-rated corporate	45,000,000	6.23	0.56	(28,035)	2,520
Total				*5,940*	*(1,492)*

We mismatch durations by about the same amount for each maturity category. The size of the mismatch reflects our view on overall tens–twos spread narrowing, and we go long 10-year relative spreads and short 2-year relative spreads. We make money when the relative spread between As and AAAs narrows and the 10-year spread narrows more.

Table 5.20   Low-grade–high-grade spread trade

Bond	Duration	30 bp A–AAA-rated narrowing		+10 bp flattening	
		Move (bp)	$ Profit	Move (bp)	$ Profit
2-year AAA-rated corporate	1.68	30	(751,948)	30	(751,948)
2-year A-rated corporate	1.53	0	—	0	—
10-year AAA-rated corporate	6.89	30	930,150	30	930,150
10-year A-rated corporate	6.23	0	—	−10	280,350
Total			*178,202*		*458,552*

When relative spreads narrow by 30 bp across the maturity spectrum, we make

$178,202. When, in addition, the 10-year spread narrows by 10 bp more (i.e., 40 bp), we make $458,552.

5.2 EQUITY PORTFOLIO STRATEGIES

Benchmarking in equity markets commonly refers to strategies aimed at outperforming a stock index. The performance of a portfolio is measured in terms of excess returns over those of the index. The objective is not necessarily to have positive returns, but to have the largest excess return (the index itself could have a negative return) over a target horizon (i.e., the objective is to beat the index).

Market-neutral hedge funds often go long a selected portfolio and short the index portfolio (in cash or futures markets) in order to make an explicit outperformance profit. If the underlying long portfolio is closely related to the index, then sometimes it is cheaper to net all individual longs against the shorts and to long/short the net positions. The market-neutral hedge fund can be highly leveraged as the value of longs and short is approximately equal and the capital required to maintain the position is minimal.

Lacking a concept like duration in fixed income markets, in equities relative value arbitrageurs rely on statistical measures of market exposure to match longs against real or benchmarked shorts. This is accomplished with the use of a "market model" where each stock is considered as having exposure to a set of factors. In the classic capital-asset pricing model (CAPM),[1] familiar from college finance textbooks, there is only one such factor and it is the market index itself. The benchmark market portfolio has a factor loading of 1, and the stocks' loadings (betas) are estimated using a regression on market returns.

Suppose we compute the monthly returns on MSFT and on the S&P 500 index for the period of Jan-1995 through Dec-2002 and plot them on a scatter diagram, as in Figure 5.1. Each dot represents the returns for MSFT and S&P 500 for a given month. Also suppose we then run a linear regression of MSFT on S&P 500 to fit a straight line through the scatter. The slope of the line is the beta of MSFT and is supposed to tell us how MSFT stock will perform as a function of S&P. For the 95-02 period, the monthly return on MSFT is related to the monthly return on S&P 500 through the following equation of the line:

$$\tilde{r}_{MSFT} = 0.915\,599\% + 1.588\,493 \cdot \tilde{r}_{S\&P500}$$

As can be seen from the plot, the historical data points do not lie on a straight line; rather, they are scattered around the line defined by the regression results. This means that MSFT returns may be driven by factors other than the general uncertainty of stocks portrayed by the market index.

A California company, BARRA, has popularized a more complicated, macro-economic factor-based model, in which each stock's and the index's return are functions of several factors (stock market index, spread between 2-year and 10-year bond, real estate index, etc.), allowing us to come up with factor loadings through a multiple regression (a subplane in a multi-dimensional scatter space). In a more abstract

---

[1] See any college finance text for a CAPM exposition. For example, Richard A. Brealey, Stewart C. Myers, and Alan J. Marcus, *Fundamental of Corporate Finance* (4th edn), 204, McGraw-Hill Irwin, Chicago.

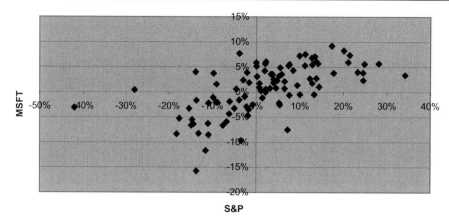

Figure 5.1   MSFT vs. S&P 500 monthly returns.
Source of data: Yahoo!Finance.

Arbitrage Pricing Theory, or APT, model, factors are defined only implicitly, but the loadings can be estimated through a principal component decomposition. Most market models relate the return on any stock $\tilde{r}$ to a set of k factors and can be written as:

$$\tilde{r} = b_0 + b_1\tilde{f}_1 + b_2\tilde{f}_2 + \cdots + b_k\tilde{f}_k + \tilde{\varepsilon}$$

Each stock has a unique set of factor loadings, $(b_0, b_1, b_2, \ldots, b_k)$, which can be estimated from historical data. Once we know the set of returns on the factors, $(\tilde{f}_1, \tilde{f}_2, \ldots, \tilde{f}_k)$, we automatically know the return on each stock. Over time, the errors from this assumption are assumed to cancel out, $E[\tilde{\varepsilon}] = 0$.

The role of the model in all cases is to estimate the co-movement of the portfolio with the benchmark, similar to the way duration predicts the price change of the bond as a result of a yield change. Here one statistic is not enough. For each stock, unique factor loadings are used to predict the change in the price of the stock as a function of the factor changes. Similarly, the factor loadings for the benchmark are used to estimate the change in the benchmark as a function of the factors. This way of approaching the problem ensures that we have some *ex ante* measure of how the portfolio is related (matched or mismatched) to the benchmark. It also allows quantification of the comparison of two completely different portfolios to each other and to a benchmark in terms of factor overloading and underloading.

Example: A non-diversified portfolio and benchmarking

Suppose we are managing a portfolio consisting of 15 U.S. stocks. (There are many mutual funds specializing in 15- to 30-stock portfolios.) The portfolio is somewhat diversified to eliminate large specific risks (exposures to single stocks), but much less than a broad market index. Suppose our performance is judged against the S&P 500 index.

Let us use a model, stylized on the Fama–French[2] setup popular in academic

---

[2] Eugene F. Fama and Kenneth R. French, "Common risk factors in the returns on stocks and bonds", *Journal of Financial Economics*, February, 1993, 33(1), 3–56.

literature, to explain long-term stock returns. Three factors are assumed to affect the variability of a stock's return: the market index, firm size (small is better) and book-to-market value (high book/market value ratio is better), both relative to the average. The firm size factor is defined as the return on a zero-net-investment portfolio long on small and short on large stocks. The book-to-market factor is defined as the return on a zero-net-investment portfolio long on high book-to-market (value) and short on low book-to-market (growth) stocks. The S&P 500 index has factor loadings of (1, 0, 0). The S&P returns vary one for one with the first factor. They are unrelated to the second and third, as the last two are defined in terms of the average and the S&P is the average. A stock with factor loadings (0.88, 0.12, −0.08) varies less than one-for-one with the S&P 500, is positively correlated with small firms' returns and negatively correlated with high book-to-market value stocks. In any given period, knowing the realizations of the factors, we are able to compute the forecast returns of the 15 stocks in the portfolio and the benchmark index. The model is used to construct the equivalent of a duration match, by picking stock in such proportions as to eliminate the exposure to all three factors in a market-neutral strategy or to match the factor loadings of the benchmark portfolio in a benchmark outperformance strategy.

Table 5.21 contains an example of a $16,200,000 portfolio of 15 stocks benchmarked against the S&P 500 index. With 15 stocks, there are many ways to eliminate exposure to the three factors. We choose the proportions in each stock, so that the net dollar exposure to each factor matches that of the benchmark: in this case (1, 0, 0).

Table 5.21 Long a 15-stock portfolio—Short S&P 500 index. Stock amounts chosen to eliminate factor exposures

Stock	Factor loadings			$ Position	$ Exposure			Profit from factor move		
	1	2	3	1	1	2	3	5.00%	1.00%	−2.00%
1	0.78	0.12	−0.22	1,800,000	1,404,000	216,000	(396,000)	70,200	2,160	7,920
2	0.81	0.07	−0.08	1,700,000	1,377,000	119,000	(136,000)	68,850	1,190	2,720
3	1.17	0.02	0.06	1,600,000	1,872,000	32,000	96,000	93,600	320	(1,920)
4	1.21	−0.04	0.20	1,330,000	1,609,300	(52,500)	266,00	80,465	(525)	(5,320)
5	1.25	−0.08	0.18	1,400,000	1,750,000	(112,000)	252,000	87,500	(1,120)	(5,040)
6	0.84	0.11	0.07	1,300,000	1,092,000	143,000	91,000	54,600	1,430	(1,820)
7	0.87	0.04	−0.08	1,200,000	1,044,000	48,000	(96,000)	52,200	480	1,920
8	0.90	−0.07	−0.15	1,150,000	1,035,000	(80,500)	(172,500)	51,750	(805)	3,450
9	1.07	−0.10	0.11	500,000	535,000	(50,000)	55,500	26,750	(500)	(1,110)
10	1.21	−0.17	0.18	900,000	1,089,000	(153,000)	162,000	54,450	(1,530)	(3,240)
11	1.34	0.33	−0.10	800,000	1,075,700	264,00	(80,000)	53,785	2,640	1,600
12	1.49	0.11	−0.15	700,000	1,043,000	77,000	(105,000)	52,150	770	2,100
13	0.93	−0.11	0.14	600,000	558,000	(66,000)	84,000	27,900	(660)	(1,680)
14	0.64	−0.33	0.11	500,000	320,000	(165,000)	55,000	16,000	(1,650)	(1,100)
15	0.99	−0.55	−0.19	400,000	396,000	(220,000)	(76,000)	19,800	(2,200)	1,520
Index	1.00	0.00	0.00	(16,200,000)	(16,200,000)	—	—	(810,000)	—	—
Total				—		(0)	—	—	(0)	0

We show that for any move in the market the portfolio is immunized (i.e., it will perform just like the index). Suppose the market overall moves up by 5% over the investment horizon. At the same time, small stocks outperform large by 1% and the growth stocks outperform value stocks by 2%. Our portfolio gains $810,000 which matches the 5% index performance and we have no exposure to the firm size or book-to-market value factors.

Example: Sector plays

There are a few commercial providers of return databases and optimization software aimed at performing portfolio selection in a factor-based model (e.g., BARRA, CRISP). These can be used in benchmark matching or other quantitative arbitrage strategies. These techniques may also be combined with and aid in the fundamental stock research within an asset management company. In that case, we use the statistically obtained factor loadings to choose investments to immunize against market factors, but opt to reallocate the thus-prescribed amounts in favor of positively evaluated stocks (through fundamental analysis). The resulting mismatch in the loadings provides a measure of exposure to the risk factors. The optimization software allows us to select portfolios not only with target exposures to the underlying predefined risk factors, but also with a particular relationship to other portfolios (e.g., industrial sectors). This is accomplished through what is called *factor rotation*. The logic is the following. If we know the exposure of our portfolio to the factors and we know the exposure of another portfolio to the factors, then we are able to determine the necessary reallocation of our portfolio to obtain the same exposure to the factors as that of the other portfolio. If the comparison portfolio is identical to an industrial sector or a benchmark, we are able to define our portfolio in terms of the exposures to that sector or benchmark, and not only the factors.

Suppose we want to construct a 15-stock portfolio whose exposure is roughly equal-weighted to sector 1 (telecom), sector 2 (semiconductor), and sector 3 (software). The easiest way to do this is to use a factor model, define each sector in terms of factor exposures, and match the factor exposure of our portfolio to that of the sectors. As there are 15 stocks and 3 factors, there are many solutions to this problem. Often we insist that certain stocks be included and allocated some dollar minimum (e.g., for liquidity reasons). One solution is given in Table 5.22. In principle, this is identical to the benchmarking exercise. The procedure allows us to claim that our portfolio has the same performance profile as a portfolio with weights 50/162 in sector 1, 58/162 in sector 2, and 54/162 in sector 3. Instead of in terms of macroeconomic factors, we are able to define risk in more familiar terms: telecom, semiconductor, and software. Notice that we can define the target any way we want. For example, the target can be long telecom–short semiconductor; or we can define the target as long S&P 500 with 10% overweight in telecom and 10% underweight in semiconductor. The method is quite general in that we can construct sector spread portfolios, underweighted portfolios, etc. All we need to do first is to decompose the target into the factor exposures and then match those through optimized stock selections.

One word of caution is that equity models rely on statistics. Models based on different factors may come up with different proportions of the same stocks, given the same target. This is the main difference between the statistics of equity approaches and the mathematics of fixed income.

Table 5.22 Matching a 15-stock portfolio to a portfolio equal-weighted in three industrial sectors. Stock positions chosen to eliminate factor exposures

Stock	Factor Loadings			$ Position	$ Exposure			Profit from factor move		
	1	2	3		1	2	3	5.00%	1.00%	−2.00%
1	0.78	0.12	−0.22	1,800,000	1,404,000	216,000	(396,000)	70,200	2,160	7,920
2	0.81	0.07	−0.08	1,700,000	1,377,000	119,000	(136,000)	68,850	1,190	2,720
3	1.17	0.02	0.06	1,600,000	1,872,000	32,000	96,000	93,600	320	(1,920)
4	1.21	−0.04	0.20	1,330,000	1,609,300	(52,500)	266,000	80,465	(525)	(5,320)
5	1.25	−0.08	0.18	1,400,000	1,750,000	(112,000)	252,000	87,500	(1,120)	(5,040)
6	0.84	0.11	0.07	1,300,000	1,092,000	143,000	91,000	54,600	1,430	(1,820)
7	0.87	0.04	−0.08	1,200,000	1,044,000	48,000	(96,000)	52,200	480	1,920
8	0.90	−0.07	−0.15	1,150,000	1,035,000	(80,500)	(172,500)	51,750	(805)	3,450
9	1.07	−0.10	0.11	500,000	535,000	(50,000)	55,500	26,750	(500)	(1,110)
10	1.21	−0.17	0.18	900,000	1,089,000	(153,000)	162,000	54,450	(1,530)	(3,240)
11	1.34	0.33	−0.10	800,000	1,075,700	264,000	(80,000)	53,785	2,640	1,600
12	1.49	0.11	−0.15	700,000	1,043,000	77,000	(105,000)	52,150	770	2,100
13	0.93	−0.11	0.14	600,000	558,000	(66,000)	84,000	27,900	(660)	(1,680)
14	0.64	−0.33	0.11	500,000	320,000	(165,000)	55,000	16,000	(1,650)	(1,100)
15	0.99	−0.55	−0.19	400,000	396,000	(220,000)	(76,000)	19,800	(2,200)	1,520
Sector 1	1.20	0.06	0.03	(5,000,000)	(6,000,000)	(300,000)	(150,000)	(300,000)	(3,000)	3,000
Sector 2	0.87	−0.05	−0.02	(5,800,000)	(5,070,000)	300,000	116,000	(253,500)	3,000	(2,320)
Sector 3	0.95	0.00	−0.01	(5,400,000)	(5,130,000)	—	34,000	(256,500)	—	(680)
Total				—	—	—	—	—	(0)	—

5.3 SPOT CURRENCY ARBITRAGE

Spot currency trading is dominated by speculation on the future direction of foreign exchange (FX) rates. Only a small component of trading is related to inventory adjustments of large wholesalers executing FX transactions on behalf of their correspondent banks and retail customers. The speculation is mostly macroeconomics-driven both in the short and long run. Bank economists and central bank watchers disseminate arriving economic data and their commentary to the trading desks, and currency traders take bets on the effect of the information on FX rate movements.

At the same time, an important activity called *triangular arbitrage*, introduced in Chapter 2, takes place on the cross-currency desks. This activity ensures that FX rates, whether quoted relative to a vehicle or directly, stay in line with each other. Triangular arbitrage is an artifact of the essence of an FX quote as a price of money in terms of other money. With so many monies around, opportunities in the wholesale market arise when a currency may become relatively cheap when purchased with one currency, but not with another. Our description of the strategy will be static in that we will assume that all quotes arrive at the same time. In reality, the arbitrage may be less than perfect as traders acquire one currency for another in anticipation of being able to sell it for another. Thus often there will be a time lapse between a purchase and a sale. The principle of arbitrage may be used to aid in setting up very short-timed speculative positions. In our illustration of pure triangular arbitrage, we ignore transaction costs and assume that we can transact at mid-prices (i.e., there is no bid–ask spread). In the interbank market, although the bid–ask spread is very small (of the order of the third decimal place), it is not insignificant and it is the source of most of the trading profit for large institutions. It often renders a lot of triangular strategies unprofitable.

Suppose we observe that in New York the dollar/euro FX rate is [USD/EUR] 1.1235 and the yen/dollar rate stands at [JPY/USD] 119.03. At the same time, in London the yen/euro cross rate is at [JPY/EUR] 132.85. How can we profit?

First, let us determine the yen price of the euro in New York. One euro costs 1.1235 dollars and each dollar costs 119.03 yen. So, 1 euro can fetch $1.1235 \times 119.03 = 133.73$ yen. This is more than the 132.85 that it can fetch in London. The same good, the euro, sells for two different prices. If we can buy and sell it in both places, we would like to buy the euro in London and sell the euro in New York. Suppose we are endowed with EUR 1,000,000. We sell the euros in New York for dollars to get:

$$1,000,000[\text{EUR}] \times 1.1235[\text{USD/EUR}] = \text{USD } 1,123,500$$

We then sell the dollars for yen to get:

$$1,123,500[\text{USD}] \times 119.03[\text{JPY/USD}] = \text{JPY } 133,730,205$$

Lastly, in London we sell the yen for euros in the cross-market to get:

$$133,730,205[\text{JPY}]/132.85[\text{JPY} * \text{EUR}] = \text{EUR } 1,006,626$$

and we end up with an instant profit of EUR 6,626. If we could, we would want to do this transaction in much larger size; and everyone else would want to copy it.

The strategy is self-correcting. All three transactions in it act to move the FX rates in line with each other. The sale of euros for dollars will increase the supply of euros and tend to reduce the price of euros in dollars (e.g., to [USD/EUR] 1.1185). The sale of dollars for yen will reduce the price of dollars in terms of yen (e.g., to 118.83). Overall this will decrease the indirect value of the euro in New York to [JPY/EUR] 132.91. If, at the same time, the yen value of the euro increases in the cross market in London as a result of the third transaction (the purchase of euros), then the arbitrage opportunity will disappear. In the dynamic world of currency trading, where FX rates change every instant, the opportunity of triangular arbitrage may depend on the speed of execution and a bit of luck.

The principle of triangular arbitrage is used by wholesalers in executing customer cross-transactions and competing for retail business. Suppose a Polish trading company is looking to exchange PLZ 5,000,000 into Swiss francs. The company obtains from a money bank indirect quotes of [PLZ/EUR] 4.3545/4.3615 and [CHF/EUR] 1.1492/1.1505. In exchanging PLZ into CHF, the company would have to incur two bid–ask spreads, resulting in the following effective market quotes: [PLZ/CHF] 3.7849/3.7952 (bid for CHF: 4.3545/1.1505; offer of CHF: 4.3615/1.1492). By calling several money banks, the company can put them in competition to give up some of the profit. If a bank were willing to do the more liquid CHF/EUR transaction at the mid of [CHF/EUR] 1.1499, then it could offer the Polish company a lower price for purchasing Swiss francs of [PLZ/CHF] 3.7929. The wholesaler that maintains large inventories of CHF and EUR, but not PLZ, gives up the profit on the CHF/EUR leg, but still ends up with a profit on the PLZ/CHF leg of the trade. The customer gets a lower effective cost of exchanging PLZ into CHF.

5.4 COMMODITY BASIS TRADES

Commodity basis trades are often entered into by non-financial institutions whose business depends on commodity prices. These trades can be executed with the use of futures markets, but are governed by spot principles. The futures contract is used not because of the economics of the strategy, but mainly out of convenience and may be a source of additional risk. The trade is normally a hedge for revenues or costs. Large commodity dealers execute similar strategies for speculative reasons.

Consider a small experimental heating solutions company. Its heaters use specialized fuel similar to heating oil, but more refined, to supply heat to customers at fixed pre-contracted rates. If the cost of the fuel it uses goes up, its profits will suffer. The company wants to eliminate the price risk of the specialty fuel. However, the specialized fuel is not widely traded, but the standard #2 heating oil is.

Let us assume that the price of the specialty fuel is equally volatile as that of the #2 heating oil. A 10% rise in the price of the heating oil is accompanied by a 10% rise in the specialty fuel price. Suppose that, currently, heating oil trades spot at $0.85 per cubic meter and the specialty fuel trades at $1.34. The company needs 50 million cubic meters of the fuel. Let us also assume that there is an active heating oil futures market and the price of a 6-month contract is equal to $0.05 more than the spot price, due to financing costs and storage conditions (i.e., $0.90). The size of the contract is 1 million cubic meters. The company cannot use heating oil, but it can use the market for heating oil as a hedge.

The difference between the price of the specialty fuel and the heating oil, equal to 1.34 minus 0.85, or $0.49, is called a *basis*. The existence of a basis will lead to a hedge ratio that is not one for one, similar to a hedge of two bonds with different durations. Let us denote the heating oil futures contract size, or the multiplier, as $m = 1,000,000$, the price of the hedge instrument as $H = 0.85$, the *absolute basis* as $B = 0.49$, and the *percentage basis* as $b = 0.49/0.85 = 57.65\%$. In order to hedge its cost exposure, the company buys:

$$50 * \frac{H+B}{H} = 50 * \frac{(1+b)H}{H} = 50 * \frac{1.34}{0.85} = 78.90$$

or, rounding, 79 heating oil contracts. Notice that on a per-contract basis, the hedge ratio will be more or less than unity depending on whether the basis b is positive or negative.

Suppose the price of specialty fuel increases by 15%, which translates into a potential cost increase of $50,000,000 * 1.34 * (0.15) = \$10,050,000$, and that the percentage basis holds (i.e., the heating oil price increases also by 15% from $0.85 to $0.9775). The futures price, assuming a constant futures basis, rises from $0.90 to $1.0275. The company's gain on the long contracts is:

$$79(1,000,000)(1.0275 - 0.9000) = 10,072,500$$

The precise setup of the hedge depends on whether we believe that the relative or absolute basis holds. It also depends on the assumed relationship of futures to spot for the hedge instrument. The hedge is designed to work for any increase in the price of the underlying cost determinant.

Commodity trading houses use the concept of a basis to set up speculative trades with one commodity bought and another shorted. The basis is the hedge ratio used in determining the relative proportions of the trade. In this application, the basis is used as a statistical concept, akin to the relationship of stock returns to factors through loadings, rather than a mathematical one, akin to the duration in bonds. Current basis is compared with historical basis levels estimated using the price history of the underlying and hedge instruments. It cannot be computed by discounted cash flow arguments.

Part Two
Forwards

6

Financial Math II—Futures and Forwards

The greatest misconception about the futures and forward markets is that they predict the prices of commodities or other financial instruments in the future while spot markets, separately, establish their value now. In this view, corn can trade at one price today and at a totally different price for a 6-month delivery, presumably reflecting future supply conditions (e.g., poor crops due to a drought). While it is true that future demand and supply conditions enter the equation, what is important to note is that they are joint determinants of both futures and spot prices. If everyone expects the drought that will drive up the price of the corn over the next 6 months, then why wouldn't some enterprising farmers buy up the corn now and pay for storing it in a silo, to sell it at a profit at a later date, resulting in a bid-up spot price today?

The fact is that spot and forward prices are tied together through a cost-of-carry relationship. The futures price must always be equal to the spot price grossed up by the cost of financing to purchase the commodity now and storing it, net of any cash flows from holding the commodity. Thus, if there is an expectation of any impending supply shocks, their impact is automatically translated not just into futures and forwards, but into spot prices as well.

The *cost of carry* is defined as the cost of financing and storing a commodity or a financial instrument net of any cash flows accruing from the instrument between now and some future date. In the spot–forward analysis, that future date is the delivery date of the forward contract or the expiry date of the futures. A *cash-and-carry transaction* consists of borrowing funds and purchasing an asset today, paying for storing it and potentially receiving cash flows from it (dividends or coupons) between today and a future date. A *reverse cash-and-carry transaction* consists of short selling an asset and lending the proceeds today, compensating the lender of the asset for storage costs and cash flows from the asset between today and a future date. The cash-and-carry argument is fundamental for establishing a *fair value* of futures and forwards.

A *forward* contract is defined as a contract to buy and sell an asset at a price agreed on today, but for a delivery at some future date. On the delivery date, the seller of the asset delivers the asset and receives cash for it. Today, no asset or cash changes hands. The two parties only agree on the sale price. The seller of the asset is said to go short, the buyer of the asset is said to go long on the forward contract. A *futures* contract is analogous to a forward contract in that there is a buyer and a seller of some underlying commodity and that they agree on a future price (or other variable) today. Subsequent to that agreement, at the end of each day, they exchange cash flows equal to the movement in the price of that commodity (or in the movement of the variable) times a multiplier. The process is referred to as *marking-to-market*; the settlement cash flows are referred to as the *variation margin*. On the futures expiry date, the futures price of the commodity is set equal to the current spot (by definition), so that the net cumulative variation margin exchanged between the expiry date and the original date is equal to the difference between that future spot price and the original agreed-on price. This elaborate mechanism allows farmers to lock in the sale price of a future crop. The farmer sells futures contracts at today's futures price. By the time of the futures expiry, the farmer will have received or paid the amount equal to the difference between today's futures price and the then prevailing spot price. When he sells his crop spot, the marking-to-market cash flows compensate him for any difference between that spot and the original futures price, so that effectively he sells for the original futures price. This was the original purpose of organizing the futures markets in Chicago in the mid-1800s. Since then, futures markets expanded geographically around the world and product-wise to cover non-commodity prices (like bonds and stock indices) as well as non-prices (like interest rates and atmospheric temperature readings).

Futures contracts on non-price variables, like temperature readings, are the best examples to study, because they expose the contracts for what they really are: bets on future outcomes. In that aspect, they are very similar to horse racing and sporting event bookmaking. In the latter, an underlying event's outcome will be revealed on a given future date. Today, buyers and sellers can agree through a trading mechanism on today's mean expectation of the outcome. If more people believe that team A will win against team B they will push up the spread in team A's favor until the spread reflects the mean number of points by which team A is expected to beat team B. As information arrives in the market between now and the event date, the spread will vary reflecting the changing expectation of the betting public. Sports betting does not provide for automatic marking to market. It is rather like a forward market with dealers willing to close out bets prior to maturity at the current mark.

A futures contract on the temperature, like the one traded on the Chicago Mercantile Exchange (CME), is very similar to a soccer match bet. When the soccer match ends, its outcome is revealed. When the expiry month ends, the temperature readings in a given location have been observed. Homes and apartments require heating when the temperature outside is low. A heating degree day (HDD) is defined as the number of days in a given month when the temperature falls below 65°F times the difference between 65°F and the actual temperature reading on a given day. On the CME, contracts are traded for several U.S. cities and several winter months. Buyers of the futures contracts can bet that the actual HDDs in a particular month is above a certain number (the spread), while sellers believe that the actual number of heating days will be below that implied by today's spread. The contract has a *multiplier* of $100 per HDD which translates the differences between HDDs into dollars of payout. Suppose today two parties enter into a 3-month expiry futures contract at a "price" of 52 HDDs. One party goes long (buys) one contract, the other goes short (sells) one contract. Each day until expiry, the parties will exchange cash flows equal to today's closing futures price minus yesterday's times the multiplier. For example, if the next day's price is 56 HDDs, then the long party will pay and the short party will receive $(56 - 52) \times \$100 = \$400$. They will continue exchanging cash flows until the expiry date. On that date, the last cash flow will be exchanged equal to that day's closing price, equal to the actual number of HDDs in the expiry month on which they had bet in the first place minus the previous day's price times the multiplier. Because all the intermediate cash flows will wash, the total sum of all the cash flows received by the long party and paid by the short party since inception will be equal to the difference between the actual number of HDDs during the expiry month and the original bet price of 52 HDDs times the multiplier. If the result is negative, then the long party will have paid and the short party received. Similar futures contracts trade for all major U.S. cities based on cooling degree days (CDDs) defined analogously to HDDs.

Stock index futures contracts work exactly the same way. Buyers bet that an index (a number, not a price of anything) will go up and sellers that the index will go down. The payout is equal to the value of the index less the bet price, times a multiplier specified by the exchange (e.g., $250 per point of the S&P 500 index per futures contract). Private forward contracts analogous to futures contracts may be easily established between two parties. There is no marking to market (intermediate cash flows) for forwards. Instead, there is only one settlement at the end, equal to the final price minus the bet (forward) price, times the notional amount of the contract (the multiplier). For most liquid financial instruments, an intermediate settlement may occur if requested by one party.

Apart from the marking to market which is automatic with futures and only if mutually agreed to with forwards, there is one more fundamental difference between the two vehicles: credit exposure. Futures are typically traded on an exchange that operates a clearinghouse. When two parties enter into a futures trade, even though they must find each other on the floor and agree on the price, legally each transacts not with the other, but with the clearinghouse that guarantees the payments. Neither party is exposed to the other in case one defaults on its obligations. The clearinghouse's guarantee is backed by a good faith futures margin each party and other parties maintain with it. The existence of a clearinghouse also enables parties to close out contracts with counterparties other than the original one as each transaction is a zero-sum game with the same number of longs as shorts and each is a legal transaction between a party and the clearinghouse. Futures contracts are standardized as to maturity dates and contract amounts (multipliers). Forwards can be custom-tailored, but each party bears credit exposure to the other because they are private contracts between two parties.

Futures exchanges in the U.S. typically have physical trading floors and the method of trading is referred to as open outcry. The biggest electronic futures exchange is operated by EUREX which after years of operating in Europe debuted successfully in the U.S. in February of 2004 competing head to head with the Chicago Board of Trade (CBT) in the U.S. bond contract. Both forms, physical or electronic, operate a clearinghouse that mitigates credit exposure and allows closing positions with any participant. The only real difference is that on an electronic exchange the bids and offers are displayed and transactions are entered into on computer screens rather than by people gesturing to each other.

Despite being bets on future events, futures and forwards perform a very important risk-sharing function. Parties unwilling to take the risk of future price or interest rate changes or the risk of changing raw material costs due to temperature variations can lock in future spot prices at today's futures and forward prices. They do not have to wait to see what future spot prices will obtain. They can lock in their cost of borrowing or lending, or the price they pay for coffee or oil. They cannot lock that cost at any level, but only at that equal to today's price in the forwards or futures market.

In turn, the forward price is tied to the spot price through the cost of carry. Suppose we think of the S&P 500 index level as the price of a tiny basket of 500 stocks in the proportions represented in the index and that we want to lock in a price of acquiring 250 of such baskets at a future date. We do not want to own the baskets today, but we want to know for sure at what price we can buy them 3 months from today. By going long 1 futures contract (the multiplier is equal to $250 per index point), we are transferring the price risk to the short party. If the index value is higher on the purchase date we will have received cash flows from the futures contract, compensating us exactly for the price increase. If the index value is lower, we will have paid into the futures contract giving up any potential savings we could have gained. At what price are we going to be able to lock in the purchase price 3 months hence? The answer is price equal to today's index value adjusted for the cost of borrowing money between now and the futures expiry date. This follows from a simple arbitrage relationship. Instead of going long 1 futures contract, we could borrow an amount of money equal to 250 times today's value of the index and purchase the baskets today. On the expiry date we have to return the borrowed cash, which is equivalent to a known cash outflow and a stock inflow, the same as in the future purchase of the index. The cost of carry is thus the financing cost of pre-purchasing the underlying commodity in the futures contract, net of any cash flows. In the case of the stock index, the extra cash flows are positive to us in the form of intermediate dividends earned on the component stocks, which reduces our cost of carry (interest cost minus the cash flows).

6.1   COMMODITY FUTURES MECHANICS

Let us consider an example of a corn contract traded on the CBT. As reported in the *Wall Street Journal* on Thursday, October 25, 2001, the December 2001 delivery corn settled at $206\frac{1}{2}$ cents per bushel. Each contract represents a claim on 5,000 bushels of corn.

Table 6.1   Grain and oilseeds futures prices for Thursday, October 25, 2001

Contract month	Open	High	Low	Settle	Open interest
Corn (CBT) 5,000 bushels (cents per bushel):					
Nov01	$201\frac{3}{4}$	$202\frac{1}{2}$	$201\frac{1}{2}$	202	2,429
Dec01	206	$207\frac{1}{2}$	$205\frac{1}{2}$	$206\frac{1}{2}$	211,016
Jan02	211	$212\frac{1}{4}$	$210\frac{1}{2}$	211	680
Mar02	$218\frac{3}{4}$	$220\frac{1}{4}$	$218\frac{1}{4}$	219	112,379
...					
Soybean meal (CBT) 100 tons (in $ per ton):					
Dec01	157.50	161.80	157.50	161.30	46,639
Jan02	156.00	159.20	154.50	158.60	20,156
Mar02	153.30	156.20	153.10	155.50	15,653

Source of data: Wall Street Journal, October 26, 2001.

The *multiplier* in the contract is $50 per 1 cent change in the futures price (5,000 bushels, but the price is in 0.01 of a dollar).

Suppose we buy one December contract (*car*) at the close price of $206\frac{1}{2}$ and observe the following December settlement prices on the following two business days:

Friday, October 26, 2001	207.30
Monday, October 29, 2001	206.80

Let us also assume that corn closed at 210.00 cents per bushel on the December expiry date (third Friday in December) which was also the spot price for corn on that day. This equivalence is assured because any outstanding long contract at expiry is a contract to purchase corn with a spot delivery from the short party.

Here is how marking to market works. At the time we "bought" the contract, our broker on the exchange floor found a seller and agreed to the transaction. We did not receive any corn and *we did not pay cash for any corn*. We merely agreed on the size of the transaction (*1 car*) and the price (206.5). Since we bought the contract at the close, after the close on Thursday we did not pay or receive any cash flows (if the contract is bought in the middle of the day and the close price is different from the transaction price, marking to market starts the same day). We bought one contract and the price goes up on Friday. On Friday after the close of the market, we receive from the clearinghouse a *variation margin* check for:

$$(207.30 - 206.50) \times 50 = \$40$$

The clearinghouse has received a check for $40 from a short party. On Monday, the price goes down, so we compute our cash flow as:

$$(206.80 - 207.30) \times 50 = \$ - 25$$

After the close of the market we send a check to the clearinghouse for $25 (which is forwarded to a short). Our *net variation margin* after 2 days is equal to $15 (= 40 − 25). Notice that this amount is also equal to the close price on Monday minus the original futures purchase price times the multiplier:

$$(206.80 - 206.5) \times 50 = \$15$$

as Friday's close price of 207.30 washes out. It will be true for any day until expiry that the net variation margin, or the cumulative total sum of all the cash flows, will be equal to that day's close price minus the original price times the multiplier. On the expiry date, with the corn price at 210.00, our net variation margin will be equal to:

$$(210.00 - 206.5) \times 50 = \$175$$

Suppose we are a popcorn maker and the original purpose of entering into the long corn contract was for us to lock in a purchase price of $206\frac{1}{2}$ cents per bushel for 5,000 bushels of corn, our main raw material. Did we accomplish that? On the expiry date we purchase corn in the spot market for 210 cents per bushel. The total we pay is:

$$5,000 \times 2.10 = \$10,500$$

At the same time we have collected $175 from our hedge strategy, so that our net cost was $10,325. That cost translates into:

$$\$10,325 \text{ net total}/5,000 \text{ bushels} = 2.065 = 206\frac{1}{2} \text{ per bushel}$$

Had the price of corn gone to 200 cents per bushel by December, we would have still locked in our price of $206\frac{1}{2}$ since we would have collected from the long futures contract:

$$(200.00 - 206.50) \times 50 = \$ - 325$$

so that our cost of acquiring corn spot inclusive of the futures loss would have been the same:

$$5,000 \times 2.00 + 325 = \$10,325$$

(i.e., $206\frac{1}{2}$ cents per bushel). In fact, no matter at what price corn would end up in December, our cost would be $206\frac{1}{2}$ cents. We would be happy with the hedge if the spot price in December is higher than the original futures price (as we would save). We would be unhappy if the spot price of corn in December is lower, as we would have foregone a potential savings. Hedging in futures can be viewed as a two-way insurance strategy. If the price moves as you anticipated (relative to the lock-in value), you get reimbursed; if the price moves in the opposite direction, you reimburse someone else. You lock in a cash flow, but you do not eliminate the possibility of a mark-to-market loss. In that sense, locking future cash flows can be viewed as speculation.

Let us test our understanding of the mechanics of commodity futures by answering the following questions related to the same excerpt from the *Wall Street Journal*:

Q1. What is the multiplier for soybean meal?
Q2. If you sell 5 cars of Mar02 soybean meal futures at 155.50 and tomorrow the price goes to 158, what is your cash flow (variation margin)?
Q3. If at expiry in March, soybean meal trades at 160, what is your net variation margin?
Q4. What sale price did you lock in on the sale of 500 tons?

Here are the answers:

A1. Each contract is for 100 tons of soybean meal and prices are in \$/ton, so the multiplier is 100.
A2. If we shorted 5 contracts at the close on Thursday at 155.50 and the next day the price went down, then we lost money (i.e., had a negative cash flow, or variation margin) for that day of:

$$(-5) \times 158 - 155.50) \times 100 = \$ - 1,250$$

A3. If the price at expiry is 160, then between October and March we have accumulated a net variation margin of:

$$(-5) \times (160 - 155.50) \times 100 = \$ - 2,250$$

A4. If we sell 500 tons of soybean meal at \$160/ton for \$80,000 and we lost \$2,250 on futures, then the total price per ton we locked in is:

$$(80,000 - 2,250)/500 = \$155.50$$

The word *multiplier* is not commonly used with commodity futures. Instead, we refer to the *contract size* (i.e., the amount of commodity represented in each contract). Contract size can always be translated into a multiplier. We use the latter exclusively to make the understanding of the next sections easier and to emphasize that futures contracts can be written on any variable (e.g., index, temperature, interest rate) whose changes have to be translated into dollars to settle the variation margin every day. With non-price variables, the multiplier is explicitly defined.

6.2   INTEREST-RATE FUTURES AND FORWARDS

Overview

Most interest rate-related futures contracts around the world are defined based on actual or artificial bond prices, not directly on interest rates. For example, on the LIFFE in London, the long gilt contract is defined on GBP 500,000 face value of the long bond of the U.K. government. On the EUREX, one 10-year Euro-Bund futures contract represents EUR 100,000 of the euro-denominated bond of the German government. Like spot, bond futures prices are quoted as a percentage of par value. In Chicago, on the CBT, one Treasury Bond contract represents USD 100,000 face value of a 30-year Treasury bond. The futures price is quoted as a percentage of par value (with fractions in 32nds). To compute the variation margin for a given day, we first have to translate it to a straight percentage and then multiply by the size of the contract. For example, if we shorted five contracts at 112-03 and the price changed to 112-27, then we would have a loss, or a negative variation margin amount, of:

$$(-5) \times (112\tfrac{27}{32} - 112\tfrac{3}{32})\% \text{ of } 100,000 = (-5) \times (0.75/100) \times 100,000 = \$ -3,750$$

Note that the multiplier, as defined before, is in this case equal to 1,000. A 0.75 change in the price represents \$750 variation margin per contract. If we wanted to speculate directly on a specific size of an interest rate change and not a bond price change, we would have to scale our bet based on the current duration of the underlying bond. To bet on an interest rate *increase* of 1% for \$1,000,000 face value of bonds, one would have to *short* $[(1/\text{Duration}) \times 10]$ bond contracts. As interest rates increase by 1% the value of each of the 10 contracts representing \$100,000 face value, for a total of \$1,000,000 par value, would decrease by 1 times the duration number of points, producing the desired dollar gain.

All U.S. Treasury bond and note contracts, and many other government bond contracts, are defined not on one underlying bond, but on a set satisfying certain maturity and coupon criteria (e.g., close in maturity and coupon to the 30-year 6% mark). The short party to the contract is given an option to choose which of the eligible bonds to deliver to the long party on the futures expiry date. The short party is also given additional timing options that complicate the analysis of these contracts. The reason behind this complication is to ensure the liquidity of the delivery instruments which are considered fungible.

Besides the government bond futures for the benchmark issues in each market (U.S., U.K., Bunds in Germany, JGBs in Japan), the most popular futures contracts are those written on Eurocurrency deposits. The contract with the most turnover in the world is that on the 3-month Eurodollar deposit rate (i.e., the 3-month USD LIBOR). It is traded on the CME and is fungible with the same contract traded on the SIMEX in Singapore. Similarly, contracts are traded on yen- and euro-denominated Eurodeposits as well as other Eurocurrencies. Next we review the somewhat peculiar mechanics of Eurocurrency futures.

Eurocurrency deposits

Recall from Chapter 3 that a Eurodollar deposit (a "depo") is a non-negotiable, U.S. dollar-denominated, interest-bearing loan on deposit outside of the U.S. regulators' reach. The interest rate is fixed and quoted on an *Act/360* basis and paid as add-on interest at the end. There is a variety of terms available ranging from overnight, tomorrow/next day, 1 day, and so on, all the way to 12 months. The most popular one is a $1,000,000 3-month deposit with a 2-London-business-day settlement. Euro-dollar lending rates are fixed daily by the group of London banks most active in this market in the form of a London interbank offered rate (*LIBOR*), widely published by all financial services and newspapers; the bid on borrowed funds is referred to as LIBID, but rarely quoted. The LIBOR rate is the benchmark rate for unrestricted 3-month deposits and swap payments' settlements. The Eurodollar market is the largest global money market by volume outstanding and turnover. The interest mechanics work as follows. Suppose on Thursday, October 25, 2001 you called a bank to borrow Eurodollars at the interest rate of 2.31% for a term of 3 months. Your interest accrual period ran from Monday, October 29, 2001, to Tuesday, January 29, 2002. This reflects the customary 2 business day settlement period. Assuming there were 92 days in the period, your payment of interest and principal on January 29, 2002 was equal to:

$$1,000,000 \times (1 + 0.231 \times 92/360) = \$1,005,903.33$$

In the following, we will ignore the 2-day settlement delay. We will pretend that a 3-month deposit arranged today starts today and ends 3 months later. Actually, it would start 2 days after today and end 3 months after that. We will also assume that 3 months equals exactly 90 days.

Eurodollar futures

The Chicago Mercantile Exchange (CME) Eurodollar contract was designed to allow locking in the rate paid or received on a $1,000,000 3-month Eurodollar (ED) deposit starting on the futures expiry date and ending 90 days later. To that end, it is quoted on an artificial price basis. The futures "price" is defined only for the expiry date as:

$$F = 100 - L$$

where L is the 3-month LIBOR rate. Note that on the expiry date, F is *not* the price of a $1,000,000 deposit or even the price of a discount instrument promising to pay 100 at L percent interest 3 months later. Instead, on the expiry date, $L = 100 - F$. Every day we can interpret $100 - F$ as the LIBOR rate L that can be locked in on that day for a forward deposit starting on the futures expiry date. For example, a price of 97.69 means that a rate of 2.31% can be locked in. The stated size of the contract of $1,000,000 is also somewhat misleading unless we know from the fine print that the *multiplier* is $2,500 per point or $25 per basis point. Let us consider some real quotes as of the close of day on Thursday, October 25, 2001.

Table 6.2   Interest rate futures prices for Thursday, October 25, 2001

Contract month	Open	High	Low	Settle	Open interest
Eurodollar (CME) $1 million (in points of 100%)					
Nov01	97.79	97.83	97.78	97.81	41,554
Dec01	97.81	97.87	97.80	97.85	836,180
Jan02	97.86	97.88	97.86	97.87	7,080
Mar02	97.71	97.80	97.71	97.77	628,766
Jun02	97.41	97.51	97.41	97.48	588,920
Sep02	96.98	97.12	96.98	97.09	398,280
Dec02	96.50	96.63	96.47	96.60	378,297
Mar03	96.14	96.25	96.14	96.24	243,043
. . .					
Euroyen (CME) ¥100 million (in points of 100%)					
Dec01	99.91	99.91	99.91	99.91	19,080
. . .					

Source of data: Wall Street Journal, October 26, 2001.

The June 2002 contract closed at 97.48. That contract covers a forward deposit starting on June 19, 2002 and ending on September 19, 2002. The implied forward rate for that deposit is $100 - 97.48 = 2.52\%$. The spot LIBOR rate on October 25, 2001 was 2.31%. For simplicity let us assume that there are exactly 90 days in the June 19–September 19 period.

Suppose at the close on Thursday, we go long on one ED contract and over the following two business days we observe these futures prices:

Friday, October 26, 2001	97.44
Monday, October 29, 2001	97.55

Our variation margin on one long contract would be:

$$\text{October 26, 2001} \quad (1) \times (9744 - 9748) \times 25 = \$-100$$
$$\text{October 29, 2001} \quad (1) \times (9755 - 9744) \times 25 = \$275$$

We dropped the decimals to convert from points (bp) to basis points and then used the multiplier in $/bp. Our net variation margin as of Monday would be $175 which also could be computed simply from the Monday close price and the original price as:

$$(1) \times (9,755 - 9,748) \times 25 = \$175$$

Locking in a deposit rate

We consider two scenarios for LIBOR as of June 19, 2002.

LIBOR = 3%   First suppose that on June 19, 2002 the 3-month LIBOR rate is 3.00%. That automatically means that the last futures price is $F = 100 - L = 100.00 - 3.00 = 97.00$, and our net variation margin over the October–June period is:

$$(1) \times (9,700 - 9,748) \times 25 = \$-1,200$$

Suppose the original reason that we had entered into the long contract was to lock in the rate of 2.52% we would earn on a $1,000,000 90-day deposit, and as planned on June 19 we deposit $1,000,000 at 3.00%. Our interest on that deposit will be:

$$1,000,000 \times 0.03 \times 90/360 = \$7,500$$

Including our loss of $1,200 on the futures contract, our effective interest rate earned is:

$$(7,500 - 1,200)/1,000,000 \times (360/90) = (6,300)/1,000,000 \times (360/90) = 2.52\%$$

LIBOR = 2%   If the LIBOR rate on June 19 is 2.00%, then the last futures price on that day is $F = 100 - L = 100.00 - 2.00 = 98.00$, and our net variation margin over the October–June period is:

$$(1) \times (9,800 - 9,748) \times 25 = \$1,300$$

If on June 19 as intended we deposit $1,000,000 at 2.00%, our interest on that deposit will be:

$$1,000,000 \times 0.02 \times 90/360 = \$5,000$$

Including our gain of $1,300 on the futures contract, our effective interest earned is again:

$$(5,000 + 1,300)/1,000,000x \times (360/90) = (6,300)/1,000,000 \times (360/90) = 2.52\%$$

In fact, no matter what LIBOR is on June 19, our effective interest rate earned inclusive of the futures gain/loss is $6,300, or 2.52%. If we had wanted to lock in the rate on a $25 million deposit, we would have had to buy 25 contracts. Next let us look at an example of a borrower of Eurodollars.

Locking in a borrowing rate

On October 25, 2001 you want to lock in an interest rate on a $20 million loan starting on June 19, 2002 and ending on September 19, 2002. You can lock in a rate of 2.52% (but not any other rate) by shorting 20 ED contracts and waiting to borrow spot on June 19.

LIBOR = 3%   If on June 19 the 3-month LIBOR is at 3.00% and the futures price is at 97.00, then you have a positive total cash flow from your futures contracts:

$$(-20) \times (9,700 - 9,748) \times 25 = \$24,000$$

You borrow $20 million at 3.00% to incur interest cost on the loan of:

$$20,000,000 \times 0.03 \times (90/360) = \$150,000$$

Including your futures gain your effective borrowing rate is:

$$(150,000+24,000)/20,000,000\times(360/90)=(126,000)/1,000,000\times(360/90)=2.52\%$$

LIBOR = 2%   If, instead, on June 19 LIBOR is at 2.00% and the futures price is at 98.00, then you have a negative total cash flow from your futures contracts:

$$(-20) \times (9,800 - 9,748) \times 25 = \$26,000$$

You borrow $20 million at 2.00% to incur interest cost on the loan of:

$$20,000,000 \times 0.02 \times (90/360) = \$100,000$$

Including your futures gain your effective borrowing rate is:

$$(100,000 + 26,000)/20,000,000 \times (360/90) = (126,000)/1,000,000 \times (360/90) = 2.52\%$$

So, we lock in a rate of 2.52% no matter where Libor ends up on June 19. Let us provide another application of Eurodollar contracts, that of a lending or borrowing extension at a guaranteed rate through a rollover or bundling strategy.

Loan extension

Suppose a London bank quotes a rate of 2.38% on deposits for the 237-day period starting on October 25, 2001 through June 19, 2002. You have excess funds of $600 million that you want to deposit through December 19, 2002. Using the ED futures contracts, your strategy is the following:

- Deposit $600 million spot @ 2.38%.
- Do long Jun02 ED futures @ 97.48 and Sep02 ED futures @ 97.09 today to lock in reinvestment rates.
- As the spot deposit matures in June, reinvest in a 3-month deposit at the then-prevailing spot LIBOR rate.
- As the June deposit matures in September, reinvest in a 3-month deposit at the then-prevailing spot LIBOR rate.

We need to compute the number of June and September futures contracts we are going to enter into. Our spot deposit will by June 19 accrue to:

$$\$600,000,000[1 + 0.0238(237/360)] = \$609,401,000$$

So, we need to guarantee a reinvestment rate for the June–September period for that amount. We do that by going long 609 June02 ED contracts at 97.48. This ensures that including any gain or loss on the futures, we will reinvest at 2.52%. By September 19, 2002 our reinvested deposit will accrue to:

$$\$609,401,000[1 + 0.0252(92/360)] = \$613,325,542$$

Now, to lock in the rate of 2.91%, inclusive of any futures gain or loss, for the September–December period, we will go long 613 Sep02 ED contracts at 97.09. This will ensure that by December 19 we can expect to withdraw from our deposit account:

$$613,325,542[1 + 0.0291(91/360)] = \$617,837,063$$

We have effectively locked in a rate of $(17,837,063/600,000,000)(360/420) = 2.5482\%$ on an Act/360 basis for the entire period from October 25, 2001 through December 19, 2002. To lock in a borrowing rate we would have computed the same amounts, but we would have had to short futures. Also notice that in our strategy we assumed that we roll the interest over in the way money market accounts do when investors select reinvestment of interest and dividends. Had we chosen to "consume" accrued interest in the form of cash withdrawals along the way, the number of futures contracts to be shorted would have been a constant 600.

It is easy to show that no matter what future spot LIBORs are, the rollover strategy produces the desired result subject to a small error due to the fact that we cannot buy fractional ED contracts as required by our calculations.

Certainty equivalence of ED futures

It is important to notice one fundamental relationship governing the Eurocurrency futures contracts. An investor expecting to have excess funds available for deposit on June 19, 2002 has two choices: to wait till June and invest the funds at the then-prevailing LIBOR rate (i.e., to bear the risk that the 3-month deposit rate will change between now and then) or to lock in the rate by buying ED futures. He cannot choose the rate that he can lock in; a seller has to agree to it too. (The rate is thus determined in the ED futures market.) It costs the investor *nothing* to enter into the futures contracts. He merely needs to agree on the number of contracts and the price with a futures seller.

Instead of buying futures, the investor could call a bank and ask the bank to quote a rate on a forward 3-month deposit starting on June 19. The bank would have to quote 2.52%. If the bank were to quote more, the investor could arbitrage the bank by agreeing to the banks higher rate and shorting futures. This would earn him certain positive cash flows on June 19. If the bank were to quote less than 2.52%, the investor would go to the futures market to buy contracts and could again try to arbitrage the bank by trying to borrow from the bank at the quoted rate. The important observation here is that the bank and the investor must be indifferent between the uncertain future spot rate or today's known rate implied in the futures price, as it costs nothing to convert one into the other. This relationship will prove of paramount importance when valuing forward rate agreements and swap contracts whose one leg contains a string of LIBOR-dependent cash flows. Although the future LIBORs are unknown today, the present value of these cash flows will be computed by replacing the unknown future LIBORs by today's forward rates or those implied in today's futures contracts. We can say that the market *places a value* on the unknown June 19 LIBOR. It equates it to a known rate of 2.52%. That rate is not determined in the spot market, but by the demand for and supply of deposits in a separate market for delivery of funds in the future.

Let us show one example of arbitrage forcing the rate of 2.52% to prevail in the bank market. Suppose we find a bank that offers a rate of 2.64% on June–September deposits. We agree to deposit $1,000,000 with a delivery of June 19. At the same time, we short one ED contract to guarantee a borrowing rate of 2.52%. On June 19, we borrow $1,000,000 in the spot deposit market at the then-prevailing LIBOR and we deposit that $1,000,000 at our bank at a rate of 2.64%. We know that no matter what LIBOR is on June 19, our cost of borrowing is guaranteed to be 2.52%, assuming for simplicity exactly 90 days. If LIBOR is 2.00%, we lose $1,300 on futures and pay $5,000 in interest, making it a total of $6,300. If LIBOR is 3.00%, we gain $1,200 on futures, but pay $7,500 in interest, again making it a total of $6,300, which is equivalent to 2.52%. The bank guarantees to pay us:

$$1,000,000\,[1 + 0.0264(90/360)] = \$1,006,600$$

So we earn $6,600 and we pay only $6,300, ensuring a $300 profit.

Borrowers and lenders in the Eurodollar market can share the risk of future interest rates with other investors by locking their funding rates in the futures and forward markets. If they desire to lock in rates different from those quoted in the futures, then they have to compensate or are compensated for the present value of the difference between their desired rate and the certainty equivalents quoted in those markets times the appropriate day-count fraction.

Forward-rate agreements (FRAs)

In the over-the-counter (OTC) forward markets, the equivalent of the Eurocurrency futures contract is a forward-rate agreement (FRA). FRAs (pronounced "frahs") are more flexible than futures in that they can be entered into for any future dates and for any notional principal amount. The disadvantage is there is no credit risk mitigation by a clearinghouse, as they are private contracts between two private parties. In order to unwind them, the two original parties have to agree on the mark-to-market value. Many of these issues are addressed by the use of contracts standardized by an international industry association. These provide for netting for credit purposes (cash inflows and outflows for all contracts with the same counterparty are netted in case of default and only the net amount is exposed to default) and using reference dealers in case the two parties cannot agree on the mark-to-market value for the unwinds of previous transactions. FRAs can be arranged by mutual agreement for any future dates. Standard maturities are quoted daily on financial screens by larger dealers. These are listed for different start and end date combinations, relative to today, using the convention of "start month × end month". For example, in the quotes:

1 × 4	2.75/2.76
2 × 5	2.82/2.83
3 × 6	2.84/2.85

the "2 × 5" contract is bid at 2.82 and offered at 2.83. In this case, 2 × 5 means a contract with a start date of exactly 2 months from today and the end date of exactly 5 months from today (plus the number of days to settlement[1]). Just like the futures contract, the FRA allows us to lock in a borrowing or lending rate for a future 3-month period for indicated dates. The convention is for the dates to be defined relative to today's date. In the futures markets, these are defined absolutely in terms of actual calendar dates. Other standard forward periods are quoted in the market, for 1-, 6-, and 12-month intervals (e.g., 2 × 3 or 1 × 7), following deposit maturity dates in the Eurodollar, Euroeuro, or Euroyen markets. The language convention in the FRA market differs from that in the futures in that a dealer does not go long or short, but quotes the rates he is willing to "pay" or "receive" on the FRA. This is similar to the convention used in interest rate swap markets.

Let us describe the exact mechanics of a FRA contract. A FRA is equivalent to a cash-settled fixed-for-floating swaplet (i.e., a swap with only one rate set and only one

---

[1] This is governed by the FRABBA rules of the British Bankers Association (BBA) for FRAs. These are identical to those for LIBOR deposits and swaps. For example, for U.S. dollars, FRA spot is 2 days after the trade date and LIBOR is set 2 days prior to spot and roll dates (for swaps). For pound sterling, spot is same date with same date LIBOR sets. The payout is made on the settlement date at the start of the FRA contract period.

exchange of cash flows on the pay date; see Chapter 8 for swap definitions). One party agrees to pay and the other agrees to receive a fixed rate of interest applied to a notional principal amount over a 3-month period in exchange for receiving (the other party paying) a floating rate equal to the spot 3-month LIBOR rate on the forward start date, applied to the same principal amount. The pay and receive amounts are netted, present-valued by the spot LIBOR on the forward start date, and settled in cash on that date. Suppose on March 19, 2002 we entered into a 3×6 FRA to pay 2.52% on $20,000,000. The start date of the forward is June 19 and the end date September 19. The amount the "FRA payer" will pay to the "FRA receiver" is defined as:

$$20,000,000 \times [(2.52 - L)/100] \times (Act/360) \times [1/(1 + L \times Act/36,000)]$$

The payment has the difference between the agreed-on rate and LIBOR applied to the notional principal, scaled by the appropriate day-count fraction, and multiplied by the present value factor for 3 months. The payment is computed on June 19, when the LIBOR rate L is revealed, and remitted 2 business days later on June 21. The cash flow can be positive or negative depending on the LIBOR rate on June 19 relative to the upfront forward rate.

Suppose both parties wait till June 19 to observe the then-prevailing spot 3-month LIBOR to turn out to be 3.00%. The settlement cash flow is then computed as:

$$20,000,000 \times [(2.52 - 3.00)/100] \times (92/360) \times [1/(1 + 0.03 \times 92/360)] = \$-24,346.68$$

The FRA payer would thus receive a check for $24,346.68 from the FRA receiver. This is almost exactly the $24,000 that the seller of 20 ED futures contracts would receive in the form of net variation margin by June 19. The difference is that the FRA cash flow is (1) computed for 92 days and not for 90, as with a $25 multiplier, (2) it is present-valued by 3 months (from the end date to the start date), and (3) it is received all at once on June 19, instead of over time in the form of daily variation margin checks. For short forward start dates, the difference between forwards and futures is negligible. For longer forward start dates, 2 years and beyond, the difference grows and the two rates start diverging. The difference between the quoted FRA and futures rates for the same dates is referred to as *futures convexity* and is largely due to the timing mismatch of the cash flows causing futures to be price–yield convex instruments relative to forwards. This is analogous to viewing bonds as having a convex price–yield relationship and forwards as having a straight-line relationship to forward yields. The futures convexity charge can be quite large (in the order of several tens of basis points for 5- to 7-year futures) if the interest rate volatility between now and the expiry date is high.

It is easy to compute in our example that if the LIBOR rate ends up at 2.00 on June 19, then the FRA payer will have to send a check to the FRA receiver for the amount of:

$$20,000,000 \times [(2.52 - 2.00)/100] \times (92/360) \times [1/(1 + 0.02 \times 92/360)] = 26,442.63$$

which is close to the $26,000 we computed in the ED futures example, except for a small difference due to the same factors. We can conclude that, just like the ED futures contract, the FRA allows us to *lock in a net borrowing/lending rate* for a future period by simply matching the principal amount and choosing the correct side of the contract. The FRA payer locks in a *borrowing* rate, while the FRA receiver locks in the lending or deposit rate. The easiest way to remember which side is which is to think of *borrowing* as issuing a bond and *paying a fixed rate* on it, hence locking in a borrowing rate requires paying on the FRA or selling futures. The latter can be thought of as selling a forward discount bond. We can think of *lending* as buying a bond and *receiving a fixed rate* on it, hence locking in a lending rate requires receiving on the FRA or buying futures. The latter can be thought of as buying a forward discount bond.

Certainty equivalence of FRAs

We use the term *certainty equivalence* to mean that the market determines today a fixed rate at which it is indifferent to exchange (i.e., willing to exchange at no charge) future known cash flows for future unknown cash flows based on future spot deposit rates. The certainty equivalence of FRAs is even more obvious than that of the ED futures, simply by looking at the settlement formula. The formula reflects the exchange of the forward rate known today for a future LIBOR rate, not known until the start of the forward interest accrual period. The exchange of the rates is applied to the same notional principal and scaled by the appropriate day-count fraction. It is present-valued by 3 months to correct for the fact that, normally, interest is computed at the beginning of the accrual period, but paid at the end, whereas the FRA settles at the beginning of the period. The correction is exact, not approximate, since we apply the correct 3-month LIBOR rate as of the beginning of the accrual period (i.e., the rate at which we could borrow/lend against cash flows occurring 3 months later). The certainty equivalence of future spot LIBOR to today's forward rate comes from the fact that the FRA settlement formula is agreed on today, but with no cash changing hands today. That is, the two parties to an FRA are indifferent between the two rates.

We will come back to the certainty equivalence of futures and forwards later in this chapter when we discuss their relationship to spot zero instruments.

6.3   STOCK INDEX FUTURES

There are futures contracts traded on all major stock indexes around the world. In Chicago and New York, futures contracts are traded on a variety of U.S. stock indexes ranging from the most popular S&P 500 to the broad Russell 2000. The CME trades also a Nikkei 225 contract. In Europe, there are futures on the FTSE 100 on LIFFE, CAC-40 on MATIF, DAX on EUREX, and a variety of others.

All stock index futures are defined with the use of a multiplier that converts the points of the index into a currency of denomination. The CAC-40 futures on MATIF are defined as €10 times the index. The FTSE 100 contracts on LIFFE are £10 times the index. The Mini-NASDAQ 100 contract on the CME is $20 times the index. An interesting one is the Nikkei 225 on the CME which is defined as $5 times the index. While the other examples convert an index into its "home" currency, the Nikkei contract converts it into a "foreign" currency. This is not as peculiar as we might think. The outcome of a Real Madrid vs. Juventus soccer match is converted into British pounds by a London bookmaker and into euros by an Irish one. The outcome of a sporting event cannot be traded in the spot market, neither can a stock index. However, financial dealers can buy and sell baskets of stocks in their home currency in the exact proportions of the index, creating synthetic spot trading in the index (they cannot buy the Nikkei stocks for dollars). This has implications for the spot–futures price relationship through the cost of carry.

On July 22, 2003 the *Wall Street Journal* reported the following futures settlement prices for the S&P 500 index equal to 978.80 (spot) as of the close of the previous day, Monday, July 21, 2003:

S&P 500 Index (CME)—$250 × index	
Sep03	978.00
Dec03	976.10
Mar04	974.20

On that same day, the U.S. dollar LIBOR rates stood at:

1-month	1.100 0%
3-month	1.110 0%
6-month	1.120 0%
12-month	1.211 25%

To simplify the analysis, we will use a continuously compounded rate of 1.13% for all expiry dates (1.1293% is the continuously compounded equivalent of the 6-month rate of 1.12% on an Act/360 basis assuming 182 days).

Locking in a forward price of the index

The index futures market allows investors to lock in a price at which they can buy or sell a basket of stocks represented in the index. Today's value of an index of 978.80 can be thought of as a $978.80 price of a basket of 500 stocks bought in very small quantities but in the right proportions. By going long one December futures contract we can lock in today the price of acquiring 250 such baskets on the expiry date in December (using the multiplier of $250 per index point). The argument here is similar to that used above for soybean meal. The net variation margin will compensate us for any loss or take away any gain we may face as a result of the price difference between the future spot price and today's futures price.

Suppose we go long one December contract at 976.10 and on the December expiry date the spot index value is 1,000.00. Our net variation margin will be an inflow of:

$$250 \times (1,000.00 - 976.10) = \$5,975$$

If in December we buy 250 baskets at $1,000 per basket we will pay $250,000, which combined with a savings of $5,975 will yield a price per basket of:

$$(250,000 - 5,975)/250 = \$976.10$$

Fair value of futures

Let us now review the theory of futures pricing based on arbitrage, which can be found in finance textbooks. This states that, for an asset that can be stored at no cost and which does not yield any cash flows, the futures price F must be equal to the spot price S plus the cost of financing the purchase of the underlying asset spot between the spot date and the expiry date; that is:

$$F = S + (Financing)$$

Equivalently, this is equal to the spot price that is future-valued to the expiry date. This theoretical futures price is commonly referred to as *fair value*. For an asset whose purchase can be financed till expiry with a loan rate of LIBOR L, the definition translates into the following intra-year equation:

$$F = S\left(1 + L \times \frac{Act}{360}\right)$$

Note that the right-hand side has two components: S, the spot price, and $SL \times \frac{Act}{360}$, the interest cost on borrowing the amount S till expiry. Using an equivalent continuously compounded rate r, the equation is often written as:

$$F = Se^{rt}$$

where t is the time to maturity in years (e.g., $t = \frac{1}{2}$ for 6 months). Recall from Chapter 2 that when using continuous rates the discrete rate $(1 + r)^n$ expressions get replaced by e^{rt}). The theoretical futures price expression, which simply reflects the *cost of carry*, is guaranteed by an arbitrage or a synthetic replication argument.

Let us numerically illustrate the replication argument. Suppose today's value of an index is 978.80; this can be thought of as a $978.80 price of a basket of 500 stocks bought in the right proportions. We want to replicate exactly the cash flows of one futures contract with a multiplier of $250 per index point and expiry of 3 months. The continuously compounded rate at which we can borrow or lend funds is equal to 1.13%. Instead of going long one futures contract, we can do the following:

• We borrow $978.80 \times 250 = \$244,700$ at a rate of 1.13%.
• We purchase 250 baskets of stocks in the index (i.e., 250 times the numbers of shares represented in one basket) at a cost of $978.80 \times 250 = \$244,700$.

This results in a zero net cash flow today. On the futures expiry date:

• We pay off the principal and interest on the loan with a cash outflow of:

$$250 \times Se^{0.0113 \times (1/4)} = 244,700e^{0.0113 \times (1/4)} = \$245,392.25$$

• We sell the stock baskets at the spot index price per basket S_t on the expiry date and receive cash for them.

Our net cash flow on the expiry date is: $250 \times S_t - \$245,392.25$.

Assuming that the entire net variation margin is received/paid on the expiry date, going long one futures contract can be seen to be equivalent to the above strategy, in that it results in a net cash inflow equal to $250 \times S_t$, unknown today, minus 250 times some amount of dollar amount, equal to the original futures price. If there exists a futures market, then traders will have a choice of engaging in the above replicating strategy or going long futures. The two options must yield the same cash flows at all dates (spot and future), otherwise people would choose only the one with a higher net cash inflow. By equating the two, we get that:

$$250 \times S_t - \$245,392.25 = 250 \times (S_t - F)$$

The left-hand side is the cash flow for the replicating strategy on the expiry date, and the right-hand side is the definition of the net variation margin. This yields us the posited futures–spot equation and the futures price of:

$$F = 978.80e^{0.013 \times (1/4)} = 981.57$$

Thus we have shown that a long futures contract can be replicated through a cash-and-carry transaction. That is, a buyer of futures, in effect, does not need the futures market; he can accomplish the same by buying the underlying asset in the spot market, combined with a credit market transaction (borrowing). In order for the fair value relationship to hold, we must show that the seller of futures does not need the futures market either, in that he can guarantee the same spot and future cash flows as the *redundant* futures contract by short selling the underlying asset spot and lending in a credit market. This is called a *reverse cash-and-carry* strategy. For pure assets like stocks, this is quite easy. The amounts are the same; only the direction of the transactions is the opposite (short the asset and lend to earn interest).

Instead of the replication argument, we can also use a direct arbitrage argument by considering and refuting two alternative cases: (1) $F > 981.57$ and (2) $F < 981.57$. Suppose that (1) is true. Then we can profit by buying stock baskets using the replicating strategy and shorting futures. The replication strategy will lock in the price of acquiring each basket on the expiry date at a price of $981.57 (the loan repayment value divided by the number of baskets). Meanwhile the futures price will lock in a higher price of selling each basket resulting in sure profit. Everyone would try to pursue this trade, forcing the futures price down or the spot price up. The opposite strategy will be taken in case (2). We would go long futures, short the baskets at 978.80 spot, and lend money at a rate of 1.13%. We would lock in a forward sale price of 981.57 per basket through the replication strategy and a lower price of acquiring them in the futures market, resulting in sure profit.

Fair value with dividends

The fair value equation must be amended for stock index futures to reflect the fact that some of the stocks in the index may pay dividends. In the replicating strategy, this means that the guaranteed cost of acquiring the baskets on the expiry date, by buying them spot and holding them till futures expiry, will be lower by the amount of dividends received between now and expiry. In other words, the cost of financing the purchase now will be equal to the interest charge less any dividends received:

$$F = S + (\text{Financing}) - (\text{Dividends})$$

There are two ways of including dividends into the fair value or cost-of-carry equation, depending on our confidence in the future dividend estimates. For shorter expiries, we can typically predict very accurately the dollar amounts and the dates of the dividends D. In this case, we can present-value them to today, subtract them from the spot price, and future-value the net amount that must be borrowed to purchase the stock basket. This logic can be represented as:

$$F = [S - PV(D)]e^{rt}$$

For longer expiries, we may feel more confident, assuming that the dividend rate will be a constant or at least a predictable percentage of the stock price. Assuming we express that rate as a continuously compounded and annualized rate d, we can subtract it from the interest charge like this:

$$F = Se^{(r-d)t}$$

Suppose that, in the above replicating strategy example, over the next 3 months we expect to receive dividends whose present value we estimate to be $4 per basket. Then we can borrow $250 \times \$4$ less, or:

$$978.80 \times 250 - 4 \times 250 = \$243,700$$

and use the $1,000 in present value from expected dividends in addition to the borrowed funds of $243,700 to acquire 250 baskets at $978.80 per basket for a total cost of $244,700. The future payoff will still be the same. But, now, the futures break-even price that will make us indifferent between synthetic replication and futures will be lower to reflect the lower cost of replication by acquiring the securities spot:

$$F = (978.80 - 4)e^{0.0113\times(1/4)} = 977.56$$

Instead, suppose that, in the above replicating strategy example, over the next 3 months, we expect a continuously compounded, annualized dividend yield of 1.6371% per basket. Then we can also borrow less than in the no-dividend case. The futures break-even price or fair value becomes:

$$F = 978.80e^{(0.0113-0.016371)\times(1/4)} = 977.56$$

Notice in our examples that the $4 present value was chosen to be equivalent to the 1.6371% continuous rate. The choice of the form of the fair value equation depends on our confidence in which is a more reliable estimate of the dividend payout: the PV amount or the dividend yield.

Single stock futures

In the early 2000s, following the lifting of a ban on such products by U.S. regulators, futures contracts on narrow indexes (custom baskets and exchange-traded funds, or ETFs) and single stocks began trading on the OneChicago (ONE) and NASDAQ LIFFE (NQLX) futures exchanges.[2] As of late 2003, there were close to 100 single stock futures contracts traded on each of the exchanges and fewer than 100 narrow

---

[2] Single stock futures traded on LIFFE in London before they were introduced in the U.S.

index futures altogether. Each futures contract represents 100 shares of a stock (or ETF) delivered on a stated expiry date. There are only two or at most three sequential expiry dates available, but the market is growing. Single stock futures compete directly with a lucrative OTC forward market in which dealers quote forward bids and asks on individual stocks to institutional investors.

The *Wall Street Journal* of July 22, 2003 quoted the following futures prices for eBay's stock (ticker: EBAY) on the ONE exchange as of the close of the previous day (EBAY closed at 111.06):

	OPEN	HIGH	LOW	SETTLE	CHG	VOL	OPEN INT
Aug	109.43	111.00	109.43	111.11	−0.96	302	800
Sept	109.91	111.00	109.91	111.20	−0.87	138	1,243

Note that the increasing prices for farther maturities reflect a positive cost of carry for EBAY (no dividend and positive interest rate). Volume and open interest are still quite low compared with major contracts, like the S&P 500, and they tend to be even lower for some lesser known custom indexes.

6.4   CURRENCY FORWARDS AND FUTURES

As on stock indexes and commodities, there are futures contracts on currencies traded on major futures exchanges in the U.S., Europe, and Asia. The unique feature in currency trading is that the market is dominated by OTC forwards, rather than standardized futures, and that a significant share of the volume of transactions (about 30% as opposed to less than 5% in other markets, the rest being interbank or dealer-to-dealer activity) is linked directly to retail demand of non-financial corporations, managing their foreign exchange (FX) exposure. Outright forwards represent only 7% of the total volume, but forwards are packaged with spots or forwards for other dates to form short-term currency swaps, which are the main instruments traded in pure non-spot FX transactions.

Spot and forward FX rates are quoted continuously in the interbank market and are observable on many financial screens, like Bloomberg or Reuters. Normally, only forwards for standard maturities of 1-, 3-, 6-, and 12-months may be displayed, but forwards for customized expiry dates, potentially all the way out to 10-years, can be easily arranged on most major currencies. Transaction sizes are large with $10 million being a basic lot.

On August 7, 2003 a UBS website[3] contained the following quotes for the USD/EUR market:

---

[3] Go to http://quotes.ubs.com/quotes/Language=E then click on Forex/Banknotes and Forwards USD.

Table 6.3   UBS FX forwards EUR/USD for August 7, 2003

Type	Expiry date	Points	Bid	Ask	Time
Spot			1.1374	1.1381	19:31:00
ON	08.08.2003	−0.36/−0.33	1.1374	1.1381	15:49:00
TN	11.08.2003	−1.06/−1	1.1373	1.1380	18:42:00
SN	12.08.2003	−0.34/−0.31	1.1374	1.1381	04:43:00
SW	18.08.2003	−2.3/−2.21	1.1372	1.1379	19:31:00
2W	25.08.2003	−4.63/−4.48	1.1369	1.1377	19:03:00
1M	11.09.2003	−12.5/−7.5	1.1361	1.1374	13:41:00
2M	14.10.2003	−23.2/−18.2	1.1351	1.1363	15:08:00
3M	12.11.2003	−32.3/−27.3	1.1342	1.1354	18:19:00
4M	11.12.2003	−41.4/−36.4	1.1333	1.1345	19:31:00
5M	12.01.2004	−50.5/−45.5	1.1323	1.1336	19:12:00
6M	11.02.2004	−58.9/−53.9	1.1315	1.1327	19:29:00
9M	11.05.2004	−82.27/−77.27	1.1292	1.1304	19:32:00
1Y	11.08.2004	−103.22/−98.22	1.1271	1.1283	19:32:00
2Y	11.08.2005	−151/−136	1.1223	1.1245	19:30:00
3Y		−130/−96	1.1244	1.1285	19:27:00
4Y		−53/−7	1.1321	1.1374	19:00:00
5Y		53/111	1.1427	1.1492	19:12:00

http://quotes.ubs.com/quotes/Language = E then click on Forex/Banknotes and Forwards USD.
ON = Overnight, TN = Tomorrow/next, SN = Spot/next, SW = Spot/week.

Valid quotes go out 2 years (3-, 4-, and 5-year quotes were not updated that day) and all forwards are related to the spot quotes of USD/EUR 1.1374/81 (bid/ask) through *forward points*. These are decimals to be added to the significant digits of the spot rate. For USD/EUR, there are four significant digits after the decimal. For example, to arrive at the 9-month forward bid, we have to take the forward points of −82.27, which are shorthand for −0.008 227, and add that to the spot bid of 1.1374 to get 1.1292. Dealers shout only the forward points to each other over the phone. Just like spot, the USD/EUR forwards are quoted here in American terms (i.e., with USD being the *pricing currency* of the "commodity" EUR). In this example, the EUR can be said to be trading at a *forward discount* as forward prices of EUR in dollars are lower than spot prices (all points are negative). Alternatively, the USD is trading at a *forward premium*. What is special for currencies is that assets underlying the forward contracts are currencies themselves. Quotes and points measuring the premium/discount magnitudes can thus be inverted easily to suit the viewpoint of the customer. This dual nature of FX rates also has implications for the cost-of-carry arbitrage link between spot and forward FX.

Fair value of currency forwards

The fair value equation for currency forwards is analogous to that for stocks and stock indexes. It reflects the cash-and-carry argument. Currency forwards are redundant contracts; they can be synthesized from spot FX and interest rate transactions. Instead of locking in the FX rate at which we can exchange USD into EUR 3 months from today through a forward contract, we can borrow funds in USD today and buy the target currency, EUR, in the spot market. But just like stocks that generate cash yields in the form of dividends, the target currency, EUR, can generate a cash yield in the form of an interest accrual on a 3-month investment in a risk-free asset denominated in EUR. With stocks the dividend accrues automatically over the carry period once they are purchased. With currencies, we invest idle cash denominated in the target currency in a short-term deposit with a maturity equal to the forward expiry date. In 3 months we have an inflow of EUR from the deposit and an outflow of USD for the repayment of the USD borrowing. On the spot date, the cash flows in both currencies net to zero. Dollars are borrowed and used completely to purchase euros; euros are bought, but immediately deposited. The three simultaneous spot transactions (borrow USD, exchange USD into EUR, and lend EUR) replicate exactly the redundant forward. The cost-of-carry link between forward and spot FX rates, both expressed in terms of units of currency FX_1 per unit of currency FX_2, can in general be written as follows:

$$F\left[\frac{FX_1}{FX_2}\right] = S\left[\frac{FX_1}{FX_2}\right] + (Financing\ in\ FX_1) - (Financing\ in\ FX_2)$$

Note that the last term in this equation is equivalent to the dividend term in the stock index futures fair value. We show the discrete interest rate version of that equation in the next section. For interest compounded continuously in both currencies, the cost-of-carry link between forward and spot FX rates reduces to:

$$F\left[\frac{Currency_1}{Currency_2}\right] = S\left[\frac{Currency_1}{Currency_2}\right] e^{(r_{Currency_1} - r_{Currency_2})t}$$

The cash-and-carry arbitrage spot–forward link for currencies is referred to by financial economists as covered interest rate parity.

Covered interest-rate parity

Suppose we observe that today's JPY/EUR spot FX rate stands at 100. At the same time, 1-year deposit rates are 2% in yen and 4% in euros. The *covered interest rate parity* (CIRP) principle states that the 1-year forward rate must be equal to:

$$F\left[\frac{JPY}{EUR}\right] = S\left[\frac{JPY}{EUR}\right] \times \frac{1 + r_{JPY}}{1 + r_{EUR}} = 100\frac{1.02}{1.04} = 98.0769$$

This is guaranteed as long as borrowing and lending in each currency is unrestricted and there are no FX controls. The argument is replication or arbitrage. In the replication strategy, we can synthesize a long forward by borrowing in yen, selling yen spot for euros, and investing idle euros till the expiry. We can synthesize a short forward by borrowing in euros, selling euros spot for yen, and investing idle yen till the expiry. If both sides of the forward can do it on their own synthetically, then the forward is a redundant contract. The forward rate agreed on by both parties must reflect the cost of the replication strategy.

The arbitrage argument underscores the fact that the forward FX rate of 98.0769 is not just a mathematical fiction, but will be ensured by dealers seeking riskless profit. Suppose a dealer quotes a forward of 98.0000. This is lower than the theoretical CIRP rate. The interpretation can be that the EUR can be bought for less in the forward market than through a spot-and-carry transaction. The arbitrage strategy will thus involve buying euros forward and selling them spot. In order to offset FX cash flows, we will have to borrow euros today, agree to pay interest on the borrowing, and deliver the borrowed euros to the spot FX transaction. We will deposit the obtained yen, earn interest on the deposit, and deliver the yen from the maturing deposit into the forward FX contract to sell yen for euros. Let us say that an "errant" dealer quoted the forward of 98.0000 for the maximum size of EUR 10,000,000. Here is how we profit:

- Borrow EUR 9,615,384.62 at a rate of 4% for 1 year.
- Spot sell EUR 9,607,843.14 at JPY/EUR 100 for JPY 960,784,313.73.
- Deposit JPY 960,784,313.73 at a rate of 2% for 1 year.
- Enter into a forward contract to sell JPY 980,000,000 at a rate of JPY/EUR 98 for EUR 10,000,000.

Net cash flows in yen are zero as we purchase yen in the spot FX market and immediately lend out the entire purchase. In euros we borrowed more than we sold in the spot FX market, resulting in a positive cash flow of EUR 7,541.48. In 1 year, we have net zero cash flows in both currencies:

- We collect the yen deposit, which accrued to: $960,784,313.73 \times 1.02 = $ JPY 980,000,000.
- Deliver JPY 980,000,000 to the forward contract to receive EUR 10,000,000.
- Pay off the borrowing, which accrued to: $9,615,384.62 \times 1.04 = 10,000,000$.

We keep the EUR 7,541.48 as riskless profit. Note that by going long the forward to purchase euros we are bidding the price of euros in yen up, and by selling euros spot we are putting a downward pressure on spot euro and bidding up spot yen. We are also putting an upward pressure on EUR deposit rates and downward pressure on JPY deposit rates. All these four effects would tend to bring the prices into a parity with respect to each other as defined by the CIRP. The most obvious effect is that the errant dealer may adjust his forward quote up after seeing our demand for forward euros. The reader should be able to determine how to profit, had the dealer erred in the opposite direction and shown a forward rate higher than that posited by the CIRP.

The CIRP equation for intra-year periods needs to be amended to reflect the accounting for interest using money market rates. For example, for 3-month strategies using LIBOR rates the JPY/EUR example would look like this:

$$F\left[\frac{JPY}{EUR}\right] = S\left[\frac{JPY}{EUR}\right] \times \frac{1 + L_{JPY}\frac{Act}{360}}{1 + L_{EUR}\frac{Act}{360}}$$

Let us apply the logic of that equation to the FX rates for August 7, 2003 as quoted by UBS in Table 6.3. The spot ask FX rate is USD/EUR 1.1374 bid and USD/EUR 1.1381 ask. Within the same UBS site, we could find the 3-month LIBOR rates: 1.14 for USD and 2.1613 for EUR. We will ignore the fact that LIBOR quotes and FX quotes may not be from the same exact time of the day. Using 97 as the actual number of days between August 7 and November 12, the stated expiry of the 3-month FX forward, we obtain the fair forward bid rate:

$$F\left[\frac{USD}{EUR}\right] = 1.1374 \times \frac{1 + 0.0114\frac{97}{360}}{1 + 0.021\,613\frac{97}{360}} = 1.1343$$

and for the fair ask rate:

$$F\left[\frac{USD}{EUR}\right] = 1.1381 \times \frac{1 + 0.0114\frac{97}{360}}{1 + 0.021\,613\frac{97}{360}} = 1.1350$$

The actual forward bid–ask quotes of USD/EUR 1.1342/1.1354 contain a wider spread, reflecting the potential mark-up charged by UBS for unsolicited orders. They also ensure that on August 7, 2003 we could not have "picked UBS off" to earn riskless profit. The interbank market has already arbitraged out all riskless profit opportunities ensuring that the cash-and-carry CIRP holds!

Currency futures

Currency futures trade on two U.S. exchanges. On the CME, all currency pairs are against the U.S. dollar with foreign currency as the underlying commodity and the dollar as the pricing currency; on the FINEX, there are a few cross-pairs, all against the euro, with the euro as the underlying commodity and the other currency as the pricing currency of denomination. Contract sizes are large by retail standards, but relatively small by wholesale market standards. For example, on July 22, 2003 the *Wall Street Journal* reported the following settlement prices for the previous business day:

	OPEN	HIGH	LOW	SETTLE	CHG	LIFETIME HIGH	LIFETIME LOW	OPEN INT
Japanese yen (CME)—¥12,500,000 ($ per ¥)								
Sept	.8437	.8471	.8432	.8448	−0.0010	.8815	.8220	81,966
Dec	.8478	.8486	.8465	.8471	−0.0010	.8915	.8350	20,435
Est vol 8,659; vol Fri 19,005; open int 102,436, −4,422								
. . .								
Euro/US dollar (CME)—€125,000 ($ per €)								
Sept	1.1239	1.1338	1.1226	1.1326	.0057	1.1896	.8780	92,581
Dec	1.1265	1.1310	1.1213	1.1299	.0057	1.1860	.9551	1,550
Mr04	1.1218	1.1270	1.1218	1.1275	.0057	1.1795	1.0425	253
Est vol 33,046; vol Fri 41,304; open int 94,456, −2,557								

On that same day, the spot FX rate for USD/EUR was 1.1347, and the U.S. dollar and euro LIBOR rates stood at:

	Dollar	Euro
1-month	1.1000%	2.1205%
3-month	1.1100%	2.12275%
6-month	1.1200%	2.10938%
12-month	1.21125%	2.11313%

We can use the CIRP equation:

$$F\left[\frac{USD}{EUR}\right] = S\left[\frac{USD}{EUR}\right] \times \frac{1 + L_{USD}\frac{Act}{360}}{1 + L_{EUR}\frac{Act}{360}}$$

to come up with the fair value of the futures. Using interpolated interest rates for 2-, 5-, and 8-month expiries, we get for September:

$$F\left[\frac{USD}{EUR}\right] = 1.1347 \times \frac{1 + 0.011\,050\,0\frac{2}{12}}{1 + 0.021\,216\,25\frac{2}{12}} = 1.13278$$

For all three delivery months we compute:

Sept	1.13278
Dec	1.13003
Mr04	1.12754

Note that LIBOR rates and futures settlement prices are not from the same times (LIBOR settles from 3 p.m. GMT and futures 3 p.m. CDT), so our calculation produces a small error (which is the greatest for the shortest maturity). All numbers are within the low and the high for the day.

Let us briefly review the mechanics of daily settlement for currency futures. These are identical to those for commodities with the currency in the denominator treated as the underlying commodity. Suppose on July 21 we entered into five long December USD/JPY contracts right at the close at .8471. Note that for JPY, the .8471 price is in dollars per 100 yen, or it is shorthand for .008471 in USD/JPY, which is equivalent to JPY/USD 118.05. Suppose by the next day the JPY/USD settlement rate changed to 119.25, or equivalently to USD/JPY .008386 or USD/100JPY .8386. We have a negative cash flow in the form of a variation margin settlement of:

$$5 \times 12{,}500{,}000(0.8386 - 0.8471)/100 = \$ - 5{,}328.48$$

The multiplier for the price as stated in the contract is thus 125,000. Note that for the USD/EUR contract, the multiplier is simply equal to the size of the contract, which is 100,000 as the price is stated in dollars per 1 euro. It can be shown in a manner analogous to the commodity arguments that going long five December JPY contracts allowed us to lock in an exchange rate of 118.05 on JPY 62,500,000 for delivery on December 19, 2003. The net variation margin accumulated by that expiry date will offset any difference between the spot FX rate on that date and the original rate of 118.05 on the purchase of JPY 62,500,000.

6.5 CONVENIENCE ASSETS—BACKWARDATION AND CONTANGO

Financial assets, like stocks, gold, fixed income instruments, and currencies, are examples of *pure assets*. They are held purely for investment purposes. Investors are indifferent between holding the assets themselves and claims on them. For example, most stock investors hold shares in their brokerage accounts in *street name*. They rarely ask for stock certificates in order to exercise their voting rights. What matters to them is that they receive dividends and that they are able to sell their positions on demand. In the meantime, brokerage houses are free to lend these shares to others who can then short-sell them. As long as there are people holding these assets for investment purposes (i.e., they are long these assets), there will be no restrictions on short sales and no additional costs to shorting. For pure assets, both cash-and-carry and reverse cash-and-carry strategies are executable and at approximately the same cost. This is perhaps the most obvious with currencies where a purchase of one currency automatically means a sale of another. For pure assets, the general form of the fair value equation looks like this:

$$F = S + (Financing) + (Storing) - (Cash\ yield)$$

where *Financing* = interest paid on funds used to purchase the asset spot or interest earned on proceeds from a short sale of the asset spot; *Storing* = storage cost equal to 0 for most financial assets except gold; and *Cash yield* = dividends or coupon interest from the underlying asset (e.g., dividends from stocks and interest from currencies or bonds). We have already seen some specific guises of this equation.

Most agricultural, energy, and metal commodities are not pure, but rather *convenience assets*. Holders of these commodities own them not only for investment purposes, but to be used in production. Any disruption in that production may be costly. There may thus be an additional value, which varies from user to user, to owning the physical asset. That value, called a *convenience yield*, can be most easily viewed as an additional cash yield or dividend; the owner of the asset has a valuable insurance policy that his business will not be disrupted. When lending out the asset to be shorted spot by someone else, the owner has to be compensated for the loss of this convenience. The reverse cash-and-carry strategy may not be executable at all or may lead to very high costs. The general fair value equation for futures and forwards has to be amended to include the convenience yield, which reflects the implicit value of the convenience benefit to the marginal investor in the market (the most willing to lend the asset out in sizable quantity):

$$F = S + (Financing) + (Storing) - (Cash\ yield) - (Convenience\ yield)$$

For most commodities, the convenience yield tends to be large resulting in subsequent futures prices to be smaller than the previous ones and the spot price. This is called *normal backwardation*. There are many economic explanations for the predominance of backwardation in commodity futures, the most popular being that most hedgers are producers of commodities who tend to short futures at a discount to fair value in order to compensate speculators for accepting the risk.

There are times when the convenience value is small relative to the financing cost net of storage, resulting in a situation where futures prices increase with maturity. This is called a *contango*. Note that financial assets are more likely to be in this category as long as the cost of financing exceeds any cash yield. There are also special situations leading to a contango (e.g., resolutions of wars, expectations of new supply lines, etc.). We can also come up with examples of contangos due to negative convenience yields, like holding wheat right before a plentiful harvest.

6.6 COMMODITY FUTURES

Most commodities in the world are priced in U.S. dollars. The exchanges for rare agricultural or mineral products, or for local physical delivery points, can be scattered around the world (e.g., groundnuts and safflower oil in Mumbai, or olein in Jakarta), but by far the main centers for futures trading are Chicago, New York, and London. On the exchanges, producers and users of commodities can hedge their price risks in agricultural, petroleum, and metal commodities. While only a small percentage of trading activity (5%) is related to hedging and the rest is related to speculation, the existence of speculators is fundamental for price risk sharing. In each commodity market, there tends to be an imbalance of economic power between producers and users which is filled by the speculators. The most typical situation in a commodity market is normal backwardation whereby futures prices decrease with the contract maturity date due to a convenience yield of owning the physical asset. On July 22, 2003 the *Wall Street Journal* reported the following information for the crude oil futures traded on the NYMEX exchange:

	OPEN	HIGH	LOW	SETTLE	CHG	LIFETIME HIGH	LIFETIME LOW	OPEN INT
Crude oil, light sweet (NYM)—1,000 bbl ($ per bbl)								
Aug	32.00	32.10	31.25	31.78	−0.18	32.35	21.16	45,102
Sept	31.05	31.17	30.33	30.83	−0.20	31.53	21.05	190,648
Oct	30.52	30.64	29.95	30.40	−0.09	30.93	20.55	55,331
Nov	30.03	30.05	29.50	29.93	−0.01	30.40	20.70	28,262
...								
Dc07	23.80	23.80	23.80	24.04	+0.18	24.20	19.50	2,590

Est vol 191,187; vol Fri 156,891; open int 536,775, +11,528.

On that date, West Texas Intermediate Oil traded spot at 31.98. Let us use the estimate for financing cost based on **LIBOR** as in the stock index futures example (i.e., 1.13% continuously compounded) and assume that storage costs run $2 per barrel per year. This is equivalent to 6.10% continuously compounded. We can compute the fair value of futures without the convenience yield using a continuous formula:

$$F_{fair} = Se^{(r-sy)t}$$

where sy = storage cost expressed as continuous yield give-up. We can also back out the convenience yield, by solving for cy such that:

$$F_{actual} = Se^{(r-sy-cy)t}$$

Applying the formula for 1-, 2-, 3-, and 4-month delivery periods we get the following results:

Table 6.4 Fair values and convenience yields for NYMEX oil futures as of July 22, 2003

Month	Fair	cy
Aug	31.85	
Sep	31.72	17.00
Oct	31.59	15.30
Nov	31.45	14.90

The results show a pretty substantial convenience yield value for the near months. As this number is difficult to determine from fundamentals and dominates the easily estimatable financing and storage costs, it renders the spot–futures and futures–futures cash-and-carry arbitrage highly speculative. The convenience yield drops with maturity to less than 3.5% for the December 2007 contract (using $r = 3.13$), reflecting the fact that futures–futures arbitrage involving farther months is mostly financial (borrowing for Dec 2007 and lending for Dec 2006 or vice versa), with future convenience value severely discounted at this point.

On July 22, 2003, the news of the day was a substantial drop in coffee prices as expectations of frost affecting the August crop in Brazil faded. Traders dumped coffee in the spot markets. This resulted in a contango for coffee prices which were reported to be:

	OPEN	HIGH	LOW	SETTLE	CHG	LIFETIME HIGH	LIFETIME LOW	OPEN INT
Coffee (CSCE)—37,500 lb (cents per lb)								
July	60.00	60.00	60.00	59.15	−3.15	79.00	55.80	201
Sept	62.85	63.00	59.70	60.25	−2.95	80.50	57.30	44,656
Dec	65.25	65.40	62.00	62.85	−2.75	81.50	59.50	13,222
...								
Dc04	73.50	73.50	73.00	72.55	−2.25	80.50	71.50	1,490
Est vol 16,058; vol Fri 6,298; open int 69, 251, −343.								

Assuming zero storage costs, the September–July price difference reflected the convenience yield of minus 9.92%.

6.7 SPOT–FORWARD ARBITRAGE IN INTEREST RATES

In this section, we show how futures and forwards can be used in lieu of spot zero-coupon instruments in zero-vs.-coupon strategies of coupon stripping and replication. This leads us directly to establish tight arbitrage relationships between interest rate futures/forwards and coupon and zero-coupon spot rates.

Recall from Chapter 2 that purchases and sales of zeros can be synthesized from purchases and sales of coupon instruments, and vice versa. For example, the purchase of a 3-year semi-annual coupon bond can be replicated by the purchase of six zero-coupon bonds, with face values equal to the coupon amounts and maturities matched to the coupon dates, and one zero-coupon bond matched with the principal repayment. We argued that the price of such a package of zero-coupon securities must be identical to that of the coupon instrument. Similarly, we argued that any zero-coupon instrument can be replicated by the right combination of coupon instruments and other zeros. For the remainder of this section we will restrict our focus to the relationship of zeros to forwards and futures, and skip the obvious extension of the arbitrage equations of coupon instruments as packages of zeros and, thus, by extension as functions of forwards and futures. We also defer the discussion of credit spread issues by assuming that zero-coupon bonds, spot and futures LIBOR deposits, forwards, and futures are all entered into between parties of the same credit quality.

Synthetic LIBOR forwards

We start with a rather concocted example that will lead us later to more advanced topics. Suppose a customer appears at the ABC Bank to ensure that the bank will lend him $100 million 1 year from today for 1 year. The customer is willing to let the rate on the loan float for 1 year. He will be charged the spot rate 1 year from today and will repay the principal and interest based on that rate at the end of the interest-accrual period 2 years from today. The bank, in order to ensure the availability of funds as provided for by the contract with the customer, may choose to engage in the following strategy with third parties (assume a simple day-count):

- Borrow for 2 years at today's 2-year zero-coupon rate of 6.5163%.
- Lend for 1 year at today's 1-year zero-coupon rate of 6.0000%.

Let us compute the face values of the borrowing and lending by working backwards:

- In order to have $100 million on hand 1 year from today, ABC will have to lend today:
$$100,000,000 \times [1/(1+0.06)] = \$94,339,622.64$$

- ABC will have to borrow that amount for 2 years (i.e., it will have to agree to repay in 2 years):
$$94,339,622.64 \times (1+0.065163)^2 = \$107,035,114.80$$

By borrowing $94,339,622.64 today for 2 years at 6.5163% to repay $107,035,114.80 in 2 years and lending $94,339,622.64 today for 1 year at 6.0000% to receive $100,000,000 in 1 year, the bank locks in a certain cost of borrowing funds. That cost is equal to the rate r such that:
$$100,000,000 \times (1+r) = 107,035,114.80$$

We solve to get $r = 7.0351\%$. In 1 year's time, when the customer comes to collect the promised $100 million, ABC agrees to charge him the then-prevailing LIBOR. So, for the accrual period, the bank will pay a rate of 7.0351 to a third party and receive LIBOR from the customer. This set of cash flows is equivalent to entering a 12×24 FRA as a payer of fixed on $100 million. If the FRA market did not exist, then LIBOR forwards could with some effort be synthesized by borrowing and lending in the zero market for the right terms.

In our example, the bank had two other choices:

- Do nothing; wait till 1 year from today, borrow at LIBOR, and provide the funds to the customer at LIBOR at a complete wash (i.e., net zero cash flows today, 1 year from today, and 2 years from today).
- Lock in the lending rate to the customer, by entering a 12×24 FRA to receive fixed on $100 million against 12-month LIBOR; the LIBOR received from the customer would then offset that paid into the FRA and the bank would net receive fixed on the loan-cum-FRA bundle.

In the latter case, the rate fixed in the FRA would have to be 7.0351% in order for the bank to have net zero cash flows at all three points in time.

We can extend the preceding example to show that any forward lending (receiving on a FRA) can by synthesized in the zero-coupon market by borrowing for the short term and lending for the long. That strategy is equivalent to an outflow (repayment of the borrowing) on the forward start date and an inflow (receipt of the deposit plus interest) on the forward end date (i.e., a loan (out)). The mathematics of the synthetic FRA for simple annual periods reflect the spot borrowing and lending:

$$(1 + z_{n_1})^{n_1} (1 + f_{n_1 \times n_2})^{n_2 - n_1} = (1 + z_{n_2})^{n_2}$$

where z_n is a spot borrowing/lending rate and $f_{n_1 \times n_2}$ is an $n_1 \times n_2$ FRA rate. In the above example, we had $n_1 = 1$ year, $n_2 = 2$ years. The equation looked like this:

$$(1 + 0.060\,000)(1 + f_{1 \times 2}) = (1 + 0.065\,163)^2$$

Solving, we get $f_{1 \times 2} = 0.070\,351$. To determine a forward rate for the period of 2 years starting in 3 years knowing the 3-year zero and the 5-year zero, we would have to solve for $f_{3 \times 5}$:

$$(1 + z_3)^3 (1 + f_{3 \times 5})^2 = (1 + z_5)^5$$

The equations are more complicated for intra-year periods and when the right day-counts are used, but in a predictable way. For example, suppose that we know a 6-month zero compounded quarterly z_6 and a 9-month zero compounded quarterly z_9, both on an *Act/360* basis. Then the 6×9 forward could be derived from:

$$\left(1 + z_6 \times \frac{Act_{0-3}}{360}\right)\left(1 + z_6 \times \frac{Act_{3-6}}{360}\right)\left(1 + f_{6 \times 9} \times \frac{Act_{6-9}}{360}\right)$$

$$= \left(1 + z_9 \times \frac{Act_{0-3}}{360}\right)\left(1 + z_9 \times \frac{Act_{3-6}}{360}\right)\left(1 + z_9 \times \frac{Act_{6-9}}{360}\right)$$

where we substitute the correct number of days in each interest compounding period.

Synthetic zeros

We can reverse the above relationships to synthesize zeros from forwards. If a 3×6 forward pay is a combination of a long 3-month zero (lending) and a short 6-month zero (borrowing), then we can also construct a long 6-month zero (lending for the long term), by a long 3-month zero (lending for the short term) and receiving on a forward (guaranteeing the lending rate for the intervening 3×6 period).

Suppose a customer of the ABC Bank requests a $100 million spot loan for a 2-year period. ABC charges 6.00% on 1-year loans (equal to its own cost of borrowing funds for 1 year). It also realizes that 12×24 FRAs are quoted at 7.0351%. What rate should it charge the customer?

In order to write its customer a check for $100 million today in exchange for a 2-year IOU, ABC can borrow funds for 1 year at 6.00% and can lock in the rate on a rollover of that borrowing at 7.0351% by paying fixed on a FRA or shorting ED futures. The borrowed $100 million will have to be repaid in 1 year with:

$$100,000,000 \times (1 + 0.06) = \$106,000,000$$

ABC can agree to pay 7.0351% on a 12×24 FRA with a notional principal of $106 million or short 106 12-month ED futures contracts (the futures strategy translates in reality to a string of 3-month LIBOR futures with expiries in 12, 15, 18, and 21 months). In 1 year's time, in order to repay the original $100 1-year borrowing, ABC will have to borrow $106 million for one year at the then-prevailing 12-month LIBOR rate. But, we know from our previous discussion that no matter what the 12-month LIBOR is 1 year from today, ABC will have been guaranteed a net interest charge at the rate of 7.0351%. Thus its borrowing will accrue over the second year to:

$$106,000,000(1 + 0.070\,351) = \$113,457,206$$

In order for the ABC Bank to break even, it has to charge its customer on a 2-year spot loan of $100 million a rate z_2 such that:

$$100,000,000 \times (1 + z_2)^2 = 113,457,206$$

Solving, we get $z_2 = 6.5163\%$.

The above relationships hold for zeros and forwards of all maturities, whether short or long. We can use that fact to construct synthetic zeros in a variety of different ways. If a 2-year zero can be constructed using a 1-year zero and a 1-year-by-2-year forward, then a 3-year zero can be constructed either as:

- A 2-year zero and a 2-year-by-3-year forward.
- Or a 1-year zero, a 1-year-by-2-year forward and a 2-year-by-3-year forward.

Let us continue with the numerical example. Suppose that prior to signing the 2-year loan agreement, our customer changes his mind and asks for a 3-year $100 million loan instead. ABC can turn to the 24×36 FRA market, currently trading at 7.4674%, to lock in the rate for the forward 1-year period starting in 2 years on a $113,457,206 principal. It will have to borrow that amount in the spot market, but its net rollover rate will be guaranteed. In order to satisfy its borrowing repayment 3 years from today, it will have to receive from its customer exactly:

$$113,457,206 \times (1 + 0.074\,674) = \$121,929,528.70$$

That means, it will quote today a 3-year zero-coupon rate z_3 such that:

$$100,000,000 \times (1 + z_3)^3 = 121,929,528.70$$

or $z_3 = 6.8324\%$. The rollover strategy for the first 2 years is at the bank's discretion. ABC can either:

- Borrow $100 million in the 2-year zero market at 6.5163%.
- Or borrow $100 million in the 1-year zero market at 6.00% and roll it over in the 1-year-by-2-year forward market at 7.0351%.

The result will be the same: $113,457,206 owed after 2 years. This will be rolled over at the guaranteed (upfront) rate of 7.4674% for the third year.

It should be clear by now that any zero can be synthesized by a zero of shorter maturity and a string of forwards for the intervening period.

Floating-rate bonds

A floating-rate bond is a bond whose coupon is not known in advance, but is tied to the future performance of an index or a rate. In the standard floating-rate bond, the coupon accrual period is matched to the maturity of the short-term interest rate used to determine the coupon. The short-term rate is set at the beginning of each coupon period and the coupon based on that rate is paid at the end of the coupon period. The coupon payment is computed as the set rate times the face value of the bond times the appropriate day-count fraction. Compared with a fixed rate bond, the valuation of the floating rate bond may appear difficult as we do not know the cash flows of the bonds in advance. However, the forward certainty equivalence principle makes valuation of most floating rate bonds straightforward.

Let us consider a 10-year, $100 face value, annual coupon bond whose floating rate is tied to the 12-month LIBOR. The coupon rate is known only for the first year as it is based on today's 12-month deposit rate. The rate for the second year, not known today, will be based on the LIBOR rate 1 year from today and paid 2 years from today. The rate for the third year, not known today, will be based on the LIBOR rate 2 years from today and paid 3 years from today. And so on. There are two ways to look at this bond today, exactly 1 year prior to the next cash flow.

One is to recognize that a floating rate bond is equivalent to an artificial rollover strategy. The issuer borrows $100 for 1 year. The fair rate on that borrowing is today's LIBOR which is set to be today's coupon for the first year. In 1 year's time, the issuer borrows $100 again for 1 year in order to repay the original loan of $100 obtained at time zero for 1 year. He also pays the coupon interest equal to time zero LIBOR. The rate set for year 2 is equal to the 1-year LIBOR 1 year from today which is a fair rate for a new 1-year loan. The issuer then proceeds with rolling over the loan every year, each time at a new, fair, 1-year rate. Each year, right after the loan is rolled over, the value of the issuer's IOU for the next year is equal to $100. He promises to repay the principal of $100 and the interest on that principal set at that time; this is to be paid a year later. The total discounted back by 1 year at the prevailing 1-year rate is $100.

Another way to look at the floating rate bond is to recognize that both the issuer and the buyer of the bond have the option to lock in, at no cost, the uncertain cash flows of the bond into their certainty equivalents through the FRA market or the ED futures market. A buyer of the bond could convert the unknown future LIBOR payments into fixed cash flows, which would most likely be different each year, but known in advance and equal to today's FRA rates spanning the respective coupon periods. Using the numbers from our previous example, the investor can lock in the following coupon payments for the first 3 years:

- For year 1, today's LIBOR or zero rate of 6.00%.
- For year 2, the 1-year-by-2-year forward rate of 7.0351%.
- For year 3, the 2-year-by-3-year forward rate of 7.4674%.

And so on. A floating rate bond is thus equivalent to a bond for which the coupon rates are fixed today, but vary each period. If the floating rate bond has a spread (i.e., is quoted as, say, LIBOR plus 1.5%), then such floating rate bond is equivalent to a sum of two fixed coupon bonds: one with varying coupons equal to the forward rates and one with all coupons equal to the spread of 1.5%, net of the short zero to offset the double-counted principal.

Synthetic equivalence guaranteed by arbitrage

The equivalence of spot zero strategies with synthetic forwards leads to the following summary of important findings:

- The payoff on a Eurocurrency forward (FRA) contract can be synthetically replicated by borrowing and lending the appropriate amounts in the zero-coupon market.
- Since forwards and futures are almost perfect substitutes, the payoff on a Eurocurrency futures contract can be synthetically replicated by borrowing and lending the appropriate amounts in the zero-coupon market.
- Given the forward and futures certainty equivalence and that the market places no cost on converting future spot to today's futures or forwards, a bank will not charge the customer for locking in the future unknown loan rate.
- Longer term zero rates can be costlessly synthesized from shorter-term zeros and intervening forwards.
- Longer term zero rates can be costlessly synthesized from shorter-term zeros and intervening futures.
- Coupons, zeros, floating-rate bonds, forwards and futures are all synthetic equivalents of the appropriate combinations of longs and shorts with each other (i.e., all can be replicated at no cost with packages of the other instruments).
- The possibility of arbitrage profits ensures that the mathematical relationships implied in the above statements hold.

6.8 CONSTRUCTING THE ZERO CURVE FROM FORWARDS

In Chapter 2, we showed how quotes for coupon bonds can be used sequentially to compute discount rates for present value calculations through a process called a zero curve bootstrap. In this section, we revisit the construction of the zero curve, this time with the use of futures and forwards. Like before, we will use observed quotes in chronological order in order to create a set of rates or, alternatively, discount factors, appropriate for computing the present values of cash flows set for future dates. This is a fundamental task in any valuation process of not only money market instruments, bonds, structured securities and swap derivatives, but also in equity, currency and commodity forwards and options.

The great insight of Chapter 2 was that coupon securities are packages of zeros. Let us assume semi-annual coupons. By knowing the yield on a 6-month coupon we automatically know the rate for a 6-month zero. A 12-month coupon was a package of two zeros: one with 6-month maturity and a face value equal to the 6-month coupon cash flow, and one with 12-month maturity and a face value equal to the 12-month coupon cash flow plus the principal. If we knew the "blended" yield on the coupon security and the yield on the first zero in the package, then we could back out the yield on the second zero, since the price of the package had to equal the sum of the parts. Similarly by knowing the price of and the yield on a 18-month coupon security and previously computed yields of the 6- and 12-month zeros, we could back out the yield on the 18-month zero. We could continue like that all the way to the coupon bond with the longest maturity, creating a set of zero-coupon yields. Using zero yields, we could then discount cash flows scheduled for any future dates and compute the prices of any fixed income security.

The coupon bootstrap is typically used in constructing the curve for dates past the 1-year or 5-year point to the 30-year point. It is considered too crude for shorter maturities, as our first observation point is 6 months out for U.S. semi-annual coupon bonds and often 12 months out for European and Canadian markets where bonds typically pay coupons annually. A forwards- or futures-based bootstrap for shorter dates dovetails nicely with the coupon bootstrap further out. It provides liquid futures points every 3 months for 10 years for U.S. markets (CME ED futures) and liquid futures points every 3 months out to the 3-year or 5-year mark for the pound and the euro. Finer observations can be obtained from 1-month LIBOR futures and FRAs whose dates do not correspond to the futures calendar. The choice of where the two methods meet, the short bootstrap based on forwards, and the long bootstrap based on coupons depends on the relative liquidity of the instruments used. Their liquidity ensures that packages can be easily constructed to create synthetic securities. That is, it ensures that the whole process is not just a mathematical exercise, but a market reality guaranteed by potential arbitrage. Let us turn to the details of the forwards/futures-based bootstrap of the zero curve.

We are going to proceed in a manner similar to the coupon case. We will use the first zero rate known and then forwards and/or futures with ever-increasing start and end dates to construct a discount curve of zero-coupon yields or discount factors. As it is good practice to avoid confusion with day-counts, we will compute discount factors and not yields for different dates. Discount factors, which are present value equivalents of $1 received on a given future date, are unambiguous. Any rate with an arbitrary maturity, compounding, and day-count can be recovered from them.

We use the futures quotes from the October 25, 2001 *Wall Street Journal*. In addition, we use three spot zero rates as starting points for our curve. The maturities of these spot rates match the expiry of the first three futures contracts (i.e., November, December, and January). We will only use the November and January quote to compute discount factors for November and January, and for periods extending 3 months after that (i.e., February and April). The December spot will be used to compute the discount factors for December and for all periods ending in 3-month intervals following the quarterly futures expiries of March, June, September, and December. For simplicity, we assume that the LIBORs implied in the futures contracts are for forward deposits spanning roughly 3 months from the futures expiry to the next contract's expiry, and not for 90-day deposits as assumed by the $25 multiplier. The quote information is summarized in Table 6.5.

Table 6.5 Spot LIBORs and futures prices for October 25, 2001. Discount factors computed for forward start dates and for spot date to forward end date

Start date	End date	Days in forward period	Actual quote	Yield (Act/360)	Forward discount factor	Spot discount factor
Spot						
15-Oct-01	21-Nov-01	37	2.05	2.05	0.997 897	0.997 897
15-Oct-01	19-Dec-01	65	2.12	2.12	0.996 187	0.996 187
15-Oct-01	16-Jan-02	93	2.15	2.15	0.994 477	0.994 477
Futures						
21-Nov-01	19-Feb-02	90	97.81	2.19	0.994 555	0.992 464
19-Dec-01	20-Mar-02	91	97.85	2.15	0.994 595	0.990 802
16-Jan-02	19-Apr-02	93	97.87	2.13	0.994 528	0.989 034
20-Mar-02	19-Jun-02	91	97.77	2.23	0.994 395	0.985 248
19-Jun-02	18-Sep-02	91	97.48	2.52	0.993 670	0.979 012
18-Sep-02	18-Dec-02	91	97.09	2.91	0.992 698	0.971 863
18-Dec-02	19-Mar-03	91	96.60	3.40	0.991 479	0.963 582

We are given three zero yields: 2.05, 2.12, and 2.15. We are also given futures quotes. These allow locking in the rates for the periods starting on the futures expiry date and ending 3 months later. We compute the actual number of days in each forward period spanned by the futures quote and the yield implied for each of those periods as 100 minus the futures price. We also compute forward discount factors (the first three using the spot zero rates are actually spot factors with the start date equal to the spot date of today). These are present values as of the start date of $1 received on the end date using the futures-implied yield. The logic follows from arbitrage as we would be able to synthesize a $1 face value loan for the forward period by locking in the rate in the futures, and borrowing or lending at future LIBOR. From forward discount factors we can compute spot discount factors that are present values as of today, October 25, 2001, of $1 received on the end date. These are products of appropriate forward discount factors spanning successive periods. For example, the spot discount factor of 0.979 012 for September 18, 2002 is the product of the spot factor of 0.996 187 for December, the forward factor of 0.994 595 for December–March, the forward factor of 0.994 395 for March–June and the forward factor of 0.993 670 for June–September. From the discount factors we are able to recover discount rates based on any convention. As is traditional, we show the continuously compounded yields (also unambiguous) which have the nice property that the spot continuous yield is an average of the appropriate forwards. We also show simple interest Act/360 yields.

Table 6.6 Continuous and simple yields implied by the computed spot discount factors

End date	Days from spot	Spot discount factor	Continuous yield	Simple yield (Act/360)
21-Nov-01	37	0.997 897	2.0763	2.0500
19-Dec-01	65	0.996 187	2.1453	2.1200
16-Jan-02	93	0.994 477	2.1738	2.1500
19-Feb-02	127	0.992 464	2.1741	2.1525
20-Mar-02	156	0.990 802	2.1620	2.1423
19-Apr-02	186	0.989 034	2.1637	2.1459
19-Jun-02	247	0.985 248	2.1961	2.1822
18-Sep-02	338	0.979 012	2.2906	2.2833
18-Dec-02	429	0.971 863	2.4283	2.4295
19-Mar-03	520	0.963 582	2.6040	2.6166

Note that by definition the first three simple yields match the inputs.

We have thus constructed the yield curve for the first 520 days. It should be clear that we could have substituted FRAs for futures or used them in addition to futures for some of the in-between dates. We also could have used more coupon instrument dates or know spot points. The result is the graph of the zero-coupon yield curve for October 25, 2001 (Figure 6.1).

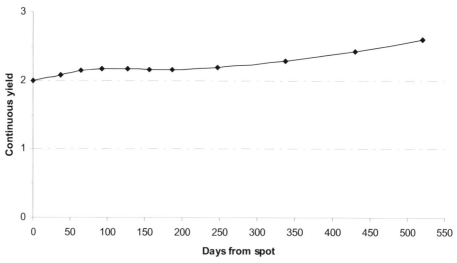

Figure 6.1   Zero-coupon curve.

Once we have the yield curve, the valuation of fixed income securities with no options embedded in them becomes trivial. Suppose someone offers us a structured note promising to pay $3,500 twice, 182 days from today and 365 days from today, plus the principal of $100,000. How much would we pay for it?

Since we do not have the exact discount factors for 182 days and 365 days, we use the arithmetic interpolation of the continuous yields to obtain these two factors. For 182 days, we use the rates for 156 days and 186 days to get the interpolated yield of 2.1635, which translates into a discount factor of 0.989 270. For 365 days, we use the rates for 338 days and 429 days to get the interpolated yield of 2.3314, which translates into a discount factor of 0.976 955. The present value of the note's cash flows is then equal to:

$$3,500 * 0.989\,270 + (3,500 + 100,000) * 0.976\,955 = \$104,577.33$$

We would be willing to pay 104.5773 of the face value for the note.

6.9   RECOVERING FORWARDS FROM THE YIELD CURVE

Once the yield curve is constructed (i.e., we have obtained a set of discount factors for all future dates), we can not only value securities with known future cash flows, but also those whose cash flows float with LIBOR rates (floating rate bonds, inverse floaters, leveraged floaters, etc.). We can do that because we can recover the forwards implied by the yield curve and substitute them for future unknown LIBORs using the certainty equivalence argument. Since all future spot LIBORs can be costlessly converted to today's forwards, the present value of an artificial security with forwards substituted for the unknown future LIBORs must be the same as that of the actual security with unknown cash flows.

The valuation of a floating-rate bond

Let us consider the following example. On October 25, 2001 we are offered a 1-year floating rate note with a face value of $200,000 whose quarterly coupon is equal to the 3-month LIBOR. The coupon payment dates are January 25, April 25, July 25, and October 25, 2002, set 3 months prior. How much are we willing to pay for it? The analysis of the bond is summarized in Table 6.7.

For the given set and pay dates, we compute the numbers of days from spot and the number of days in each accrual period. We interpolate the continuous yields and compute the interpolated present value (PV) factors to each set and pay date. From each pair of PV factors, we can compute the implied LIBOR set (i.e., today's forward 3-month LIBOR) for the set date. These are obtained from the arbitrage equation:

$$PV(\$\ on\ pay\ date) = PV(\$\ on\ set\ date) \times \frac{1}{1 + f_{set\ date \times pay\ date}\frac{Act}{360}}$$

Each cash flow is set, based on the implied LIBOR forward on the set date, to be equal to:

$$200{,}000 \times f_{set\ date \times pay\ date} \times \frac{Act}{360}$$

and paid on the pay date, 3 months later. We can then compute the PV of each cash flow by multiplying each cash flow by the discount factor to the pay date. We sum the PVs to obtain the price of the note. This turns out to be exactly $200,000. This should be no surprise given our previous argument about the nature of the floating rate note as a revolving loan always worth par.

Including repo rates in computing forwards

This generic arbitrage analysis is very general and applies to all credit markets. There is, however, one situation where the analysis has to be modified to take into account *special repos* (repurchase agreements) that render forward replication strategies more expensive. Recall from the discussion of the U.S. Treasury market in Chapter 3 that supply and demand forces may make a bond scarce, which means that a lender of funds through a reverse repo (buyer of securities to resell tomorrow) will sometimes lend funds at a zero interest rate just to be able to temporarily own the desired bond. His resale price will include a rebate that will make it equal to today's purchase price, thus earning him no interest.

Let us consider a simplified numerical example. Assume that a 1-year zero yielding 6% enjoys general repo while a 2-year zero yielding 6.5% is expected to be on special for the next month. You want to replicate a 1-year-by-2-year forward deposit by buying the 2-year zero and shorting the 1-year zero. If neither bond were on special, then we could lock in a rate $f_{12\times24}$ such that:

$$(1 + 0.06)(1 + f_{12\times24}) = (1 + 0.065)^2$$

Table 6.7 One-year floating-rate bond, quarterly coupons, face value: $200,000

Set date	Pay date	Days from spot to set date	Days from spot to pay date	Days	Interpolated continuous yield to pay date	PV factor to set date	PV factor to pay date	Implied LIBOR set	CF on pay date	PV of CF
25-Oct-01	25-Jan-02	0	92	92	2.1728	1.000000	0.994538	2.1489	1,098.34	1,092.34
25-Jan-02	25-Apr-02	92	182	90	2.1635	0.994538	0.989270	2.1302	1,065.08	1,053.65
25-Apr-02	25-Jul-02	182	273	91	2.2231	0.989270	0.983510	2.3170	1,171.38	1,152.06
25-Jul-02	25-Oct-02	273	365	92	2.3314	0.983510	0.976955	2.6252	201,341.78	196,701.94

Sum of PVs = *200,000,00*

CF = cash flow and PV = present value.

or $f_{12\times24} = 7.0024\%$. Alternatively, we can write this in terms of discount security prices as:

$$\frac{1}{(1+0.06)}\frac{1}{(1+f_{12\times24})} = \frac{1}{(1+0.065)^2}$$

The interpretation of the last equation can be that \$1 of principal and interest to be received 2 years from today can be guaranteed by spending $1/(1+0.065)^2$ on a 2-year bond or by spending $[1/(1+0.06)][1/(1+f_{12\times24})]$ on a 1-year bond to be rolled over into $1/(1+f_{12\times24})$ of a 1-year-by-2-year forward bond after 1 year. However, in order to own the 2-year zero we have to give up interest for 1 month. That is equivalent to paying a higher price for the 2-year bond today and is equal to the non-special value that we have grossed up plus the lost interest fraction; that is:

$$\frac{1}{(1+0.06)}\frac{1}{(1+f_{12\times24})} = (1+0.065)^{1/12}\frac{1}{(1+0.065)^2}$$

The forward that we can really lock in to the market is $f_{12\times24} = 6.4423\%$.

When including special repo situations, calculations can get quite complicated, especially when dealing with coupon securities and trying to compute their forward prices, which themselves are packages. However, nowhere in this more complicated analysis should the principle of arbitrage be violated. We need to be careful to include in the mathematics any repo rebates that would have to be given when replicating a forward. The "specialness" of repo cuts both ways: the forward depositor (lender) locks in a lower forward rate; and the borrower does likewise because he uses the hotly desired security as collateral in a repo transaction. The equations above hold for both forward lenders and forward borrowers.

6.10 ENERGY FORWARDS AND FUTURES

In addition to crude oil and gas products and their refined derivatives, like gasoline and heating oil, and with the deregulation of electricity markets in the developed world, the last 5 years have seen the emergence of energy forwards and futures trading for delivery of electric power to specific points on national grids. Forwards and futures contracts on electric power inherit certain features from the somewhat complicated spot markets. In the U.S., these trade on both a firm and a non-firm basis, depending on whether power interruptions are guaranteed by liquidating damages or not. They trade for peak and non-peak periods which divide each 24-hour period into 16 hours of heavy demand and 8 hours of light demand. In Europe, electricity markets trade for base load and peak load periods, the latter being $8:00$–$20:00$ CET. In addition, geography plays a role as national grids have natural gridlock points. For example, in the U.S., power to California is delivered through a limited number of access points, like the California–Nevada or California–Arizona borders. Each market may have its own "convenience yield" issues determined by local deregulation rules concerning power generation and transmission. In some OTC cases, there are also options embedded in the contracts giving the short party choices pertaining to the timing of the energy delivery. This can potentially lead to price manipulation attempts (as claimed in the 2001 Enron scandals in the U.S.). Most exchange contracts are cash-settled. To prevent settlement price disputes, exchanges have special provisions for the final futures settlement price. For example, EUREX contracts are settled based on the spot prices for base and peak loads over the entire delivery month. The NYNEX 40-MW contracts for the Pennsylvania–Maryland–New Jersey hub settle based on the arithmetical average of prices over the peak days during the delivery month. The COB (California–Oregon border) and PV (Palo Verde, Arizona) contracts call for 432 MWh delivered at the rate of 1 MWh per hour during 16 peak hours spread over 27 non-Sunday days. While such tight standardization is desirable for liquidity and price stability, it often means that the futures contracts may not be the best hedge instruments for power generators and transmitters who face specific local conditions. That is, perhaps, why the market is dominated by customized OTC contracts. These are arranged through a small number of players who act almost like exchanges (before its collapse, Enron established itself as such an exchange).

Studies show that futures prices do in fact converge to the spot prices for the delivery points on the grid by the expiry month. That is, at least one part of the cost-of-carry equation is satisfied: the financing cost; this, inclusive of the convenience yield, goes down to zero. But studies also show that hedging with futures does not reduce the volatility of the average price paid, especially if hedgers take basis risk between the actual delivery point and time, and the contract specifications. This is because both spot and futures prices are highly variable at all times. Power suppliers can only reduce this risk by trading off the stability of long-term contracts for higher overall cost, supplemented with some futures hedging.

7
Spot–Forward Arbitrage

he *cash-and-carry* trade is arguably the most important principle linking spot and
rward markets for all securities. Its essence lies in going long a synthetic forward
nd short a real forward, or short a synthetic forward and long a real forward. The
ynthetic side of the trade relies on cash flow replication through a spot position
ombined with borrowing or lending. A synthetic long forward is constructed using a
pot purchase and a spot borrowing transaction. A synthetic short forward is con-
tructed using a spot sale and a spot lending transaction. For example, a forward
urchase of a bond is replicated by borrowing money to buy the bond now and
:paying the borrowing at a future date. A forward sale of a stock is replicated by
:lling the stock now and investing the proceeds at some interest rate. A forward
ommodity purchase is constructed by borrowing the money to buy the commodity
ow and paying for storing it between now and a future date. The synthetic side, which
iimics the forward completely, is traded against the forward; the sides are chosen
ased on the relative costs of the two. The trade is viable until the costs are the same
nd money cannot be made; that is, when the markets adjust to follow the mathe-
iatical cost-of-carry formulae we have laid out: spot and forward foreign exchange
FX) rates fall in line with (borrowing and lending) markets; spot stock indexes
iaskets) and index futures adjust to rates for borrowing and lending against equity
ollateral; coupon bonds, zeros, forward bond sales and purchases, and forward deposit
ites fall in line with spot and repo (repurchase agreement) rates.

The cash-and-carry building blocks can also be combined to perform *forward–
rward* arbitrage where the cost-of-carry is locked in today, but for forward periods.
his can be viewed as two cash-and-carry transactions in opposite directions combined
i one package (with spots canceling out). The forward–forward mechanism strength-
is the arbitrage relationships between various markets as the forward replication is
erformed using not just spots, but also other forwards, and the spot replication can be
erformed by using an entire menu of forwards on the same underlying cash instru-
ient. For example, stock index arbitrage cannot only tie the spot value of the index to
ie index futures price through borrowing/lending markets, but also index futures of
ifferent maturities to each other through forward borrowing/lending transactions,
xecuted in the forward rate agreement (FRA) or Eurocurrency markets.

In this chapter, we use the mathematics of Chapter 6 to identify cash-and-carry
rbitrage in a variety of markets. We start with currencies where the synthetic
rward always combines spot with *both* borrowing and lending. We cover a simpler
ise of stock index arbitrage where the synthetic forward combines spot with *either*
orrowing or lending, and the other part is replaced by dividends. We describe a similar
ise of bond futures arbitrage where dividends are replaced by coupons. We also
rward trades that link zeros and coupons. All four of these trades are benchmark
ises in their own markets. Relative value trades deviate from these pure arbitrage cases

due to imperfect synthetic replication or basis risk on one side of the trade. We devote two short sections to dynamic hedging with a Eurodollar strip and via duration matching. The latter are examples of imperfect replication through continuous rebalancing and as such are relative value strategies. In those cases, a series of risks (e.g., exposure to many points on the yield curve) is reduced to its main components (e.g., only the 2-year and the 10-year point) and hedged as such. This is expedient and involves smaller transaction costs, but requires rebalancing over time and leads to a tracking error. It is the most common method for hedging large fixed income portfolios.

7.1 CURRENCY ARBITRAGE

To review the spot–forward currency arbitrage based on the covered interest rate parity (CIRP) principle, let us use the data for USD and EUR as of August 13, 2003.[1] Here are our quotes.

FX rates [USD/EUR]			FX (CME) futures (settle)	
	Bid/Ask	Mid		
Spot	1.1308/1.1315	1.131 15		
1m (18-Sep)	1.1296/1.1307	1.130 05	Sept (19-Sep)	1.1300
2m (20-Oct)	1.1285/1.1297	1.129 1		
3m (18-Nov)	1.1276/1.1288	1.128 2		
4m (18-Dec)	1.1267/1.1279	1.127 3	Dec (19-Dec)	1.1272
5m (20-Jan)	1.1257/1.1269	1.126 3		
6m (18-Feb)	1.1249/1.1261	1.125 5	Mr04 (19-Mar)	1.1248
9m (18-May)	1.1224/1.1236	1.123 0		
1y (18-Aug)	1.1202/1.1214	1.120 8		
2y (18-Aug)	1.1172/1.1193	1.118 25		

We also have the following **LIBOR** (London interbank offered rate) (ask) rates:

	Dollar (UBS&WSJ)	Euro (UBS)	Euro (WSJ)
1-month	1.100 0%	2.144 76%	2.115 38
2-month	1.120 0%	2.157 43%	
3-month	1.130 0%	2.162 12%	2.132 50
4-month	1.148 75%	2.169 98%	
5-month	1.168 75%	2.182 4%	
6-month	1.180 0%	2.188 73%	2.158 75
12-month	1.36%	2.281 64%	2.250 38

Let us just check a few CIRP equations of the form:

$$F^{N\text{-}month}\left[\frac{USD}{EUR}\right] = S\left[\frac{USD}{EUR}\right] \times \frac{1 + L_{USD}^{N\text{-}month}\dfrac{Act_{0 \times N}}{360}}{1 + L_{EUR}^{N\text{-}month}\dfrac{Act_{0 \times N}}{360}}$$

---

[1] The source is the August 14, 2003 issue of the *Wall Street Journal* and a UBS website: http://quotes.ubs.com/quotes/ Language=E accessed on August 13, 2003.

where $L_{CURR}^{N\text{-}month}$ is an N-month **LIBOR** for currency $CURR$, and $Act_{0\times N}$ is the number of days between month 0 (i.e., today) and the end of month N, which is the maturity of the forward for the implied borrowing/lending transactions. For FX forwards with 3- and 6-month expiries, we get:

$$F^{3m} = 1.131\,15 \frac{1 + 0.011\,300 \times \dfrac{97}{360}}{1 + 0.021\,6212 \times \dfrac{97}{360}} = 1.128\,023$$

$$F^{6m} = 1.131\,15 \frac{1 + 0.011\,800 \times \dfrac{189}{360}}{1 + 0.021\,8873 \times \dfrac{189}{360}} = 1.125\,228$$

Ideally, we would want to write two separate equations for each maturity: one assuming a spot bid for euros, a lending rate for euros (i.e., London interbank bid rate or LIBID, not LIBOR), and a borrowing rate for dollars (i.e., a LIBOR which is ask); and another assuming a spot ask for euros, a borrowing rate for euros (LIBOR) and a lending rate for dollars (LIBID), as these would precisely reflect our synthetic forwards. This would produce bid and ask quotes for the synthesized forwards and would define a no-arbitrage *zone*. For simplicity, we assume that we can trade at mid-rates (averages of bids and asks), whether buying or selling, or borrowing or lending.

The calculated fair value forward rates fall within the actual forward quotes, reflecting no arbitrage. Now suppose that the dealer changes the quotes for 3- and 6-month forwards to mid-rates of:

Spot	1.131 15	(Size: EUR 100,000,000)
3m	1.129 7	(Size: EUR 50,000,000)
6m	1.124 0	(Size: EUR 50,000,000)

Note that for the 3-month quote the fair value of 1.128 023 is well below the actual quote of 1.1297. That means that in the forward market euros are *rich* (expensive relative to synthetic). This sets the direction of our arbitrage: we will want to sell euros forward. To match the flows, we use circular thinking. In order to sell euros 3 months forward, we need to deposit them today to earn interest. In order to deposit them today, we need to buy them spot by selling dollars. In order to sell dollars spot, we need to borrow them. If we borrow dollars today, we will have to repay the principal and interest 3 months from today. By selling euros forward, we will obtain dollars to repay the borrowing. That completes the circle. Now all we have to do is to compute the amounts in such a way that we have net zero cash flows in both currencies 3 months from today and such that we have a positive cash flow in one or both currencies today. Suppose we are a New York dealer and want to earn profit in dollars. We compute the amounts by working backwards from the forward transaction whose size is limited by the quote size of EUR 50,000,000 (we would like that size to be unlimited to make the most money!). Today, we enter into the following contracts:

- Sell EUR 50,000,000 3-month forward at EUR/USD 1.1297 for USD 56,485,000.

- Deposit (lend) EUR 49,710,401.51 at 2.16212% for 3 months, since

$$50,000,000/(1 + 0.021\,621\,2 \times 97/360) = 49,710,401.51$$

- Borrow USD 56,313,540.91 at 1.13% for 3 months, since

$$56,485,000/(1 + 0.0113 \times 97/360) = 56,313,540.91$$

- Sell USD 56,229,920.66 spot at USD/EUR 1.13115 to buy EUR 49,710.401.51 in order to cover the EUR deposit.

In 3 months' time, we have zero net cash flows in both currencies:

- The EUR deposit accrues with interest to EUR 50,000,000 and is withdrawn to deliver to the forward contract.
- The USD 56,485,000 obtained from the forward contract is used to pay off the accrued loan liability of exactly that amount.

Today, we have a zero net cash flow in euros, but a positive cash flow in dollars:

- The EUR 49,710,401.51 purchased spot is deposited for 3 months.
- We borrow USD 56,313,540.91, but sell spot for euros only which gives us USD 56,229,920.66, resulting in a profit of USD 83,620.25.

The flow of the transactions is portrayed in Figure 7.1 (+ is a cash inflow, − is an outflow).

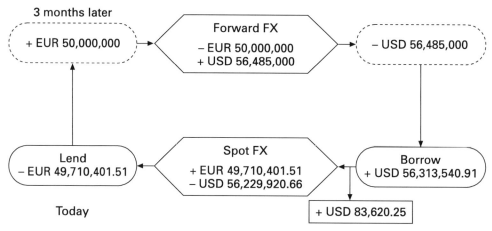

Figure 7.1 Spot–Forward currency arbitrage based on covered interest-rate parity for 3 months.

Note that a dealer based in Europe would have spot-exchanged all of the borrowed USD 56,313,540.91 into EUR 49,784,326.49 and lent out the same EUR 49,710,401.51, resulting in a net profit of EUR 73,924.98. Also note that the fact that we are lending in EUR with a higher interest rate and borrowing in USD with a lower interest rate is coincidental here and in and of itself did not determine the direction of the transactions. It was strictly the comparison of the fair value forward to the actual forward. The next example will make that point clear.

Let us now create profit out of the 6-month quote. The fair value of 1.125 228 is well above the actual quote of 1.1240. That means that in the forward market euros are *cheap* relative to the synthetic strategy. This time we will want to buy euros forward. In order to sell dollars 6 months forward, we need to deposit them today to earn interest. In order to deposit them today, we need to buy them spot by selling euros. In order to sell euros spot, we need to borrow them. If we borrow euros today, we will have to repay the principal and interest 6 months from today. By selling dollars forward, we will obtain euros to repay the borrowing. Again we work backwards from the FX forward to have net zero cash flows in both currencies 6 months from today and to have a positive cash flow in one or both currencies today.

The flow of the transactions for a New York dealer locking in profit in dollars is portrayed in Figure 7.2 (+ is a cash inflow, − is an outflow).

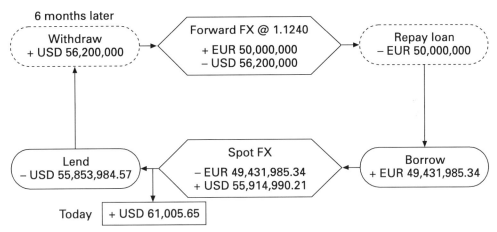

Figure 7.2 Spot–Forward currency arbitrage based on covered interest-rate parity for 6 months.

The borrowing and lending amounts are computed, like in the 3-month example, by taking the present values of the forward amounts at the respective interest rates, i.e.:

$$50{,}000{,}000/(1 + 0.021\,887\,3 \times 189/360) = 49{,}431{,}985.34$$

$$56{,}200{,}000/(1 + 0.011\,800\,0 \times 189/360) = 55{,}853{,}984.57$$

The spot FX transaction results in dollars in excess of the amount needed to deposit, resulting in a profit of USD 61,005.65. (Here a European dealer would have spot-exchanged a smaller amount of euros needed to generate exactly USD 55,853,984.57 required for deposit, leaving himself with a profit in euros.)

Note that in this example the arbitrageur borrows in the high interest rate currency, the euro, and lends in the low interest rate currency, the dollar. Although this may seem counterintuitive, this yield loss is already taken into account in the fair value equations which consider the total cost of synthesizing forward dollars and euros. Based on that, euros turn out to be expensive and dollars cheap. The dealer synthesizes an outflow of euros and an inflow of dollars (i.e., a forward sale of euros for dollars), and offsets these flows with a transaction in the forward market in the opposite direction. In the process of creating the synthetic forward, he borrows in euros and lends dollars, locking in a yield loss. He is more than compensated for that loss by the difference between the actual and the synthetic forward. Going in the other direction would lock in a riskless loss of the same amount.

Note also that both American and European dealers would perform the same trans-actions, selling euros spot and buying them forward, as well as borrowing euros and lending dollars for 6 months. All would exert pressure on the FX and interest rates to move into parity with each other. The very attempt to lock in profit may eliminate its possibility.

Let us now illustrate forward–forward arbitrage with FX rates. Suppose that there are no arbitrage opportunities in the interest rate market. That is, based on our spot LIBOR quotes, 3×6 FRAs are quoted 1.228 976% for U.S. dollars and 2.203 947% for euros. We obtain these numbers by solving for $f_{3\times6}$ in the following fair value equation for interest rates applied to both currencies:

$$\left(1 + L_{3m}\frac{Act_{0\times3}}{360}\right)\left(1 + f_{3\times6}\frac{Act_{3\times6}}{360}\right) = 1 + L^{6m}\frac{Act_{0\times6}}{360}$$

For dollars, we have:

$$f_{3\times6} = \frac{360}{92}\left(\frac{1 + 0.0118 \times \frac{189}{360}}{1 + 0.0113 \times \frac{97}{360}} - 1\right) = 0.012\,289\,76$$

and for euros we have:

$$f_{3\times6} = \frac{360}{92}\left(\frac{1 + 0.021\,587\,5 \times \frac{189}{360}}{1 + 0.021\,325\,0 \times \frac{97}{360}} - 1\right) = 0.022\,039\,47$$

We assume that we can lock in borrowing and lending rates in both currencies at these levels. Suppose also that we get quotes for 3- and 6-month FX forwards:

Spot	1.131 15	(Size: EUR 100,000,000)
3m	1.129 7	(Size: EUR 50,000,000)
6m	1.124 0	(Size: EUR 50,000,000)

We have already computed fair value forwards using the CIRP link to the spot. These were 1.128 023 and 1.125 228. We can also write a 3-month-by-6-month forward CIRP link with $n = 3$ and $N = 6$ in the following way:

$$F_{N\text{-}month}\left[\frac{USD}{EUR}\right] = F_{n\text{-}month}\left[\frac{USD}{EUR}\right] \times \frac{1 + f_{n\times N}^{USD}\frac{Act_{n\times N}}{360}}{1 + f_{n\times N}^{EUR}\frac{Act_{n\times N}}{360}}$$

We can synthesize the 6-month FX forward with a strategy involving a 3-month FX forward and forward borrowing/lending in the two currencies. Relative to the quoted 3-month FX forward, the fair value of the 6-month forward should be:

$$F_{6m} = 1.1297 \times \frac{1 + 0.012\,289\,76\frac{92}{360}}{1 + 0.022\,039\,47\frac{92}{360}} = 1.126\,901$$

(i.e., much higher than the actual 6-month forward of 1.1240). The price of the euro in dollars for the delivery in 6 months synthesized from a 3-month forward and deposit transactions is higher than the actual forward price. To profit, we will buy euros through the actual 6-month forward and sell them forward synthetically. Like before, this sets the circular direction of all transactions.

To buy euros (sell dollars) 6 months forward, we will need to deposit dollars 3 months from today for 3 months. To supply dollars to the deposit, we will buy dollars by selling euros 3 months forward. We will borrow euros forward 3 months from today for 3 months. We will earn interest on the deposited dollars and pay interest on the borrowed euros. We can lock in those rates in today's FRA markets (or further synthesize the forward loan in each currency by two offsetting spot deposit transactions for 3 and 6 months). All the contracts are entered into today, and the profit is locked in 3 months from today.

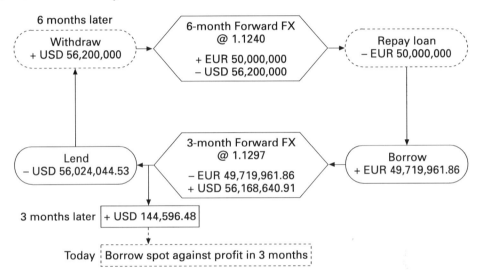

Figure 7.3 Forward–Forward currency arbitrage based on covered interest-rate parity in 3 months for 3 months.

Against the anticipated profit of USD 144,596.48, we can borrow today in the Euro-dollar market the amount $144{,}596.48/(1 + 0.011\,300 \times 97/360) = 144{,}157.56$. This borrowing locks in a profit of USD 144,157.56 today.

In Figure 7.3, we lend dollars forward at 1.228 976% and borrow euros forward at 2.203 947%. In reality, we will lend dollars in 3 months at the then-prevailing 3-month LIBOR rate, but we lock in the net interest rate by contracting today to receive fixed 1.228 976% on a 3×6 dollar FRA. Similarly, we will borrow euros at the then-prevailing LIBOR rate, but we lock in the net interest rate by contracting today to pay fixed 2.203 947% on a 3×6 euro FRA. Each FRA is written for the principal amount computed above as the borrowing/lending amount 3 months from today.

As before, all dealers will enter into the same trades causing the FX and money rates to fall in line. The spot–forward and the forward–forward arbitrage will act in the same direction, further strengthening the CIRP relationships (and eliminating the very arbitrage opportunities).

7.2 STOCK INDEX ARBITRAGE AND PROGRAM TRADING

Stock index arbitrage follows the same cost-of-carry logic as CIRP-based currency arbitrage. The only difference is that the role of foreign currency lending/borrowing is played here by the anticipated stock dividends. To profit from a situation of futures price exceeding its fair value we short actual futures contracts and synthesize a long futures position: we borrow cash by agreeing to pay interest, we buy a basket of stocks to mimic the performance of the index, and we earn dividends on holding the basket to the maturity date. We match the amounts involved in such a way that we have zero net cash flows on the futures expiry date and a positive cash flow today. To profit from a situation of futures price being below its fair value, we reverse the strategy. We buy actual futures contracts and synthesize a short futures position. We short an index-mimicking basket by borrowing the physical assets (i.e., stocks), we invest the proceeds from the short sale at an interest, and we reimburse the lender of the stocks for the cash dividends until the maturity date.

   We will illustrate this using the same July 21, 2003 data as in Chapter 6. Let us recall that with the S&P 500 index equal to 978.80 at the close of the day, the futures settlement prices were:

S&P 500 index (CME)—$250 × index	
Sep03	978.00
Dec03	976.10
Mar04	974.20

and the U.S. dollar LIBOR rates stood at:

1-month	1.100 0%
3-month	1.110 0%
6-month	1.120 0%
12-month	1.211 25%

We consider the September contract with 2 months left to expiry. We use an inter-polated LIBOR rate of 1.105% and 60 as the number of days left to the September 19 expiry date. We also assume that if we were to spend exactly $978.80 to buy the 500 stocks represented in the index in the proportions as defined by the index (admittedly this would mean buying very tiny amounts of each stock, but we will deal with much larger dollar amounts so that everything will scale up to realistic numbers), then, over the holding period between today and September 19, we would accumulate dividends from the constituent stocks in the amount of $D = \$2.50$ as of September 19.[2] We can compute the fair value of the futures to reflect the cash-and-carry strategy as:

$$F = \left(S - \frac{D}{1 + L \times \frac{Act}{360}} \right) \times \left(1 + L \times \frac{Act}{360} \right)$$

---

[2] Almost all stock indices around the world are based purely on stock prices and exclude dividends. Our treatment assumes that this is the case and we treat dividends as "interest" earned on holding stocks. The DAX index is an exception as dividends are assumed to be reinvested and are thus included in the index itself.

and specifically in our case:

$$F = \left(978.80 - \frac{2.50}{1 + 0.011\,05 \times \dfrac{60}{360}}\right) \times \left(1 + 0.011\,05 \times \frac{60}{360}\right) = 978.1026$$

Analogously to investing in a **LIBOR** deposit in a foreign currency, we can think of the $2.50 total dividend as "interest" earned on holding stock. Note that the $2.50 is a precise estimate based on the schedule of dividend payments announced by each company in the index for the period from July 21 to September 19. This number might vary throughout the year as each company would follow its own calendar of ex-dividend dates. These may or may not coincide with the calendar year. Over longer holding horizons, say a few years, we may be less confident about our future dividend estimates. In that case, it is more common to be certain about dividend yields than dollar amounts (dollar amounts are likely to grow over many years as stock prices grow). To illustrate working with dividend yields, we can convert the $2.50 amount to a yield d on a discount instrument with a face value equal to the current price of the share (i.e., $978.80) sold today for the current price of the share, $978.80, minus the present value of the anticipated dividends. Dividend yield d can be defined on any day-count or compounding basis, including continuous. Here we use an *Act/365* basis. The dividend yield d must thus satisfy the following equation:

$$\left(S - \frac{D}{1 + L \times \dfrac{Act}{360}}\right) \times \left(1 + d \times \frac{Act}{365}\right) = S$$

or specifically in our case:

$$\left(978.80 - \frac{2.50}{1 + 0.011\,05 \times \dfrac{60}{360}}\right) \times \left(1 + d \times \frac{60}{365}\right) = 978.80$$

Solving, we get $d = 1.554\,881\%$. By defining the dividend yield in this manner, we can rewrite the fair value equation for stock and stock index futures to look analogous to that based on CIRP for currencies:

$$F = S \frac{1 + L \times \dfrac{Act}{360}}{1 + d \times \dfrac{Act}{365}}$$

Substituting the numbers we get as before:

$$F = 978.80 \frac{1 + 0.011\,050\,00 \times \dfrac{60}{360}}{1 + 0.015\,548\,81 \times \dfrac{60}{365}} = 978.1026$$

The actual September futures price is 978.00. Comparing the fair value to the actual price, we can make the following statement. The S&P 500 basket can be bought for delivery in September for $978.00 by going long September futures; this is cheaper than by synthesizing the purchase with the use of spot equity markets and the money markets for borrowing against stock collateral. In order to profit, we will want to buy stocks forward (i.e., by going long in the futures and sell stock through a synthetic futures contract). To maximize our profit, we would want to buy as many futures contracts as possible at the "unfairly low" price of 978.00 and short as many baskets as possible at the "unfairly rich" synthetic forward price of the basket of 978.1026, based on the spot index value of 978.80. By attempting this strategy, we would most likely drive the futures price up and the spot index basket price down to bring the two in line with the cost-of-carry equation. With shorting 500 stocks we would inevitably encounter thin markets in some of the component stocks so that our realized index value (average actual sale price of the basket) may already be lower than the published index value. This is why the speed of execution and size of orders sent to the floor of the exchange matter so much for spot–futures arbitrageurs.

Let us now determine the amounts of the transactions for one futures contract with a multiplier of $250 per index point. As with currencies, we will work backwards by matching future cash amounts and stock flows first, leaving ourselves with profit today:

- Go long one futures contract to lock in a price of buying 250 stock baskets forward for

$$250 \times 978.00 = \$244,500$$

- We reimburse the lender of the stocks for lost dividends on the forward date

$$250 \times 2.50 = \$625$$

- The total (principal and interest) we need to receive from a deposit on a forward date is thus

$$244,500 + 625 = \$245,125$$

- This means we can lend (invest) today

$$245,125/(1 + 0.011\,05 \times 60/360) = \$244,674.39$$

- We short-sell 250 index baskets at $978.80 each for $244,700.

This leaves us with a zero net cash and stock flow on the forward date (futures expiry):

- We buy the stocks back at the then-current spot price (say $980.35), but we have net variation margin flow (of $980.35 - 978.00 = \$2.35$ per basket); our net cost of acquiring the baskets is exactly the original futures price of $978.00 times the number of baskets, 250, or $244,500. This, together with the dividend reimbursement of $625, is paid for in full by the maturing LIBOR deposit.
- The stocks purchased in the open market are returned to the lender of the stock.

Today, we have a positive cash flow of $25.61, equal to the excess of our proceeds from the short sale over the amount we lend to the LIBOR deposit. Stocks are borrowed and sold (short) in the market leaving us with no net stock flow.

We summarize the amounts in the now-familiar Figure 7.4:

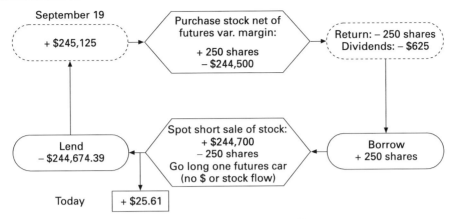

Figure 7.4   Stock index futures arbitrage.

Let us now show an arbitrage strategy for the situation where the fair price is lower than the futures price. Suppose that on July 21, 2003 the September S&P 500 futures settle at 978.30 and we are able to short contracts right at that price. Since the fair value of 978.1026 is lower than the actual of 978.30, we would want to go short futures and long synthetic forwards. We compute the amounts backwards by matching flows:

- Go short one futures contract to lock in a price of buying 250 stock baskets forward for
$$250 \times 978.30 = \$244,575$$

- We will receive dividends on the forward date
$$250 \times 2.50 = \$625$$

- Total (principal and interest) that we can repay on an interest deposit on a forward date is thus
$$244,575 + 625 = \$245,200$$

- This means we can borrow today
$$245,200/(1 + 0.011\,05 \times 60/360) = \$244,749.25$$

- We buy 250 index baskets at $978.80 each for $244,700.

This leaves us with a zero net cash and stock flow on the forward date (futures expiry):

- We sell the stocks held at the then-current spot price (say, $980.35), but we have net variation margin flow of $(-1) \times (980.35 - 978.00) = \$-2.35$ per basket. Our net cost of selling the baskets is exactly the original contracted futures price of $978.00 times the number of baskets, 250, or the total of $244,500. This, together with the received dividends of $625, is used to pay off the maturing **LIBOR** borrowing.

Today, we have a positive cash flow of $49.25, equal to the excess of **LIBOR** borrowing over the purchase price of the stocks. Stocks are purchased and deposited in our account to earn dividends, leaving us with no net stock flow.

Again we summarize the amounts in a diagram (Figure 7.5):

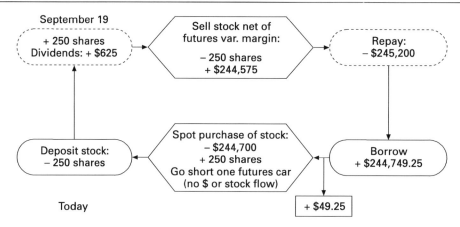

Figure 7.5 Stock index futures arbitrage with dividends.

Note that the above discussion is simpler in the case of individual stock futures, like those on eBay's shares. We do not need to trade a whole basket of stocks, but simply a certain number of shares of the same stock (100 shares of eBay per one futures contract). The borrowing/lending amounts are arrived at analogously to the index case, working backwards from the forward amounts.

Stock index arbitrage is primarily executed with the use of program trading. A dealer continuously computes the fair value of futures, adjusting it for his estimated execution cost. The latter is related to the speed of execution, the depth of the market in each constituent stock, and the dealer's own settlement costs. If the program is slow, the realized price of each basket traded may be different from the one assumed in the fair value calculation. The dealer's estimated profit must exceed all these costs. A dealer may at times resort to mildly speculative tricks of the trade, like sending some orders as market and some as limit, front-running the anticipated moves in the futures price, etc., in order to beat his costs. A dealer may also take on what is called a *tracking*, or *correlation* risk. Instead of sending a program order for all stocks in the index (500 for S&P 500), he may trade in only a subset of the stocks. This can be justified on two grounds. Defensively, as some stocks may have thinner markets (fewer bids and offers) and the price concessions or markups when trying to replicate the index may be large. Offensively, the dealer, based on fundamental research, deletes stocks from the program believing that his imperfect basket will outperform the prescribed one. For example, if a stock is rated "sell", the dealer may want to exclude it from a buy program. Exclusions may also be driven by external factors, like regulation. A broker-dealer engaged in an investment banking transaction (bond or stock issue) with a particular company may be prohibited from transacting in the company's stock (the stock may be placed "on the restricted list" to prevent new issue price manipulation).

Program trades can also be netted. If an SPX transaction calls for spot basket sales, but a Dow futures strategy calls for spot basket purchases, the two can be netted to yield a net basket sale. This may happen especially when the dealer takes on a tracking error risk.

The risks of program trading—stock index arbitrage and customer program execution—are related to external execution risks and deliberate risk taking. External execution risks are always present and are amplified during large market dislocations, like market crashes. When stocks fall rapidly, it is much easier to sell futures than to sell 500 different stocks, some of which may trade on different exchanges. At that moment, the futures price is a more reliable determinant of the spot fair value than vice versa. This is also true for after-hours trading (e.g., right before cash markets open). TV commentators make predictions for the stock market openings based on this reversed fair value calculation, by knowing the current futures price. For example, at 9 : 20 EST in New York, the U.S. stock markets are closed but the futures are not. By computing the fair value of spot, using the reverse cash-and-carry argument, we can make a prediction about the stock market opening 10 minutes later.

Deliberate risk taking by assuming a tracking error is a form of relative value trading, or quasi-arbitrage. This case should be viewed as two separate strategies, futures against the correct basket and the correct basket against the simplified tracking basket. The former should result in sure profit, the latter can be a source of profit or loss. When performing index arbitrage or customer program execution, dealers compete with each other not only on pure execution costs, but also on this extra "skill" of outperforming the market. Bids for customer programs submitted by large dealers often reflect their perceived advantage in a market segment in which the program is concentrated. The dealer may be a large-volume market-maker or possess superior execution technology (high speed of execution and error control).

7.3 BOND FUTURES ARBITRAGE

Bond futures arbitrage is a classic example of a cash-and-carry trade described in professional fixed income textbooks. Yet it is quite a bit more complicated than its currency and stock index counterparts. There are two reasons for this. First, the computation of the forward price of the bond relies on the reinvestment rate for the intermediate coupon accrual or receipt (between now and futures maturity) and, more importantly, the repo rate for the bond. And since the repo market tends to be very short-term (overnight or a few days), the actual repo interest paid/received on lending/ borrowing the bond may not be known in advance unless we can negotiate a term repo to the futures maturity. Second, most bond futures have delivery and timing options embedded in them which afford the short-futures party the right to choose a bond to be delivered from a long list of eligible bonds and the timing of the settlement. These options may result in a mismatch between the bond chosen for the synthetic cash-and-carry strategy and the actual bond delivered to the futures contract, resulting in an unknown profit or loss at expiry.

Let us take a close look at the U.S. long-bond contract traded on the CBT (Chicago Board of Trade). In order to prevent a squeeze on any one bond, the contract specifies that the deliverer of the bonds on the expiry date may choose from a list of eligible bonds of similar maturity (minimum 15 years). The long party receives a bond with a face value of $100,000 and pays an invoice price equal to the final futures settlement price times a *conversion factor*[3] for the bond delivered (plus accrued interest), just as if

---

[3] They are called price factors on LIFFE.

the quantity of the delivered bond were different. The conversion factor is the percentage price of the bond computed at an artificial yield of 6%. (A bond priced at 6% to $109\frac{16}{32}$ has a conversion factor of 1.0950.) This is meant to make all bonds close substitutes of an artificial 6% par bond and of each other (i.e., to have the same value). In reality it does not, making some bonds more likely to be delivered (i.e., cheaper) than others.[4]

The most common, albeit not the best, way to determine which of the eligible bonds is the *cheapest-to-deliver* (CTD) is to compute each bond's basis. The *basis* for a given bond is the difference between the actual price of the bond in the market and the futures price times the conversion factor for that bond:

$$\text{Basis in ticks} = (\text{Bond price} - \text{Futures price} \times \text{Conversion factor}) \times 32$$

The higher the basis, the costlier it is for the short-futures party to purchase the bond in the market and sell it through futures for the settlement price times the factor. A better way to determine the CTD is to find the highest repo rate implied in purchasing a bond and selling futures.[5] The amount of futures sold is equal to the conversion factor for the cash-and-carry bond. The cash-futures trade is equivalent to lending cash/borrowing the bond in the repo market.

Once we have decided on the CTD, the mechanics of the bond–futures arbitrage are analogous to stock futures. Similar to dividends received between the spot date and the futures expiry date, we have to account for the coupon accrual between those two dates. The fair value of the futures can be written as:

$$F_{fair} = \frac{1}{CvFactor} \times \left[B \times \left(1 + r \times \frac{Act}{360} \right) - FV(Accr) \right]$$

where the future value of the bond's spot price B is taken using the repo rate r. We subtract the future value of the accrual, $Accr$, to reflect the portion of the coupon accrued by the bond holder between now and expiry (i.e., the difference between the accrued interest on the expiry date and accrued interest on the spot date). The treatment varies if there is an actual coupon received in the interim period. The conversion factor, $CvFactor$, scales the number of futures contracts in the cost-of-carry relationship.

We will dispense with an actual numerical example here only to state that the cash-and-carry arbitrage can take two forms. If the fair value is lower than the actual futures price, we go *long the basis* (i.e., purchase a deliverable cash bond, financing it in the repo market, and sell a factor-weighted number of futures). If the fair value exceeds the futures price, we go *short the basis*, by shorting the bond, receiving the repo interest, and buying a factor-weighted number of futures contracts. We match the amounts for the expiry date. Without using numbers, we can summarize the long-basis trade in Figure 7.6:

---

[4] For a good discussion of factors and delivery issues, see an older text by Daniel R. Siegel and Diane F. Siegel, *The Futures Markets*, 1990, Probus Publishing, Chicago.
[5] Bloomberg screens can order bonds from the highest to the lowest *implied repo rate* (i.e., from the most likely to be the CTD to the least likely).

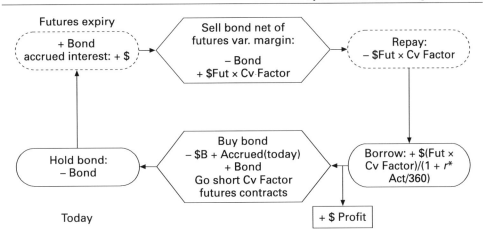

Figure 7.6   Bond futures arbitrage.

7.4. SPOT–FORWARD ARBITRAGE IN FIXED INCOME MARKETS

In Chapter 6, we described the linkages between the zero and coupon instruments of the spot market and the forwards and futures on deposit rates. We covered the synthetic replication of spots from forwards and vice versa as well as the bootstrap of the zero-coupon curve from forwards. In addition, in Chapter 2, we covered the bootstrap of the zero-coupon curve from the spot coupon bonds. If any of the synthetic structures described in these linkages do not result in the same exact financing rates as their actual counterparts, temporary riskless profit opportunities arise.

Zero–Forward trades

Suppose we observe the following set of zero rates and a set of FRA rates (Table 7.1) on a given day, all on a 30/360 basis.

Table 7.1   Spot and forward zero-coupon rates

Zero rates (semi except *)		FRAs (semi)	
3 month*	2.454 47		
6 month	2.500 0		
1 year	2.520 0	6 × 12	2.5400
18 month	2.550 0	12 × 18	2.6100
2 year	2.575 0	18 × 24	2.6030
30 month	2.594 6	24 × 30	2.7200
3 year	2.621 3	30 × 36	2.7550

We use the familiar no-arbitrage condition for all successive zero rates (ignoring the 3-month rate):

$$\left(1+\frac{z_n}{2}\right)^{n/6} = \left(1+\frac{z_{n-6}}{2}\right)^{n/6-1}\left(1+\frac{f_{n-1\times n}}{2}\right)$$

where z_n is a zero rate with a maturity of n months and $f_{n-1\times n}$ is an FRA rate with a start maturity of $n-1$ months and end maturity of n months. For example, for the 18-month zero, we use:

$$\left(1+\frac{z_{18}}{2}\right)^{3} = \left(1+\frac{z_{12}}{2}\right)^{2}\left(1+\frac{f_{12\times18}}{2}\right) = \left(1+\frac{0.0252}{2}\right)^{2}\left(1+\frac{0.0261}{2}\right)$$

resulting in a fair 18-month zero of $z^*_{18} = 2.55\%$. This happens to be equal to the actual 18-month zero of 2.55%. But when we apply the equation one more time to compute the fair 2-year zero, we get $z^*_{24} = 2.5632\%$ instead of the actual 2-year zero of 2.575%. We have discovered an arbitrage opportunity. We cannot claim that the 2-year zero is "unfair" or "too high". We could just as easily claim that the 1-year zero and the 12×18 FRA are "too low", producing a low synthetic rate. We are simply observing that the 2-year zero can be manufactured from other instruments, or synthesized, to yield less than the actual 2-year zero-coupon bond.

In our example, we have only one "misquote", and it happens to be the 2-year zero. This can be verified by checking alternative ways of synthesizing zeros. The 30-month zero rate could be synthesized from the 2-year zero and the 24×30 FRA. It can also be synthesized from a 1-year zero, 12×18, 18×24, and 24×30 FRA, or any other combination of lower maturity zeros and forwards. By performing the calculations for all these combinations, we will discover that the only one that produces a rate not equal to the actual is the one involving the 2-year zero. All the others will yield a fair 30-month zero rate of exactly 2.5946%. The same is true for the 36-month zero rate.

We can structure several distinct arbitrage strategies. All strategies will involve lending at the 2-year rate of 2.575% and synthetic borrowing through a combination of zeros and forwards. One example is to borrow for 3 years at 2.6213% and shorten the borrowing maturity to 2 years, by receiving on the 24×30 FRA at 2.72% and on the 30×36 FRA at 2.755%. The simplest strategy is to:

- Lend for 24 months by buying a 2-year zero yielding 2.575%.
- Borrow for 18 months by selling an 18-month zero yielding 2.55%.
- Extend the borrowing for another 6 months by agreeing to pay 2.603% on an 18×24 FRA.

We match the amounts for future dates, leaving us with a borrowed amount in excess of the lent amount as riskless profit. The limiting factor is the depth of the quotes. Suppose that at most we can buy $100 million face value of the 2-year zero. We compute the rest of the numbers working backwards from $100 million:

- The notional principal on the 18×24 FRA will be $100,000,000/(1+0.026\,03/2) = \$98,715,221.39$.
- That will also be the face value of the 18-month zero for which we will receive

$$98,715,221.39/(1+0.0255/2)^{3} = \$95,033,648.12$$

- The 2-year zero with a $100 million face value, yielding 2.575%, will cost us

$$100,000,000/(1 + 0.025\,75/2)^4 = \$95,011,591.39$$

All cash flows in the future are matched. When the 18-month borrowing of $98,715,221.39 matures we will pay it off by borrowing that amount in the 6-month LIBOR market at the then-prevailing rate. However, by signing the 18 × 24 FRA today (to pay fixed) we are guaranteeing the effective rate on that borrowing (our net cost including the FRA settlement amount) to be 2.603%. We will thus owe exactly $100 million in 2 years. That is exactly the face value of the 2-year zero-coupon we are investing in today. Our riskless profit from the strategy is $22,056.73. The strategy is a disguised cash-and-carry trade where we buy a 2-year bond in the cash market and carry (finance) it by borrowing for 18 months. Against that we sell forward bonds by agreeing to pay fixed. The same strategy executed with Eurodollar (ED) futures on 6-month LIBOR, instead of FRAs, would involve selling 98.715 contracts at 97.397 (i.e., 100.000 − 2.603). We discuss in the next sections how the actual ED futures on 3-month LIBOR are used in locking rates.

Coupon–Forward trades

To the extent that coupon bonds are packages of zero-coupon bonds and we have just shown that zero-coupon bonds are packages of forwards, we can construct a two-layer strategy involving coupon bonds traded against forwards. The arbitrage can arise when coupons are mispriced relative to zeros, but we prefer to use forwards or futures, or when coupons are mispriced relative to forwards. We discover the latter when we observe par coupon rates, construct the discount curve, and discover that the latter does not agree with the forwards and futures. Let us look at this case more closely.

Suppose that we obtain the following quotes (Table 7.2), all semi-annual on a *30/360* basis:

Table 7.2 Spot coupon and forward zero rates

Coupon rates (semi)		FRAs (semi)	
6 month	2.5000		
1 year	2.5199	6 × 12	2.5400
18 month	2.5495	12 × 18	2.6100
2 year	2.5628	18 × 24	2.6030

Using the par coupon rates, we bootstrap the semi-annual zero-coupon (discount curve) as described in Chapter 2. That is, the subsequent zero rates are backed out using the following no-arbitrage equation:

$$\frac{c_n/2}{(1 + z_6/2)} + \frac{c_n/2}{(1 + z_{12}/2)^2} + \cdots + \frac{c_n/2}{(1 + z_n/2)^{n/6}} + \frac{100}{(1 + z_n/2)^{n/6}} = 100$$

with the first zero with a 6-month maturity being automatically equal to the first par rate (i.e., $Z_6 = 2.50\%$ ($\Leftarrow c_6 = 2.50$)). For example, the 12-month zero is obtained from:

$$\frac{c_n/2}{(1+z_6/2)}+\frac{c_n/2}{(1+z_{12}/2)^2}+\frac{100}{(1+z_{12}/2)^2}=\frac{2.5199/2}{(1+0.0250/2)}+\frac{2.5199/2}{(1+z_{12}/2)^2}+\frac{100}{(1+z_{12}/2)^2}=100$$

and so on. By following this procedure, we come up with the following (Table 7.3) set of zeroes (FRAs repeated for completeness):

Table 7.3   Synthetic spot zeros and actual forward zeros

Zero rates (semi)		FRAs (semi)	
6 month	2.5000		
1 year	2.5200	6×12	2.5400
18 month	2.5500	12×18	2.6100
2 year	2.5750	18×24	2.6030

As this happens to be the same as in the previous section, we can conclude that the 2-year zero synthesized from coupon rates is too high relative to the 2-year zero synthesized from forwards. Our strategy will involve lending at the high 2.575% rate for 2 years against borrowing at the 2.5632% rate for 2 years. Let us again assume $100 million as the principal of the synthetic 2-year zero. The first part of the strategy remains the same. We:

- Borrow for 18 months by selling $98,715,221.39 face value of an 18-month zero yielding 2.55% for $95,033,648.12.
- And extend the borrowing for another six months by agreeing to pay 2.603% on $98,715,221.39 of an 18×24 FRA.

This ensures that we will owe exactly $100 million in 2 years' time. Against that, we have to lend synthetically $95,011,591.39 on a zero basis for 2 years in the coupon market. We:

- Buy $100 million face value of the 2-year 2.5628% par coupon bond and strip the coupons.
- Sell $2.5628/2 = $1.2814 face value of a 6-month zero (synthetic or real) yielding 2.50%.
- Sell $2.5628/2 = $1.2814 face value of a 12-month zero (synthetic or real) yielding 2.52%.
- Sell $2.5628/2 = $1.2814 face value of a 18-month zero (synthetic or real) yielding 2.55%.
- And sell $2.5628/2 = $1.2814 face value of a 24-month zero (synthetic or real) yielding 2.575%.

Each sold zero, if synthetic, would involve additional trades in shorter maturity coupons.

Exercise   Assume that the sold zeros are synthesized from coupons. Refer to Chapter 2 to compute face amounts and the cost today. Verify that the total cost, netted against the purchase of the $100 million 2-year coupon bond, is $95,011,591.39.

7.5 DYNAMIC HEDGING WITH A EURO STRIP

The arbitrage strategies described in the last two sections when applied to longer maturities can easily involve a large number of securities. A dealer executing many trades back and forth a day might have to enter into hundreds of largely offsetting synthetic hedges. This can be cumbersome and result in significant transaction costs. In this and the next section, we describe two methods of reducing the dimensionality of the hedge problem. We pretend that all securities, no matter what their maturities or coupon structures, can be perfectly represented as sets of sensitivities to a few common building blocks. The idea is analogous to our chessboard of contingent claims of Chapter 1. All securities are viewed as subsets of the entire board, with some squares overlapping and some not. Furthermore, the board consists of perhaps only as few as 20 squares. Because of this oversimplification, the replication is not going to be perfect. The hedge will deteriorate over time and will have to be continuously rebalanced. But it will be extremely simple. In this section, the set of canonical hedges is defined as the set of all ED futures contracts. In the following section, it is a set of a few selected benchmark bonds. These dynamic hedging techniques are used widely by swap, corporate bond, mortgage bond, and all option traders. The only thing different in each case is the set of building blocks.

Let us consider the common way of dealing with short-term swaps. The technique is called *blipping the curve* (i.e., blipping the ED futures inputs). This starting point is the zero-coupon (discount) curve, obtained by bootstrapping the ED futures. ED futures are assumed to be the most basic building blocks for all complex instruments; we can synthesize all other instruments from ED futures. If a resultant synthesized instrument yields a rate different from the actual one, then that rate can be viewed as "wrong" and arbitrage exists. However, instead of computing the exact amount of each ED contract needed for the synthetic side of the trade at the outset, the last step involves the computation of the sensitivities (durations) of the instrument to a small change in each ED futures rate, taken one at a time. Each time the ED rate is perturbed, or blipped, the zero curve is rebootstrapped and the value of the synthetic is recomputed. The present value changes relative to the base case (i.e., the sensitivities determine the amount of futures to be entered into as hedges).

Suppose we have an opportunity similar to the one described previously, except we only observe the following (Table 7.4):

Table 7.4 Spot zero rates and ED futures prices

Zero rates (semi except *)		ED futures	
3 month*	2.454 47	3 month	97.47
6 month	2.500 0	6 month	97.47
1 year	2.520 0	9 month	97.47+
18 month	2.550 0	12 month	97.40
2 year	2.5750	15-month	97.40
30 month	2.594 6	18-month	97.41
3 year	2.621 3	21 month	97.40

where 97.47+ means 97.475. ED futures allow us to lock in borrowing and lending rates equal to 100 minus the ED price, quarterly compounded, for 3-month forward periods starting on the futures expiry dates. By using the first zero rate with the maturity of 3 months and the futures rates starting with the 3-month futures rate (which locks in the rate of $100 - 97.47 = 2.53\%$ for the 3×6 period) and using all the subsequent futures rates, we can compute, using the familiar recursive formula from Section 6.7; with $n = 3, 6, \ldots, 24$:

$$\left(1 + \frac{z_n}{4}\right)^{n/3} = \left(1 + \frac{z_{n-3}}{4}\right)^{\frac{n}{3} - 1}\left(1 + \frac{f_{n-3\times n}}{4}\right)$$

the following set (Table 7.5) of quarterly compounded synthetic zero rates and their semi-annual equivalent rates:

Table 7.5 Actual and synthetic zero rates

Zero rates	Actual semi	Synthetic semi	Synthetic quarterly
3 month			2.454 47
6 month	2.5000	2.5000	2.492 2
9 month			2.504 8
12 month	2.5200	2.5177	2.509 9
15 month			2.527 9
18 month	2.5500	2.5480	2.539 9
21 month			2.547 1
24 month	2.5750	5.5618	2.553 7

We added the actual semi-annual zero rates in the first column. The biggest discrepancy between the actuals and the synthetics is in the 24-month maturity.

Let us attempt the usual static arbitrage first. To profit, we borrow for 2 years in the synthetic market (by borrowing for 3 months and locking in the rates for the rollover borrowings in the futures market) at 2.5618% and lend in the actual zero market (by buying a 2-year zero) at 2.575%. We borrow more than we lend for the same face value (today's discounted value of $1 to be received 2 years from today would be higher using the lower synthetic rate than that using the higher actual rate) locking in a sure profit. On the face value of $100 million that profit would be:

$$100,000,000/(1 + 0.025\,618/2)^4 - 100,000,000/(1 + 0.025\,750/2)^4 = \$24,707.60$$

As before, we work backwards from the $100,000,000 at 2 years to compute the principal, or equivalently the number of contracts, for each ED futures by discounting sequentially at the implied forward rate. The results are summarized in Table 7.6:

Table 7.6 Face amounts for forward borrowing

Period	Borrow at start time	Face at end time	No. of cars
0×3	95,036,299	95,619,458	
3×6	95,619,458	96,224,251	95.62
6×9	96,224,251	96,832,870	96.22
9×12	96,832,870	97,444,127	96.83
12×15	97,444,127	98,077,514	97.44
15×18	98,077,514	98,715,018	98.08
18×21	98,715,018	99,354,198	98.72
21×24	99,354,198	100,000,000	99.35

We reborrow the amounts shown in the first column at the start of each period to pay off the loan maturing from the immediately preceding period at the then-prevailing 3-month rate, but we have locked in the net borrowing cost equal to that implied by today's futures prices by shorting futures today. Against this synthetic borrowing strategy, we buy a 2-year zero yielding 2.575% with a face value of $100,000,000 for $95,011,591.39.

Let us now illustrate dynamic arbitrage with the same replicating instruments. The essence of the curve-blipping method is that instead of statically locking in the profit today, we commit to a dynamic strategy over the life of the trade. The dynamic strategy means selling a strip of futures today and rehedging (buying back some or selling more) every day between now and the maturity of the trade (2 years). Dynamic rehedging will generate profits and losses over time. The present value (PV) of the difference between the spot trade in the actual security and the sum of all the profits/losses over time is equal to the computed lockable profit. We book a paper profit today, but we realize it over time.

Let us take a 2-year zero trade and compute the sensitivity of the value of the 2-year zero to a 1 basis point (bp) change in the 12-month ED price (= rate). Before the blip the ED rate is 97.40. We assume that the synthetic zero rates are fair. The fair value of $100 million to be received at 2 years is thus $95,036,298.99. Now let us perturb the 12-month ED price to be 97.39 and recompute the set of synthetic zero rates. These become (Table 7.7):

Table 7.7 Synthetic zero rates with a 1 bp blip to the 12-month ED price

Zero rates	Actual semi	Synthetic semi	Synthetic quarterly
3 month			2.4545
6 month	2.5000	2.5000	2.4922
9 month			2.5048
12 month	2.5200	2.5177	2.5099
15 month			2.5299
18 month	2.5500	2.5496	2.5416
21 month			2.5485
24 month	2.5750	2.5631	2.5549

The fair value of $100 million to be received at 2 years changes to $95,033,938.48. The dollar sensitivity of the 2-year zero price to the 1 bp blip is $2,360.51. Given that each futures contract has a sensitivity of $25 per 1 bp, if we short $2,360.51/25 = 94.42$ contracts today we will have immunized the value of our 2-year zero to a 1-bp change in the 12×15 forward rate.

We perform the same sequence of calculations for each futures contract, one at a time, arriving at a set of futures contract amounts to be shorted. That is, for each contract, we blip the futures price by -0.01, we reconstruct the zero curve, we revalue the 2-year zero with the face value of $100,000,000, take the difference between its new blipped value and the original value of $95,036,298.99, and divide the resultant dollar sensitivity by $25 to get the number of futures to be traded. The final result is given in Table 7.8:

Table 7.8   Hedge of a 2-year zero with an ED futures strip

Futures blipped	Recalculated PV of 2-year zero	Sensitivity	No. of cars
3m	95,033,938	2,361	94.44
6m	95,033,938	2,361	94.44
9m	95,033,938	2,361	94.44
12m	95,033,938	2,361	94.42
15m	95,033,938	2,361	94.42
18m	95,033,938	2,361	94.42
21m	95,033,938	2,361	94.42

Just like in the static lock-in arbitrage strategy, at the outset we would short an entire strip of ED futures with the amounts shown and sell a 3-month zero (to buy the 2-year zero). But we would also commit to perform the same blipping procedure every time futures prices change (for simplicity assume every day) for the next 2 years. Each time we would compute a new set of contract numbers, compare it with the previous set, and make adjustments to our positions by trading contracts that need rebalancing. The logic is that we are buying the actual 2-year zero unfairly cheaply to yield 2.575%, and dynamic trading will result in cumulating the profit from converging to the fair value. The convergence is guaranteed by maturity when the 2-year's price will be 100.

With the simple cash-and-carry trade like ours, the dynamic hedge will not be very dynamic. We start by shorting futures in the amounts very close to those computed in the static lock-in. The subsequent adjustments are most likely going to be negligible and our daily profits/losses close to 0. In essence, we are immunizing against fair movements in the value of the actual 2-year (due to interest rate changes), incurring no profits or losses, and waiting for the 2-year to adjust its value in the market up to the fair level. Once that happens, our long position will gain in value more than the dynamic hedge will lose. We can then lift the hedge, sell the zero, and walk away with the profit. (Of course, it can be that the 2-year will not adjust, but the hedge will adjust down, resulting in profit coming from the short side.) Sometimes we have to wait for the full adjustment all the way to maturity.

The blipping method explained here would rarely be used with a one-off, statically lockable cash-and-carry arbitrage. However, for large swap or bond portfolios, with non-coinciding maturity and coupon dates, complex coupon formulae, and mismatched day-count conventions and coupon frequencies, it is a convenient way of reducing the number of hedge instruments to a bare minimum and to ensure that intermediate points on the yield curve are hedged. As the blipping and hedging is performed with a small set of instruments, the replication requires adjustment over time.

The computation of ED sensitivities is also a way of characterizing disparate portfolios in the same terms. Different portfolios, reduced to the same set of sensitivities, can be compared as to their exposure to different points on the yield curve. This is a more detailed characterization than that obtained by portfolio duration calculations (here we have price values of basis points, or PVBPs, to all quarterly points of the yield curve).

The discussion in Chapter 9 will make it clear that the blipping method is a version of the dynamic delta-hedge used by option dealers applied to simpler non-contingent securities.

7.6   DYNAMIC DURATION HEDGE

A dynamic duration hedge is a simplified version of the strip hedge, relying on the same principle. We illustrate it by considering a rather obvious example. We get quotes on par coupon bond yields from a dealer:

5-year	3.00%
7-year	5.00%
10-year	3.00%

Clearly the 7-year seems to be an obvious candidate for purchasing and the 5-year and 10-year for shorting. To profit, first we compute the durations of the bonds. Let us assume that they are the following:

5-year	4.3
7-year	6.1
10-year	8.5

To be precise we would want to compute the duration of the 7-year in terms of its sensitivity to the 5-year and the 5×10 forward and then reconstitute it in terms of the duration with respect to the 5-year and the 10-year. Let us ignore non-parallel curve movements.

We buy $100 million of the 7-year. This position will change in value by 6.1 bp per 1 bp change in yields in the opposite direction. Based on the computed durations we short $90.5 million of the 5-year and $26 million of the 10-year resulting in zero net sensitivity to yield changes (Table 7.9):

Table 7.9 Duration hedge of a 7-year bond with 5- and 10-year bonds

Bond	Duration	Face	Sensitivity
5-year	4.3	−90.5	−3.89
7-year	6.1	100	6.10
10-year	8.5	−26	−2.21

The next day, as yields change, we recompute the durations and the face amounts so that we are left with no exposure to yield changes. Every day we realize a net profit or loss on the portfolio which is close to 0 since the portfolio is immunized against yield curve movements. We are buying time waiting for a big adjustment in yields. This can be by the 7-year moving down to yield 3%, realizing a big net gain in our long position, or the 5- and/or 10-years moving up to yield closer to 5%, realizing a big net gain in our short positions. If the movement is not big but gradual, we keep holding the position, rebalancing continuously. Over time we accumulate a profit.

8

Swap Markets

A swap is an agreement to exchange two streams of cash flows: one paid and one received. These streams can be customized to suit the parties involved. Usually, they are designed to resemble coupon interest streams on bonds. As such, the swap is a synthetic exchange of two non-identical securities. The value of the swap is equal to the difference in the values of the two securities. A swap can also be dissected one cash flow exchange at a time and defined as a set of interest rate or currency forwards packaged together to create bond-like coupon exchanges (*swaplets*). From this perspective, forwards (future cash flow exchanges) are the building blocks for swaps, and the value of the swap is equal to the sum of the present values of all the exchanges. The valuation of swaps can be made simple or difficult depending on how cleverly we exploit this dual nature of swaps.

To make things easy, we do not immediately jump to definitions, but instead start this chapter with common applications of swaps in corporate finance decisions. We turn to flow diagrams to abstract from the details of cash flow computation. We begin with the starkest example of a currency swap, where the two cash flow streams are in two different currencies. We define a plain vanilla interest swap, the most common type of swap, where the two streams are in the same currency, but one is based on a fixed rate and the other on a floating rate. Then we discuss the pricing and hedging of swaps. The pricing involves computing the present values of both sides of the swap. The hedging is done by blipping the underlying discount curves and computing the sensitivities and hedge ratios with respect to a set of predefined hedge instruments. Once we understand the pricing basics, we look at more complicated applications of swaps, where they are combined with each other to form complex bonds or they combine asset classes as in equity swaps (synthetic exchanges of bonds for stock baskets). We end with swap market statistics. These show the enormous growth of swap markets in the last 20 years. By some measures, swaps now represent the largest segment of all financial markets.

8.1 SWAP-DRIVEN FINANCE

A corporation that has decided to raise new debt finance faces many choices. It can go to the bank to get a credit line or a revolving loan. The bank (or a syndicate of banks) will set the maximum amount the corporation can borrow and the final maturity of its commitment. Every month or quarter, the corporation will be able to draw the amount of funds equal to the limit amount or less. If it chooses to draw the funds, it will agree to pay an interest rate tied to the short-term borrowing rate, like *Prime* in the U.S.

domestic credit market or *LIBOR* in the Eurocurrency market, plus a spread reflecting the corporation's credit rating. The corporation will also pay a small fee per month or quarter for the unused amount of funds, simply for the fact that the bank stands ready to provide the funds on demand (*commitment fee*). From the bank's perspective, this arrangement will entail that, any time the corporation draws the loan, the bank will turn to money markets to borrow short term to fund it. If the corporation reduces the level of funds used, the bank will repay the borrowed funds. If the corporation keeps borrowing, the bank will roll over its obligations and borrow new funds. The interest rate that the corporation is charged and the bank incurs in the money market floats month to month or quarter to quarter, depending on rollover rates.

Instead of going to the bank, the corporation may decide to issue bonds directly in the credit markets with the help of an investment banker. Here the corporation faces a few choices. It can issue a fixed coupon bond or a floating coupon bond in the domestic market. It can issue a fixed or a floating coupon bond in a foreign market. It can issue a bond with a complicated, formula-driven coupon structure or zero-coupon, formula-driven, principal structure. Apart from the corporation's exact timing and cash flow-matching needs, the structure of the debt will depend on the relative cost of the alternatives.

Suppose a French company, in desperate need of new money, has borrowed heavily in France in the past and French investors are not demanding new bonds; but American investors are demanding new bonds and are willing to accept an interest rate 10 bp lower than on comparable credits, simply to be able to diversify their risks. Suppose the Americans want a floating coupon bond because they perceive their interest rates low by historical standards and want to be able to benefit from potential rises in interest rates. Ideally, the company would like to borrow fixed in France as most of its cash flows are relatively constant and most of its customers pay in euros. Can the company benefit from the American appetite, but have its liabilities tailored to its needs?

Enter the swap market. The company can sell U.S. dollar-denominated floating coupon bonds in the U.S. and enter into a floating dollar–fixed euro currency swap with a global bank, matching the dates of swap cash flows to the bond coupon dates.

More often than not, the process will work in reverse. Large corporations are on a continuous hunt to discover cheap sources of finance, whether they need it or not. The relative cheapness depends on swap rates offered to convert the available source (floating dollar) into a desirable one (fixed euro). The attractiveness of the swap rates may make the new issuance desirable, potentially to retire previously issued debt at a higher cost. This is referred to as swap-driven finance.

Fixed-for-fixed currency swap

A U.K.-based company wants to issue new debt with a maturity of 5 years to finance an expansion of its American operations. The company is relatively unknown in the U.S. and there is not much demand currently for its debt in the U.S. markets. The company is expecting that the funds to repay the new debt issue would come from its North American operations.

Suppose the current exchange rate is $1.50/£ and the company's credit rating is AA (i.e., the same as that reflected in swap rates). The company needs to raise $150 million now. We observe the following zero-coupon interest rates in the U.S. and U.K. (rates are usually quoted annual in the U.K. and semi-annual in the U.S., we show both equivalents):

Table 8.1 Zero rates in the U.K. and U.S.

Term	Zero rates		Zero rates	
	U.K. semi	U.S. semi	U.K. annual	U.S. annual
6m	3.000 000	2.200 000	3.022 500	2.212 100
1y	3.200 000	2.450 000	3.225 600	2.465 006
18m	3.400 000	2.700 000	3.428 900	2.718 225
2y	3.600 000	2.950 000	3.632 400	2.971 756
30m	3.800 000	3.200 000	3.836 100	3.225 600
3y	4.000 000	3.450 000	4.040 000	3.479 756
42m	4.200 000	3.700 000	4.244 100	3.734 225
4y	4.400 000	3.950 000	4.448 400	3.989 006
54m	4.600 000	4.200 000	4.652 900	4.244 100
5y	4.800 000	4.450 000	4.857 600	4.499 506

By the arbitrage arguments of Chapter 2 imply that if the company were to issue 5-year coupon bonds and wanted to sell them at par, it would have to offer the following coupon rates:

Table 8.2 Five-year bond coupon rates

	U.K.	U.S.
Semi	4.722 118	4.359 746
Annual	4.780 222	4.409 975

Suppose that investors do not demand U.S. dollar bonds from the company. If the company were to issue them, they would demand rates higher than 4.359 746% semi. The company can obtain dollar financing at that rate by issuing U.K. bonds and swapping their cash flows into dollars. The company issues £100 million face value of 4.780 222% annual coupon bonds (or 4.722 118% semi). For the 5-year 4.780 222% bond, it receives from investors £100 million; the bonds sell at par. This obligates the company to the following set of coupon payments:

Table 8.3 GBP payments

1y	4.780 222
2y	4.780 222
3y	4.780 222
4y	4.780 222
5y	104.780 222

The company exchanges the £100 million received from the sale of the bonds into $150 million at today's exchange rate of $1.50/£. At the same time, the company enters into a swap agreement with a financial institution to exchange a stream of GBP-denominated cash flows for a stream of USD-denominated cash flows. Specifically, it agrees to the following schedule of cash flows:

Table 8.4   Five-year fixed $-fixed £ swap

	Receive in GBP	Pay in USD
1y	4.780 222	6.614 962
2y	4.780 222	6.614 962
3y	4.780 222	6.614 962
4y	4.780 222	6.614 962
5y	104.780 222	156.614 962

The swap receipts are identical to the coupon and principal payments owed on the bonds and will offset with each other, leaving the company with zero net GBP cash flows. The USD payments are equivalent to 4.409 975% coupon and principal payments on a $150-million face value bond.

The dealer will not charge anything (or pay anything) to enter into this swap with the company because the present value of the USD stream is equal to $150 million (based on the fair par coupon rate in USD) and the present value of the GBP stream is equal to £100 million (based on the fair par coupon rate in GBP), as each is the present value of a par coupon bond and the two present values are equal to each other based on today's exchange rate of $1.50/£.

With the bond and the swap in place, the company's net obligations are identical to those of a USD $150-million, 5-year, 4.409 975% annual coupon bond. The net of the transactions is summarized in the following diagram.

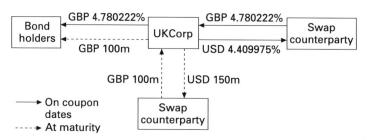

Figure 8.1   Summary of the net of transactions.

The receipts from the swap counterparty are passes to the bond investors. What is left is the dollar obligation in the form of a dollar coupon stream and principal payment at the end.

Note that the scheduled swap cash flows for year 5 consist on both sides of the swap of the regular coupon interest and the principal repayment. The company's coupon cash flow is £4.780 22 million on the receive side and $6.614 962 (4.409 975% on $150 million) on the pay side. The principal exchange is £100 million on the receive side for $150 million on the pay side. In currency swaps, the principal exchange at the end of the swap is standard, unless specifically deleted in the swap agreement. In interest rate swaps, the principal exchange never takes place as it is in the same currency and is an exact zero-flow offset.

Technically, even though swaps can be easily customized to customers' needs, they follow certain conventions. In our example, if the company wanted to replicate a dollar bond exactly which would have had semi-annual coupons, as is common with U.S. corporate bonds, it would have most likely issued a GBP bond and swapped it into a GBP–USD, fixed–fixed swap with annual GBP receipts and semi-annual USD payments. For the swap to have been par (i.e., be entered into with no compensating payment by either counterparty), the swap's USD rate would have to be set at 4.359 746% semi-annual, instead of 4.409 975% annual. Thus the company would have ended up with annual GBP cash flows on the receive side, which it would have passed on to its bondholders, and semi-annual USD cash flows on the pay side, its net liability. The cash flows would have been as follows (Table 8.5).

Table 8.5   Five-year fixed $–fixed £ swap

	Receive in GBP	Pay in USD
6m		3.269 809
1y	4.780 222	3.269 809
18m		3.269 809
2y	4.780 222	3.269 809
30m		3.269 809
3y	4.780 222	3.269 809
42m		3.269 809
4y	4.780 222	3.269 809
54m		3.269 809
5y	104.780 222	153.269 809

For many counterparties, currency swaps are a way of speculating on currency rates and interest rate differentials. By swapping into dollars, the company may be gambling that the dollar is going to weaken so that the GBP value of its USD liabilities is going to decrease. It may also be fearing that the interest rate differential between the rates in the U.K. and in the U.S. may decrease without an offsetting currency move, so the company wants to lock it in today.

Fixed-for-floating interest-rate swap

Let us alter the above example to present a rationale for interest-rate swaps: different cost of capital in floating and fixed rate markets in the same currency. Our U.K. company now wants to issue new fixed rate debt with a maturity of 5 years to finance an expansion of its U.K. operations into a government contract business. The funds to repay the new debt issue would come from these new operations. The company knows the schedule of government payments it is to receive. The company has previously used bank loans and floating rate debt to match its liabilities to the general state of the economy. Investors are comfortable evaluating the company's floating rate debt. The company reckons that if it were to issue fixed rate debt it would have to pay a premium in the form of a coupon rate above that for corporations with a similar credit rating. The solution is to issue a floating rate bond and swap it into a fixed rate liability.

The company issues a 5-year, £100 million bond whose annually adjusted interest rate is equal to 12-month LIBOR (London interbank offered rate). Recall from prior chapters that such a floating rate bond prices to par as long as each coupon rate is set at the beginning of the interest accrual period and each interest payment is made at the end of the accrual period. This is because the bond is equivalent to an annually revolving loan where the loan is regranted every year at the then-prevailing 1-year rate. The company thus receives £100 million (par or face value) for the bond.

The company also enters into a £100-million, notional principal, fixed-for-floating interest rate swap whereby it agrees to receive an annual floating coupon stream equal to LIBOR and pay an annual 4.780 222% fixed rate coupon stream. The flows are summarized in Figure 8.2.

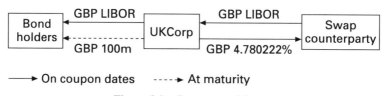

Figure 8.2   Summary of flows.

The company's LIBOR coupon flows, to the bond holders and from the swap counterparty, are unknown in advance. But they will offset each other exactly. The fixed payments on the swap and the face value repayment to the bondholders leave the company with a net liability equivalent to a fixed rate bond.

Viewing the swap as an exchange of two bonds, all the floating rate coupon receipts on the swap plus £100 million received once in year 5 represent an asset priced to par today. The 4.780 222% fixed coupon payments on the swap and the £100 million paid once to the counterparty in year 5 represent a liability priced to par today. No payment to or receipt from the dealer is needed today to compensate for the difference in the present values. The one-time £100-million flows cancel each other and are not made. The remaining flows, floating on the receive side and fixed on the pay side, constitute the swap.

Fixed and floating rate cash flows do not have to have the same periodicity. Often their structure is determined by market convention. So is the day-count used to compute the exact flows. In our example, it is more likely that the floating rate bond and the floating interest receipts on the swap would be quarterly, while the fixed coupon on the swap would be semi-annual or annual for GBP-denominated bonds and swaps. In the U.S., the fixed coupon would typically be semi-annual while the floating coupon would be set and paid quarterly. In the U.S., the fixed coupon would use a *30/360* day-count while the floating LIBOR side would use *Act/360*. The quoted semi-annual swap rate would reflect these conventions. Swaps following a market convention for a given currency's interest rates are labeled *plain vanilla*.

For many counterparties, interest rate swaps are a way of speculating on interest rates. By swapping into fixed, the company may be gambling that the 5-year rates are going to rise, so it wants to lock the rate in today. (We could also view a decision not to swap as a gamble on the rates going down.)

Off-market swaps

Both prior examples assumed no exchange of any compensatory cash flow upfront. That was due to the fact that the bond issue and the swap occurred at the same time and the rates on the swap were set to equal current market rates. This need not be the case. Bond issuers can choose to come to the swap market at any time to alter the structure of their liabilities back and forth between fixed and floating and one currency vs. another. This may be because of their internal cash flow needs or because they want to speculate on the direction of currency and interest rates.

Suppose our U.K. company with American operations issued a 5-year, £100-million, 4.780 222% fixed rate GBP bond a year ago. At that time, the company converted the £100 million proceeds into $150 million to invest in the project, but as it anticipated the widening of the interest rate differential between the U.K. and U.S. it left the bond issue unswapped. Suppose today the foreign exchange (FX) rate is still $1.5/£, but interest rates in the U.K. have risen by 50 basis points (bp) while interest rates in the U.S. stayed the same, as in Table 8.6.

Table 8.6 New zero rates in the U.K. and U.S.

Term	Zero rates		Zero rates	
	U.K. semi	U.S. semi	U.K. annual	U.S. annual
6m	3.500 000	2.200 000	3.530 625	2.212 100
1y	3.700 000	2.450 000	3.734 225	2.465 006
18m	3.900 000	2.700 000	3.938 025	2.718 225
2y	4.100 000	2.950 000	4.142 025	2.971 756
30m	4.300 000	3.200 000	4.346 225	3.225 600
3y	4.500 000	3.450 000	4.550 625	3.479 756
42m	4.700 000	3.700 000	4.755 225	3.734 225
4y	4.900 000	3.950 000	4.960 025	3.989 006
54m	5.100 000	4.200 000	5.165 025	4.244 100
5y	5.300 000	4.450 000	5.370 225	4.499 506

These rates imply that the 4-year par swap rates in the U.K. and the U.S. are:

Table 8.7 Four-year bond coupon rates

	U.K.	U.S.
Semi	4.849 306	3.898 814
Annual	4.910 531	3.939 253

The company enters into a 4-year GBP–USD fixed–fixed swap. The principal is £100 million on the receive side and $150 million on the pay side. The coupon on the receive side is not the current on-market 4.910 531% rate. Rather, the company asks the counterparty to match the bond coupon rate of 4.780 222% which is now *off-market* (i.e., unfair). As it is willing to accept a rate that is lower than the fair market rate, the company will have two choices (the dealer should be indifferent as to which one it chooses). One will be to pay the current on-market USD rate on the pay side of the swap, but receive a one-time payment from the dealer to compensate the company for the present value differential. The other choice is to receive no payment today, but to pay a lower USD rate on the pay side of the swap. Let us examine each choice.

Receive an upfront payment for an off-market swap with a positive PV

The payment will be equal to the present value of the difference between the 4-year par swap rate and the off-market 4.780 222% rate. Using the above zero rates:

Table 8.8   Present value of coupon differences (on- vs. off-market)

	Payment difference	Present value
1y	0.130 309	0.125 618
2y	0.130 309	0.120 150
3y	0.130 309	0.114 024
4y	0.130 309	0.107 369
Sum of present values		*0.467 161*

this turns out to be £467,161. This number is also equivalent to £100 million, which is the value of a 4-year 4.910 531% par coupon bond, minus £99.532 839, which is the value of a 4-year 4.780 222% coupon bond:

Table 8.9   Present value of the off-market bond's cash flows

	Payments	Present value
1y	4.780 222	4.608 143
2y	4.780 222	4.407 538
3y	4.780 222	4.182 810
4y	104.780 222	86.334 348
Sum of present values		*99.532 839*

The present value of the USD side remains $150 million, which is equivalent to £100 million.

Receive nothing upfront and pay a lower USD rate

Instead of being taken out, the £467,161 can be used to lower the present value of the USD side of the swap by $700,742. That is, the company will pay a USD coupon rate such that the present value of those payments and the principal repayment will be equal to $149.299 258 million.

Table 8.10 Present value of the cash flows of a $150 million 3.812 193% coupon bond

	Payments	Present value
1y	5.718 289	5.580 724
2y	5.718 289	5.392 993
3y	5.718 289	5.160 597
4y	155.718 289	133.164 944
Sum of present values		*149.299 258*

The coupon rate is 3.812 193%. Note that the rate is lower than the par rate of 3.939 253% by 0.127 060%, which is not equal to the 0.130 309% U.K. rate differential.

The company need not stop here. It could take out £467,161 or lock in its USD coupon to a low rate of 3.812 193%, and then further swap into floating USD by entering into a 4-year USD fixed-for-floating interest rate swap. This additional step would leave it with a floating dollar liability for the remainder of the term or until it decided to swap again. If the company decided to take £467,161 out of the currency swap, then it would enter into an interest rate swap to receive a par rate of 3.939 253% in USD and to pay LIBOR *flat*. If it did not take any money out and locked in an off-market 3.812 193% in USD on the fixed–fixed currency swap, then it could enter into a USD interest rate swap to receive 3.812 193% and pay LIBOR minus a spread whose present value in today's terms is equal to $700,742. The same dealer could offer a combined package of the two swaps in one *GBP fixed–USD floating currency swap*.

8.2 THE ANATOMY OF SWAPS AS PACKAGES OF FORWARDS

So far we have viewed swaps as exchanges of two fictitious bonds. In the fixed–fixed currency swap, it was an exchange of a fixed rate bond in one currency for a fixed rate bond in another currency. In a plain vanilla interest rate swap, it was an exchange of a fixed rate bond for a floating rate bond in the same currency. In a fixed–floating currency swap, it was an exchange of a fixed rate bond in one currency for a floating rate bond in another currency. If the fictitious bonds' coupons were set to match market par rates, then the exchanges were made with no upfront payments. If one or both of the exchanged bonds' coupons were not set to par rates, then the swap was off-market with a potential upfront payment or coupon adjustment to compensate for the deviation of the present value of the bonds from par.

Instead of treating swaps as exchanges of streams of cash flows, we will now look at each cash flow exchange. In this light, we will treat swaps as strings of consecutive forward contracts. For market swaps, each forward may be off-market, but the total sum of the mark-to-markets (MTMs) (present values) of the component forwards will sum to zero. For all swaps, the present value of the swap will be equal to the sum of the MTMs of the building block forwards. This way of looking at swaps will invoke the same arbitrage relationships as when we built coupon bonds from forward-rate-agreements (FRAs) and FX forwards from deposits.

Fixed-for-fixed currency swap

Let us examine the currency swap entered into by our U.K.-based company with American operations. The cash flows on the swap are given in Table 8.11:

Table 8.11 Five-year fixed $–fixed £ swap

	Receive in GBP	Pay in USD
1y	4.780 222	6.614 962
2y	4.780 222	6.614 962
3y	4.780 222	6.614 962
4y	4.780 222	6.614 962
5y	104.780 222	156.614 962

The forward FX rates the company is locking in are equal to the coupon ratios for the coupon related flows and to the original spot \$1.50/£ rate for the final principal exchange:

Table 8.12 Forward FX rates locked in for coupon and principal exchanges

	Receive in GBP	Pay in USD	FX forward $/£
1y	4.780 222	6.614 962	1.383 819
2y	4.780 222	6.614 962	1.383 819
3y	4.780 222	6.614 962	1.383 819
4y	4.780 222	6.614 962	1.383 819
5y	4.780 222	6.614 962	1.383 819
5y	100.000 000	150.000 000	1.500 000

These are not real forwards quoted by anyone. The real forwards that would be quoted can be arrived at using the spot rate and pairs of zero-coupon rates in the covered interest rate parity (CIRP) relationship. Using these actual FX forward quotes, we can calculate the GBP equivalent of the USD payments that can be locked in today, the net GBP cash flow for each future date that can be locked in today, and thus the MTM on each forward cash flow exchange locked in the swap. The MTM is the amount the company would have to pay upfront if it were to enter into each GBP-for-USD cash flow exchange separately in the FX forward market.

Table 8.13 Swap MTM broken down to individual FX forward MTMs

	Receive in GBP	Pay in USD	CIRP: FX forward $/£	£ equivalent of $ outflow	£ equivalent received–paid	FX forward MTM in £
1y	4.780 222	6.614 962	1.488 948	4.442 710	0.337 512	0.326 965 523
2y	4.780 222	6.614 962	1.480 936	4.466 743	0.313 479	0.291 888 597
3y	4.780 222	6.614 962	1.475 898	4.481 991	0.298 231	0.264 820 891
4y	4.780 222	6.614 962	1.473 784	4.488 421	0.291 801	0.245 177 133
5y	4.780 222	6.614 962	1.474 561	4.486 054	0.294 168	0.232 057 754
5y	100.000 000	150.000 000	1.474 561	101.725 158	−1.725 158	−1.360 909 897
				Sum of MTMs		*0.000 000*

The sum of all the MTMs is equal to 0. The 5-year swap can be viewed as a package of six forwards to sell USD forwards for GBP forwards with the amounts set by the swap cash flow schedule as shown in the table. Each forward is off-market (i.e., it has a non-zero PV). The first five have a positive PV to the company. Any dealer willing to take the other side would have to be compensated by upfront receipts of the MTMs of the forwards. For example, for year 1 the company is to receive £4.780 222 million and pay $6.614 962 million, which at today's forward FX rate is equivalent to £4.442 710 million. Thus the company is scheduled to receive a bargain positive flow of £0.337 512 million. It would have to compensate a dealer by paying him the present value of that amount or £0.326 966 million. The same logic applies to the rest of the flows. The last component forward is a large negative PV contract: the company is to receive £100 million and pay £101.725 158 million. To accept that, the company would have to be paid £1.360 910 million. Today, the net of all settlements of off-market forwards is 0.

Fixed-for-floating interest rate swap

Let us turn to the interest rate swap entered into by our U.K. company that issued a floating rate bond to investors. To convert its liabilities to fixed, the company agreed to the following schedule of cash flows.

Table 8.14   Pay fixed–receive floating GBP swap

	Receive in GBP: 12-month LIBOR × 100 million		Pay in GBP
	Set at time	Paid at time	
1y	0	1	4.780 222
2y	1	2	4.780 222
3y	2	3	4.780 222
4y	3	4	4.780 222
5y	4	5	4.780 222

Taking each cash flow exchange at a time, an agreement to receive a floating rate set and paid in such a way in exchange for paying a fixed rate at the end of the interest accrual period is equivalent to an FRA. Even though we do not know the future cash flows (e.g., the third one will be known in 2 years to be paid in 3 years), we know the equivalent fixed rate that an FRA dealer would let us eliminate that uncertainty into at no cost. That rate is the forward 1-year rate for the interest accrual period. We can compute the market forward rates for each period as equivalent to floating rate receipts. Then we can proceed in a way analogous to what we did with the currency swap. We can compute the differences between the forward-equivalent receipts and the scheduled fixed rate payments, and mark-to-markets on these fixed–fixed exchanges by discounting the differences to today. These amounts are how much the company would have to pay a dealer to enter into the exchanges of floating-for-fixed (the floating-for-fixed forward costs nothing as that is a fair FRA, but the fixed forward for fixed 4.780 222% has a non-zero PV).

Table 8.15   Swap MTM broken down to individual FRA MTMs

	Receive in GBP	Pay in GBP	Forward rate: zero PV equivalent of LIBOR receipts	Equivalent received–paid	MTM: PV of differences
1y	LIBOR set at 0	4.780 222	3.225 600	−1.554 622	−1.506 043
2y	LIBOR set at 1	4.780 222	4.040 803	−0.739 419	−0.688 493
3y	LIBOR set at 2	4.780 222	4.860 016	0.079 794	0.070 855
4y	LIBOR set at 3	4.780 222	5.683 244	0.903 022	0.758 737
5y	LIBOR set at 4	4.780 222	6.510 494	1.730 272	1.364 944
			Sum of MTMs		*0.000 000*

The sum of the MTMs is 0.

Another way to look at this swap is to recognize that each LIBOR receipt balanced against a fixed forward rate payment has a zero MTM (fair FRA). The remainder of the fixed payment to be made over the forward has value to the swap parties. For example, for the second year the receipt of the floating LIBOR set one year from today to be paid 1 year later is covered by £4.040 803 million out of the total of £4.780 222 million paid. The excess of £0.739 419 paid to the swap counterparty 2 years from today can be settled today by an immediate receipt of £0.688 493. The same logic applies to all five exchanges. In early years, these have a negative PV to the company; in the last 3 years, they have a positive PV to the company as the forward equivalent of floating receipts greatly exceeds scheduled fixed payments.

The interest rate swap can thus be viewed as a package of off-market FRAs settled through a set of upfront payments summing up to 0 or a package of on-market FRAs and a string of discount bonds with face values equal to the differences between the stated fixed rate and the forward rates.

Other swaps

It can be stated in general that any swap, currency, interest rate or other can be viewed as a package of forwards with consecutive maturity dates. The forwards in the swap are off-market, and the sum of the MTMs is equal to the PV of the swap. If the swap is an on-market or a par swap, then the sum of the MTMs on the constituent forwards is equal to zero.

Swap book running

An interest rate swap dealer may trade many swaps a day paying fixed on some and receiving fixed on others. Similarly, a currency swap dealer may, in any given currency, pay on some swaps and receive on others. Both will deal with hundreds of pay and receive dates, a variety of quoted rates, on- and off-market, several day-counts, etc. Some pays and receives offset each other partially and some are for similar dates. The dealers are only left with residual positions to expose them to interest rate or currency risks.

At the time of each swap, recognizing that swaps are synthetic packages of forwards, dealers can eliminate their exposure by entering into reverse synthetic transactions in the forward markets. For example, a fixed rate payer on an interest rate swap may enter into a string of FRAs on which he agrees to receive a fixed rate. The dealer makes a profit on the swap by charging a few basis points running (i.e., offering to pay a few basis points less on the fixed side of the swap) over the cost of his replicating strategy. This covers the risk that if he is slow to execute the reverse transaction, the zero and forward rates that he uses to compute the swap rate may run away from him and he may have to transact at less advantageous terms when executing the offsetting synthetics. The dealer has to transact in offsetting synthetics every time he enters into a swap. This is very unwieldy and costly.

Suppose a dealer has a portfolio of two swaps: a pay-fixed swap maturing on December 15, 2014, with coupon dates on June 15 and December 15, and a receive-fixed swap maturing on December 3, 2014, with coupon dates June 3 and December 3. If hedged through replication, the dealer would have to enter a lot of nearly offsetting FRAs with close but not identical roll dates.

To avoid the execution costs (bid–ask spreads) that static replications would entail and to reduce the dimensionality of the problem, most dealers choose to run their books using dynamic hedging with a small group of most liquid instruments. The dealer computes his net PV sensitivities resulting from these two swaps or, in general, from thousands of swaps on his books to a set of common inputs, typically Eurocurrency futures and government bonds. The dealer then hedges with that reduced set of instruments. This way, all swaps are approximated as constructed from the same building blocks. On a daily basis, the PV changes of all the swaps taken together will be exactly offset by the sum of the PV changes of the selected set of hedge instruments held in quantities determined by the sensitivities (duration-like hedge ratios).

The building blocks are not perfect (only the exact static replication would have been), and so this approach requires daily rebalancing of the hedge. The rebalancing consists of computing new sensitivities and adjusting the quantities of the hedge instruments held by buying more of some and selling more of some. The advantage of avoiding thousands of bid–ask spreads on FRAs or futures is enormous. This is reflected in the very tight market-making quotes of dealers in the institutional markets. In a way, they compete with each other by showing the tightest bid–ask spread that reflects their lowest costs of manufacturing the swaps.

Another great advantage to this approach is in risk definition. The risk of a swap portfolio can be described with respect to a reduced set of hedge instruments.

8.3 THE PRICING AND HEDGING OF SWAPS

Swap rates always reflect the cost of replicating strategies. We have already shown how the rate on a currency swap and an interest rate swap is determined using quoted zero rates. In reality, to reflect the actual process of hedging the swaps, the pricing of a swap typically requires one other initial step: that is the building of the zero curve from the rates on the hedge instruments.

Here is the thinking process behind the selection of liquid hedge instruments. Zero-coupons reflecting swap parties' credits are generally traded only for maturities less than 1 year. These are Eurocurrency (LIBOR) deposits that trade freely in both directions (i.e., borrowing and lending at tight spreads). Maturities longer than 1 year have to be synthesized from Eurocurrency futures or FRAs. This is achievable with the use of liquid futures or forwards for up to 10 years for the U.S. dollar, 5 years for the euro, and 2 years for the Japanese yen, the Swiss franc, and a few other currencies. Beyond that, dealers rely on the existence of long-term government bonds that can be bought and shorted at tight spreads. These bonds reflect the credit rating of the sovereigns, and not swap parties, and thus require a "plug" of a swap spread which itself is continuously determined in the market.

We illustrate the process of pricing a U.S. interest rate swap, its execution, and the subsequent hedging involved.

Suppose in September of 2003, a New York dealer is contacted by ABC Corp. to provide a quote on a 5-year, $200-million notional principal, interest rate swap where ABC will pay the dealer a fixed rate, semi-annually, and will receive a floating rate of 3-month LIBOR. This is a plain vanilla swap.

Suppose at the time the dealer is faced with the following set of rates on the "building blocks". These are taken for this illustration from the September 26, 2003 issue of the *Wall Street Journal*.

Table 8.16 US "building block" rates taken from the *Wall Street Journal*, Friday, September 26, 2003

Eurodollar (CME)		US Treasury issues		
		Maturity	Coupon	Yield
Dec03	98.83	9/30/2005	1.625	1.657
Mar04	98.75	9/15/2008	3.125	3.030
Jun	98.51	8/15/2013	4.25	4.099
Sep	98.19	2/15/1931	5.375	5.000
Dec	97.77			
Mar05	97.35	Money rates		
Jun	96.96	3-month LIBOR	1.1400%	
Sep	96.65			
Dec	96.35			
Mar06	96.10			
Jun	95.87			
Sep	95.65			
Dec	95.44			
Mar07	95.25			
Jun	95.08			
Sep	94.92			
Dec	94.77			
Mar08	94.64			
Jun	94.51			
Sep	94.41			
Dec	94.31			
Mar09	94.22			
Jun	94.14			
Sep	94.07			
Dec	94.00			

We assume that Eurodollar (ED) expiry dates correspond to the swap roll dates. If not, we would interpolate. First, we need to determine the forward rates that can be locked in for future 3-month periods. If we had FRAs, we could use those directly. Here we do not. We must correct the forward rates implied in the ED futures prices by what is called a futures convexity adjustment. The correction takes into account the fact that the MTM settlement on the futures takes place at a constant dollar amount per 1-bp change in the interest rate every day until the futures expiry, while on a FRA the adjustment is a one-time event on the FRA start date: the longer the expiry date, the bigger the adjustment, and the greater the volatility of the short-term discount rate, the greater the deviation of the MTM present value from that of the forward.[1] The ultimate check if the adjustment is correct is the comparison to FRA rates, if available.

From the money market and futures (or forward) inputs we build the zero-coupon curve. That is, we compute the discount factors to a sequence of future dates (3 months, 6 months, ..., 60 months). We also show the set of quarterly compounded zero rates to those dates.

Table 8.17   Zero-coupon curve derived from ED futures

Forward period time (months from today)		100 ED	Convexity adjustment	FRA rate	Zero rate (to end time)	Discount factors (to end time)
Start	End					
0	3			1.140	1.140 000	0.997 158 1
3	6	1.17	0.000	1.170	1.155 000	0.994 249 9
6	9	1.25	−0.008	1.242	1.183 998	0.991 172 3
9	12	1.49	−0.016	1.474	1.256 479	0.987 533 3
12	15	1.81	−0.024	1.786	1.362 327	0.983 143 5
15	18	2.23	−0.032	2.198	1.501 485	0.977 770 7
18	21	2.65	−0.040	2.610	1.659 657	0.971 432 1
21	24	3.04	−0.048	2.992	1.825 959	0.964 219 7
24	27	3.35	−0.056	3.294	1.988 810	0.956 344 2
27	30	3.65	−0.064	3.586	2.148 245	0.947 846 8
30	33	3.90	−0.072	3.828	2.300 660	0.938 861 9
33	36	4.13	−0.080	4.050	2.446 149	0.929 451 2
36	39	4.35	−0.088	4.262	2.585 540	0.919 652 3
39	42	4.56	−0.096	4.464	2.719 426	0.909 502 2
42	45	4.75	−0.104	4.646	2.847 578	0.899 059 7
45	48	4.92	−0.112	4.808	2.969 826	0.888 381 3
48	51	5.08	−0.120	4.960	3.086 624	0.877 500 3
51	54	5.23	−0.128	5.102	3.198 326	0.866 448 8
54	57	5.36	−0.136	5.224	3.304 687	0.855 278 8
57	60	5.49	−0.144	5.346	3.406 508	0.843 998 8

The interpretation of the results is that we know the present value of $1 received or paid on any future date as simply an outcome of a static strategy to replicate that receipt/payment (through lending/borrowing for 3 months and locking in the

---

[1] The theoretical argument for the convexity adjustment is quite complex and beyond the scope of our discussion.

refinancing rate by buying/selling a strip of ED futures with all intermediate maturities).

We are now ready to price the 5-year swap with a fixed semi-annual rate. "Pricing the swap" here means determining the fixed semi-annual coupon coupon rate that would make a 5-year semi-annual bond have a value of par. The bond would have 10 equal coupon cash flows, first paid 6 months from today and last 5 years from today and one principal cash flow in 5 years. We want to determine what coupon rate divided by two would produce the 10 coupon cash flows so that the sum of their present values together with the present value of the principal cash flow at the end would equal to 100. We have already determined the discount rates and factors for all the semi-annual dates. All we need to do is to pick a rate and discount cash flows based on it. We can easily verify that the rate of 3.3636% is the desired coupon rate. The cash flow discounting is portrayed in the following table.

Table 8.18 PV of 3.3636% coupon bond using derived zero rates

Zero rate (to end time)	Discount factors (to end time)	Par swap rate = 3.3636	
		Cash flow	PV of cash flow
1.140 000	0.997 158 1		
1.155 000	0.994 249 9	1.6818	1.6721
1.184 664	0.991 167 4		
1.257 978	0.987 518 5	1.6818	1.6608
1.364 726	0.983 114 2		
1.504 816	0.977 722	1.6818	1.6443
1.663 938	0.971 359 6		
1.831 202	0.964 119 1	1.6818	1.6215
1.995 023	0.956 211 2		
2.155 433	0.947 677 4	1.6818	1.5938
2.308 828	0.938 652 2		
2.455 132	0.929 202 2	1.6818	1.5627
2.595 214	0.919 365		
2.729 692	0.909 177 7	1.6818	1.5291
2.858 358	0.898 698 9		
2.981 055	0.887 985 3	1.6818	1.4934
3.098 249	0.877 070 2		
3.210 303	0.865 985 6	1.6818	1.4564
3.316 980	0.854 783 6		
3.419 085	0.843 472 7	101.6818	85.7658

Sum = 100.0000

The dealer quotes ABC Corp. a fixed rate of 3.39%. ABC accepts and the swap is done. ABC Corp. has agreed to pay a fixed rate of 3.39 semi to receive a floating 3-month

LIBOR. The dealer computes his profit relative to his estimated cost of manufacture as 2.64 bp running, or 12.28 bp upfront; that is:

$$0.001\,228 \times 200,000,000 = \$245,639$$

This comes from repricing the swap using the agreed-on rate.

Table 8.19 PV of 3.39% coupon bond using derived zero rates

Zero rate (to end time)	Discount factors (to end time)	Par swap rate = 3.3900	
		Cash flow	PV of cash flow
1.240 000	0.997 158 1		
1.155 000	0.994 249 9	1.6950	1.6853
1.184 664	0.991 167 4		
1.257 978	0.987 518 5	1.6950	1.6738
1.364 726	0.983 114 2		
1.504 816	0.977 722	1.6950	1.6572
1.663 938	0.971 359 6		
1.831 202	0.964 119 1	1.6950	1.6342
1.995 023	0.956 211 2		
2.155 433	0.947 677 4	1.6950	1.6063
2.308 828	0.938 652 2		
2.455 132	0.929 202 2	1.6950	1.5750
2.595 214	0.919 365		
2.729 692	0.909 177 7	1.6950	1.5411
2.858 358	0.898 698 9		
2.981 055	0.887 985 3	1.6950	1.5051
3.098 249	0.877 070 2		
3.210 303	0.865 985 6	1.6950	1.4678
3.316 980	0.854 783 6		
3.419 085	0.843 472 7	101.6950	85.7770
		Sum =	100.1228
		Profit =	0.1228

In order for the dealer to realize this profit, he will need to manufacture the swap at the estimated cost. That is, he will have to hedge the PV change on the swap so that every time rates change the PV change on the swap will be exactly offset by the change in the PVs of the hedge instruments held. Immediately after or at the time of the swap, the dealer has to sell a strip of futures. The amounts are computed by blipping the curve one instrument at a time. Let us change the price of the first ED Dec03 contract by −0.01 to 98.82. We rebuild the zero curve and reprice the swap. The change in the present value of the swap in dollars divided by $25 gives us the number of December contracts that need to be sold to hedge the swap.

Table 8.20 PV of 3.39% coupon bond using zero rates derived by blipping Dec03 ED contract

| Forward period time (months from today) | | 100 ED | Convexity adjustment | FRA rate | Zero rate (to end time) | Discount factors (to end time) | Par swap rate = 3.3900 | | 0.026 |
Start	End						Cash flow	PV of cash flow	
0	3			1.140	1.140 000	0.997 158 1			
3	6	1.18	0.000	1.180	1.160 000	0.994 225 1	1.6950	1.6852	
6	9	1.25	−0.006	1.244	1.187 998	0.991 142 7			
9	12	1.49	−0.012	1.478	1.260 479	0.987 493 9	1.6950	1.6738	
12	15	1.81	−0.018	1.792	1.366 727	0.983 089 6			
15	18	2.23	−0.024	2.206	1.506 484	0.977 697 6	1.6950	1.6572	
18	21	2.65	−0.030	2.620	1.665 369	0.971 335 4			
21	24	3.04	−0.036	3.004	1.832 454	0.964 095	1.6950	1.6341	
24	27	3.35	−0.042	3.308	1.996 137	0.956 187 4			
27	30	3.65	−0.048	3.602	2.156 435	0.947 653 8	1.6950	1.6063	
30	33	3.90	−0.054	3.846	2.309 739	0.938 628 8			
33	36	4.13	−0.062	4.068	2.455 968	0.929 179 1	1.6950	1.5750	
36	39	4.35	−0.070	4.280	2.595 986	0.919 342 1			
39	42	4.56	−0.078	4.482	2.730 409	0.909 155	1.6950	1.5410	
42	45	4.75	−0.086	4.664	2.859 027	0.898 676 5			
45	48	4.92	−0.094	4.826	2.981 683	0.887 963 2	1.6950	1.5051	
48	51	5.08	−0.102	4.978	3.098 840	0.877 048 3			
51	54	5.23	−0.110	5.120	3.210 862	0.865 964	1.6950	1.4678	
54	57	5.36	−0.118	5.242	3.317 510	0.854 762 3			
57	60	5.49	−0.126	5.364	3.419 588	0.843 451 6	101.6950	85.7748	

Original
Sum = 100.1203   100.1228
PV change in % of par   (0)
PV change in $ (4,991)
No. of cars   (200)

Next, we return the Dec03 futures value back to 98.83 and change the price of the Mar04 contract by −0.01 to 98.74. We rebuild the curve and reprice the swap. The change in the present value of the swap in dollars divided by $25 gives us the number of Mar04 contracts that need to be sold to hedge the swap.

Table 8.21 PV of 3.39% coupon bond using zero rates derived by blipping Mar04 ED contract

| Forward period time (months from today) | | 100 ED | Convexity adjustment | FRA rate | Zero rate (to end time) | Discount factors (to end time) | Par swap rate = 3.3900 | | 0.026 |
Start	End						Cash flow	PV of cash flow	
0	3			1.140	1.140 000	0.997 158 1			
3	6	1.17	0.000	1.170	1.155 000	0.994 249 9	1.6950	1.6853	
6	9	1.26	−0.006	1.254	1.187 997	0.991 142 7			
9	12	1.49	−0.012	1.478	1.260 478	0.987 493 9	1.6950	1.6738	
12	15	1.81	−0.018	1.792	1.366 726	0.983 089 7			
15	18	2.23	−0.024	2.206	1.506 484	0.977 697 7	1.6950	1.6572	
18	21	2.65	−0.030	2.620	1.665 369	0.971 335 4			
21	24	3.04	−0.036	3.004	1.832 454	0.964 095 1	1.6950	1.6341	
24	27	3.35	−0.042	3.308	1.996 137	0.956 187 4			
27	30	3.65	−0.048	3.602	2.156 435	0.947 653 8	1.6950	1.6063	
30	33	3.90	−0.054	3.846	2.309 739	0.938 628 8			
33	36	4.13	−0.062	4.068	2.455 968	0.929 179 1	1.6950	1.5750	
36	39	4.35	−0.070	4.280	2.595 986	0.919 342 1			
39	42	4.56	−0.078	4.482	2.730 409	0.909 155	1.6950	1.5410	
42	45	4.75	−0.086	4.664	2.859 027	0.898 676 5			
45	48	4.92	−0.094	4.826	2.981 682	0.887 963 2	1.6950	1.5051	
48	51	5.08	−0.102	4.978	3.098 840	0.877 048 3			
51	54	5.23	−0.110	5.120	3.210 862	0.865 964	1.6950	1.4678	
54	57	5.36	−0.118	5.242	3.317 509	0.854 762 3			
57	60	5.49	−0.126	5.364	3.419 588	0.843 451 7	101.6950	85.7748	

Original
Sum = 100.1204   100.1228
PV change in % of par   (0)
PV change in $ (4,906)
No. of cars   (196)

We return the Mar04 futures value back to 98.75 and change the price of the Jun04 contract by −0.01. We continue the process, each time rebuilding the curve and re-pricing the swap. We observe the changes in the present value of the swap. We divide these by $25 to get the number of all contracts that need to be sold to hedge the swap. Starting with Sep08 the PV changes will be 0. The results are summarized in Table 8.22.

Table 8.22 Summary of results (EDs on the CME)

Hedge	No. of cars	Hedge	No. of cars	Hedge	No. of cars
Dec03	−200	Dec	−185	Dec	−172
Mar04	−196	Mar06	−182	Mar08	−169
Jun	−196	Jun	−182	Jun	−169
Sep	−193	Sep	−179	Sep	0
Dec	−192	Dec	−179	Dec	0
Mar05	−189	Mar07	−175	Mar09	0
Jun	−189	Jun	−175	Jun	0
Sep	−185	Sep	−172	Sep	0
				Dec	0

We also compute the hedge for the change in the spot LIBOR. A 1 bp blip in the 3-month spot rate results in a swap PV change of $−4,992, which is equivalent to −200 contracts. Trading in spot deposits can be costly, so dealers normally hedge this part with the first available ED contract as a proxy for spot (a serial October contract if available, or stack on top of the other December contracts) or leave it unhedged.

Table 8.23 Additional hedge (ED on the CME)

Hedge	No. of cars
Oct03	−200

Each day after the inception of the swap and every time interest rates change dramatically, the dealer will repeat the entire exercise to compute the new hedge amounts and trade the appropriate number of contracts to ensure that his holdings are equal to the currently computed hedge. Every day the profits and losses on the futures will exactly offset the PV changes on the swap. As the swap ages and actual cash flows drop off, fewer maturities of the futures will be held. Daily adjustments to the positions will be small, but over time all hedges will be liquidated.

8.4 SWAP SPREAD RISK

Swap spread is defined as the difference between the par rate on a swap of a given maturity and the yield on a risk-free government security with the same maturity. In our example above, the fair 5-year swap rate was 3.3636% while the 5-year yield on the 5-year U.S. Treasury was 3.03. The 5-year swap spread in this case was 33.4 bp. Dealers continuously quote the spreads over governments they are willing to pay (bid) and receive (ask) on swaps with all standard maturities. The spread is quoted on the same basis as the governments (e.g., semi-annual *30/360* in the U.S., semi-annual *Act/365* in the U.K, annual *Act/Act* for German Bunds and French OATs). The assumption is that the underlying government rates are quite variable while the spreads are not, so it is convenient to quote just the "add-ons". But at the time a swap is executed, the actual swap rate is agreed on. In the U.S., all annual maturities up to 15 years plus the 30-year are shown routinely on financial screens. All other maturities are quoted on request. In the U.K., maturities up to 5 years and the 10-year are quoted routinely. In Japan, maturities up to 2 years and the 10-year are quoted routinely. The availability of the hedge instruments dictates which maturities are considered liquid enough to make markets in.

Swap spread risk refers to the possibility that the PV of the swap will not be offset by the PV change in the underlying hedge instruments because those instruments are government securities with no default premium allowed for in the yield. Let us illustrate this by extending the above example.

Suppose the dealer had quoted the 5-year spread of 33/36. ABC Corp. accepted the offer and agreed to pay 36 bp over the current 5-year Treasury note yielding 3.03% (i.e., 3.39%). The dealer could have chosen to hedge the 5-year receive-fixed swap, by shorting the 5-year government note. He would have had to compute the change in the value of the swap and the change in the price of the 5-year note resulting from a 1-bp change in the yield to maturity. The ratio of these two sensitivities would have given him the amount of the 5-year note to be shorted. The procedure would be repeated every day ensuring that swap PV changes would be offset by Treasury PV changes. This would only be true if yields on swaps moved one for one with yields on Treasuries (i.e., only if there were no swap spread changes). If the 5-year swap spread were to rise, resulting in the swap yield moving up by more than the Treasury yield or the swap yield moving down by less than the Treasury yield the dealer would incur a loss.

The ED hedge chosen by the dealer for the 5-year swap did not expose him to the spread risk, because ED contracts reflect the same credit as swaps (i.e., they implicitly include a default premium).

Most dealers get naturally exposed to swap spread risk on swaps with long maturities. Eurocurrency contracts are neither available nor liquid enough, and dealers have no choice but to use government securities as hedges. Governments are also more convenient as they require one trade instead of many, potentially saving cost and effort. For that reason and for speculative reasons, dealers choose them for swaps with shorter maturities, too.

A dealer computes and monitors closely his exposure to swap spreads of all maturities. Often he actively seeks out swaps that might reduce those exposures by offering tighter spreads for the desired maturity. Swap spread risk is the secondary risk swap a dealer is left with after hedging the primary interest rate risk. It can be his strategic advantage or disadvantage when competing with other dealers. It is the main risk of a well-run swap book.

8.5 STRUCTURED FINANCE

Just as forwards and zeros can be viewed as building blocks for swaps, swaps can be viewed as building blocks for structured bonds. We showed in the swap-driven finance examples how one liability can be turned into another with the use of swaps: fixed into floating, one currency into another, etc. In those situations, corporations use swaps at the time of or subsequent to a bond issuance to match the demand of their bond investors to their own funding needs. This wizardry can take advanced forms by combining several swaps with each other and with options to create highly complicated bond structures (we discuss option pricing later). The driver here is investor demand for a particular exposure scenario. The issuer's objective is simply a lower cost of financing.

Inverse floater

As the first example we consider an inverse floater. This is a bond whose coupon payout is equal to a formula of some fixed rate minus a short-term floating rate. Such coupon structure is often demanded during times of low rate volatility, a steep yield curve, and when investors expect the short-term rates to decrease. The pricing is attractive then, as forwards increase with maturity.

Using the rate inputs as of September 26, 2003 an investor may be offered by ABC Corp. a 5-year bond whose quarterly coupon is equal to:

$$6.52 - \text{LIBOR}_{3m}$$

Let us explain this structure in a diagram.

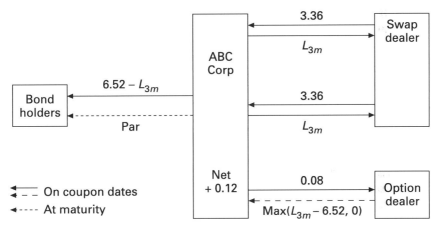

Figure 8.3   An inverse floating bond.

On the issue date ABC sells the inverse floater bonds with a coupon of $6.52 - L_{3m}$ for 100. It enters into a swap with a notional principal of 200 to receive 3.36 and pay L_{3m} on the same dates (times the appropriate day-count). At the same, it buys a cap for which it pays upfront or over time the equivalent of 8 bp running. The cap provides protection for the scenario that L_{3m} is above 6.52 on any coupon date. In those cases, the option dealer who provided the cap will compensate ABC for the difference. If L_{3m} stays below 6.52, ABC will receive nothing. ABC nets 12 bp running which reduces its cost of funding. The swap dealer makes a profit on the swap (paying 3.36 while the fair rate is 3.3636); the option dealer makes a profit on the cap. The investor gets a desired coupon formula, paying well above today's 1.14 LIBOR. To make the cash flows clear, let us examine two scenarios.

First, assume that on some coupon date L_{3m} is 1.25 (i.e., lower than 6.52). The bond holder coupon is 5.27. ABC receives 3.36 on the two swaps (i.e., a total of 6.72). It pays

0.08 out of that for the cap and keeps 0.12. With the remainder, equal to 6.52, it pays 1.25 twice on the two swaps and 5.27 to the bond holders (i.e., it pays exactly $L_{3m} = 1.25$ minus the 0.12 it kept).

Next, assume that L_{3m} is 8.50 (i.e., higher than 6.52) on some coupon date. The bond holder coupon is 0. ABC receives 3.36 on the two swaps (i.e., a total of 6.72). It pays 0.08 out of that for the cap and keeps 0.12. The remainder is equal to 6.52, but ABC also collects 1.98 on the cap. It pays the sum of the two, equal to 8.50, on the first swap and another 8.50 out of its own pocket on the other swap.

The net financing cost to ABC is L_{3m} minus 0.12 irrespective of the level of L_{3m} on any coupon date. The coupon on the bond looks attractive to most investors who do not believe in short-term rates going up from the currently low level. The fixed portion of the coupon reflects double the current term swap rate net of the cost of the cap. Cap protection tends to be cheap as it has a high strike price. In most cases, the swap and the option dealer are the same, providing the issuer with a competitive quote on the entire behind-the-scenes part of the deal (in our case the 3.36 swap level is very close to the fair level and the dealer makes most of his profit on the cap).

Leveraged inverse floater

The leveraged inverse floater combines three or more swaps and a cap into a single bond. Consider the following quarterly coupon formula offered by ABC to its investors:

$$9.80 - 2 \times L_{3m}$$

It is easy to see that, compared with the leveraged floater, all we need to do is to add another swap and lower the strike on the cap. Here is the summary diagram.

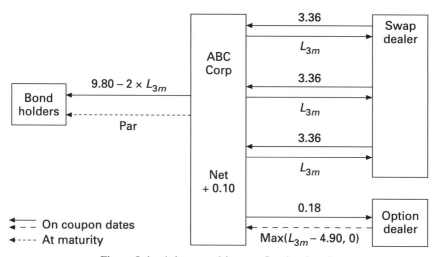

Figure 8.4   A leveraged inverse floating bond.

The structure works for everyone involved. The investors' coupon on day 1 is $9.80 - 2 \times 1.14 = 7.52$, which is very attractive compared with the alternatives of 3.36 fixed or L_{3m} floating. The dealer sells a cap and enters into a profitable swap with a notional principal equal to three times that on the bond. The issuer gets

L_{3m} − 10 bp financing. The investors bear the risk in this structure that short rates increase rapidly, which would sharply reduce or potentially eliminate the coupon payout.[2]

Capped floater

A capped floater is a bond whose coupon is floating but capped. The investor gives up potentially increased coupon payouts for a larger coupon now. The issuer desires reduced cost of financing. This structure is simpler than an inverse floater.

Suppose investors demand a floating rate. For a little extra spread on top of the floating rate, they are willing to give up upside potential. If ABC needs floating rate financing, then it can simply sell the cap embedded into the coupon formula to the dealer and use the proceeds to enhance the coupon offered. If ABC needs fixed rate financing, then it can purchase a cap and swap the floating rate on the bond into a fixed liability. The next diagram shows this more complicated scenario.

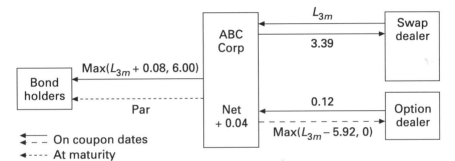

Figure 8.5 A capped floating bond.

The investor's coupon is L_{3m} plus 8 bp, but no more than 6.00. ABC get financing equal to 3.35 fixed. The swap dealer receives the ask side of the fixed rate, 3.39, and pays LIBOR. The option dealer buys a cap. If LIBOR on any coupon date is below 5.92, the cap does not pay. ABC simply passes the L_{3m} coupon it receives on the swap to the bond holders, enhanced by 8 bp out of the 12 bp it receives as the payment for the cap. If LIBOR on a coupon date is greater than 5.92, say 7.00, the situation is only a little more complicated. ABC receives 7.00 from the swap dealer and passes 6.00 to the bond holders. It also receives 0.12 from the cap dealer. Out of the 1.12 total, it pays $7.00 − 5.92 = 1.08$ on the cap back to the option dealer, leaving it with 0.04 which reduces its net fixed rate liability.

Callable

Fixed rate bonds, floating rate bonds, and all the structured bonds can be issued in a callable form. In this case, ABC has the right to call the bonds from the bond holders at par or a price specified in advance in a call schedule. ABC can choose to retain that

---

[2] Consider the duration and convexity of a leveraged inverse floater. A small rate increase may render the PV of future coupons 0.

right (in which case it will bear the cost of a higher coupon demanded by the investors) or sell it to the dealer (in which case the dealer will cover that cost, leaving ABC with a straight fixed rate liability). The choice depends on ABC's needs and on the deal's pricing. If interest rates are currently volatile, the dealer will be willing to pay a lot for the call right, potentially reducing ABC's fixed financing cost in a significant way.

Range

A range bond pays a coupon that depends on how many days during the interest accrual period a floating rate stayed within a pre-specified range. In this case, the issuer simply desires low cost of floating financing. It offers investors an enhanced floating (LIBOR plus spread) or fixed coupon rate for each day the floating rate does not leave the range bounds. Investors get no interest rate accrual for days when the rate goes outside the range. They are betting that the rate will not jump up and/or down. The range can have upper or lower bounds or both. The coupon formula might read as follows:

$$L_{3m} + 100 \text{ bp} \qquad \text{but only for days where } 0.75 < L_{3m} < 2.75$$

The range option embedded in the coupon is sold to an option dealer in exchange for the spread and some extra that reduces the issuer's financing. This is similar to a capped floater except the option is a lot more complicated from the dealer's perspective.

Index principal swap

A structure attractive to mortgage bond investors who want the enhanced yield of a prepayment-exposed investment, but want to limit the unpredictability of prepayments is called an index principal swap (IPS) or index-amortizing swap (IAR). As is often the case, this structure is driven by this specific investor demand, while the issuer simply wants reduced floating financing. The issuer issues a bond with a formula coupon and principal to the bond holders, but reverses the cash flows of the bond by entering into an IPS with a dealer.

The swap is a fixed-for-floating swap, except the notional principal of the swap changes over time. To compute the principal for each period, one takes the principal as of the last period times one minus a percentage taken from an amortization table that might look like this:

Rate	Percent of notional amortized
3	0
2	50
1	100

Suppose the last period's principal was 100 and the index rate L_{3m} of this period is 1.14%. We use 1.14 to interpolate between 1 and 2 in the table to obtain the notional percentage equal to 93%. This period, the new notional principal used to compute interest flows on both sides of the swap is equal to the last principal times 100 minus the amortized percentage of 93, or 0.07. The new principal is thus 7.

This procedure is intended to mimic the prepayment behavior of fixed rate mortgages. As rates go down, homeowners refinance their mortgages. Mortgage bonds' principals are reduced. Similarly, IPS bonds principals will be reduced, but based on a pre-specified amortization table rather than the actual behavior of homeowners who often do not refinance optimally.

The IPS was first popularized in the mid-1990s in the U.S. where over 50% of morgages are fixed, with no prepayment penalties, and a large securitized mortgage bond market exists.

8.6   EQUITY SWAPS

Some investors desire equity market exposure in a bond form. This can be accomplished by defining the formula for a bond coupon payout as the appreciation of the stock index over the accrual period times the principal of the bond and times the appropriate day-count fraction. In this case, the issuer of the bond desires a low cost of financing that has nothing to do with equities. The dealer packages the bond by entering into an equity swap with the issuer. In the *equity swap*, every coupon period, the dealer pays the stock index appreciation on a notional principal of the swap and receives a floating interest rate (e.g., LIBOR) times the appropriate day-count fraction times the same notional principal. The stock return each period is passed on to the bond holders in the form of a bond coupon. The LIBOR-based interest is the issuer's net cost of financing. The structure naturally includes an at-the-money option given that the coupon paid to the bond holder cannot be negative. Alternatively, the bond holder gets a fixed rate plus only a predefined portion of the appreciation combined with out-of-the-money options. The option is paid for by the bond holder through a reduced coupon formula (negative spread).

Here is a diagram for an S&P 500 index-based coupon assuming the (European) put cost is 1.3% running. SPX stands for the percentage change in the S&P 500 for the coupon year. The investor receives the excess of SPX over 2%, floored at zero.

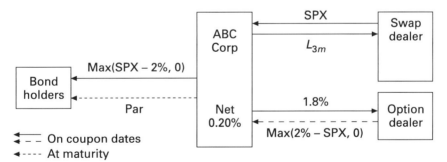

Figure 8.6   An S&P 500-linked coupon bond.

Let us distinguish two scenarios. First, let us look at SPX > 2% (e.g., SPX = 14%). The investor gets a 12% coupon. ABC receives 14% on the swap, pays 1.8% for the put, receives no payout from the put, and keeps 0.20%, which reduces its floating financing cost. Second, let us look at SPX < 2% (e.g., SPX = 0.5%). The investor gets a 0%

coupon. ABC receives 0.5% on the swap and 1.5% payout from the put, pays 1.8% for the put, and keeps 0.20%, which reduces its floating financing cost. Similarly, if SPX turns out negative for the year, the bond holder gets no coupon and ABC keeps a 0.20% reduction in its financing cost.

The pricing on the swap works as long as we can show, similarly to what we have established for the fixed-for-floating par swap, that the SPX-for-L_{3m} swap is fair (i.e., it has a zero PV).

This follows directly from the cash-and-carry relationship for stock index futures. The equity swap can be viewed as a string of 1-year synthetic forward (or futures) contracts. In our case, from the dealer's perspective, the swap's cash flows—pay SPX, receive LIBOR—are equivalent to a string of short index forwards or reverse cash-and-carry transactions. In the reverse cash-and-carry transaction, the dealer borrows a basket of stocks, sells the stocks short, and invests the proceeds to earn LIBOR. At the end of the year, he covers the short by buying the basket in the spot market. The initial sale and subsequent repurchase of stocks are equivalent to paying out the appreciation on the basket. The interest on short-sale proceeds is equivalent to receiving floating LIBOR. In order to hedge the string of short forwards packaged into the swap, the dealer has to hedge by doing the opposite (i.e., he has to receive the SPX appreciation and pay LIBOR). He does that by entering each year into a 1-year cash-and-carry. He borrows the principal to pay LIBOR. He buys the stocks at the beginning of each year and liquidates them on each coupon payout date. The profits on stocks are passed to ABC to satisfy the swap obligation. The LIBOR receipt from ABC covers the borrowing cost. Each year the dealer repeats the exercise for the following year. (In reality, on the coupon pay date, the dealer liquidates only the appreciated part of the holdings and pays the proceeds to ABC and holds the rest for the following year.)

8.7 COMMODITY AND OTHER SWAPS

There are parallels of equity swaps that involve other asset classes. They are always fixed income hybrids in that one side of the swap is a floating interest rate stream, while the other is some other asset return stream. A common example is a commodity swap, potentially linked to a bond issuance, whose coupon payout is a formula based on a percentage change in the price of a commodity over the coupon period. Structures sold in the past 10 years have involved oil, gold, and a variety of financial assets (e.g., weather-related contracts, total-rate-of-return contracts). Many have been partly hedgeable with existing exchange-traded or over-the-counter (OTC) forward and futures structures. All have been statically replicable with cash-and-carry purchases of the underlying assets against borrowing in the LIBOR markets.

Increasingly, dealers push the envelope of innovation by looking to secondary and unhedgeable variables on which to write swaps. One such variable is the historical volatility of an interest rate or a price; another is the inflation rate in an economy. There is no market in volatility or inflation forwards; one side of the swap cannot be synthetically replicated or dynamically hedged. The trading of such products is more akin to bookmaking and insurance sales than to swap trading. In most cases, risk management relies on book-matching or diversification. If both sides of the trade can be found and the dealer can find two counterparties willing to take the opposite sides of swap, then the dealer simply extracts the bid–ask spread on the bet the way a book-maker does on a sporting event. If the offsets are not identical, then the dealer tries to diversify the risks across the events and calendar dates, in effect pooling unhedgeable risks the way an insurer does.

8.8   SWAP MARKET STATISTICS

The global OTC derivatives market is enormous. According to a paper in the *BIS Quarterly Review* of June 2003 titled "International banking and financial market developments", the total notional principal outstanding reached over $140 trillion by the end of 2002.

The biggest category is interest rate derivatives accounting for over $100 trillion. Of that, euro-denominated interest rate swaps accounted for over $30 trillion and U.S. dollar-denominated swaps for under $25 trillion. The vast majority of swaps are under 5 years of maturity, with only 20% over that mark. That, however, includes aged long-term swaps. The maturity differential is also related to the availability of hedge instruments in various currencies.

Table 8.24   Notional amounts outstanding of OTC derivatives by risk category and instrument (in billions of U.S. dollars)

	Dec. 1998	Dec. 1999	Dec. 2000	Dec. 2001	Dec. 2002
Foreign exchange	18,011	14,344	15,666	16,748	18,469
Outright forwards and FX swaps	12,063	9,593	10,134	10,336	10,723
Currency swaps	2,253	2,444	3,194	3,942	4,509
Options	3,695	2,307	2,338	2,470	3,238
Interest rate contracts	50,015	60,091	64,668	77,568	101,699
Forward-rate agreements	5,756	6,775	6,423	7,737	8,792
Interest-rate swaps	36,262	43,936	48,768	58,897	79,161
Options	7,997	9,380	9,476	10,933	13,746
Equity-linked contracts	1,488	1,809	1,891	1,881	2,309
Forwards and swaps	146	283	335	320	364
Options	1,342	1,527	1,555	1,561	1,944
Commodity contracts	415	548	662	598	923
Gold	182	243	218	231	315
Other commodities	233	305	445	367	608
Forwards and swaps	137	163	248	217	402
Options	97	143	196	150	206
Other	10,389	11,408	12,313	14,384	18,337
Total contracts	*80,318*	*88,202*	*95,199*	*111,178*	*141,737*

Source: http://www.bis.org/publ/qcsv0306/anx1920a.csv

Most single-currency interest rate swaps and FX derivatives were dealer-to-dealer or dealer-to-other financial institution.

Table 8.25 Notional amounts outstanding of OTC single-currency interest rate derivatives by instrument and counterparty (in billions of U.S. dollars)

	Dec. 1998	Dec. 1999	Dec. 2000	Dec. 2001	Dec. 2002
Forward rate agreements	5,756	6,775	6,423	7,737	8,792
With reporting dealers	2,848	3,790	3,035	3,658	4,579
With other financial institutions	2,384	2,596	2,851	2,955	3,540
With non-financial costumers	523	389	537	1,124	673
Swaps	36,262	43,936	48,768	58,897	79,161
With reporting dealers	18,310	23,224	24,447	27,156	36,321
With other financial institutions	13,971	16,849	20,131	25,197	34,383
With non-financial costumers	3,980	3,863	4,190	6,545	8,457
Options	7,997	9,380	9,476	10,933	13,746
With reporting dealers	3,283	3,503	4,012	4,657	5,781
With other financial institutions	3,435	4,566	4,066	4,358	5,684
With non-financial costumers	1,279	1,310	1,399	1,918	2,281
Total contracts	*50,015*	*60,091*	*64,668*	*77,568*	*101,699*
With reporting dealers	24,442	30,518	31,494	35,472	46,681
With other financial institutions	19,790	24,012	27,048	32,510	43,607
With non-financial costumers	5,783	5,562	6,126	9,586	11,411

Source: http://www.bis.org/publ/qcsv0306/anx21a21b.csv

Table 8.26 Notional amounts outstanding of OTC FX derivatives by instrument and counterparty (in billions of U.S. dollars)

	Dec. 1998	Dec. 1999	Dec. 2000	Dec. 2001	Dec. 2002
Outright forwards and FX swaps	12,063	9,593	10,134	10,336	1,072
With reporting dealers	5,203	3,870	4,011	3,801	431
With other financial institutions	5,084	4,123	4,275	4,240	436
With non-financial costumers	1,777	1,600	1,848	2,295	204
Currency swaps	2,253	2,444	3,194	3,942	450
With reporting dealers	565	651	881	1,211	141
With other financial institutions	1,024	1,072	1,410	1,674	190
With non-financial costumers	664	721	904	1,058	118
Options	3,695	2,307	2,338	2,470	323
With reporting dealers	1,516	871	838	900	110
With other financial institutions	1,332	908	913	842	133
With non-financial costumers	847	529	588	728	80
Total contracts	*18,011*	*14,344*	*15,666*	*16,748*	*1,846*
With reporting dealers	7,284	5,392	5,729	5,912	683
With other financial institutions	7,440	6,102	6,597	6,755	760
With non-financial costumers	3,288	2,850	3,340	4,081	403

Source: http://www.bis.org/publ/qcsv0306/anx1920a.csv

Most single-currency interest rate swaps and FX derivatives were dealer-to-dealer or dealer-to-other financial institution.

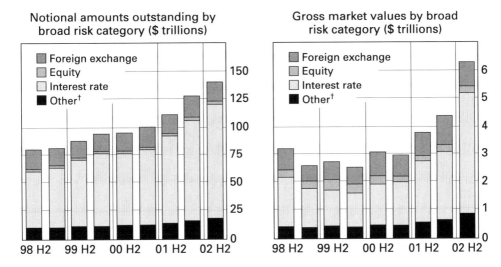

Figure 8.7 Notional amounts outstanding by broad risk category ($ trillions) and gross market values by broad risk category ($ trillions). † Estimated positions of non-regular reporting institutions.
Source: BIS

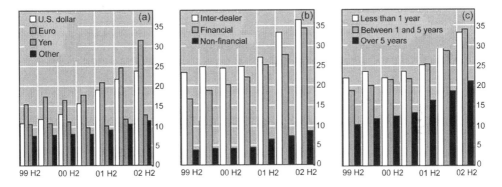

Figure 8.8 Interest rate swaps, notional amounts outstanding (in trillions of U.S. dollars): (a) by currency; (b) by counterparty; and (c) by maturity. The latter includes FRAs, which in December, 2002 accounted for approximately 6% of the total notional amount outstanding.
From *BIS Quarterly Review*, June, 2003, "International banking and financial market developments".

While dealer-to-dealer trades offset some risks, exchange-traded short-term interest rate futures, and in particular Eurocurrency (Eurodollar, Euroeuro, Euroyen, etc.) contracts, remain the main hedge instrument of choice for the residual exposure on most swaps under 5 years (under 10 years in the U.S.). This is evidenced in the continuing growth in the turnover of those contracts among other futures and options, representing around $100 trillion worth of contracts per quarter. These are split equally between the dollar and the euro-denominated interest rate contracts.

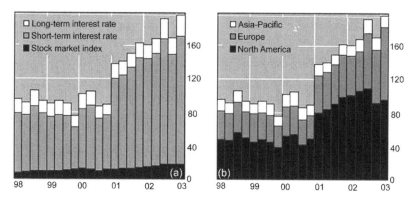

Figure 8.9 Turnover of exchange-traded futures and options, quarterly date (in trillions of U.S. dollars): (a) by contract type and (b) by region.
Sources: FOW TRADE data, Futures Industry Association, BIS calculations. From *BIS Quarterly Review*, June, 2003, "International banking and financial market developments". Reprinted with permission from BIS.

For long-term swaps, spot long-term government bonds are the main hedge instruments. While the turnover of the note and bond futures has increased in the U.S., this has not been the case universally. Swap hedgers have always preferred spot bonds to futures in order to avoid delivery and embedded option risk.

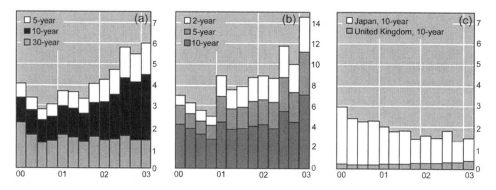

Figure 8.10 Turnover in government bond contracts, quarterly futures contract turnover (in trillions of U.S. dollars): (a) U.S.; (b) Germany; and (c) Japan and the U.K.
Sources: FOW TRADE data, Futures Industry Association, BIS calculations. From *BIS Quarterly Review*, June, 2003, "International banking and financial market developments". Reprinted with permission from BIS.

The post-technology boom era of the early 2000s has ushered in very low short-term interest rates, resulting in fairly steep swap yield curves for most currencies, even in Japan where interest rates on all maturities have remained under 1%.

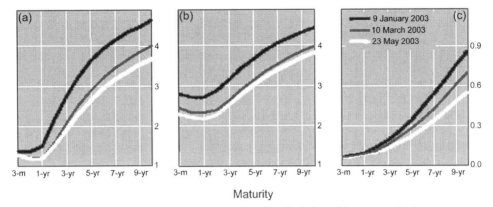

Figure 8.11 Swap yield curves (in percentages): (a) U.S. dollar; (b) euro; and (c) yen.
Note: For 3-, 6-, and 12-month U.S. dollar and yen maturities, LIBOR; for 3- and 6-month euro maturities, euro deposit rates. *Source*: Bloomberg. From *BIS Quarterly Review*, June, 2003, "International banking and financial market developments". Reprinted with permission from BIS.

Part Three

Options

9

Financial Math III—Options

Options are bets on the direction of prices of securities, interest, and currency rates, index levels, and non-financial variables. There are two types of participants in the options markets. Speculators (here called by their proper name, but euphemistically referred to as investors in cash markets for stocks or bonds) buy or sell options and wait for the desired outcome at maturity (a price rise or a rate drop). When their bets prove right, they get a payout; when their bets prove wrong, they do not get a payout or have to make one themselves. The dealers, or market-makers, do not take outright bets on the direction of underlying securities. They buy and sell bet tickets, and then manufacture the payouts for the holders of those tickets. Their risk is that they may over- or underestimate the cost of the manufacture of the payoffs on the bets that they sold or bought. If they estimate that cost correctly, they always earn a profit, whether prices go up or down, by simply charging a small margin over the cost.

This chapter has two central ideas.

The first is that there is a big difference between option dealers and insurance sellers or sports bookmakers. Option dealers buy and sell bets whose payoffs depend on the prices or rates of instruments that themselves can be bought and sold throughout the life of the option. Insurance companies and bookmakers sell bets on the outcomes of future events (earthquakes, floods, fires, soccer games). They cannot trade in these events; they can only adjust the odds (payoff) or premiums (prices of bets) they offer to reflect the demand and supply for bets. An option dealer who sold a bet that the stock will go up can buy the stock so that if indeed the stock goes up he can profit from the appreciation and pass the gain on to the option (bet) buyer. In contrast to a static cash-and-carry trader who buys the asset once and locks in financing once, the option dealer does it dynamically. This means that, as the stock rises more, he buys more of it, and when it falls he sells it, expecting not to have to pay on the sold bet. This is what we will refer to as manufacturing the payoff of the options and what is commonly known as *delta-hedging*. The cost of this manufacture depends directly on how volatile the underlying stock or interest rate is. The more it moves up and down, the more it costs the dealer to manufacture the desired payoff by the option expiry time. The important point is that the dealer does not speculate on the direction of the stock price.[1] If he sells a bet on the stock going down, he shorts the shares to benefit from the price going down so that he can pass the benefit to the bet buyer. He computes the cost of selling more shares as they go down and buying them back as they go up. His profit is the margin he

---

[1] Most dealers actually do. The market is so competitive that making profit solely through delta-hedging is very hard. Most dealers use their knowledge of demand and supply flows to their advantage. This extra profit comes on top of *revenue from customer flow*.

charges over what he expects the cost of financing the purchases and sales will be.[2] Once he sells an option, he follows a "recipe" of how to manufacture the payoff. We will present the recipe in detail.

The second, related idea is that speculators and dealers in the options markets do not act the same way. The dealer manufactures the payoff by actively trading the underlying asset while the option is alive. He does not care which way the asset price or rate goes, but he is busy accumulating gains (or losses) which by the expiry date are equal to what he pays to (receives from) the speculator. The speculator buys (or sells) the bet from the dealer in order to profit from his view, similar to the way the homeowner purchases an insurance policy in order to "profit" from a fire in his house. The speculator acquires a directional bet and engages in no further trading. He waits for the outcome to materialize. If he is right, he gets (or pays) a payout specified as some formula that depends on the outcome. For example, if he owns a call option, he gets the excess of the stock price over some level (strike price).

The central idea here is that the price of the bet the speculator buys from the dealer does not depend on the subjective probability or the expected value of the outcome, but only on the dealer's cost of manufacture. The latter fluctuates with the perceived volatility of the underlying asset. Sometimes bets may seem cheap, sometimes dear, relative to the hoped-for future payoff. When the speculator is right in his prediction about the event and comes to receive his payoff, the dealer has manufactured that payoff through the dynamic hedge strategy (i.e., has accumulated a profit exactly equal to the promised payoff). When the speculator is wrong and is not owed any payoff, the dealer has also manufactured that payoff. He has dynamically traded the underlying asset, in the process losing the entire amount of money received for the bet upfront, except for his extra margin (i.e., accruing a zero profit). No matter what happens, at option expiry or payout time, the dealer has on hand the exact amount the speculator demands.

Options are *redundant* securities in the sense that their payoffs can be replicated through dynamic trading strategies. As such, they are not needed. The profit the dealer earns can be thought of as a charge for convenience of having the ready security, so that the speculator does not have to manufacture it himself. This is just like the markup for ready-made clothes bought off the rack so that we do not have to tailor them individually. Redundant does not mean useless, however. Options allow very complicated *risk-sharing* schemes for investors. Let us remember that the primary function of securities markets is to channel savings (excess funds) to where they are needed, whether in productive ventures (ownership shares of small and large businesses) or housing construction (mortgage loans). In order for the original investors (or on their behalf, for banks or brokers) to be willing to put their money in those investments, they need to know that they can sell their participation on open markets. That is why we have stock exchanges and bond markets (see Chapter 1). Having options further strengthens that process. Original investors know that they will be able to sell part of their risk in a stock by selling a limited-time bet to give up the upside over a certain desired level or by buying put options to protect the value of their investments in case

---

[2] The *premium* (price) of the option reflects his profit and the cost of hedging. This is different from an insurance premium, which reflects the profit plus an unhedgeable bet on the event itself, with the insurer diversifying to improve his chances of winning, but nonetheless playing the odds. The option is more akin to a Dell computer. The buyer pays upfront; Dell assembles the computer according to customer specifications and delivers it on the due date.

they go sour. The best analogy is the decision to purchase a house for $1 million knowing that we can also buy fire and flood insurance, or borrow money against the house in case of dire need. Without these possibilities, spending $1 million on a house would be a much rarer occurrence.

This chapter is organized as follows. We start with option markets terminology, payoff diagrams, and static arbitrage parities. In Section 9.7, we turn to the binomial option pricing model, the most intuitive way of presenting the dynamic replication argument and the hedge recipe approach, as trading takes place at discrete times, the way it does in reality. We tie the binomial model to its celebrated continuous-time cousin, the Black–Scholes model. We discuss the residual risks (vega, volatility skew, gamma) of hedged option portfolios. At the end of the chapter, we turn to standard interest rate options. These, like swaps within spot and forward markets, represent a huge and fast-growing component of the options markets; yet most readers are only familiar with basic stock option examples. We also discuss some more common, exotic payoffs.

9.1 CALL AND PUT PAYOFFS AT EXPIRY

Tickets sold by national and state lotteries around the world are bets on a set of numbers. The payoff is a fixed monetary amount if the lottery ticket buyer is right in choosing the right combination. Such bets are called *binary* or *digital*. It does not matter how "close" to the right combination the better is, all that matters is whether he is right or wrong in guessing five or six numbers.

Most common options sold in financial markets work a little differently. The bettor can also be "right" or "wrong", but the "more right" he is, the bigger his payoff is. A *call* option on the price of an asset (e.g., stock) pays on the *expiry date* the greater of zero and the difference between that asset's price and a pre-specified strike price (bet level). If we want to bet that the price of ABC will go over $60 per share, we buy a call *struck* at 60. If the price on the expiry date is 67, we get $7; if the price is 74, we get $14. If the price is below 60, whether at 40 or 50, we get nothing. A *put* option on a price of an asset pays on the expiry date the greater of zero and the difference between a pre-specified strike price and that asset's price. If we want to bet that the price of ABC will go under $60 per share, we buy a put struck at 60. If the price on the expiry date is 47, we get $13; if the price is 54, we get $6. If the price is above 60, whether at 65 or 80, we get nothing. We graph the payoff the buyer of the option (bet) gets as a function of the *underlying asset*'s price in the following *payoff diagrams*.

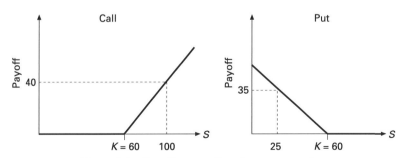

Figure 9.1   Payoff on a call and a put at expiry.
K = Strike price; S = Spot price at expiry.

Options that pay only at expiry are called *European*; those that pay prior to and on the expiry date are called *American*. Neither notion has any connection to a location.

At any given time, there may be options trading on the same underlying asset price (event), but with different strikes and expiry dates. On the exchanges, options follow a certain schedule of dates and strikes. Over the counter (OTC), they can be arranged for any payoff date and strike (bet level). The intrinsic value of an option is defined as the payoff the option would have if it were immediately exercisable based on today's price of the underlying asset. Options with a positive intrinsic value are called *in-the-money*; options with no intrinsic value are called *out-of-the-money*; options whose strike price is equal to the asset price are called *at-the-money*. Note that options cannot have a negative intrinsic value. If the better is wrong he simply does not exercise his option and gets no payoff.

Most individual stock options and many others have a *physical settlement* provision; that is, they are not pure bets, but give the holders (buyers) the right to buy (call) or sell (put) the asset to the *option writer* (seller) at the strike price on (or prior to) the expiry date. This is tantamount to receiving the payoffs as described above. For example, a 60 call, when the price is 67, gives the holder the right to buy the stock from the writer for 60 (a private transaction). Once bought, the holder can sell the stock immediately for 67 in the spot market (open market), realizing a profit of 7. A 60 put, when the price is 47, gives the holder the right to sell the stock to the writer for 60 (a private transaction). To deliver, the holder can buy the stock immediately for 47 in the spot market (open market), realizing a profit of 13. Many options written on non-price financial variables (stock indices, interest rates, etc.) are settled in cash. The settlement features of options are similar to futures that can also have cash settlement or physical settlement. We always need to check contract provisions for both, as they may not follow the same rules.

9.2 COMPOSITE PAYOFFS AT EXPIRY

Long and short positions in calls and puts can be combined to achieve a narrowly tailored bet on the range of the asset price in the future. It is important to realize that speculators can both buy (hold) and sell (write) options. They can combine long and short positions. Here are some examples.

Straddles and strangles

Suppose we believe that between now and the expiry date, the price of ABC, currently 60, is going to jump dramatically, but we do not know which way. Suppose we buy a put struck at 55 and a call struck at 65. This is called a 55–65 *strangle*.

On the expiry date, if the price is very low or very high we get a payoff; if the price stays between 55 and 65 we get nothing. If the price is 30 at expiry, we collect 25 on the 55 put and nothing on the 65 call. If the price is 80, we collect nothing on the 55 put and 15 on the 65 call. If the price is 62, we get nothing on both options.

Because we bought both options, we incurred an upfront cost of the bet. So our profit is reduced by the total price of the options. An option price is called a *premium* (like with insurance).

Next suppose that we believe that on the expiry date the price of ABC is going to stay around 62. To give ourselves some room for error, we sell a 60–65 strangle (60 put and 65 call) and receive premiums for both options. If we are right and the price does not go below 60 or above 65, we get to keep the total premium and make no payoff; if we are wrong we have to make a payout on one of the options. The payoffs on the long 55–65 strangle and short 60–65 strangle are shown in Figure 9.2.

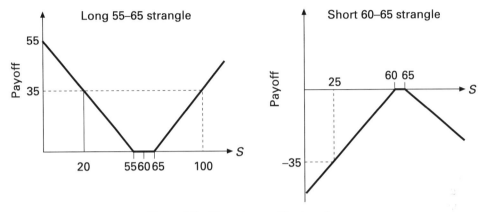

Figure 9.2 Strangle payoffs at expiry.

A strangle where the call strike and the put strike are the same is called a *straddle*. Short straddles and strangles are bets that the price will not fluctuate much from some level. Long strangles and straddles are bets that the price will move away from the anticipated level.

Note that it is not the direction of the position, long or short, which distinguishes the speculator from the dealer, but it is their actions after the bet is arranged and paid for. The speculator statically waits for the payout; the dealer manufactures it through dynamic trading.

Spreads and combinations

Another set of popular speculative strategies includes call and put spreads. These combine long and short positions in options of the same type.

A long *call spread* consists of a long low-strike call and a short high-strike call. Suppose we believe that ABC's price will rise by expiry, but will not exceed 80. We can buy a 65 call and sell an 80 call. Any outcome between 65 and 80 will yield an increasing payoff; we will have given up any increase at and above 80. If the stock ends up at 76, we will collect 11 from the 65 call and we will pay nothing on the 80 call. If the stock ends up at 88, we will collect 23 from the 65 call, but we will pay 8 on the 80 call, leaving us with 15, the maximum payoff from the strategy reached at 80. Below 65 both options are worthless.

A long *put spread* consists of a long high-strike put and a short low-strike put. Suppose we believe that ABC's price will drop by expiry, but not below 35. We can buy a 55 put and sell a 35 put. Any outcome between 35 and 55 will yield an increasing payoff; we will have given up any increase below 35. If the stock ends up at 46, we will collect 9 from the 55 put and we will pay nothing on the 35 put. If the stock ends up at 28, we will collect 27 from the 55 put, but we will pay 7 on the 35 put, leaving us with 20, the maximum payoff from the strategy reached at 35. Above 55 both options are worthless.

The payoffs on the long 65–80 call spread and short 35–55 put spread are shown in Figure 9.3.

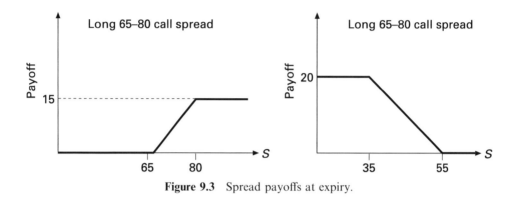

Figure 9.3   Spread payoffs at expiry.

We can package puts and calls into other combinations. If we sell a low-strike put and buy a high-strike call, we will have no payout over a wide intermediate range of prices (but perhaps a net premium received), we will benefit on the upside, and pay out on the downside.

Options can also be combined to form *calendar spreads*. In this case, we buy an option with one expiry date and sell an option with the same (or different) strike, but with a different expiry date. For example, if we believe that ABC's price might first go up but then come down, we can buy a call with short maturity and sell one with a longer maturity. Or if we believe that neither option will ever pay, we may want to sell the more expensive (longer) one and buy the cheaper (shorter) one to pocket the difference.

Options can be combined with long and short positions on the underlying asset and in leveraged proportions.

A *buy–write* is a strategy where we buy the stock and sell a high strike call. As the stock rises, we are exposed to the possibility that it will rise above the strike of the call. At that level, we will forgo any further appreciation in the stock as we will be forced to pay out on the call. If we believe that the stock will appreciate over time but not rapidly, we can opt to sell a string of calls with increasing strikes and maturities. We collect lots of premium and hope that the options never pay off. This strategy is popular with asset managers (e.g., insurance companies) who naturally hold long portfolios of stocks and want to gain extra income for some extra risk. The strategy is called *covered call writing*.

In a leveraged buy–write, we buy the stock and sell two calls with the same strike and the same maturity. If the stock price rises above the bet level we may lose any of the prior appreciation we have gained.

The payoffs on a long, 80-strike buy–write and a 2-to-1 leveraged version of that are shown in Figure 9.4.

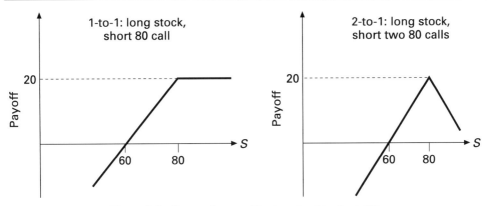

Figure 9.4 Buy–write payoffs at expiry (stock at 60).

We can also combine a put with a long stock position to obtain protection against the stock falling. The strategy works for holders of concentrated wealth (e.g., private stocks of wealthy families) who cannot or do not want to sell their holdings. If we are afraid that ABC's price may drop below 50, we can buy a 50 put to protect our long stock position. To reduce the cost of the protection we can sell a 40 put.

Options help with investment-timing decisions. Suppose we researched ABC's stock and consider it a solid long-term investment. Based on our analysis, we would like to buy it at 56 or below, but the price has run up to 60. The stock is highly volatile in the short run. Suppose we sell (write) a 60 put for 5. If the stock continues to go up, at least we collected 5; we have to chase the stock up, but we enjoy a defrayment of cost. If the stock goes down to 57, we will be exercised against, having to pay 3. Our net profit is 2 and we can use it to buy the stock, effectively paying 55. If the stock goes down even further to 50, we pay out 10. This leaves us with a loss of 5, but we can buy the stock for 50, effectively paying 55.

The payoffs on a 50 put-protected stock and a long, 40–50 put-protected stock are shown in Figure 9.5.

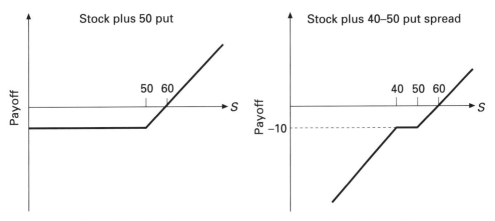

Figure 9.5 Payoffs on put-protected stock at expiry (stock at 60).

Binary options

OTC, we can purchase options with fixed monetary payoffs. Suppose we pay 3 to get 20, if ABC's stock goes to or above 70, or we pay 2 to get 20, if ABC's stock goes down to 50 but not below 40. The payoffs on these two options are in the following diagrams. Binary options are more common with interest rates, where a version of them is called a *range*.

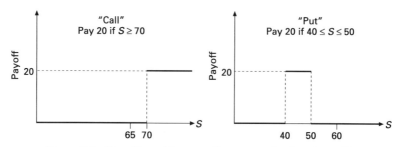

Figure 9.6 Payoffs on binary options at expiry (stock at 60).

9.3 OPTION VALUES PRIOR TO EXPIRY

In all the above diagrams we showed the payoff of the options on the expiry date. Prior to expiry the option value will have to be higher than the present value (PV) of the payoff and in most cases even higher than the intrinsic value (equal to the payoff computed with today's stock price). For American options, which can be exercised immediately, this should be obvious. We can always exercise the option for its intrinsic value, so the value cannot be lower than that. Then there is a possibility of an even greater payoff. For European options, the argument is a little more subtle. For options on assets with no intermediate payouts, it can be shown that European calls should not be exercised early and are thus equally valuable as American calls.[3] American puts may be optimal to be exercised early and so the European options price can be lower than its American version.

In general, the value of the option prior to expiry can be represented as a line above the intrinsic value bound.

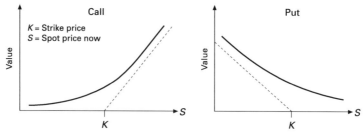

Figure 9.7   Value of a call and a put prior to expiry.
K = Strike price; S = Spot price now.

---

[3] For example, an American call on a stock that pays no dividends should not be exercised early and is thus just as valuable as a European one.

Option prices observe certain obvious arbitrage rules. A higher strike call will always be worth less than a lower strike call with the same expiry. If ABC's stock is at 60, then a 70 call will be worth more than an 80 call because the 70 call will always pay more than an 80 call. If the stock ends up at 75, the 70 call will pay 5 while the 80 call will pay nothing. The two will pay the same only if they both pay nothing. A lower strike put will be always worth less than a higher strike put with the same maturity. The reasoning is analogous to the call case.

An option with a longer maturity will always be worth at least as much as an otherwise identical option with a shorter maturity. If the options have the same strikes, then their intrinsic values will be the same, but the longer option will allow more time for the underlying asset to move to generate a higher payoff. The analogy is the insurance policy comparison between short- and long-term coverage. Since long-term coverage allows for a greater possibility of a payoff, it will cost more. Insurance has a similarly asymmetric payoff. It pays nothing if the desired event does not take place, no matter how "close" to it we got; on the other side, the payoff depends on how deep in-the-money we get. It is only one side of the probability distribution that determines the value of the policy.

We will discover a few more arbitrage rules later.

9.4   OPTIONS, FORWARDS, AND RISK SHARING

Suppose we buy a European call and sell a European put on the same asset. Suppose that we also search among all possible strike prices and find one strike price K, such that the premium on the call struck at K that we buy is exactly paid for by the premium on the put struck at K that we sell. Let us examine the payoff of our strategy at expiry for physical-settle options.

If $S \geq K$, then the call option is in-the-money and we buy the stock for the amount K. If $S \leq K$, then the put option is in-the-money. We are exercised against, and we buy the stock for the amount K. By buying the call and selling the put, we are in effect agreeing to buy the stock for the amount K on the expiry date. In a cash settle case, this means that no matter whether the stock price is above or below the strike price, our payoff is $S - K$ on the expiry date.

Our strategy is equivalent to entering a long forward on the stock. Net, we pay nothing today, and on a future date we deliver the sum of money K for one share of the stock. The forward is on-market (zero PV upfront).

If we were slightly less careful in our search for the perfect strike and, instead, picked one at random, but made sure that the strike on the long call is the same as the strike on the short put, then we would have in effect entered into an off-market forward with the mark-to-market value (PV) equal to the difference between the premium on the call and that on the put.

$$Call - Put = Forward$$

We can think of the forward value of the stock as the median separating two possibility regions for the future stock price. The long call covers the part of the region to the right of the strike (i.e., with stock values greater than the strike). The short put covers the part of the region to the left of the strike (i.e., with stock values lower than the strike). Traders can synthesize forwards from options or they can enter into forwards and synthesize options by selling off the undesirable probability regions. For example, to synthesize a call a dealer may enter into a forward and buy a put to offset the short put implicit in the forward. To synthesize a put, a dealer may enter into a short forward and buy a call to offset the short call implicit in the short forward.

This is an advanced way of risk arbitrage. The prices of calls and puts have to be in line with on- and off-market forwards and futures. The arbitrage is executable by combining futures and options on the same underlying asset and choosing to buy the side that is cheaper relative to the other.

This is also an advanced way of broad risk sharing. When a stock is bought in an IPO providing capital to a growing business, the buyer may not think much of options and forwards. He does, however, appreciate the existence of a secondary market for stocks (stock exchange), so that he can sell the stock when he no longer wants to bear the risk of the stock. The person he sells to may, however, be an option player who wants the stock, but only for a certain amount of time or only in a certain scenario. The fact that he can customize his participation in the stock may be the main reason that he purchases the stock. He does not buy another stock that does not have options trading on it, because that would force him into an all-or-nothing risk.

9.5   CURRENCY OPTIONS

Options on currencies work the same way as options on other assets. However, just like in spot and forward foreign exchange (FX) rates, we need to be careful to distinguish the pricing currency (numerator) and the priced one (denominator). With other assets, this is natural: the underlying price and the strike price of a stock option are expressed in dollars per share of ABC's stock. We are never interested in inverting the price or the strike to know how many shares per dollar we can buy. With currencies we often do. Because of that, each currency option (i.e., its strike rate) can be defined in two different ways (e.g., in yen per dollar and in dollar per yen). To keep things straight, one should think of the denominator currency as the underlying asset and the numerator currency as a price unit.

Let us consider a call option on the U.S. dollar with a strike of 110 Japanese yen per dollar (think of the dollar as the underlying asset) with one call covering $1,000 (think of dollars as shares and each call is on 1,000 shares). If the dollar's price rises above ¥110, the holder gets a payoff, otherwise not. The payoff, as with any call is equal to the difference between the spot price of the underlying asset S (i.e., the spot FX rate in ¥/$) on the expiry date minus the strike K, or nothing, times the number of units of the underlying asset (principal amount or size). That is, just like with any call, it is:

$$Call^{JPY/USD} = Size^{USD} \times Max(S^{JPY/USD} - K^{JPY/USD}, 0)$$

where both S and K are in ¥/$. The payoff is denominated in ¥. If the spot FX rate at expiry is ¥117, we get ¥7 times the 1,000 unit size, or ¥7,000, equivalent to $59.82905983 at the ¥/$117 FX rate; if the spot FX rate at expiry is ¥102, we get nothing. A physical-settle version of this option would be the right to buy 1,000 dollars for ¥110 a piece, which would be exercised only if the spot value of the dollar is greater than ¥110. But the right to buy the dollar is automatically equivalent to the right to sell the yen.

The call on the dollar struck at ¥/$110 *is* also a put on the yen struck at $1/110 = $/¥0.009 090 91$. If the size of the call is 1,000 dollars, then the size of the put is ¥110,000 (converting using the strike FX rate):

$$Call^{USD/JPY} = Size^{JPY} \times Max(K^{USD/JPY} - S^{USD/JPY}, 0)$$

When the value of the yen goes down to $0.008 547 01 (i.e., the spot FX rate moves to ¥/$117), we get a payout of $0.009 090 91 - 0.008 547 01 = \$0.000 543 90$ per unit of yen. This times the size of the option, 110,000 units of yen, gives us the total payoff of $59.829 059 83, which is the same as ¥7,000 at the ¥/$117 FX rate. When the spot FX rate goes up to $/¥0.009 803 92 (i.e., ¥/$102), we get nothing.

Call on currency₁ = Put on currency₂
Size converted at the strike FX rate (strike rate inverted)

This rule is true for all currency options, standard or not.

9.6   OPTIONS ON NON-PRICE VARIABLES

Options can be written on any variable, not just a price of some asset. Suppose we write a put option on the temperature reading in Paris on July 15, 2008 with a strike temperature of 23°C. We need to define how the outcome of the event will be translated into a monetary payoff. With stocks or currencies, this is automatic. Once we know the size of the option, say 100 shares or £62,500, the payoff is equal to the price difference per unit times the size. With options written on non-price variables, we have to define a number that translates the units of the non-price variable into money. Once we specify a *multiplier* of €500 per one degree centigrade, the definition of our option is complete. If the temperature in Paris on the expiry date is 17°C, our put option pays $23 - 17 = 6$ times 500, or €3,000. If the temperature is 26°C, the put pays nothing.

The first, most common example of a non-price variable is a stock index. A stock index is not a price of anything, but a normalized number designed to track the percentage changes in a particularly defined basket of stocks. The basket changes over time as some stocks come in and some are removed. Consider the Nikkei 225 index. In order to define a payoff of an option we need to translate the index points into yen. For example, we may specify that an 11,000 call will pay the difference between the index value and strike level times ¥10,000, or 0, whichever is greater. So if the index hits 11,078.23 on the expiry date of the call, the holder would get:

$$(11,078.23 - 11,000) \times ¥10,000 = ¥782,300$$

Note that the multiplier need not be specified in what seems natural. Suppose a U.S. investor wants exposure to the Japanese stock market, but does not want to bear currency risk. We could define the multiplier in dollars per Nikkei point (e.g., $250 per point). The holder would then get:

$$(11,078,23 - 11,000) \times \$250 = \$19,557.50$$

(For a dealer, this dollar option is much harder to hedge. The yen option is hedged by buying stocks in the right proportions, using the multiplier to define the yen amounts to be spent on shares. The dollar option involves additional currency exposure as yen gains and losses on the stocks have to be translated into dollars at a fictitious one-for-one fixed rate.)

Another non-price-based option example is an interest rate. Options can be written on the price of a bond, in which case we only need to specify the face value of the bond as the size. But options can also be written directly on the interest rate, whether spot or forward. The rate cannot be bought or sold (only an instrument whose value depends on it), so we cannot specify a "size". But we can specify a multiplier, say as $100 per 1 basis point (bp) of the difference between the underlying rate and the strike rate. (Hedging may be difficult. The option fixes a linear yield–payout relationship; the price–yield relationship for the hedged instrument is non-linear, so a $1 price change does not translate to a 1% yield change.)

Sometimes an interest-rate-based option's multiplier is implicit. A *cap* is a multi-period "call" option on a short-term rate which consists of several caplets. Each caplet provides a payment for one interest accrual period equal to 0 or the difference between the rate and a strike, whichever is greater, times the notional principal amount times the appropriate day-count. A 5-year, $100 million 4% cap on the 3-month U.S. dollar LIBOR (London interbank offered rate) consists of 20 caplets, one for each subsequent 3-month period. Caplet 9's payout will be based on the greater of zero and the difference between the 3-month LIBOR 2 years from today and 4%, and will take place 3 months later (i.e., in 2 years and 3 months); this is designed to mimic the way swaps and floating rate bonds pay. The multiplier for each caplet is equal to $100 million times the day-count for the relevant 3-month interest period (e.g., *Act/360*). Suppose 2 years from today LIBOR sets at 4.34%. The payout on the cap for that interest period assuming it has 92 days will be:

$$\$100,000,000 \times (4.34\% - 4\%) \times 92/360 = \$86,888.89$$

The multiplier on the cap changes slightly for each period as the day-count fraction changes.

9.7 BINOMIAL OPTIONS PRICING

The option premium charged by a dealer reflects his cost of manufacturing the payoff. The dealer sells (or buys) the option, then borrows or lends money, and takes a partial position in the underlying asset. By the expiry time, his hedge is worth exactly the same as the payoff on the option he owes or receives. We will illustrate the mechanics of payoff manufacturing with increasingly more revealing examples of binomial trees.[4] All examples use stocks, but are equally applicable to other traded assets.

One-step examples

We use the following assumptions for Examples 1–3. The underlying stock sells currently for $S = \$50$ a share. The expiry of the option is 1 year from today (or one period with no trading in the underlying between now and expiry). The dealer sells the option,

---

[4] The examples follow the notation and exposition used by many option textbooks, notably the "bible" of John C. Cox and Mark Rubinstein, *Option Markets*, 1985, Prentice Hall, Englewood Cliffs, NJ, and Martin Baxter and Andrew Rennie, *Financial Calculus*, 1996, Cambridge University Press, Cambridge, U.K.

collects the premium, and then follows a set of instructions. For Examples 1, 2a, and 3a, we also assume that the dealer can borrow or lend money at no interest. On the expiry date, one period from today, the stock can take on two values $S_{up} = \$70$ or $S_{dn} = \$20$. The dealer believes that the up probability is $\frac{1}{4}$ and the down probability is $\frac{3}{4}$. He takes the following steps:

(1) Given the potential stock outcomes $S_{up} = \$70$ or $S_{dn} = \$20$ for the up and down states tomorrow and given today's stock price of $S = \$50$, the dealer computes a number:

$$q = \frac{S - S_{dn}}{S_{up} - S_{dn}}$$

We will refer to q as the risk-neutral[5] probability of the up state and to $1 - q$ as the risk-neutral probability of the down state. These are the only probability-like numbers that the dealer uses in his weighted average calculations, not his subjective beliefs $\frac{1}{4}$ and $\frac{3}{4}$ (he could easily be wrong). The risk-neutral probability q has no meaning outside the context of this six-step procedure (i.e., it is not a real probability of anything). In our examples, we compute q to be:

$$q = \frac{50 - 20}{70 - 20} = \frac{3}{5} = 0.60$$

(2) Given the strike level K and the potential stock outcomes $S_{up} = \$70$ or $S_{dn} = \$20$ for the up and down states, he assigns the call payoffs C_{up} and C_{dn}, or put payoffs P_{up} or P_{dn}, for the corresponding states of nature in the expiry period.

(3) He computes the premium on the option by taking the average of the future option outcomes weighted by the risk-neutral probabilities of the states; that is:

$$C = qC_{up} + (1 - q)C_{dn} \qquad \text{or} \qquad P = qP_{up} + (1 - q)P_{dn}$$

(4) He computes a hedge number

$$\Delta = \frac{C_{up} - C_{dn}}{S_{up} - S_{dn}} \qquad \text{or} \qquad \Delta = \frac{P_{up} - P_{dn}}{S_{up} - S_{dn}}$$

which tells him how many shares of stock he needs to hold (buy or sell) today.

(5) He buys/sells the prescribed number of shares by paying/receiving $\Delta \times S$. He uses the collected premium in the purchase or sale. If necessary, he borrows/lends $\Delta \times S$ minus the option premium, so that his cash position today is 0.

(6) He liquidates his hedge one period from today when the state of nature is revealed (i.e., the stock either goes up or down). He uses the proceeds to settle his borrowing/lending and to pay the agreed-on payoff to the option buyer.

We will show that if he faithfully follows steps 1–5, then in step 6 he will always have on hand the exact amount of money demanded by the option holder, no matter what happens to the stock price. He will not have used his subjective beliefs to gamble on the direction of the stock.

---

[5] The word "risk-neutral" reflects a complicated mathematical concept of a probability measure change. We do not need to understand here what that is about. We simply blindly compute a number that we call q, which happens to resemble a probability. We will use it later in our mechanistic recipe.

In our illustrations, we will place all the computed numbers diagrams with nodes like this. Next to today's stock price of $S = 50$, we will show all the numbers from steps 1–5 (i.e., q, Δ, the option premium C or P, the cost of shares $\Delta \times S$, and the amount of borrowing/lending $\Delta \times S - C$ or $\Delta \times S - P$). Next to the potential future stock prices S_{up} and S_{dn}, we will show the corresponding value of the option C_{up} (or P_{up}) and C_{dn} (or P_{dn}), the value of the stock position held from the previous step $\Delta \times S_{up}$ and $\Delta \times S_{dn}$, and the cash position carried over from the previous step.

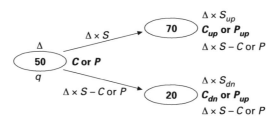

Figure 9.8   A binomial node. Current stock price $S = 50$.

Example 1 (Binary lottery, zero interest rate)   John Dealer sells a binary "call" option on the stock that pays $10 if the stock ends up at or above $60 or nothing if it ends up below $60 one period from today. John's calculations are shown in Figure 9.9.

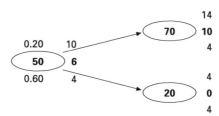

Figure 9.9   A binary call with payoff $C = 10$ if $S > 60$, otherwise zero.

The risk-neutral probability $q = 0.60$. The call payoffs 1 year from today are 10 if the stock is at 70 or 0 if the stock is at 20. So he sells the call for:

$$C = 0.60(\$10) + 0.40(\$0) = \$6$$

Given his hedge ratio:

$$\Delta = \frac{10 - 0}{70 - 20} = \frac{1}{5} = 0.20$$

he buys 0.20 shares for 0.20×50, or $10. Since he collected only $6 for the option, he borrows $10 - 6 = \$4$.

One period later, if the stock is at $70, his stock position is worth $0.20 \times 70 = \$14$. He liquidates it, pays $10 on the option, and repays the borrowing of $4. If the stock is at $20, his stock position is $0.20 \times 20 = \$4$. He liquidates it, pays nothing on the option, and repays his borrowing of $4. Collecting the premium of $6 on day 1 has allowed

John to manufacture the payoff he is obligated to make irrespective of whether the stock goes up or down.

Example 2a (call struck at 55, zero interest rate)   John Dealer sells a standard call option on the stock struck at \$55. At expiry, the call pays the value of the stock (i.e., S_{up} or S_{dn}) minus the strike ($K = 55$) if the stock ends up at or above \$55 or nothing if it ends up below \$55 one period from today. John's calculations are as follows.

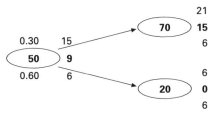

Figure 9.10   A call struck at 55. Payoff $C = \max(S - 55, 0)$. Zero interest rate.

The call payoffs are 15 if the stock is at 70 or 0 if the stock is at 20. So he sells the call for:

$$C = 0.60(\$15) + 0.40(\$0) = \$9$$

Given his hedge ratio:

$$\Delta \frac{15 - 0}{70 - 20} = \frac{3}{10} = 0.30$$

he buys 0.30 shares for 0.30×50 or \$15. Since he collected only \$9 for the option, he borrows $15 - 9 = \$6$.

One period later, if the stock is at \$70, his stock position is worth $0.30 \times 70 = \$21$. He liquidates it, pays \$15 on the option, and repays the borrowing of \$6. If the stock is at \$20, his stock position is $0.30 \times 20 = \$6$. He liquidates it, pays nothing on the option, and repays his borrowing of \$6.

Example 3a (put struck at 55, zero interest rate)   John Dealer sells a standard put option on the stock struck at \$55. At expiry, the put pays the strike ($K = 55$) minus the stock value (S_{up} or S_{dn}) if the stock ends up at or below \$55 or nothing if it ends up above \$55 one period from today. John's calculations are as follows.

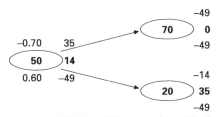

Figure 9.11   A put struck at 55. Payoff $P = \max(S - 55, 0)$. Zero interest rate.

The put payoffs are 0 if the stock is at 70 or 35 if the stock is at 20. So he sells the put for:

$$P = 0.60(\$0) + 0.40(\$35) = \$14$$

Given his hedge ratio:

$$\Delta = \frac{0 - 35}{70 - 20} = -\frac{7}{10} = -0.70$$

he shorts 0.70 shares to collect 0.70×50, or \$35. Since he collected \$14 for the option, he places the combined proceeds $35 + 14 = \$49$ in a deposit (i.e., lends).

One period later, if the stock is at \$70, his stock position is worth $-0.70 \times 70 = -\$49$. He liquidates it. He uses the \$49 from the deposit to buy the stock back and return it to the lender. He pays nothing on the option. If the stock is at \$20, his stock position is $-0.70 \times 20 = -\$14$. He uses the \$49 from the deposit to liquidate the stock position (\$14) and to pay \$35 on the option.

Let us make a few observations. Once the payoff on the option is defined, the rest is a mechanical adherence to a recipe. The recipe covers all potential payoff structures—binary, standard, or any other exotic—as well as both puts and calls and both bought and sold options. The actions for the dealer who buys the option, instead of selling, would be analogous. They are completely determined by his hedge ratio Δ. A positive delta means long stock; a negative one means short stock. The borrowing and lending simply balances the cash position resulting from the price of the Δ amount of stock and the premium on the option.

Let us now demonstrate that the recipe works with only slight modifications when we do not make the unrealistic assumption that the financing interest rate is 0. Here are the amendments:

(1) The formula for q is changed by replacing today's S with its future value equivalent (i.e., the forward). Recall that the forward is equal to the value of S multiplied by a future value factor, equal to 1 plus the interest rate r for 1 year. For fractions of a year, or special compounding and day-count conventions, it needs to be amended appropriately. For an annual period it is:

$$q = \frac{S(1 + r) - S_{dn}}{S_{up} - S_{dn}}$$

In our example, we assume that $r = 10\%$ and compute q to be:

$$q = \frac{50(1.1) - 20}{70 - 20} = \frac{7}{10} = 0.70$$

(2) No change.
(3) We compute the premium on the option by taking the average of the future option outcomes weighted by the risk-neutral probabilities of the states, present-valued to today; that is:

$$C = \frac{1}{1 + r}[qC_{up} + (1 - q)C_{dn}] \qquad \text{or} \qquad P = \frac{1}{1 + r}[qP_{up} + (1 - q)P_{dn}]$$

(4) through (6) No change, but we have to remember about interest paid or earned on borrowing or lending when carrying over the cash position from the previous step.

Let us repeat the standard call and put example with a financing cost of 10%.

Example 2b (call struck at 55, 10% interest rate)   John Dealer sells a standard call option on the stock struck at \$55. At expiry, the call pays the value of the stock (i.e., S_{up} or S_{dn}) minus the strike ($K = 55$) if the stock ends up at or above \$55 or nothing if it ends up below \$55 one period from today. John's calculations are as follows.

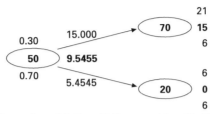

Figure 9.12   A call struck at 55. Payoff $C = \max(S - 55, 0)$. 10% interest rate.

The call payoffs are still 15 if the stock is at 70 or 0 if the stock is at 20. But he sells the call for:

$$C = \frac{1}{1.1}[0.70(\$15) + 0.30(\$0)] = \$9\frac{6}{11} = \$9.54545$$

Given his hedge ratio:

$$\Delta = \frac{15 - 0}{70 - 20} = \frac{3}{10} = 0.30$$

he buys 0.30 shares for 0.30×50, or \$15. Since he collected only \$9 $\frac{6}{11}$ for the option, he borrows $15 - 9\frac{6}{11} = \$5\frac{5}{11}$.

One period later, if the stock is at \$70, his stock position is worth $0.30 \times 70 = \$21$. He liquidates it, pays \$15 on the option, and repays the borrowing, which has by now accrued to \$6 ($5\frac{5}{11} \times 1.1$) at the 10% interest rate. If the stock is at \$20, his stock position is $0.30 \times 20 = \$6$. He liquidates it, pays nothing on the option, and repays his borrowing and interest of \$6.

Example 3b (put struck at 55, 10% interest rate)   John Dealer sells a standard put option on the stock struck at \$55. At expiry, the put pays the strike ($K = 55$) minus the stock value (S_{up} or S_{dn}) if the stock ends up at or below \$55 or nothing if it ends up above \$55 one period from today. John's calculations are as follows.

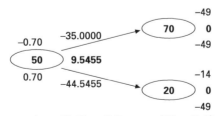

Figure 9.13   A put struck at 55. Payoff $P = \max(55 - S, 0)$. Zero interest rate.

The put payoffs are unchanged: 0 if the stock is at 70 or 35 if the stock is at 20. He sells the put for:

$$P = \frac{1}{1.1}[0.70(\$0) + 0.30(\$35)] = \$9\frac{6}{11} = \$9.54545$$

Given his hedge ratio:

$$\Delta = \frac{0 - 35}{70 - 20} = -\frac{7}{10} = -0.70$$

he shorts 0.70 shares to collect 0.70×50, or \$35. Since he collected $\$9\frac{6}{11}$ for the option, he places the combined proceeds $35 + 9\frac{6}{11} = \$44\frac{6}{11}$ in a deposit (i.e., he lends).

One period later, if the stock is at \$70, his stock position is worth $-0.70 \times 70 = -\$49$. He liquidates it. He uses the \$49 ($44\frac{6}{11} \times 1.1$) from the deposit, which has accrued interest in the meantime, to buy the stock back and return it to the lender. He pays nothing on the option. If the stock is at \$20, his stock position is $-0.70 \times 20 = -\$14$. He uses the \$49 from the deposit and interest to liquidate the stock position (\$14) and to pay \$35 on the option.

Let us make a few more observations. First, the hedge ratios are the same as in the zero interest case, but the borrowing/lending grows period to period and makes a difference in the final apportioning of the proceeds at expiry.

Second, a positive interest rate raised the price of the call and lowered the price of the put (Examples 2b and 3b relative to 2a and 3a). This is because a call seller borrows money to buy stock thereby incurring a cost, while a put seller lends money after shorting a stock accruing interest. So the cost of manufacturing the final payoff increases for the short-call hedger and decreases for the short-put hedger.

Third, the price of the call and the put in our example was the same (Examples 2b and 3b). This was not a coincidence. The strike price on both options was equal to \$55. This is the forward price of the stock for delivery on the expiry date, equal to the spot price of the stock \$50 times a future value factor reflecting the cost of carry (i.e., $50 \times (1 + 0.10) = \$55$).

This confirms our prior assertion, before we knew anything about option pricing, that a call and a put struck at a forward will have the same cost, so that we can manufacture the forward by buying a call and selling a put struck at the forward price.

Let us further show that the last property will hold no matter how volatile the stock is between now and expiry. Suppose that, instead of potential outcomes of \$70 or \$20, the stock is perceived to have potential outcomes of $S_{up} = \$80$ or $S_{dn} = \$15$. The stock is more volatile and is thus riskier. We follow our recipe using an interest rate of 10%. The forward value of the stock is still the same \$55.

Example 2c (call struck at 55, 10% interest rate)   John Dealer's calculations are as follows.

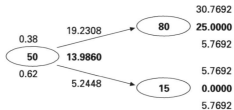

Figure 9.14   A call struck at 55. Payoff $C = \max(S - 55, 0)$. 10% interest rate. Higher volatility.

He sells the option for $13.986, a lot more than before, to reflect the increased expected value of the payoff.

Example 3c (put struck at 55, 10% interest rate)   John Dealer's calculations are as follows.

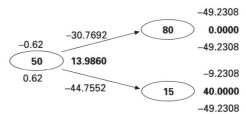

Figure 9.15   A put struck at 55. Payoff $P = \max(55 - S, 0)$. 10% interest rate. Higher volatility.

Again, he sells the option for $13.986, a lot more than before (Examples 2c and 3c relative to 2b and 3b), to reflect the increased expected value of the payoff.

In both examples, he sells the call for the same price as the put (Examples 2c and 3c). It will always be true that if the perceived riskiness of the underlying asset increases, both calls and puts will increase in value, but the price of a call struck at a forward will always be equal to the price of a put struck at a forward. This is because the forward does not have anything to do with the volatility of the stock, it simply reflects the cost of carry. A long-call–short-put position, equivalent to the forward, must carry a net zero premium (an on-market forward costs nothing to enter into).

What we have also shown is that, while the subjective probabilities of the stock outcomes are irrelevant, the volatility, or the potential dispersion of the outcomes, is not. The more volatile the stock is, the higher are the premiums on standard calls and puts (Examples 2c and 3c relative to 2b and 3b). This reflects the asymmetric nature of their payoffs. A more volatile stock means that the payoff when the option is in-the-money is likely to be larger, while when the option is out-of-the-money the payoff is still the same constant zero. Thus the expected value of the payoff is higher if the volatility is higher.

A multi-step example

Let us now demonstrate the full dynamic process of hedging an option (i.e., manufacturing its payoff). We consider a put struck at $K = 54$, an interest rate $r = 2.6\%$ per period (i.e., already de-compounded), and a stock price currently at 50, and follow the dynamics shown in Figure 9.16:

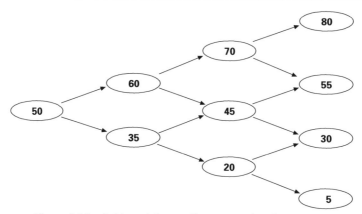

Figure 9.16   A binomial tree. Current stock price $S = 50$.

For example, an option with 3 months to expiry might be divided into monthly steps. Over the first month, the stock can go up to 60 or down to 35 (the actual probability of each step is irrelevant). If the stock went down to 35 during the first month, then it can go up to 45 or down to 20 over the second month, etc. For clarity, we will drop the arrows for the rest of the exposition.

We follow the same logic as used in the one-step examples for each subtree. We first compute the risk-neutral probability:

$$q = \frac{S(1+r) - S_{dn}}{S_{up} - S_{dn}}$$

for all subtrees. For example, for the subtree emanating from the 45 point, we have:

$$q = \frac{45(1+0.026) - 30}{55 - 30} = 0.6468$$

We also determine the payoff of the option at expiry. For example, when the stock price is 45, the payoff would be $54 - 45 = \$9$. We place the q's and the final payoffs in the diagram.

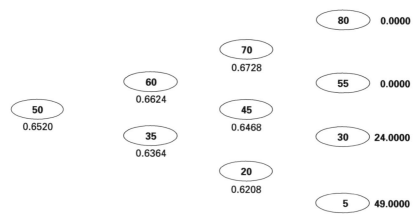

Figure 9.17   A binomial tree. Current stock price $S = 50$. Put payoff $P = \max(54 - S, 0)$. Computed q's and final payoffs.

As in the one-step examples, we sweep through the tree backward to determine the premium on the option today. We use the same equation as before for each node:

$$C = \frac{1}{1+r}[qC_{up} + (1-q)C_{dn}] \quad \text{or} \quad P = \frac{1}{1+r}[qP_{up} + (1-q)P_{dn}]$$

We start with the second-to-last date and consider the subtrees emanating from all three points. We compute put values for all three states: 70, 45, and 20. For the $45 state we compute:

$$P = \frac{1}{1+0.026}[0.6468 \cdot 0 + (1-0.6468) \cdot 24] = 8.2620$$

For the $20 state we compute:

$$P = \frac{1}{1+0.026}[0.6208 \cdot 24 + (1-0.6208) \cdot 49] = 32.6316$$

We place the values on the tree diagram. We go to one date before the one just computed and calculate the put values for each node (60 and 35) on this date, using the same equation linking a node on a given date to two future nodes. For example, for the $35 state we get:

$$P = \frac{1}{1+0.026}[0.6364 \cdot 8.2620 + (1-0.6364) \cdot 32.6316] = 16.6889$$

We proceed recursively like this until we obtain today's value of the put $P = \$7.3881$.

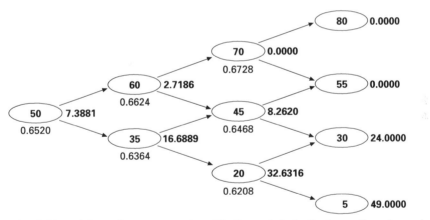

Figure 9.18 A binomial tree for a put struck at 54. Computed q's, final payoffs and premiums.

Next, we demonstrate that no matter which route the stock price takes between today and 3 months from today, the hedge will work perfectly.

For each node, we compute the hedge number:

$$\Delta = \frac{C_{up} - C_{dn}}{S_{up} - S_{dn}} \quad \text{or} \quad \Delta = \frac{P_{up} - P_{dn}}{S_{up} - S_{dn}}$$

which tells us how many shares we should hold at that node. In our put example, all deltas will be negative or 0 to reflect the fact that we will short shares. For example, for the $35 state 1 month from today the delta is:

$$\Delta = \frac{8.2620 - 32.6316}{45 - 20} = -0.9748$$

Again we place all the deltas in the diagram.

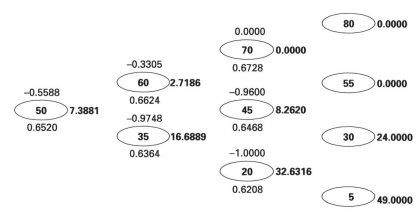

Figure 9.19 A binomial tree for a put struck at 54. Added Δ's for all nodes.

Depending on the route the stock takes, all trades are now determined by the differences between deltas at subsequent nodes. The lending amounts are determined too by the cash position at each node. Let us go through the tree forward, following one hypothetical path.

Suppose the stock price from today's level of $50 goes down to $35 1 month from today, then to $45 2 months from today, and ends up at $30 3 months from today. In order to hedge our position, we are required to short 0.5588 shares today. This will result in proceeds of $0.5588 \times 50 = \$27.9406$. We deposit that and the premium received from selling the put (i.e., a total of $27.9406 + 7.3881 = \$35.3287$) in an account earning 2.6% per month.

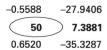

Figure 9.20 Today's node with $S = 50$, $P = 7.3881$, $\Delta = -0.5588$. Proceeds from short sale 27.9406. Total lending 35.3287.

The following month the price goes down to $35. Based on our new delta of -0.9748, we need to short an additional $0.9748 - 0.5588 = 0.4159$ shares. This results in proceeds of $0.4159 \times 35 = \$14.5590$. Meanwhile, our prior lending accrued to $35.3287 \times (1 + 0.026) = 36.2473$. We relend the sum of the two (i.e., $14.5590 + 36.2473 = \$50.8063$) for another month at 2.6%. Note that the borrowing/lending amount can also be found by subtracting the put value at a node, 16.6889, from the value of the share holding, $-0.9748 \times 35 = \$ - 34.1174$ (i.e., $-34.1174 - 16.6889 = \$ - 50.8063$).

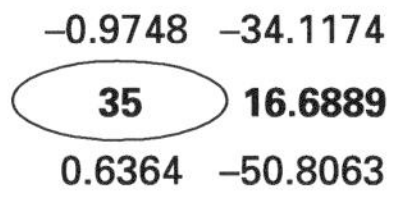

Figure 9.21   Month 1's node with $S = 50$, $\Delta = -0.9748$.

The following month, the stock price increases to $45. Based on our new delta of -0.9600, we need to buy back $0.9748 - 0.9600 = 0.0148$ shares. This costs us $0.0148 \times 45 = \$0.6653$. We take that amount from the maturing deposit which has accrued to $50.8063 \times (1 + 0.026) = \$52.1273$. We relend the remainder $52.1273 - 0.6653 = \$51.4620$ for another month at 2.6%. Again, the borrowing/lending amount can be found by subtracting the put value at a node, 8.2620, from the value of the shareholding, $-0.9600 \times 45 = \$ - 43.2000$ (i.e., $-43.2000 - 82620 = \$ - 51.4620$).

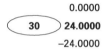

Figure 9.22   Month 2's node with $S = 45$, $\Delta = -0.9600$.

We proceed to the final step. The stock goes down to $30. We collect the deposit with accrued interest (i.e. $51.4620 \times (1 + 0.026) = \$52.8000$). We buy back the shorted shares for $0.9600 \times 30 = \$28.8000$ and pay $24 to the put holder. We are left with no stock position, no borrowing or lending position, and our put obligation is satisfied.

0.0000

(30) 24.0000

−24.0000

Figure 9.23   Final month's node with $S = 30$. Payoff of 24.

We can trace any other path through the tree to see that the result would be identical: we would end up with no stock, no cash, and we would have made a payout on the put, if any was required. The summary of all the calculations is portrayed in the completed diagram.

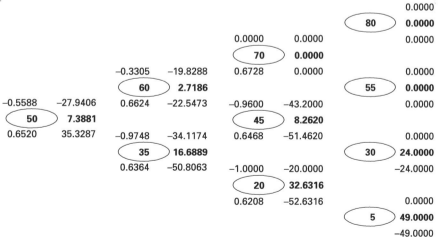

Figure 9.24   A complete binomial tree for a put struck at 54, including premiums, Δ's, totals shorted and totals lent.

The procedure of computing the q's, sweeping backward to get the option value upfront, and sweeping forward to compute the required hedges and borrowing/ lending positions works for all standard calls and puts, digital options, barrier options, American exercise style, and many other options. In all of these cases, the only thing that changes is the recursive computations of the option value during the backward sweep. For example, for American options that can be exercised early, we have to amend the option value for any given node to see if the immediate exercise value is not greater than the unexercised value; that is:

$$C = Max\left\{\frac{1}{1+r}[qC_{up} + (1-q)C_{dn}], S - K\right\}$$

or

$$P = Max\left\{\frac{1}{1+r}[qP_{up} + (1-q)P_{dn}], K - S\right\}$$

This is very easy to implement in any computer code or spreadsheet.

Black–Scholes

The well-known Black–Scholes[6] equation for calls and puts is a continuous general-ization of the binomial approach. There are at least two improvements there: first, the stock price, looking forward from one date to the next, can take on a continuum of values, not just two; and, second, there is a continuum of dates, not just month to month or day to day. The equation computes the present value of a hedge strategy where the rebalancing occurs instant by instant and over minute price changes. The overriding principle of payoff manufacturing remains the same. An option payoff is replicated by a position in a stock combined with borrowing or lending. The stock and bond position is adjusted continuously and for infinitesimal value changes. The value of the option today is equal to the cash required to start this dynamic hedge process. For options on a non-dividend-paying stock, it is equal to:

$$C = SN(d_1) - Ke^{-rT}N(d_2)$$

$$P = Ke^{-rT}N(-d_2) - SN(-d_1)$$

where $d_1 = \dfrac{\ln(S/K) + (r + \sigma^2/2)T}{\sigma\sqrt{T}}$, $d_2 = d_1 - \sigma\sqrt{T}$, r is a continuously compounded interest rate, and T is time to maturity (in years). The formula provides an explicit link between the annual volatility of the stock return σ and the value of the option. In the Black–Scholes model, the continuously compounded return on the stock over an in-finitesimal interval dt is assumed to be normally distributed. What this means is that, instead of the stock price taking on potentially only two values when moving from time t to time $t + dt$, the stock can take on a continuum of values such that the continuously compounded return on the stock over that interval, $\ln(S_{t+dt}/S_t)$, has a standard devia-tion of $\sigma\sqrt{dt}$. This is portrayed in Figure 9.25.

[6] Fischer Black and Myron Scholes, "The pricing of options and corporate liabilities", *Journal of Political Economy*, **81**, 637–659, May/June, 1973. The model is also attributed to Robert C. Merton, "Theory of rational option pricing", *Bell Journal of Economics and Management Science*, **4**, 141–183, Spring, 1973.

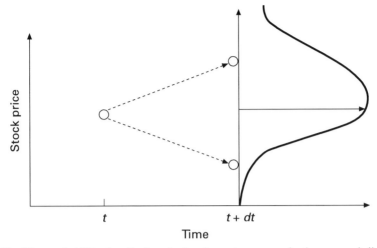

Figure 9.25 The probability density for stock price outcomes under log-normal distribution.

The probability mass curve in the graph is not the normal bell curve but rather that of a log-normal. The minimal stock price is 0, the maximal price is ∞. The percentage return is normal and would have a bell-shaped curve.

The inclusion of price volatility in arriving at the value of the option was implicit in our binomial trees, where the width of each branch depended on the variability of the stock. If we set:

$$u = e^{\sigma\sqrt{\Delta t}}, \qquad d = 1/u, \qquad q = \frac{e^{r\Delta t} - d}{u - d}$$

then it is easy to show that our binomial model with a time step of Δt is just a discrete approximation of and will converge to the Black–Scholes equation[7] as we shorten Δt (i.e., increase the number of rehedging times in the tree). That is why we chose to present the binomial approach to option pricing first, rather than go the continuous equation route. The discrete model is intuitive and more general, as it allows American exercise options to be valued; the continuous approach relies on a stochastic calculus argument. The two can be made equivalent to each other. That is, they come up with the same answer to the premium and hedge ratios.

Dividends

The inclusion of dividends in option pricing is straightforward, assuming that dividends are a known cash payout between now and the option expiry. Their effect on option prices should be intuitive. Because they are an outflow of value from the stock, they reduce the potential future outcomes for the stock. As such, their impact is to decrease the call values and to increase the put values. This can also be argued by considering the delta hedge. The call writer shorts less of the stock, and the put writer buys more of

---

[7] This is only one of many possible ways of making the binomial tree converge to the Black–Scholes equation. For a discussion, see John C. Hull, *Options, Futures, and Other Derivatives* (4th edn), 2000, Prentice Hall, Englewood Cliffs, NJ.

the stock, because when they adjust the hedge the stock price will have been reduced by the amount of the dividends, whether the stock has gone up or down.

There are two ways to correct option valuation for dividends, depending on whether their amount is known in dollars or as a percentage of the stock price (analogously to the forward discussion in Chapter 6). Consider dividends paid at a constant continuous rate δ. In the Black–Scholes model, the inclusion of dividends is accomplished[8] by multiplying each occurrence of the stock price S by the continuous compounding term $e^{-\delta T}$. In the binomial model, the correction is the same. Each node's stock value is reduced by the amount of accrued dividends. We change the definitions of the upstate and the downstate to $u = e^{-\delta \Delta t + \sigma \sqrt{\Delta t}}$, $d = e^{-\delta \Delta t - \sigma \sqrt{\Delta t}}$.

9.8   RESIDUAL RISK OF OPTIONS: VOLATILITY

Can anything go wrong with the hedge? If the dealer adheres strictly to the algorithm and as long as the stock follows one of the considered paths, then the answer is no. And, if the Black–Scholes model considers a continuum of paths, doesn't the algorithm consider all possible paths? Unfortunately, the answer is no.

The range of possible outcomes considered is determined by the assumed volatility of the stock. Volatility is the square root of variance. Variance is the expected value of squared deviations of the stock's return from the mean return over a given period. The Black–Scholes model requires volatility as an input. It then considers all the stock price paths that are within a certain range bounded by the volatility. That is, stock price movements period to period are restricted not to jump discontinuously. Graphically, this can be portrayed as all the paths within an expanding cylinder of outcomes, with the greatest density of paths close to the center. The edges of the cylinder are not binding, but the probability of outcomes outside or far from the center is minuscule (i.e., we assume a bell-shaped normal curve for the path of stock returns).

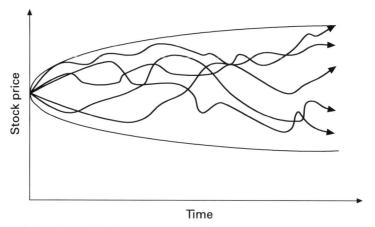

Figure 9.26   Stock price paths for constant σ. Paths are bound not to jump discontinuously.

[8] See R. Roll, "An analytic formula for unprotected American call options on stocks with known dividends", *Journal of Financial Economics*, **5**, 251–258, 1977; R. Geske, "A note on an analytic valuation formula for unprotected American call options on stocks with known dividends", *Journal of Financial Economics*, **7**, 375–380, 1979; and R. Whaley, "On the valuation of American call options on stocks with known dividends", *Journal of Financial Economics*, **9**, 207–211, 1981.

In the binomial setup, volatility translates directly to the width of the span of potential outcomes. Thus a 30% annual volatility may translate into a 70–20 span as in Example 2b and a 40% volatility may result in a wider span of 80–15 as in Example 2c.

If a dealer underestimates the actual volatility the stock will experience during the life of the option, then he will discover that he has sold the option too cheaply. The premium he has charged will not cover the cost of the replicating strategy. In the Black–Scholes model, that means the dealer should have used a higher volatility input. In the binomial model, the assumed span should have been wider. Note that the dealer is not asked to predict the really unpredictable (i.e., whether the stock will go up or down), but only the slightly unpredictable (i.e., whether the stock will move little or a lot between now and expiry).

Let us see in our binomial model what happens if the seller of a 55 call underestimates volatility. Suppose he uses the model as in Example 2b, describing potential outcomes as 70 and 20. He charges $9 $\frac{6}{11}$ for the call and borrows $5 $\frac{5}{11}$. With the total amount of $15 he buys the prescribed 0.3000 shares at $50 a share. But the stock proves more volatile (i.e., it attains either 80 or 15). The dealer will lose money whether the stock goes up or down. Here is the diagram.

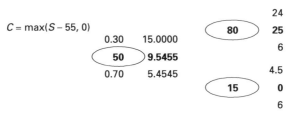

Figure 9.27   Example 2b revisited: mis-hedge.

If the stock goes up to 80, the 0.3 shares are worth $24, but the dealer owes $25 to the option holder and $6 on his borrowing. If the stock goes down to $15, the 0.3 shares are worth $4.50, but the dealer owes $0 to the option holder and $6 on his borrowing.

The primary risk of any option dealer is not the direction the underlying asset may take, but the exposure to volatility of the underlying asset. A sold option results in a *short-volatility position*. If the actual volatility of the underlying asset increases, the dealer loses money; if it decreases, the dealer makes money. A bought option results in a *long-volatility position*. If the actual volatility of the underlying asset increases, the dealer makes money; if it decreases, the dealer loses money. The sensitivity of an option to the volatility input is called the *vega* of the option. The unit is the dollar change in the value of the option per 1% change in volatility. The vega of an option depends on the maturity of the option, the strike level relative to the current underlying asset's price (*in-the-moneyness*), and the interest rate. In general, the longer the time to expiry the higher the vega, as there is more time to lose money on mis-hedging. Also, the closer the option is to the money the greater the vega. Deep in-the-money options and deep out-of-the-money options have low vegas.

Option portfolios can be described as long or short volatility, too. A long-volatility portfolio may contain bought and sold options, but the majority are bought. The "majority" here means that the net vega position in terms of net dollar sensitivity of the portfolio to a 1% change in the volatility (long-vega options minus short-vega options) is positive. A short-volatility portfolio has a net negative vega. With many bought and sold options in the portfolio, the overall vega of the portfolio changes over time and as the price of the underlying asset fluctuates.

The vega of an option is related to another "Greek": the *gamma*. The latter relates to the change in the delta of the option per unit of underlying price change. The higher the gamma, the more the delta hedge needs to be adjusted as a result of an underlying price change. High-gamma options are considered risky given that the required change in the delta hedge may be difficult to execute quickly and without a loss.[9] The vega (and the gamma) risk of an option portfolio cannot be hedged with positions in the underlying asset, but only through option positions. A position in a stock does not have any vega or gamma exposure; hence it cannot offset any option exposure. Only another option can.

Implied volatility

Running an option book is a bit of a chicken-and-egg game. In order to price the options we buy and sell, we need the volatility input into a pricing model (Black–Scholes, binomial, other). Different volatility assumptions will result in different hedge ratios (i.e., positions in the underlying assets). Suppose we have somehow guessed the right input, priced all the options, computed the hedges, and bought or shorted the right net number of shares, bonds, or currency underlying the options in our portfolio. Our portfolio is now free of directional risk. Whether the underlying asset price goes up or down, we do not show any profit or loss.

But how do we guess the volatility input? We could perform a statistical analysis of the past movements in the asset's price and compute the standard deviation of the returns on the asset. This *historical volatility* could then be input into the model. However, that would be tantamount to betting that the historical level of price variation will continue into the future. A better way is to try to get at the market's current consensus of the future price volatility. Where can we obtain that? In the option prices other people charge.

Before we use the model to price our portfolio, we examine currently quoted option prices. Dealers who quote these prices include their estimates of future volatility as input into the same models to calculate their manufacture costs. We can back out what those estimates are by using our model to see what volatility input yields the prices that they quote. This *implied volatility* can then be input into our own model to price and hedge our portfolio.

Using implied volatility is always superior to using historical volatility as an input into an option model. This is because we can actually trade the options priced using implied volatilities. After all, we obtain those implied volatilities from actual option quotes. We can use those options to eliminate our vega risk. Suppose our portfolio is long-volatility and market-neutral. That is, we have bought more options than we sold, but we bought or shorted enough of the underlying asset to eliminate the directional risk. We compute the sensitivity of our portfolio to a 1% change in the volatility input

---

[9] Gamma of options is analogous to convexity of bonds. Both can lead to considerable mis-hedging.

and sell new options at the quoted prices by choosing the amount sold so that those options have the same sensitivity to a 1% volatility change. We also neutralize the directional risk of the newly sold options. Now our combined portfolio is directional risk-free and vega risk-free!

The only way for a hedger to make money from trading options is to charge/pay for options more/less than the fair value. That is, the hedger's profit comes purely from the bid–ask spread and not from speculation on any explicit (price, rate) or implicit (volatility) market variable. Most dealers do not offset their vega risk completely and thus can be considered arbitrageurs in first-order risk (directional) and speculators in second-order risk (volatility). They can offset their volatility risk but choose not to as that would eat into their profits.

The only time we may consider using historical volatilities as inputs is when there are no options being quoted for expiries similar to the options in our portfolio. This is typical for very long-term options.

Volatility smiles and skews

In the Black–Scholes model, there is only one volatility input. This means that volatility is constant over time. This is actually not a big problem and can be easily rectified. We can assume that volatility changes over time. We can then substitute a vector of volatilities, indexed by time, for a single number. In the binomial setup, this translates into considering different widths for the tree branches as we move through time steps (left to right). A bigger problem is associated with the fact that in the Black–Scholes model we also assume that volatility is constant across different price levels (up and down in the tree). We can fix that by considering different branch widths across states. After all the "fixes", using perhaps a whole matrix of volatility inputs, the tree will most likely fall apart as different nodes will not recombine and the tree will more likely look like our graph made up of separate price paths. This can still be handled by more complicated numerical methods. But what if, in reality, prices jump discretely and by more than the normal distribution for return would allow, and what if they jump differently at different levels and different times? What if the volatility itself is random?

An option valuation model is never perfect. It is a simplification of potential price or rate movements. The total scope of those movements is constrained by probabilistic assumptions about price paths and volatility structure. Paths close to the mean may be assumed more likely than those away from the mean. Paths may be assumed continuous (i.e., prices do not jump discretely). Volatility may be assumed constant in time, returns, or prices and unrelated to the price levels. There may be other unrealistic model features. In stock and currency models, the stock price or the FX rate may be assumed to fluctuate, but interest rates may not be. In interest rate option models, all rates may be assumed to move in parallel or close to parallel. These simplifications are introduced to make the math of the models tractable.

For these and perhaps many other reasons, it is well known that options on the same underlying asset may require different volatility inputs for different strikes and expiries.

First, consider the implied volatilities as published on October 17, 2003 by the Federal Reserve for at-the-money currency options as of the end of the previous month.

Table 9.1   Implied volatility rates for foreign currency options* (September 30, 2003)

	1 week	1 Month	2 Month	3 Month	6 Month	12 Month	2 Year	3 Year
EUR	12.6	11.8	11.6	11.4	11.4	11.3	11.2	11.2
JPY	14.3	12.5	11.6	10.8	10.3	10.1	10.0	9.9
CHF	12.7	11.9	11.7	11.5	11.5	11.5	11.5	11.4
GBP	10.3	9.8	9.6	9.4	9.3	9.3	9.4	9.4
CAD	10.1	9.7	9.5	9.4	9.1	8.9	8.9	8.8
AUD	13.2	12.3	11.9	11.4	11.1	11.0	10.9	10.8
GBPEUR	8.3	7.8	7.7	7.6	7.6	7.5	7.5	7.3
EURJPY	12.8	11.6	11.1	10.7	10.5	10.3	11.6	10.3

* This release provides survey ranges of implied volatility mid-rates for at-the-money options as of 11:00 a.m. The quotes are for contracts of at least $10 million with a prime counterparty. This information is based on data collected by the Federal Reserve Bank of New York from a sample of market participants and is intended only for informational purposes. The data were obtained from sources believed to be reliable but this bank does not guarantee their accuracy, completeness, or correctness. For background information on the release, see page VBGROUND.FRB http://www.ny.frb.org/markets implied.txt
Reproduced with permission of Federal Reserve Bank of New York (http://www.newyorkfed.org/markets/impliedvolatility.html)

For each currency, the implied volatilities change with the expiry date. Generally, they decrease as the time to expiry increases. This implies that dealers estimate different replication costs for short options than for long options. This phenomenon perhaps has to do with the distinction between the *realized* and *implied* volatility and *mean reversion*. Short-term at-the-money options will require constant rebalancing as the hedge ratio computed between now and expiry will fluctuate. For longer term options, the hedge ratio day-to-day is going to change much less (longer time to expiry may make the present value of payoff less variable); therefore, while the actual volatility of the FX rate per day may be the same over a short period as over the long period, the dealer's "realized" volatility will be lower. The dealer will perform the buy-high-sell-low unprofitable trades less frequently. Therefore, his cost of manufacture or the premium will be lower. This will result in a lower computed implied volatility. *Mean reversion* refers to the possibility that, while FX rates fluctuate unpredictably in the short run, they tend to oscillate around long-term trend lines and the further they deviate from the trend lines the more they are pulled toward them (i.e., volatility depends on the level of rates). As option models cannot take all of these possibilities into account, they can be "fixed" by lowering the implied volatility for long-term options to reflect the lower cost of manufacture.

Consider another example of the computation of implied volatilities, as of October 15, 2003; this time for options on the S&P 500 index futures expiring December 18, 2003.

Table 9.2 December futures on the S&P 500

Strike	Implied volatility		Implied delta		Vega (ticks)
	Call	Put	Call	Put	
975	20.81	20.49	0.79	−0.2	1.24
980	20.48	20.21	0.78	−0.21	1.29
985	20.18	19.95	0.76	−0.23	1.34
990	19.91	19.72	0.75	−0.25	1.39
995	19.59	19.43	0.73	−0.26	1.44
1000	19.36	19.16	0.71	−0.28	1.49
1005	19.07	18.91	0.69	−0.3	1.53
1010	18.79	18.66	0.67	−0.32	1.57
1015	18.52	18.42	0.65	−0.34	1.61
1020	18.19	18.12	0.63	−0.36	1.65
1025	17.92	17.87	0.61	−0.38	1.68
1030	17.76	17.68	0.58	−0.41	1.71
1035	17.53	17.48	0.56	−0.43	1.73
1040	17.29	17.27	0.53	−0.46	1.74
1045*	17.04	17.04	0.51	−0.48	1.75
1050	16.88	16.91	0.48	−0.51	1.75
1055	16.65	—	0.45	−0.54	1.74
1060	16.46	16.54	0.43	−0.56	1.73
1065	16.3	—	0.4	−0.59	1.7
1070	16.12	16.19	0.37	−0.62	1.67
1075	15.91	16.02	0.34	−0.65	1.62
1080	15.81	—	0.32	−0.67	1.57
1085	15.75	—	0.29	−0.70	1.52
1090	15.62	—	0.27	−0.72	1.45
1095	15.53	—	0.24	−0.75	1.39
1100	15.43	15.64	0.22	−0.77	1.32

December futures = 1044.50, days = 47, at-the-money volatilities = 17.06%, interest rate = 6.50%. *Source*: http://www.pmpublishing.com/volatility/sp.html#StandardDeviations

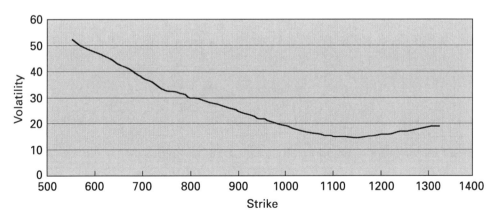

Figure 9.28   S&P 500 implied volatility skew (December 18, 2003). Puts with strikes below 1045; calls with strikes above 1045.
Source: http://www.pmpublishing.com/volatility/sp.html#StandardDeviations.

The *at-the-money* level is 1044.50 (= current value of the index). Calls/Puts with strikes higher/lower than that level are called out-of-the-money, and with strikes lower/higher than that level they are called in-the-money. The table shows the implied volatilities for different strike levels. As a general rule they decrease as the strike level increases in a *half-smile* fashion as shown on the enclosed graph (for very high strikes they start increasing again slightly). This relationship of implied volatilities to strikes is generally referred to as a *volatility smile* or *volatility skew*. It is a reflection of all the simplifications we cited above. It can, for example, be explained by the fact that as prices drop they tend to drop and fluctuate by more than assumed by the standard model (volatility is higher at lower price levels), and as prices increase they tend to increase more gradually without big jumps (volatility is lower as prices increase). The existence of volatility skew introduces additional risk to option portfolios. Options on the same underlying and with the same maturities, but with different strike prices, are not good hedges for each other. Hedging with imperfect substitutes carries basis risk (similar in a way to that of hedging one commodity with another, e.g. jet fuel with oil). Explicit modelling of the volatility skew allows dealers to minimize the tertiary risk to relative volatility changes across strikes. They involve relating different, implied volatilities through a postulated mathematical function, itself often assumed not to change over time.

Table 9.1 also shows the delta for each option sold, in units of futures contracts to be bought/shorted per one option, as well as its vega, in ticks (index points) per 1% volatility change.

9.9   INTEREST RATE OPTIONS, CAPS, AND FLOORS

The modeling of options on interest rates is more complicated than those on equity prices, commodity prices, or FX rates. There are several reasons for that. First and foremost is that interest rates are not prices of assets that can be bought and sold. Imagine in our binomial example that, instead of stock prices, we place the rate on a 10-year bond on the nodes of the tree. We build the tree using the right volatility and follow our recipe to a tee. Now we try to hedge using the recipe's prescriptions. We want to dynamically trade the underlying asset so that the dollar changes in our hedge position exactly offset the changes in the value of the option over its entire life. In the stock example, the delta of the option told us how many shares of the asset to buy or sell. In the commodity case, that would be the amount of the commodity; in the currency case, that would be the amount of foreign or domestic currency. As the price of the stock, commodity, or currency changed by one dollar, the value of our hedge position changed exactly by delta times one dollar. The complication with interest rates is that we cannot buy an interest rate. We can buy the 10-year bond whose price (PV of cash flows) depends on the rate, but not the rate itself. Suppose we try to outsmart the option model and we buy or sell some amount of the bond corresponding to the "amount" of the rate we were supposed to buy or sell as our delta. The hedge will not work because the relationship between bond price changes and rate changes is non-linear (duration is not constant in yield). As the rate changes, what seemed like the right amount of the bond to buy will prove to be slightly wrong, but will not be equally wrong, depending on whether the yield goes up or down. The dollar value change in the hedge will not be equal to the delta times 1 bp change in the rate. This convexity feature of the interest rate instruments can be partly overcome by the use of non-convex futures instruments. A Eurocurrency contract is the best example. Its value (variation margin settlement) is a constant monetary amount per 1 bp change in the interest rate change. But the application of non-convex instruments can only help in a limited number of cases. Most spot or forward rates on which options are written will be themselves complicated functions of the intermediate futures. The 10-year bond as an asset can be synthesized from shorter spot rates and lots of intermediate forwards. The 10-year par rate will still be a very non-linear function of those rates or forward prices.

The second important complication for interest rate options is that interest rates are not independent of each other. If the 10-year par rate can be synthesized from 40 quarterly forward rates, then do we have to take into account the volatilities of all those rates and their correlations? Our binomial nodes then have 40 variables on them. And, then, how do we come up with all the volatility and correlation inputs? It was hard enough with a single stock, let alone with tens of interrelated rates.

The solution is often a reduced-form model with only one or two variables driving the uncertainty in the model. All other rates are then assumed to be deterministic functions of that one *state variable*, whose implied volatility structure we are confident about (i.e., we can calibrate from other existing options). If the model has two state variables, then we must be able to observe enough prices for other options so that we can not only back out implied volatilities for both state variables, but also the correlations between the two (in a process analogous to the implied volatility computations). The assumption of one or only two state variables is clearly unrealistic, but most of the time this is the best we can do. Often, this is accurate enough. But because the math behind models like these becomes quite complicated, only experts can tell whether we are close enough to the true value of the option and the true hedge ratios.

Options on bond prices

Suppose we buy a call option on a price, not a rate, of a specific 5-year bond struck at 102. Can we price the option by assuming some volatility of the bond price and construct our binomial tree? Unless the option expiry is super-short, the answer is still probably no.

Bond prices do not fluctuate like stock prices. First, each bond has a maximum price equal to the sum of the coupons and principal (when the yield is 0, the present value boils down to a simple sum as all discount factors are equal to 1). Second, the bond price must be equal to the face value by maturity. In a way, the bond price is pulled toward that known final value. This constrains how much the bond price can fluctuate. A bond with little time to maturity cannot move much, even if the yield changes dramatically. Stocks or commodity stock prices do not have maturities and hence predetermined maturity prices.

Hence even options written on bond prices, not rates, may require a rate-driven valuation model with attendant complications as described above.

Caps and floors

Caps and floors are packages of options, calls, and puts, correspondingly, on the same underlying (mostly short-term) interest rate with sequential expiry dates. The vast majority of caps and floors have the 3-month LIBOR as their underlying rate. The expiry dates on the options, called caplets or floorlets, follow a quarterly or semi-annual schedule, typically matched to the maturity of the underlying rate, starting with immediate expiry and ending with the last expiry date being one period prior to the stated maturity of the cap. For example, a 5-year cap on 3-month LIBOR struck at 4.5%

consists of 20 caplets with expiries of 0 months, 3 months, 6 months, 9 months, and so on, all the way to 57 months. The payouts on the options are delayed by 3 months (i.e., made in arrears); the last payout is on the maturity date of the cap (i.e., in 60 months). The payoff on each caplet is equal to the greater of 0 and the difference between the underlying LIBOR rate on the expiry date and the strike rate of 4.5% times the day-count fraction on an *Act/360* basis for the period covered by the LIBOR rate. A floor is a "put" equivalent of a cap. That is, the payoff of each floorlet is equal to the greater of 0 and the difference between the strike rate of 4.5% and the underlying LIBOR rate on the expiry date times the same day-count fraction. All these details are designed to match the swap market conventions, since caps and floors are viewed as natural supplements to swaps. Let us illustrate our 4.5% cap and 4.5% floor by assuming some hypothetical LIBOR rates (in column 2) for future option expiry dates (called set dates), and day counts for the subsequent 3-month period until the pay dates. The principal amount is $100,000,000.

Table 9.3 Five-year, 4.5%, $100 million cap and floor on 3-month LIBOR (dates in months from today)

Set date	LIBOR	Cap			Floor			Pay date
		$Max(L - K, 0)$	Days	Payout	$Max(K - L, 0)$	Days	Payout	
0	4.50	0	91	0	0	91	0	3
3	4.20	0	91	0	0.3	91	75,833	6
6	4.81	0.31	92	79,222	0	92	0	9
9	5.20	0.7	90	175,000	0	90	0	12
12	5.40	0.9	89	222.500	0	89	0	15
15	5.55	1.05	91	265,417	0	91	0	18
18	5.83	1.33	92	339,889	0	92	0	21
21	6.21	1.71	91	432,250	0	91	0	24
24	6.43	1.93	90	482,500	0	90	0	27
27	6.11	1.61	92	411,444	0	92	0	30
30	5.73	1.23	91	310,917	0	91	0	33
33	5.32	0.82	91	207,278	0	91	0	36
36	5.17	0.67	89	165,639	0	89	0	39
39	4.85	0.35	92	89,444	0	92	0	42
42	4.62	0.12	91	30,333	0	91	0	45
45	4.33	0	91	0	0.17	91	42,972	48
48	4.02	0	89	0	0.48	89	118,667	51
51	3.78	0	92	0	0.72	92	184,000	54
54	3.66	0	91	0	0.84	91	212,333	57
57	3.21	0	90	0	1.29	90	322,500	60

The buyer of the cap benefits if spot LIBOR rates on future dates exceed 4.5%. The buyer of the floor benefits if spot LIBOR rates on future dates are below 4.5%. Typically, the first caplet and floorlet are deleted, unless specifically stated to the contrary (i.e., technically we have 19 optionlets). Caps can be viewed as protection against interest rate increases, while floors can be viewed as protection against interest rate declines.

The at-, in-, and out-of-the money terminology for caps and floors is a little different from stock options; there, we usually had only one option, here we have many. A cap or floor is said to be (struck) at-the-money if the strike price is chosen to be the swap rate of the same maturity as the maturity of the cap. Correspondingly, we can talk about in-the-money or out-of-the-money caps and floors, depending on whether their strike is greater or less than the swap rate. The statement applies on an aggregate basis, not to individual optionlets. In our illustration, if the 5-year swap rate on an Act/360 basis is 5%, then our cap would be called in-the-money (as the swap rate is higher than the strike), even though based on today's LIBOR the caplets are really at-the-money and, on a forward basis, some caplets may be out-of-the-money. Our floor would be out-of-the-money as the swap rate is above the strike.

Relationship to FRAs and swaps

We have shown before that a swap is a package of forward-rate agreements (FRAs). A 5-year quarterly swap can be viewed as a package of 20 FRAs with subsequent maturities. The start date of each FRA matches one set date of the swap, and the end date of the FRA matches the pay date of the swap corresponding to the given set date. The first FRA is 0×3, the next 3×6, and so on. The last one is 57×60.

Instead of dissecting swaps along set and pay dates, we can dissect them along rate levels. A pay-fixed swap can be viewed as a long cap and a short floor. Similarly, each constituent FRA can be viewed as a long-caplet and short-floorlet position. Suppose we buy a $100 million 5-year cap struck at 4.5% and sell a $100 million 5-year floor struck at 4.5%. When LIBOR exceeds the strike, the payoff on the floor is 0 and the payoff on the cap is equal to LIBOR minus the fixed rate of 4.5%. This is equivalent to a receipt of LIBOR and payment of fixed 4.5%. When LIBOR is below the strike, the payoff on the cap is 0 and the liability on the floor is equal to the fixed rate of 4.5% minus LIBOR. This is equivalent to a receipt of LIBOR and payment of fixed 4.5% (i.e., no matter where LIBOR sets, the cash flows are equivalent to those of a swap with a fixed rate of 4.5%). Table 9.4 summarizes the situation.

Table 9.4 Five-year, 4.5%, $100 million cap, floor, and swap (dates in months from today)

Set date	LIBOR	Days	Long cap		Short floor		Pay date	Swap		
			$Max(L-K,0)$	Payout	$Max(K-L,0)$	Payout		Receive	Pay	Net
0	4.50	91	0	0	0	0	3	1,137,500	1,137,500	0
3	4.20	91	0	0	0.3	−75,833	6	1,061,667	1,137,500	−75,833
6	4.81	92	0.31	79,222	0	0	9	1,299,222	1,150,000	79,222
9	5.20	90	0.7	175,000	0	0	12	1,300,000	1,125,000	175,000
12	5.40	89	0.9	222,500	0	0	15	1,335,000	1,112,500	222,500
15	5.55	91	1.05	265,417	0	0	18	1,402,917	1,137,500	265,417
18	5.83	92	1.33	339,889	0	0	21	1,489,889	1,150,000	339,889
21	6.21	91	1.71	432,250	0	0	24	1,569,750	1,137,500	432,250
24	6.43	90	1.93	482,500	0	0	27	1,607,500	1,125,000	482,500
27	6.11	92	1.61	411,444	0	0	30	1,561,444	1,150,000	411,444
30	5.73	91	1.23	310,917	0	0	33	1,448,417	1,137,500	310,917
33	5.32	91	0.82	207,278	0	0	36	1,344,778	1,137,500	207,278
36	5.17	89	0.67	165,639	0	0	39	1,278,139	1,112,500	165,639
39	4.85	92	0.35	89,444	0	0	42	1,239,444	1,150,000	89,444
42	4.62	91	0.12	30,333	0	0	45	1,167,833	1,137,500	30,333
45	4.33	91	0	0	0.17	−42,972	48	1,094,528	1,137,500	−42,972
48	4.02	89	0	0	0.48	−118,667	51	993,833	1,112,500	−118,667
51	3.78	92	0	0	0.72	−184,000	54	966,000	1,150,000	−184,000
54	3.66	91	0	0	0.84	−212,333	57	925,167	1,137,500	−212,333
57	3.21	90	0	0	1.29	−322,500	60	802,500	1,125,000	−322,500

Each row is a dissection of a FRA into a cap and a floor. The sum of the rows is equal to the swap. Each column group is a dissection of the swap into a long cap and short floor. The net receipt on the swap is identical to the net of the cap and floor positions:

Cap struck at K − Floor struck at K = Swap with fixed rate K

Suppose that we do not pick the strike rate randomly. Instead we select it in such a way that the premium we pay on the cap is equal to the premium we receive on the floor (i.e., we have no net cash flow upfront). What swap would have no net cash flow upfront? A *par* swap or an *on-market* swap. We can thus conclude the following:

Cap(with K = Swap rate) − Floor(with K = Swap rate) = Par swap

Recall the analogous relationship for stock options struck at the forward. We showed that as implied volatilities increased the values of the calls and puts, both struck at the forward, increased by the same amount as their payoff was still equivalent to the forward. The same is true for caps and floors. In order to conform to the constraint of arbitrage, if prices of caps struck at the swap rate increase (due to implied volatility rise), the prices of floors struck at the swap rate must also increase by the same amount. The pricing assumptions do not change the payout on the combined position, which is still equivalent to an on-market swap. These considerations are the basis for the in-the-moneyness language for caps and floors as defined above.

We can construct swaps out of caps and floors and vice versa. A cap can be viewed as a combination of a pay-fixed swap and a long floor position. A floor can be viewed as a combination of a long cap position and a receive-fixed swap.

An application

Bond issuers often combine a long cap position with a floating-rate bond. This ensures that the coupon payments on the bond do not exceed a certain desired level.

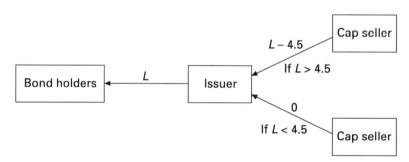

Figure 9.29   An issuer of a floating rate bond caps interest liability of 4.5%.

Suppose a company issues a 5-year bond paying quarterly floating coupons equal to LIBOR. The company also buys from a dealer a cap struck at 4.5%. If LIBOR on any coupon set date exceeds 4.5%, the company's net obligation will stay at 4.5%. If LIBOR on any coupon date is below 4.5%, the company takes advantage of the floating nature of the issue and pays less than 4.5%. Its net obligation is thus the lower of the two: LIBOR or 4.5%. The hypothetical cash flows are summarized in Table 9.5.

Table 9.5 Five-year, $100 million floating rate bond and 4.5% cap (dates in months from today)

Set date	LIBOR	Days	Long cap		Floating bond coupon	Pay date	Net
			Max(L − K, 0)	Payout			
0	4.50	91	0	0	−1,137,500	3	−1,137,500
3	4.20	91	0	0	−1,061,667	6	−1,061,667
6	4.81	92	0.31	79,222	−1,229,222	9	−1,150,000
9	5.20	90	0.7	175,000	−1,300,000	12	−1,125,000
12	5.40	89	0.9	222,500	−1,335,000	15	−1,112,500
15	5.55	91	1.05	265,417	−1,402,917	18	−1,137.500
18	5.83	92	1.33	339,889	−1,489,889	21	−1,150,000
21	6.21	91	1.71	432,250	−1,569,750	24	−1,137,500
24	6.43	90	1.93	482,500	−1,607,500	27	−1,125,000
27	6.11	92	1.61	411,444	−1,561,444	30	−1,150,000
30	5.73	91	1.23	310,917	−1,448,417	33	−1,137,500
33	5.32	91	0.82	207,278	−1,344,778	36	−1,137,500
36	5.17	89	0.67	165,639	−1,278,139	39	−1,112,500
39	4.85	92	0.35	89,444	−1,239,444	42	−1,150,000
42	4.62	91	0.12	30,333	−1,167,833	45	−1,137,500
45	4.33	91	0	0	−1,094,528	48	−1,094,528
48	4.02	89	0	0	−993,833	51	−993,833
51	3.78	92	0	0	−966,000	54	−966,000
54	3.66	91	0	0	−925,167	57	−925,167
57	3.21	90	0	0	−802,500	60	−802,500

For months 9–45, when LIBOR exceeds 4.5%, the company effectively pays a 4.5% rate times the appropriate day-count.

A mirror image application of a long floor position is on the investment side. Suppose a portfolio manager owns a floating rate bond and fears that as rates come down her income from the bond will decline. She can purchase a floor struck at the desired level to maintain her income at or above that level. In the discussion of swaps, we also showed additional uses of caps and floors in structured finance.

9.10 SWAPTIONS

Swaptions are options to enter into a swap. Unlike a cap or floor with a series of expiry dates for all optionlets, a swaption has one expiry date. Once the holder exercises a swaption, he will pay and receive multiple cash flows, like on a swap. Exercise can be European-style (once at expiry only), American-style (once any time prior to or on expiry date), or Bermudan-style (once on any swap date prior to or on the expiry date). For example, a 3-into-7, $10 million, European call swaption struck at 5% gives the owner the right to receive a fixed 5%, against floating LIBOR, on a $100 million 7-year swap. If the option is exercised on the expiry date, which is 3 years from today, the swap would start on that day and end 7 years later. The same swaption can be referred to as

3-year-10-year-final swaption to imply that the exercise right is in 3 years and the final maturity of the swap is in 10 years. A Bermudan or American version would be exercisable between today and 3 years from today, not just 3 years from today, and the swap would start immediately at exercise and end 10 years from today. The "3-into-7" language is rarely used with American and Bermudan options; the "3-year-10-year-final" language is preferable (if the option is exercised in 2 years, the swap will last 8 years).

Calls are options to receive (fixed) on the swap; puts are options to pay (fixed) on the swap. The call/put terminology corresponds to the view of swaps as exchanges of bonds. A receive-fixed swap can be thought of as a bought fixed-rate bond and a sold floating-rate bond, or a bought fixed-rate bond financed by a revolving loan. So, a call swaption is like an option to buy a fixed-rate bond, just like a call is an option to buy a stock. A put swaption is an option to sell a fixed-rate bond (i.e., the option to pay a fixed rate on an obligation, and to receive a floating financing rate).

Options to cancel

Swaptions can be packaged with swaps to provide options to cancel the swap. Suppose we pay a fixed rate of 4.5% on a 10-year quarterly swap and we receive 3-month LIBOR. Suppose also our swap counterparty sells us a 5-into-5 call swaption struck at 4.5. The call gives us the right to receive 4.5% on a 5-year swap starting 5 years from today. But if we exercise the call, then we will exactly offset the remaining cash flows on the existing 10-year swap.

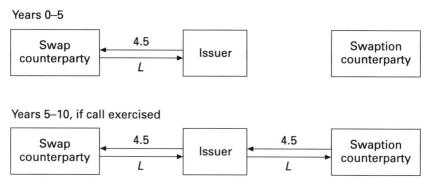

Figure 9.30 A 5-into-5 call swaption packaged with a 10-year swap.

The call swaption, which we defined as the right to enter a swap to receive fixed, can also be defined as the right to cancel a pay-fixed swap. The "call" language thus conforms to the call provisions on fixed coupon bonds. Analogously, the "put" notion for swaptions corresponds to the right of the fixed coupon bond holders to put the bonds back to the issuer at par.

Relationship to forward swaps

From the above construction, we should also be able to see the following relationship:

Call swaption − Put swaption = Forward swap

where *Forward swap* is defined as a swap with the first set date in the future (and not today).

Suppose we buy a 5-into-5 call struck at 4.5% and sell a 5-into-5 put struck at 4.5%. If 5-year swap rates are low in 5 years, say at 3%, then we will exercise our call right to receive fixed 4.5% (above market). The holder of the put we sold will not exercise. Alternatively, if 5-year swap rates are high in 5 years, say at 6%, then the holder of the put we sold will exercise his right to pay fixed 4.5% (below market). We will not exercise our call. His exercise decision will force us to receive fixed 4.5%. Thus no matter what swap rates are in 5 years, we will enter into a 5-year swap at that time. Viewed from today, this is a forward swap. It starts at a future known date and ends at a future known date, and the fixed rate on it is agreed on today.

In addition, if instead of 4.5% we choose the strike rate in such a way that the premium paid for the call equals that received for the put, then the sure forward swap will be arranged at no cost to either party (i.e., it will be a par forward swap).

This relationship will be true no matter what the level of implied volatilities used by dealers as inputs into their pricing models, as the static arbitrage constraint will not change.

Swaptions can be synthesized from forward swaps and other swaptions. A call is equivalent to a forward receive-fixed swap and a put swaption. A put is equivalent to a forward pay-fixed swap and a call swaption.

Swaptions can also be viewed as one-time options on long (swap) rates. Note that, in the above discussion, we decided that the call holder will exercise when future swap rates are lower than the strike. This guarantees that the present value of the swap he chooses to exercise into is positive (i.e., he has a positive payoff). This is true because the LIBOR leg part of the swap (equivalent to the floating-rate bond) always prices (present-values) to par, and the positive PV will come from the discounted value of the differences between the strike and the actual lower fair swap rate (i.e., the bond with a fixed coupon equal to the strike will price above par). If the fair rate were equal to the strike, the fixed bond with a coupon equal to the strike would also price to par. So the payoff of the call can be viewed as the difference between the strike and the fair swap rate times the day-count-corrected *annuity factor* (sum of discount factors for all swap payment dates):

$$Call = Max[0, K - Swap\ rate] \times Annuity\ factor$$
$$Put = Max[0, Swap\ rate - K] \times Annuity\ factor$$

Swaptions and caps and floors are also related, but not so simply. Both types of options are ways of dissecting swaps (i.e., share the risk of the swap with other players). Caps and floors can be forward starting to make them look identical to swaptions in terms of start and end dates. But caps and floors dissect swaps on the floating side, while swaptions do so on the fixed side. Caps and floors are packages of several mini-options on each swaplet (FRA), while swaptions are one-time options on the entire swap. The two are related for the following reason: the long (forward) swap rate, which is the underlying rate for the swaption, is a package of forward-starting swaplets (FRAs). That one rate can be exchanged costlessly into a series of short-term fixed rates (equal to FRA rates for the respective pay periods) or further into unknown floating-rate payments (as on-market FRAs cost nothing to enter into). A long cap and short floor position is equivalent to those floating-rate payments.

Because of these interrelationships between long and short rates, we can claim that the prices of swaptions and caps and floors are interrelated, as are their implied volatilities. The modeling of these relationships is extremely hard.

9.11   EXOTIC OPTIONS

The term "exotic options" applies to all non-standard options (i.e., with payoffs not defined like those for calls and puts) traded OTC. Exotic options include digital, or binary, options (fixed point payoffs irrespective of how far into the money the option is), barrier options, like knock-ins or knock-outs (the price or rate has to hit or avoid certain barriers prior to expiry for the payoff formula to even apply), as well as a whole variety of options that are difficult to price because the primary risk in them is not easily hedgeable. We will not attempt a complete listing of the exotics. Instead, we focus on some very popular structures that at first appear to be quite simple. But, they are anything but simple.

Periodic caps

Consider a fairly standard provision of an adjustable mortgage. The interest rate changes once a year based on some floating index, but the rate is guaranteed not to change by more than 2% per year or 6% total over the lifetime. The mortgagee has in effect issued a floating-rate bond to finance a house purchase. Every year, the interest rate he pays is based on the cost of funds for that year (set at the beginning of the year based on some 1-year money rate). Next year the rate adjusts up or down. But the rate is guaranteed not to go up by more than 2% year to year. So if the index changes from 3% to 6%, the homeowner's rate increases only by 2% instead of 3%. The option the homeowner holds is not a standard call option on a rate or a cap. The strike on the option changes every year and is based on last year's rate and last year's strike. If the following year the index changes from 6% to 9%, the mortgage rate again only goes up by 2% and only from the already "unfairly" low last year's level that did not reflect a full index increase at that time. Mortgage banks that want to protect themselves against income lost due to these imbedded options purchase periodic caps from dealers. *Periodic caps* pay the difference between the mortgage rate (with the options) and the fully indexed floating rate (without the options). The resetting strike feature changes the probability of payoff relative to a straight call. It also changes how the payoff can be manufactured. The dealer-hedger cannot compute the delta on the option until he knows the strike. Thus it is not the implied volatility over the entire life of the option that determines the cost of manufacturing, but it is the sequence of future implied volatilities on shorter 1-year options. This is true with the caveat that previous strikes also carry over as in our example. The cost of payoff manufacturing has thus a known component (stickiness of the strike) and some unknown component (future annual-rate differences). The premium quoted will reflect the subjective bet on the future path of implied volatilities.

Constant maturity options (CMT or CMS)

Constant maturity options are caps or floors with long-term government (CMT) or swap rates (CMS) as the underlying variables, but with the day-count and frequency of payoff like that of a short rate. A 5-year quarterly cap on a 10-year rate struck at 6% pays the greater of 0 and the difference between the 10-year rate and the strike every quarter for the next 10 years. The day-count used for the payoff calculations is that of a given quarter. The payoff is made in arrears, just as the case is for a simple cap. The only difference between a straight cap and a CMS cap is that, instead of comparing LIBOR to the strike, we compare the 10-year swap rate to the strike. Why does this pose problems?

The simple answer is: convexity. With a standard cap, the hedge instrument is a 3-month LIBOR deposit, a forward, or a futures on it. While these may be non-linear instruments (i.e., the PV of the position changes as the rate changes, but not as a fixed monetary amount per 1 bp rate change), the non-linearity is nowhere near as great as that of longer term instruments and can be fairly easily corrected for. With CMS rates, as we compute the delta per 1 bp move and then translate it through duration into a dollar holding of the underlying bond, our hedge will always be imperfect and differently so on the up- and downsides. These hedging errors will magnify, the longer the hedge. On a 5-year maturity option, they can be very large. The CMT options have the added difficulty of swap spread exposure.

We can argue that these instruments are more similar to swaptions than to caps. Recall that a swaption was a bet on a future long-term rate. The payoff was multiplied by the appropriate annuity factor, reflecting the final maturity of the underlying swap. Here, a CMS cap can be seen as a series of swaptions with increasing maturities and with payoffs multiplied by an "inappropriate" annuity factor, one for a cap instead of for a swaption. Because that annuity factor is correct for swaptions, they can be hedged easily with their underlying instruments (i.e., forward swaps), which in turn can be synthesized from long long-maturity swaps and short short-maturity swaps. CMS caps produce a hedge error from the mismatch of the actual annuity factor with that of the underlying forward swap.

Digitals and ranges

A *digital option* is an option with a fixed monetary payoff, if a price or rate breaches a certain strike level. A *range* is a compound version of a digital option where the underlying price or rate has to breach one level but not go over or under another level (i.e., it has to end up within a predetermined range). These structures are popular in commodity, FX, and interest rate markets. In interest rate markets, they are typically packaged into cap- or floor-like serial forms with short-term LIBOR rates as the underlyings and range levels changing period to period. These options are not difficult to price theoretically, but they pose a risk of low-probability events with highly uncertain hedge outcomes.

Suppose we sold an FX range that pays $1 if the USD/EUR rate is within 1.10 and 1.20. We price the option using a binomial tree and have followed the hedge recipe. We come to 1 day prior to expiry. The spot USD/EUR FX rate stands at 1.20. If it ticks up by tomorrow, we will owe nothing to the option holder. If it ticks down we will owe $1 (everything). There is no effective hedge strategy that will produce the desired payoff: $0 or $1. We have to gamble. At the time the option was sold, this knife-edge event had effectively a zero probability. In a standard call or put, these events do not occur because the size of the payoff changes monotonically with the level of the rate, allowing us to adjust the hedge. Here it jumps from 0 to everything over a practically non-existent move in the underlying.

Quantos

Quantos are options whose payoffs are defined in non-native currencies. A seemingly standard put option on the FTSE 100, whose payoff is in constant U.S. dollars per point of the index, is quite a bit more complicated than that whose payoff is defined in British pounds. In the latter case, the hedge is obvious. The seller of the put shorts the stocks in the index. The total change in their value in pounds dynamically produces the pound payoff at expiry. The quanto version of the option forces the dealer into an additional currency hedge as the pound payoff needs to be guaranteed in dollars. In addition, the two hedges are interrelated: as the potential payoff in dollars rises because of the FTSE change, the underlying stock hedges pound value may over- or under-compensate for a possible FX rate change when the hedge is liquidated and the payoff made.

The *quanto* label can be added to almost any option. A popular equity option that pays the best of several national indices (say, S&P 500, Nikkei 225, and FTSE 100) is often *quanto*ed into one desired currency, say the euro.

10
Option Arbitrage

We review relative value strategies with options. We start with static cash-and-carry trades where the arbitrage principles are the same as with non-option products, but we exploit the relative mispricing of forwards as long call–short put positions. This happens frequently when one or more options needed to synthetically replicate a forward can be acquired very cheaply as parts of more complex securities. Next we consider dynamic arbitrage strategies where the underlying market risk is hedged out and the trade is a relative value bet on secondary risk. The secondary risk involved can be a relative play on two related, but not identical implied volatilities: correlation risk or spread. We end with dynamic strategies spanning several asset classes and some exotic examples with truly unhedgeable risks.

To readers interested in options, our treatment of dynamic option strategies will most likely seem wanting. We only sketch out some basic trades. Relative value arbitrage in options can get very complicated. The residual risks can be significant, unhedgeable, and their understanding may require math knowledge that goes beyond the scope of this book. They can be defined in terms of exposures to volatility skews, to correlations, to local vs. term volatilities (i.e., period to period vs. total end dispersion), often in second- and third-order derivative terms. They can also involve tradeoffs between exposures from different markets, stock price correlation with interest rates, credit spread correlation with interest rates, or interest rates with currency rates. Our goal for this chapter is limited to highlighting the risks of some benchmark trades.

10.1 CASH-AND-CARRY STATIC ARBITRAGE

To make clear the static arbitrage principle, we start with a simple financing trade: borrowing or lending against a known, non-contingent cash flow constructed by combining several contingent payoffs.

Borrowing against the box

The borrowing-against-the-box strategy can be employed with options on any underlying: stocks, currencies, commodities, etc. The idea is very simple. If a long call–short put position is equal to a long forward and a short call–long put position is equal to a short forward then by combining four options with the same expiries into a synthetic long forward at one price with a synthetic short forward at another, we can generate a sure payoff at the expiry day. If the net premium (today) for the four options is positive (an inflow), then the payoff at expiry is an outflow and the strategy is equivalent to borrowing. If the net premium is paid (outflow) and the payoff is an inflow, then the strategy is equivalent to lending. The arbitrage consists of trying to lock in through this strategy a higher lending, or lower borrowing rate than our own cost of financing.

Let us consider a stock option case using the multi-step pricing model from Chapter 9. We employ a three-step binomial to price four 3-month options with the inputs as before. Stock currently trades at 50; the interest rate is 2.6% per month (de-annualized). The forward stock price for delivery 3 months from today can be computed as 54.0023. We sell a 50 call and buy a 50 put (short synthetic forward at 50). We buy a 55 call and sell a 55 put (long synthetic forward at 55). As each synthetic forward is off-market, the net premium is non-zero. Table 10.1 summarizes our position.

Table 10.1   Borrowing against the box

Position	Strike	Option	Premium
Short	55	Put	7.6497
Long	55	Call	−6.7259
Long	50	Put	−6.3419
Short	50	Call	10.0475
Net			*4.6294*

Let us consider the payoff. If the stock at expiry is 45, the calls are worthless, we pay 10 on the 55 put, and receive 5 on the 50 put; our net is an outflow of 5. If the stock is at 72, the puts are worthless, we receive 17 on the 55 call, and pay 22 on the 50 call; our net is an outflow of 5. If the stock is at 52, we pay 3 on the 55 put, the 55 call and the 50 put are worthless, and we pay 2 on the 50 call; our net is an outflow of 5. No matter where the stock ends up at expiry, out net cash flow will be an outflow of 5. So, we traded a net inflow of 4.6294 today for a net outflow of 5 three months from today. What interest rate is implied in this synthetic borrowing of 4.6294? From:

$$4.6294(1 + r)^3 = 5.0000$$

we compute the rate to be 2.6% per month. This is exactly what we assumed for valuing the four options.

Suppose we have an investment opportunity to earn 3.2% per month on comparable risk. That is, we know that if we invest:

$$5.0000/(1 + 0.032)^3 = 4.549\,157$$

the investment will accrue to exactly 5.0000. We synthetically borrow 4.6294 and invest 4.5492; our net profit today is 0.0803. When the investment matures in 3 months, we collect 5 and distribute it appropriately to the option claimants. The only risk we are facing is that of default on our investment. If, for some reason, the investment fails to produce 5, we will not be able to meet our obligations under the option contracts. We have statically eliminated any market risk of stock fluctuations by choosing a combination of options with a known payoff. We do not have any market risk of interest rate fluctuations, because we are not going to hedge the options (i.e., we are not going to finance any stock positions). We are simply left with default risk.

Index arbitrage with options

Recall from Chapter 7 that stock index arbitrage consisted of either a long index futures position against a short spot basket with lending or a short index futures position against a long spot basket with borrowing to buy the basket. The direction of the trade depended on the fair value calculation for the futures, and the spot basket plus money market transaction was equivalent to a synthetic forward. Here we are going to exploit the put–call parity of Chapter 9 to construct the forward. Since the long forward position is equivalent to a long call and short put position (both struck at the forward), we will be able to perform a static cash-and-carry by transacting in options upfront and trading them against futures or basket positions.

Suppose, as in the previous example, that the stock index trades at 50 and the interest rate is 2.6% per month. The 3-month futures contract on the index trades at its theoretical fair value of 54.0023. So we cannot make money trading futures against spot. Using our option-pricing model, we value calls and puts struck at the forward (i.e., at 54.0023). We get 7.3887 for the put and 7.3887 for the call. We notice that we can buy the put in the market for 7.39 (the asking price), and we have a customer willing to pay 7.42 for the call. One simple strategy is to sell the call to the customer for 7.42 and try to offset that by buying it in the market for less. But suppose the market is wide at 7.38/ 7.42 (i.e., the asking price is 7.42): we can still profit by establishing a synthetic short forward in the options and either going long futures or establishing a synthetic long forward in the cash markets (buying stock and financing the purchase at 2.6%). Let us consider the first choice.

We sell a call for 7.42 to the customer and buy a put for 7.39 in the market, both struck at 54.0023. We go long one futures contract with the same expiry at 54.0023 (assuming contract sizes or multipliers on the options and futures are the same). Our net premium is 0.03 which is also our net profit. If the stock (and the futures) ends up at 62 at expiry, we owe 7.9977 to the call owner, our put is worthless, and we collect 7.9977 in the futures variation margin.

If the stock ends up at 50, we owe nothing on the call, we collect 4.0023 on the put, and we have lost 4.0023 in the futures variation margin. The second choice is a little more complicated. We sell the call for 7.42 and buy a put for 7.39 to collect a premium of 0.03. We borrow money at 2.6% per month to buy the underlying stocks for 50. In 3 months we sell the stock basket (inflow) and repay 54.0023 (outflow). This, as we have shown before, is equivalent to the cumulative variation margin on the long futures position. The short call–long put option position has the opposite payoff equivalent to the cumulative variation margin on the short futures: the inflow of the strike price and the outflow of the value of the stock. The future cash flow is 0. Today's cash flow is 0.03.

Analogous strategies can be employed with commodity and currency options. We compare the cost of replicating a forward position through options to the actual forwards/futures or their synthetic equivalents in cash positions.

Options are sometimes used in index arbitrage in an attempt to better time program execution and to recoup transaction costs. Suppose we want to go long futures and short synthetic in large size. Selling a basket spot may take time and make force us to sell many stocks at the bid. Suppose, instead of buying futures, we leg into the trade by buying a call and sending a sell order. If stock prices tick up, we may be able to get better execution on the program and still sell the put at the desired price. If bids in the cash market weaken, we may still be able to hit them and sell the put at a better price. Of course, the opposite could easily happen. Legging into a trade is always a small bet on the execution costs.

Warrant arbitrage

Issuers in some markets often attach warrants to their bonds in order to make the bonds more attractive to investors. Warrants are call options that give the holders the right to buy the shares of the issuing company at a predetermined strike price. The only difference between warrants and standard calls is that the shares to be sold on exercise of the options will be newly issued. This is possible in a warrant contract because the writer of the option is also the issuer of the stock.[1] Often these "bond sweeteners" come free or close to free.

There are two distinct cases here. We illustrate the first with a fairly common situation with Japanese industrial bonds in the early 1990s.

A Samurai Co. issues a 3-year bond to investors. The bond has a warrant attached that allows investors to buy Samurai stock for ¥50 a share in 3 years. The yield on the Samurai bond is less than that on Samurai's straight bonds to reflect the value of attached warrants. We discover, by comparing the present value (PV) of the bond's coupons and principal with the PV of similar bullet bonds, that the yield give-up (i.e., the cost of acquiring the warrant) is equal to ¥1. When we price a 3-year call using the Black–Scholes or binomial model we compute the fair price of the warrant as ¥10.0475. One way to profit would be to buy the bond with the warrant, detach the warrant, and try to find buyers for the warrant at a premium close to the fair value. But other buyers may have acquired the warrants at a low cost just like we have.

Here is the simplest strategy. We short the stock today. We collect ¥50 from the short sale and invest the proceeds at 2.6%. In 3 months we have:

$$50(1 + 0.026)^3 = ¥54.0023$$

If the stock ends up in-the-money, say at 60, we exercise the warrant by buying the stock at 50 and returning the stock to the lender on our short. We pocket ¥4.0023. If the stock ends up out-of-the-money, say at 45, we buy it back in the market for 45, return it to the lender on the short, and pocket ¥9.0023. The minimum we will make is ¥4.0023.

In the 1990s, many outstanding warrant bonds issued by Japanese industrial companies offered this static arbitrage opportunity. The trade consisted of acquiring the warrants which often had many years left to maturity, shorting the stocks, and waiting to collect. The only problem with pursuing the strategy was the availability of the stock for shorting. Only those with access to large long-term holdings of the stock could execute the strategy. Insurance companies that held the stocks as investments lent them out, but often charged significant stock borrow fees. If in our example the borrow fee for the entire time to maturity were set to ¥6, then the strategy was not risk-free. It lost ¥1.9877 if the warrant ended in-the-money.

Let us briefly describe the second case. We elaborate on this case when we discuss convertible bonds later in this chapter.

Instead of gambling to make ¥4.0023 or more depending on where the stock ends up

---

[1] This leads to the dilution of earnings from existing shareholders to new shareholders.

(minus any stock borrow fees), can we somehow lock in the difference between the computed fair value of ¥10.0475 and the cost of the warrant of ¥1? The answer is yes, but again only by shorting the stock.

In the static case we shorted one full share per warrant. This time, we short only the delta number of shares (close to half a share) and adjust the amount of shorting throughout the life of the warrant (i.e., we dynamically replicate the payoff of the warrant through a delta hedge). Our cash flows at expiry will be matched. The start of the delta hedge at the outset generates an inflow (short sale minus the money lending) of ¥10.0475. We spend ¥1 on the warrant and keep ¥9.0475. The only thing that complicates things is again the stock borrow fee which is non-zero, but lower than in the static case (we start shorting only half the amount). The way the borrow fee is taken into account is to treat it like additional dividends in the option-pricing model. When we short stock we have to compensate the lender of the stock for the lost dividend. The stock loan fee is paid on top of that just for the privilege of using the stock. We have to use an amended version of the Black-Scholes model to compute the warrant's fair value and all the deltas now and in the future.

10.2 RUNNING AN OPTION BOOK: VOLATILITY ARBITRAGE

We explained in Chapter 9 that an option dealer hedges out the net price or rate risk of his option portfolio. He does this by faithfully following a delta-hedge recipe. He computes the exposures of all options to the underlying asset or assets (i.e., price sensitivities to a unit change in the underlying prices or rates), nets these across options, and takes the opposite positions in the underlying assets. Every day as the prices of stocks, currencies, and commodities or the rates on bonds change, the mark-to-market change on the options is exactly offset by the change in the value of the hedging assets. The dealer has to rebalance that portfolio daily to ensure that, as conditions change, the hedge assets will continue to offset the value of the option portfolio.

We also explained that the only risk the dealer is left with is that of the mismatch between the implied volatility used as an input into the pricing and hedging model and the actual volatility of the hedge assets. For example, if the dealer has a net short position in options (i.e., a net negative vega position) and the underlying asset prices fluctuate more than he had assumed, then his hedge will have a tracking error. It is important to realize that this error is small relative to the completely unhedged position. At the same time, if the option portfolio is very large, it can amount to substantial losses over time.

The dealer's job can be viewed as having two parts: one is fairly mechanical and involves computing the exposures every day and rebalancing the hedge portfolio according to a recipe; the other part is dynamic and involves forecasting the path of the volatility of the assets and taking pre-emptive action.

Hedging with options on the same underlying

The only perfect hedge for an option is another option. If we have an option position that is already hedged in the underlying asset, the only way we can offset the volatility exposure of that position is by buying or selling another option with a similar vega. We will illustrate this principle using our one-step binomial applied to a three-option example.

Suppose as an option dealer, we have lots of bought and sold options in our portfolio, all written on the same underlying stock. The net exposure of that portfolio can be summarized as equivalent to a short 1-year call option struck at 60 and two short 1-year put options struck at 50. We assume the current stock price is 50 and the interest rate is 10%. The up and down states, which reflect the current implied volatility, are 70 and 20 as before. We price the options using those inputs and also using the 80–15 inputs, reflecting a higher implied volatility. The results are as follows.

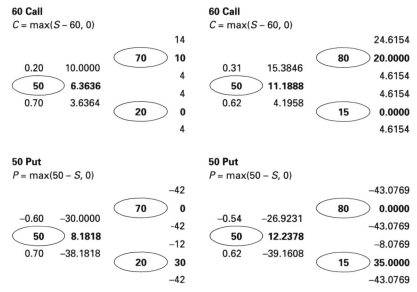

Figure 10.1   Pricing options with two volatility inputs to get the vega.

We have one short call in the portfolio worth 6.3636 and two short puts each worth 8.1818. The vega of the options is equal to the difference between the price under the increased implied volatility assumption minus that under the current one. (In reality, stock options traders plug the inputs into their Black–Scholes models and revalue the options using an implied volatility increased by 1% to determine their vega exposure.) For the call, we have:

$$11.1888 - 6.3636 = \$4.8252$$

and for the put:

$$12.2378 - 8.1818 = \$4.0559$$

We also show the deltas for each option: 0.20 for the call and -0.60 for the put. Suppose our portfolio is delta-hedged so that our combined option-and-hedge holdings are:

Table 10.2 Delta and vega of the position

Position	Security	Unit PV	PV	Unit delta	Delta	Unit vega	Vega
−1	60 Call	6.3636	−6.36364	0.20	−0.2	4.8252	−4.82517
−2	50 Put	8.1818	−16.3636	−0.60	1.2	4.0559	−8.11189
−1.00	Stock	50	−50	1	−1	0	0
Net			−72.7273		0		−12.9371

Since our combined delta from the three options was 1.0, we short one share to hedge the option exposure (we should have bought 0.20 to hedge the call and shorted 0.60 to hedge each put). We have a net vega exposure of −12.94 (i.e., if the volatility increases as expected, the short options will provide us with a mark-to-market loss of 12.94).

In order to hedge the volatility risk, we look for positive vega exposures in the market. Suppose we can buy 55 puts in the market for 9.30. We use our pricing model to verify.

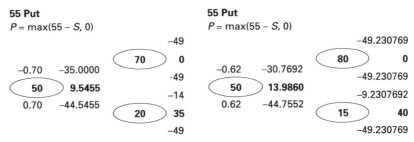

Figure 10.2 Computing the vega of the 55 put.

We apply the model twice with different volatility inputs to compute the vega of the 55 put to be:

$$13.986 - 9.5455 = 4.4406$$

We also notice that the puts are cheap relative to their fair value. We decide to hedge by buying some 55 puts. How many? We need to offset 12.94 in volatility exposure; so, given the vega of each put of 4.4406, we need to buy 2.9134 puts. But if we buy 2.9134 puts, then we need to delta-hedge them by buying:

$$2.9134 \times 0.70 = 2.0394$$

shares. Our combined portfolio now looks like this:

Table 10.3 Delta and vega of the hedged position

Position	Security	Unit PV	PV	Unit delta	Delta	Unit vega	Vega
−1	60 Call	6.3636	−6.363 64	0.20	−0.2000	4.8252	−4.825 17
−2	50 Put	8.1818	−16.363 6	−0.60	1.2000	4.0559	−8.111 89
2.9134	55 Put	9.5455	27.809 73	−0.70	−2.0394	4.4406	12.937 13
1.04	Stock	50	51.968 5	1	1.0394	0	0
Net			*57.050 96*		*0.0000*		*0.000 1*

If the volatility changes, the change in the value of the extra puts will offset the change in the value of the original options in our portfolio. Notice that this will work for a variety of volatility changes (i.e., even if the volatility decreases instead of increasing).

Volatility skew

Our primary risk (to the change in the price of the stock) and our secondary risk (to the change in the volatility of the stock price) are now eliminated. Is our portfolio risk-free?

No, our portfolio can still make or lose money if the implied volatilities on the different options change differently. We are left with a tertiary risk of relative volatility changes. Theoretically, this should not happen as the underlying asset for all options is the same and so it can have only one true volatility. But our model is not perfect. In particular, it assumes that volatilities do not change! It also assumes that volatilities are the same for any asset price. The volatility skew intends to correct for that by assigning slightly different volatilities for different strikes of the options (something we did not do).

Let us illustrate what happens when a dealer fails to include the skew in hedge calculations. We focus solely on the vega. We use the data from Chapter 9 for December, 2003 S&P 500 index futures options as of October 15, 2003. With the index at 1045, we show the implied volatilities for strikes between 1030 and 1075, and a fitted regression line $Vol = 57.638 - 0.0388 \cdot Strike$.

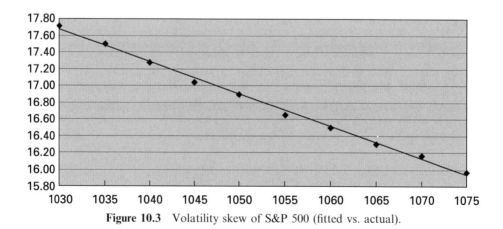

Figure 10.3 Volatility skew of S&P 500 (fitted vs. actual).

Table 10.4 Hedge performance without and with skew

Strike	Before move without skew				After move without skew				Before move with skew				After move with skew			
	Implied volatility	Vega per unit	Position	Start vega	Implied volatility	Vega per unit	Position	End vega	Implied volatility	Vega per unit	Position	Start vega	Implied volatility	Vega per unit	Position	End vega
1030	17.00	1.69	-30	-50.7	17.00	1.71	-30	-51.3	17.72	1.71	-30	-51.3	17.51	1.73	-30	-51
1035	17.00	1.71		0.0	17.00	1.73		0.0	17.51	1.73		0.0	17.28	1.74		0.0
1040	17.00	1.73		0.0	17.00	1.75		0.0	17.28	1.74		0.0	17.04	1.75		0.0
1045	17.00	1.75	100	175.0	17.00	1.73	100	173.0	17.04	1.75	100	175.0	16.90	1.75	100	175
1050	17.00	1.73		0.0	17.00	1.71		0.0	16.90	1.75		0.0	16.65	1.74		0.0
1055	17.00	1.71		0.0	17.00	1.69		0.0	16.65	1.74		0.0	16.50	1.73		0.0
1060	17.00	1.69		0.0	17.00	1.66		0.0	16.50	1.73		0.0	16.30	1.70		0.0
1065	17.00	1.66	-42	-69.7	17.00	1.63	-42	-68.5	16.30	1.70	-40	-68.0	16.16	1.67	-40	-66
1070	17.00	1.63	-33	-53.8	17.00	1.59	-33	-52.5	16.16	1.67	-33	-55.1	15.97	1.62	-33	-53
1075	17.00	1.59			17.00				15.97	1.62						
Total				*0.8*				*0.8*				*0.6*				*2*

In Table 10.4, we illustrate what happens to a dealer who does not take the volatility skew into account. We assume that we start with the index at 1045 and compute the at-the-money volatility to be 17%. We own 100 options struck at-the-money at 1045. We hedge the volatility risk by selling options struck at 1030, 1065, and 1070. If we do not include the skew, then we will assume the options with out-of-the-money and in-the-money strikes have the same volatility. We compute their vegas using that volatility; this is how we come up with the number of options to be sold to hedge. If we take the skew into account, then we come up with a different set of vegas (those in the original data) and different numbers of options to be sold. We also show what happens as the market moves. Suppose the index goes down to 1040. We assume that the implied volatilities and the vegas do not change for the same percentage of in-the-moneyness. In our case, that translates, for example, into the 1050 option having now the same implied volatility as the 1055 option had before the move. We see that a dealer unaware of the skew continues to think that he is hedged and does not rebalance, while a dealer aware of the skew sees that he is no longer vega-hedged and will most likely sell more options.

What we did not show in Table 10.4 is that not only will the volatility risk be mis-hedged, but also the deltas will be computed using the wrong σ input. The dynamic delta hedge will result in daily unexplained profit or loss (i.e., the change in the delta position in the stock will not match the change in the value of the options).

Most professional skew models do not rely on a simple regression model like ours to modify the volatilities used in computing prices and hedge ratios in a Black–Scholes model. Rather, they internalize the volatilities as stock level-dependent within one option-pricing model, used with the same inputs, to price all options with different strikes. This is equivalent to having different volatilities on different branches of our binomial trees in the up and down direction. This ensures the consistency of both delta (stock position) and vega (option position) hedges.

Options with different maturities

The comments about options with different strikes apply to options with different maturities. The implied volatilities of options on the same underlying, but with different maturities, are not the same and will change differently over the life of our portfolio. Dealers find it very hard to hedge long-expiry options with short-expiry options even though that is what they are most often asked to do by customers who can buy short-term options on the exchanges and come to dealers for longer term or more complicated bets. The implied volatilities on long and short options can be quite different. Longer options' deltas are also less volatile, so the hedge with short options requires more trading of the underlying. Dealers find themselves trading off the transaction costs of this strategy against potential benefits of the hedge.

10.3   PORTFOLIOS OF OPTIONS ON DIFFERENT UNDERLYINGS

If a portfolio contains options written on different underlying assets—some on bonds, some on stocks, and some on currencies—then each option has to be delta-hedged separately. But the notion of "different underlying" need not be so clear-cut. We consider a few cases where underlying assets are different, but at the same time similar. In these cases, the underlying assets are not completely independent of each other; they exhibit co-movement. Their volatilities can be postulated to be statistically or mathematically related.

Index volatility vs. individual stocks

Instead of a portfolio of options all written on the same stock, suppose we have a portfolio of options on a variety of stocks. Each option is delta-hedged with a position in its own underlying stock. Can we do anything about volatility exposure?

The only method that will work well is what we already described in the previous section. We have to find vega offsets for options on different underlyings one at a time. Buying options on Intel in order to hedge vega exposure on Microsoft can be a dangerous game. Ideally, we need to find options on Microsoft. But hedging all exposures separately can be prohibitively expensive. We may soon find out that we have to pay ask prices well above fair values on a multitude of individual options, incurring an instant mark-to-market loss. So, to hedge a portfolio of options we may be tempted to look for an option on the entire portfolio or an index option.

Suppose we have bought and sold a variety of options on 35 individual stocks in the S&P 100 index. We have a net short-vega exposure. So our thinking is that when the implied volatilities of the individual options rise and we stand to lose money, we can protect ourselves by buying an option with the same vega on the entire index. To a limited extent, this may work; but, in general, it will amount to a substantial bet on the correlation structure of the index. If the stocks in the index are highly positively correlated (say, they are from the same country or industry), then most likely as some stocks increase the others increase and as some stocks decline the others decline too. So the average volatility of the stocks is related to the volatility of the index. But the change in average volatility may not be so clearly reflected in the change of index volatility if the stocks in the index are not highly positively correlated; this is what we are trying to hedge. The hedge breaks down when the average volatility of the stock changes by 2%, while index volatility changes by 1%. We can try to estimate that differential and adjust for it, but the game is risky.

The strategy of hedging individual options with basket (index) options is highly speculative. The situation is similar to that with volatility skew exposure across strikes and maturities. While we know how to translate a volatility input into an option value and a delta (Black–Scholes model), we do not know the exact relationship between the volatilities within the skew (regression?). All the options within the skew are on the same underlying asset and therefore, over large movements of the underlying's price, they have to be highly correlated. Because of this high correlation, as we argued, the average volatility in the skew portfolio will move closely with the volatility of any option close to the money. This need not be the case with options on different stocks relative to average volatility and relative to the option on a basket: the reason the hedge is more speculative in this case.

Interest rate caps and floors

Portfolios of caps, floors, and certain exotic options can all be viewed as all options on short-term interest rates with different maturities. The short-term rates may be 1-, 3-, and 6-month LIBOR (London interbank offered rate) or other short rates (e.g., in the U.S., Fed Funds rate or T-Bill rate) related through a "spread". Each cap and each floor is a portfolio of caplets and floorlets seemingly on the same underlying rate (say, 3-month LIBOR). But is the 3-month deposit today the same asset as a 3-month deposit 4 years from today? The implied volatilities in the caplets of increasing maturities can be different and change differently over time. But they are related.

The procedure of *cap volatility curve calibration*, which relies on bootstrapping, is portrayed in Figure 10.4. Suppose we view the spot 3-month LIBOR as a random asset similar to a stock, subject to a volatility parameter moving through time, or a binomial tree. We observe caplet prices with 3-month, 6-month, 9-month, etc. maturities. From the 3-month caplet price we can back out an implied volatility. We can then consider the 6-month caplet. We let LIBOR fluctuate for the first 3 months with a volatility as computed in step 1, and then we imply what the volatility for the following 3 months would have to be so that the model price of the caplet would match the actual price. We then consider the 9-month caplet using the first two volatilities, for 0–3 months and for 3–6 months, and implying the 6–9 month one. In a binomial tree model we are effectively computing different volatilities for different time steps (left to right).

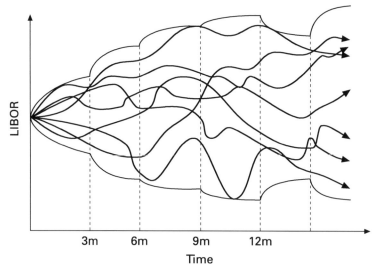

Figure 10.4 Cap volatility calibration. Term vs. local volatility.

Computed volatilities are often referred to as *local volatilities* or *forward–forward volatilities*. The single volatilities that would be required in a model to obtain the true prices are referred to as *term volatilities*. These represent the total width of the dispersion for a given point in time. Local volatilities represent the dispersion relative to the previous step. In Figure 10.4, we deliberately included one odd outcome, where the term volatility shrinks relative to a prior period. This is not unusual. We often find that long-term volatilities are lower than short-term ones. What that necessarily implies is that the local volatility for that period is negative or, alternatively, that the model has mean-reversion (i.e., outcomes are constrained from above and below).

The simplest procedure to deal with the volatility exposure for a cap portfolio is to disassemble it into caplets and compute the term vega exposures of all the options to a set of benchmark caplets with different maturities. These can then be combined to form a set of benchmark caps, those with the most liquidity in the inter-dealer market. We can then see where the bulk of the exposure is and design the start date and end date of caps or floors that would hedge the computed exposure. An analysis of an average strike for each caplet also helps select the strike of the hedging cap to minimize skew risk.

Caps and swaptions

We might think that the logic of cap and floor-only portfolios can apply to hedging entire, fixed income derivative portfolios. After all, swaptions are options on longer-term rates, and long-term rates can be replicated from forwards on short rates. So, swaption and cap volatilities should be closely related. This could not be further from the truth. The yield curve changes continuously. Long and short rates do not move together and are not equally volatile. A long par rate is a function of short-term rates over time. However, the volatility of the long rate is a function not only of the implied volatilities of forward short rates, but also the correlations between them. The best analogy here is with stock index volatility relative to individual stock volatilities. Hedging caps with swaptions and vice versa suffers from the same problems (i.e., it is a bet on the correlation structure of the rates). As much as it is clear with indices and stocks, the issues in swaptions and caps are often befuddled because the pricing models in interest rates are very complicated and at the same time not complicated enough. They try to capture all the synthetic static arbitrage relationships between rates (coupons vs. zero-coupons, short vs. long) while simplifying the volatility structure to one or at most two factors (i.e., they are arbitrage-free, but perhaps only one-factor). The simplification often leads to the omission of the rate correlation structure. Even a seemingly complicated model with both local and term volatilities can be one-factor if the only thing driving rate movement is the short-term rate. Any long-term rate for any node on a model tree is simply an arbitrage-free deterministic outcome of a present-value calculation conditioned on being at that node. Model purists often object to any violations of no-arbitrage rules. Yet allowing some arbitrages might allow easier multi-factor modeling which can then capture the calculation of the exposure to correlations. That knowledge allows us to design more complicated spread hedges consisting of both caps and swaptions with the same combined volatility and correlation exposure as the underlying portfolio.

At the present time, many dealers combine the delta hedges (in the underlying deposits, futures, and bonds) for cap and swaption portfolios, but run the volatility risk on cap and swaption portfolios separately, hedging the first (caps) exclusively with options on short-term rates (caps) and the latter (swaptions) with options on long-term rates (swaptions or CMSs/CMTs). They monitor the total vega of each portfolio and do so relative to each other. Frequently, they leave the vega of each part, viewed separately, unhedged, betting on the convergence or divergence of cap and swaption volatilities.

Explicit correlation bets

Option traders in many markets buy and sell bets whose primary risk (after delta-hedging the underlying) is the correlation risk. These bets are known as *spread options* or *best-of options*.

In equity markets, option sellers offer spread options on the difference between the prices of two stocks or indices; that is, the payoff is defined as:

$$Max[Stock_1 - Stock_2 - Strike, 0]$$

If the two underlyings are stock indices for two different national markets, then these options may be offered with quanto features. A different structure, exposing the dealer to the correlation between stocks or indices, has a "best-of" payoff:

$$Max[Index_1 - Strike, Index_2 - Strike, Index_3 - Strike, 0]$$

The owner of such a "call" is entitled to the return on the best of three indices. Apart from the current levels of the indices, the primary variable driving the price of the option is not the volatility of the indices, but their correlation structure. Similar spread structures can be written on two or more currency rates.

In commodity markets, option traders typically offer spread structures on two seemingly related commodity prices. These can be, for example, oil price and jet fuel price. Customers (airlines) demand such options to hedge the price volatility of the inputs into their business cost structure (jet fuel). As futures contracts on the commodity of interest may not exist (jet fuel), they hedge with proxy instruments (oil) by incurring *basis risk*. The spread structures allow them to close the hedging gap. But structures like these may leave the dealer with a speculative rather than a hedged position, if one or both assets in the basis do not have futures contracts on them. The dealer's job is then to protect himself by running a matched or diversified book.

In interest rates, the most common version of the spread option is that written on two different points on the yield curve. The payoff may then read:

$$Max[10\text{-}year\ rate - 5\text{-}year\ rate - Strike, 0]$$

or

$$Max[5\text{-}year\ rate - 10\text{-}year\ rate - Strike, 0]$$

The first option can be thought of as a bet on the steepening of the yield curve, or a "steepener", as it pays when the par 10-year coupon rate rises by more that the par 5-year coupon rate (or declines by less). The second option is a "flattener". It pays when the yield curve flattens (i.e., the 10-year rate rises by less than the 5-year rate).

In all these cases, the correlation exposure is unhedgeable unless there exist spot or forward instruments on the spread itself. The delta hedge can be easily constructed by buying one asset and shorting the other, but more often than not it provides insufficient protection against unpredictable relative moves.

10.4 OPTIONS SPANNING ASSET CLASSES

There exist cash securities and related derivatives that cannot be neatly classified as belonging to equity, fixed income, or currency markets. They present holders with unique risks of the interaction of prices of and secondary exposures to assets in different markets.

There are assets that appear to belong to this group, but when dissected are actually structured securities built from separate components. A bond with an equity warrant attached to it is really two separate assets that have nothing to do with each other, even though the yield on the bond part may be lower to cover the cost of the warrant. The two components can, however, be priced and hedged separately. A structured bond whose coupons are tied to the performance of a stock index, rather than an interest rate, can be easily decomposed into a string of stock index forwards or options and a set of zero-coupon bonds. Each can be priced separately to give the total price of the package, but each is then hedged separately.

However, there are certain assets that cannot be dissected into separate components.

Convertible bonds

The most common example of a security spanning asset classes is a convertible bond. When the embedded option is exercised, the bond is tendered. The holder gives up the right to further coupon interest in exchange for shares. His decision to exercise, while most often is prompted by the rise in the stock price which makes the exercise value (stock) greater than the value of the unexercised bond, can be prompted by the decline in value of the bond coupon stream due to interest rise. The embedded equity option cannot be priced as a straight call. In addition, a convertible bond may be callable, which makes the evaluation of the bond even more complex. The call provision frequently allows the issuer to force reluctant bond holders to exercise the equity option. If the intrinsic value of the equity option is above par, then the holder would, upon exercise, receive shares valued at more than par (a call by the issuer at par will prompt the holder to exercise in order to avoid the loss of value). The issuer's decision to call bonds may be driven not by equity considerations, but by a decline in interest rates and the desire to refinance debt at lower rates.

These considerations have to be taken into account in the pricing/hedging model. The volatilities and the correlation structure of the stock price and the interest rate(s) have to be modeled explicitly. The daily rebalancing of the hedges also has to take into account the movement in all related asset classes. A change in interest rates may entail a change in the position in the underlying stock and vice versa.

We describe the valuation problem for convertibles with the following diagram of a two-dimensional binomial tree. The first dimension is the interest rate, and we have up and down nodes based on its volatility. The other dimension is the stock price, and we have up and down nodes based on its volatility. We also have another condition that binds all the nodes: the correlation of the interest rate and the stock.

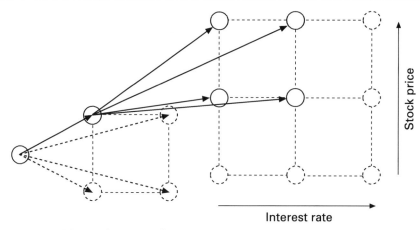

Figure 10.5 Two-dimensional pricing grid for convertibles.

We omit the math of setting up the tree. The main logic of the valuation is that, as we sweep backward in the tree, we apply the exercise condition in order to compute the value of the convertible bond on that node. The condition compares the exercise value of the bond (number of shares into which it is exercisable times the price) with the discounted expected value of the forward nodes. This is where the interaction of the stock price and the interest rate takes place. The discounted expectation includes all future coupon payments discounted to today (and all future possibilities of exercise). The delta with respect to the stock and the delta with respect to the interest rate that come up from the model are the product of the interaction of the two random variables. The model price of the convertible is equal to the amount needed to start the dynamic hedge (to be rebalanced until the maturity of the convertible), where the hedge consists of positions in the stock and in a purely interest rate-sensitive instrument (e.g., a bullet bond).

What the convertible model highlights is that, in practice, portfolios of bonds convertible into different stocks are hedged with baskets of stock and a variety of interest rate-sensitive instruments. Each bond has a delta with respect to its stock and a delta with respect to interest rates. Stock deltas call for hedges in the underlying stocks, while interest rate deltas call for hedges in bonds. The latter actually involve hedges in risk-free as well spread-sensitive bonds (i.e., interest rate deltas can be broken down into exposures to pure interest rates as well as corporate spreads).

More importantly, all the deltas are related to each other. A change in interest rates may require the hedger to change his stock position, and a change in the stock prices may require the hedger to change his bond position. The greatest danger of the hedging scheme is that the real movements in stocks and rates do not reflect the assumed statistical correlation in the model and the hedge slips (i.e., results in extra profit or loss).

Quantos and dual-currency bonds with fixed conversion rates

Any multi-currency bond that gives the holder a right to receive coupon interest in the currency of his choosing, with the foreign exchange (FX) conversion rate which is predetermined, exposes the issuer to intertwined interest rate and currency risks. If, during the life of a bond, the value of a currency declines, the bond holder may choose to have interest paid in that currency to take advantage of the rate originally contracted for and not equal to the current market rate. The risk here is the same as in quanto options where a payoff is translated into a non-native currency. A stock index quanto call gives the owner the payoff of a stock index not in the currency of the stocks in the index, but in another currency at a fixed rate. The writer-hedger of the option is exposed to the correlation of the FX rate and the index level. As the index increases his FX hedge may increase.

Dual-currency callable bonds

A single-currency callable bond is equivalent to a straight bullet bond and a call swaption. The exercise of the call swaption leads to cash flows that exactly offset those on the bond, effectively canceling the bond. The issuer normally issues a callable bond and sells the swaption to a dealer, the sole purpose of the structure being a lower cost of capital.

A single-currency callable bond in one currency swapped into another currency or a dual-currency bond with conversion rights which is callable carries the correlation risk between the FX rate and long interest rates in the two currencies.

10.5 OPTION-ADJUSTED SPREAD (OAS)

Many bonds have options embedded in them. They are sold as packages of bullet bonds and options. Sometimes these options are physically separable, as in warrant bonds. Sometimes they are not physically separable, but the components can be treated separately for valuation and hedge calculation purposes. A callable bond gives the issuer the right to call (repay) the bonds prior to maturity at par (or another *call price*). The buyer of the bond cannot be sure when he will be repaid the principal (at the latest at maturity) and how many coupon payments he will get. Even though this option is embedded, it can be treated separately. A callable bond can be viewed as a bullet bond plus a call swaption with the strike equal to the coupon of the bond sold by the bond holder to the issuer. When the bond is called, the remainder of the cash flows (which will be 0) can be constructed from the coupons on the bullet bond and the exactly offsetting payoff on the swaption. A puttable bond gives the holder the right to put (redeem) the bonds back to the issuer at par (or another *put price*). A puttable bond can be viewed as a bullet bond plus a put swaption sold by the issuer to the bond holder. Callable bonds and puttable bonds can be priced and hedged by looking at their components separately and netting the prices and deltas.

What if the bond is both callable and puttable? Then the options cannot be treated separately, because the decision to call depends on whether the bond has been put and on the future possibilities of being put. Vice versa, the decision to put depends on prior and future decisions to call. The two are intertwined. This is identical to the convertible bond situation where the decision to exercise the conversion option depends on future share prices and interest rates together. In Chapter 8, we discussed structured finance with the use of derivatives like swaps and caps. A callable inverse floater is an example of a bond with embedded options that are not separable. The inverse floater's coupon contains a cap protection as the coupon rate cannot fall below 0. On top of that, the issuer can call the entire package and his decision will depend on whether the caps are to be exercised or not.

In these and other examples, the embedded options are dealt with using the right pricing model (i.e., one that does not separate the components, but values and computes delta hedges for the whole package). To provide information to investors, dealers often compute and quote measures of optionality in bonds. The *option-adjusted spread* (OAS) is defined as the difference between the yield on the structured bond minus the yield the bond would have if all the embedded options (whether separable or not) were eliminated.[2] For example, for a convertible bond, the OAS is equal to the yield on the convertible minus the yield on an equivalent straight bullet bond with the same maturity. OASs are quoted for most bonds we have already mentioned.

They are also very popular in mortgage-backed securities (MBSs). Let us consider the simplest example of an MBS: a fixed-coupon pass-through. A pass-through is a bond whose coupon stream matches the payment stream of the underlying pool of mortgages. Each month a pass-through holder receives coupon and principal repayments. The biggest risk of fixed-coupon pass-throughs is the embedded option sold by the lender (bond holder) to the borrower (mortgagee). Any homeowner has the right to prepay the mortgage by paying it in full (e.g., when selling the property) or sending extra checks to reduce the principal. Each homeowner may have his own reasons for prepaying, but, in general, he will tend to prepay when interest rates are low (in order to refinance). The pass-through owner will be subject to the totality of the prepayment decisions coming from the entire pool. The embedded option is equivalent to a call swaption held by the homeowners who can call their loans prior to maturity. The option is not exercised optimally as soon as interest rates go down, as it depends on the sum of individual decisions.

Just as callable bonds have OASs quoted on them, so do MBSs. This allows investors to compare the level of uncertainty about the timing of the cash flows, all subsumed into one summary statistic. We need to remember that this statistic, however, hides a lot of detail about the exact reasons for exercising the embedded options. This is particularly important for MBSs where the prepayment speeds are just estimates. In contrast, true callables and convertibles are exercised rationally whenever the exercised value exceeds the unexercised value.

Just like large bond portfolios, which are often characterized by average duration and convexity numbers, portfolios of bonds with embedded options can be described by average OASs on like securities. These however are not additive and cannot be used to come up with heuristic hedges. Individually, they provide crude clues to volatility exposure.

10.6 INSURANCE?

The last section of this chapter is devoted to the discussion of financial contracts that look like other financial options; but, because they are truly unhedgeable, they are more

---

[2] Sometimes the definition is in terms of the spread over the spot model (discount) rate (rather than the quoted yield) which can value the bullet and the structured bond to the observed prices.

akin to insurance products than options. Insurance companies do not hedge their risks; they cannot take positions in underlying assets as most of the bets they sell are on events. Instead, they manage the risks through diversification and reserve management. They avoid higher probability events or accident-prone individuals; they spread risks across ages, sexes, types of liability, geography, etc.; and they build reserves in good years to use in years with high payouts. They do not manufacture payoffs the way option dealers do. Option dealers look to find underlying positions that dynamically traded can eliminate most risks. Sometimes that is not possible and they venture into insurance-like bets. This is an ever-growing segment of the market as financial engineers push the envelope of financial innovation.

We start with the simple example of an option-insurance borderline case of long-term options.

Long-dated commodity options

Suppose we sell a standard call option on the price of petroleum. Let us choose Brent crude oil whose current spot price is $28 a barrel and set the strike price equal to $35.

The hedging of commodity options with spot trading is impractical and expensive. Buying oil outright would lead to high storage costs and could only be done for a limited quantity. If we had sold a put, we would have to short oil spot which would be impossible. The standard way to deal with these problems is to buy or sell futures with the same maturity as the option expiry. The futures will converge to spot by the expiry date, and so the futures is the perfect hedge tool. It can be bought and shorted, and rebalanced quickly and with minimal transaction costs.

We set the expiry of the call option we sell to be 10 years. However, futures contracts go out at most 2 years. We are subject to unexpected supply shock risks that drive a wedge between the fair value of futures without the convenience yield and the actual price. Oil futures are subject to normal backwardation as we explained before. That is, each futures contract price deviates from its fair value based on today's spot, the financing cost and storage costs, and the convenience yield markup, reflecting no assurance of delivery of a physical commodity. So if we dynamically hedge with the traded futures, our cost of manufacturing the payoff will be a function of the convenience yield which fluctuates in an unpredictable fashion. Any supply shocks (war, supply gaps) will exacerbate the fluctuations of the futures price from fair value. None of this would matter if we had a 10-year futures contract, except for the potential "jumpiness" of its price. But because there is no 10-year contract, we have to hedge with 1- or 2-year contracts which will be subject to different convenience yields. We will roll over the hedges on their expiry, or earlier, into new 1- or 2-year contracts (this is also called *stacking*). In addition, the realized volatility of the spot price over 10 years may be much lower than the volatility of the hedge. The estimated manufacture cost based on a hedge rollover assumption (with implied volatility) will be just as inaccurate as the cost based on the spot price (with historical volatility or some other estimate). In effect, if we engage in the hedge, we are taking an outright bet on the convenience yields and historical volatility; if we do not engage in the hedge, we are taking a bet on the oil price itself. Often both choices are equally risky.

Options on energy prices

Another example of unhedgeable options—options on electricity prices—comes from the world of commodities as well. This time the spoiler is the fact that electricity cannot be stored easily and has to be delivered to a specific point on the grid. While the capacity to generate the spot product may exist, the ability to deliver it may not.

Suppose we sell an option on the spot price of electricity delivered to Los Angeles on a specific date at a specific peak time. We hedge with short-term futures contracts on the price of electricity at the California–Arizona border. In deregulated or partially deregulated markets, electricity prices for two different points on the grid are not good substitutes of each other. While they may appear to reflect the spot price of the same commodity, the supply conditions (weather-related demand, grid overload, local generation failures, etc.) may cause the prices to diverge dramatically. In short, a true hedge instrument does not exist. Although we may euphemistically refer to hedging with a substitute as "basis risk", we may not have a hedge at all. Not only is there no assurance of the convergence of the two prices, the two may fluctuate differently.

Options on economic variables

Dealers are sometimes pushed by their customers to buy or sell options on economic variables like the inflation rate, GDP level, or unemployment rate. Financial institutions that have sold client contracts with indexed payoffs (pension, health insurance) have indirect, but natural aggregate demand for such structures. Although the payoffs on such products, for example:

$$Max[U.S.\ consumer\ price\ index - 2\%, 0]$$

may look like those of standard call and put options, these are not options at all; they are essentially unhedgeable bets. Unless the dealer can find the other side of the trade to transfer the risk to (i.e., to reduce his role to a matched-book dealer—read: a broker), he is an insurance provider. Any hedge relying on some "basis risk" will be faulty. A macroeconomic model may provide a statistical relationship between the underlying rate (inflation) and some instruments (stock index, real estate index, long bond rate) which can be traded. The model will be unstable and, as a result, of limited use.

A final word

How are such products different from the previously covered spread options? The main difference is that here there is no underlying price or rate, while the spread option has two rates or prices of well-defined underlying assets. The basis risk of insurance-like products may sometimes be no larger than the correlation risk of the seemingly hedgeable options. In most cases, common sense is all that is needed to separate dynamic arbitrage from outright speculation.

Appendix
Credit Risk

11

Default Risk (Financial Math IV) and Credit Derivatives

Up to now, we have assumed that all interest-bearing securities were default-free. The prices (present values) of deposits, bonds, and swaps varied as interest rate changed, but the cash flows promised from these contracts, even those unknown at the outset (LIBOR-indexed interest), were sure to be received at the scheduled dates. Alternatively, for securities with non-guaranteed cash flows (stock dividends), we have assumed that the interest rate charged reflected the riskiness of the investment. For some transactions, we assumed that the interest rate reflected the quality of the collateral (repos) or the credit standing of the guarantor (lending against the box). In most of the discussion so far, we ignored any issues related to compensation for the risk of default (i.e., willful non-performance on the contract).

It is, however, very important to understand how the possibility of default is factored into the yields on fixed income securities. In general, the yield on any interest-bearing security can be decomposed into two parts. The first reflects the general cost of funds for a given maturity (short maturity vs. long maturity) and type (zero, coupon, or amortizing interest). This is due to supply and demand forces in money and capital markets for given maturity ranges. The second reflects the possibility that the issuer of the security will fail to pay one or all of the promised cash flows. This can be due to the short-term liquidity problems of the issuer or due to bankruptcy. Credit-rating agencies spend countless resources researching and analyzing all relevant information to assess that probability of failure to perform. The prices of fixed income securities change as a result of changes in either of the two components. In most of this chapter, we will assume that the first component does not change (i.e., default-free interest rates stay the same). The only part that changes is that due to the changing probability of default.

The default risk of the issuer is reflected in a credit spread. The *credit spread* is defined as the difference between the yield on a default-risky security and a default-free security of the same maturity and type. Any security issued by the government of the currency of denomination can be used as a default-free benchmark. One simply matches the maturity of the reference rate to the given security. For example, if the yield to maturity (YTM) on a 5-year U.S. dollar-denominated coupon bond issued by ABC Corp. is 6.35% and the YTM on a 5-year U.S. Treasury is 5.84%, then the credit spread for 5-year ABC bonds is said to be 51 basis points (bp).

This chapter consists of two main parts: sections 11.1–11.4 cover the mathematics (Financial Math IV) related to default risk; and Sections 11.5–11.7 provide an overview of credit markets arbitrage, particularly with the use of credit derivatives. We start our discussion of credit spread by developing a simple model of how a probability of default translates into spread.

11.1   A CONSTANT DEFAULT PROBABILITY MODEL

Let us examine a 3-year annual bond issued by ABC Corp. The bond carries a 5% coupon. We also observe the following rates on default risk-free securities.

Table 11.1   Rates of default-free bonds

Year	Risk-free		
	Forward yield	Zero yield	Par yield
1	2.50	2.500 000	2.500 000
2	2.75	2.624 924	2.623 305
3	3.00	2.749 797	2.745 279

Suppose we assume that the probability that ABC will go bankrupt over the next year is 0.11%. We further assume that if ABC goes bankrupt then not only will it not pay the 5% coupon due in 1 year, but it will also fail to pay any coupons after that. If, however, ABC survives the first year, then the probability that it will go bankrupt in the second year will again be 0.11%. If ABC fails in year 2, then it will fail to pay the coupon in year 2 and the coupon and principal in year 3. If it survives year 2, then it will again face the probability of default of 0.11% for year 3. For each year the survival probability is constant at 99.89%.

What follows is that the cumulative survival probability up to any given time (or year) n is equal to 0.9989^n. What also follows is that the expected present value (PV) of any coupon payment is equal to the cumulative survival probability times the promised cash flow (CF) times a discount factor (DF), where the discount factor is computed using default-free rates. This is because if ABC does not survive to pay a given cash flow then its PV is equal to 1 minus the cumulative probability of survival times 0 as the cash flow times some discount factor, or 0. The analysis is summarized in Table 11.2.

Table 11.2   PV of ABC's bond in a default probability model

Year	CF	Probability of default per year (%)	Cumulative survival probability	Risk-free		PV
				Zero rate (%)	DF	
1	5	0.11	0.998 90	2.5000	0.975 610	4.8727
2	5	0.11	0.997 80	2.6249	0.949 499	4.7371
3	105	0.11	0.996 70	2.7498	0.921 843	96.4745

Sum PV = 106.0842

Yield = 2.8550%

Risk-free yield = 2.7417%

The promised cash flows in years 1, 2, and 3 are 5, 5, and 105, respectively. We use the risk-free zero rates to discount the cash flows if they are received. The PV of each cash flow is the expected value computed as the weighted average of two possibilities: the first, weighted by the cumulative survival probability, is the PV of receiving the cash flow; and, the second, weighted by the remaining probability mass, is 0 (i.e., the PV of not receiving a cash flow). The price is 106.0842. Given that price, we can back out the YTM on the bond to be 2.8550%. Given the risk-free zero-coupon rates, we can compute the default-free yield on 3-year coupon bonds as 2.7417%. The credit on ABC's bond is 0.1133%.

Suppose ABC's rating changes to "junk" and the perceived probability of default changes to 10% per year.

Table 11.3 PV of ABC's bond after a credit downgrade

Year	CF	Probability of default per year (%)	Cumulative survival probability	Risk-free		PV
				Zero rate (%)	DF	
1	5	10.00	0.900 00	2.5000	0.975 610	4.3902
2	5	10.00	0.810 00	2.6249	0.949 499	3.8455
3	105	10.00	0.729 00	2.7498	0.921 843	70.5625
					Sum PV =	78.7982
					Yield =	14.1562%
					Risk-free yield =	2.7417%

The promised cash flows do not change, but their expected value does. The new price is 78.7982. The YTM on ABC bonds increases to 14.1562%, and the credit spread is now 11.4145%.

Our model can incorporate a deterministic scenario of changing credit quality. Suppose we believe that, while the probability of default for year 1 is 0.11%, it will increase to 6% in year 2 and 8% in year 3. We recomputed the cumulative survival probabilities, and the rest proceeds as before.

Table 11.4 PV of ABC's bond assuming known credit deterioration

Year	CF	Probability of default per year (%)	Cumulative survival probability	Risk-free		PV
				Zero rate (%)	DF	
1	5	0.11	0.998 90	2.5000	0.975 610	4.8727
2	5	6.00	0.938 97	2.6249	0.949 499	4.4577
3	105	8.00	0.863 85	2.7498	0.921 843	83.6150
					Sum PV =	92.9454
					Yield =	7.7238%
					Risk-free yield =	2.7417%

The YTM on the bond changes to 4.9821%.

In the last three examples, we showed how an estimate of default probabilities translates into the credit spread through the calculation of the bond price as the expected present value of the scheduled cash flows, where the expectation is weighted by the probabilities of receiving the cash flows. Next, we consider a model with more complicated changes to the credit quality of the issuer.

11.2 A CREDIT MIGRATION MODEL

The term "credit migration" refers to the possibility that the probability of default for a given future period depends on the default risk of the bond during the previous period. That is, if we think that a bond is likely to be upgraded from A to AA or likely to be downgraded from A to BBB over the next year, the probability of default for the following year will depend on whether the bond was upgraded or downgraded. In this approach, we consider the probabilities not only of default, but more gradual changes to the bond's credit rating, and the path of those changes. We can also take into account the changing nature of the subsequent probabilities of upgrades and downgrades.

Let us examine the following scenario. ABC has the probability of default over the next year of 0.20%. We postulate that the annual default probability for year 2 will change to 0.10% with a probability of 30% or to 0.70% with a probability of 70%. The 30–70 probabilities of period-to-period changes in the issuer's credit rating are referred to as transitional probabilities. Now, depending on where we end up in year 2, we will assume different transition probabilities for years 2–3 and different default probabilities for year 3. If we end up at 0.10% for year 2, then we postulate that the annual default probability for year 2 will change to 0.05% with a probability of 25% or to 0.30% with a probability of 75%. If we end up at 0.70% for year 2, then we postulate that the annual default probability for year 2 will change to 0.30% with a probability of 30% or to 3.00% with a probability of 70%. This way we can model a non-linear path toward credit trouble and a migration from one credit category to the next over time.

We use a decision tree similar to the binomial tree for options to depict our scenario (ours will be recombinant, but it does not have to be). On each node, we mark the probability of default for the year starting at that node and ending next year. We show transitional probabilities of going up or down. We also show the scheduled cash flow for the *next* period. The PV displayed at each node is the discounted expected value of the cash flow to be received next period, cumulated with the expected value of the subsequent period's cash flow which is probability-weighted and discounted. Graphically, each node n is represented as:

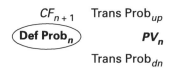

Figure 11.1 A node of a credit migration tree.

where

$$PV_n = (1 - DefProb_n)[CF_{n+1} + (TransProb_{up} \cdot PV_{up} + TransProb_{dn} \cdot PV_{dn})]/(1 + r_{n,n+1})$$

We sweep backward through the tree to compute the expected value of all cash flows under our transitional and survival assumptions.

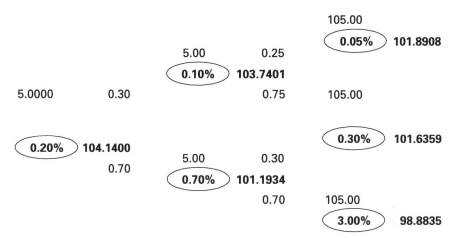

Figure 11.2 ABC's bond in a credit migration model with transitional probabilities.

Today's price of the ABC bond is 104.14 and the YTM is 3.5217%.

Note that our tree does not rely on any hedging argument. It is just a convenient graphical tool for computing weighted averages given conditional default and transition probabilities. It only coincidentally resembles option-pricing trees which are discrete approximations of price dynamics.

11.3 ALTERNATIVE MODELS

Credit migration can, of course, be a lot more complicated and depend not just on previous default probabilities, as in our model, but on other (state) variables. The latter can be market-general (e.g., interest rates or economic indicators) or issuer-specific (e.g., financial ratios, legal structure). Any model has to be a vast statistical approximation of the reality of defaults.

One particularly well-known and highly qualitative model is that used by credit-rating agencies. S&P's and Moody's assign issuers to credit quality categories with different likelihoods of default. The agencies provide past default statistics. They also painstakingly analyze all relevant financial information to determine a forward-looking forecast of an issuer's ability to repay cash flows. This includes public financial disclosure as well as general industry and economic data. We can refer to that as an expert opinion model.

An interesting option-theoretic alternative is offered by a San Francisco-based company called KMV. The approach is based on the observation that the stock of any given company is a de facto call option on the total value of the firm with a strike price equal to the value of the debt. If we know the total value of the assets of the company and the total value of the shares outstanding, then in effect we know the value of the underlying price and the value of the option. If we can further assess the volatility of the underlying assets, then, from the option-pricing model, we can back out the strike price (the value of the debt) of the option (the equity). That, in turn, can be converted to the YTM and the credit spread. It can also be converted to a forward-looking forecast of default probability. KMV claims to have superior out-of-sample predictive power for the defaults. The enormous value added by the company's service lies in extremely thorough data collection process for all debt issues and a very rigorous treatment. The approach relies on a hedging argument which, while quite impossible to implement, does offer the implied self-consistent market consensus estimate of future defaults, in the same way as the implied volatility does for future price paths (here we are interested in the implied strike and its subcomponents though).

11.4 CREDIT EXPOSURE CALCULATIONS FOR DERIVATIVES

Credit risk refers to the possibility that some cash flows that we have been promised may not be paid to us. In general, the magnitude of credit risk depends on two factors: the size of the cash flows owed to us and the default probability of the counterparty to the transaction. A loan with twice the face value issued to the same borrower has twice the credit risk. The same loan issued to two different borrowers may have different credit risks as the default probabilities of the two borrowers may be different. The price of a credit-sensitive bond compensates the owner for both factors. Credit spread implied in the bond's yield takes into account the probability of default. The yield is then used in cash flow discounting: the greater the cash flows, the greater the PV reduction due to credit spread.

The notion of *credit exposure* refers to estimation of the size of the cash flows subject to default (i.e., it only considers the first factor). In many cases, most notably in derivative contracts, cash flows are floating or contingent on market events and are not known in advance. They have to be forecast. Forecasting is a very risky business. This renders credit exposure calculations a very inexact science. All that we can do is try to come up with a metric of the relative riskiness of different assets based on the size of the exposed cash flows. Once that size is defined for a security, it can be cumulated with other securities of or contracts with the same counterparty to come up with the total size of cash flows exposed to the default of that counterparty. A bank performing such a computation can then set a limit on the exposure it is willing to take. It can define a credit line limit for a given counterparty to regulate the business behavior of its traders by inducing them to or preventing them from engaging in a particular type of deal in order to manage the concentration of credit risks. From that perspective, it is a very useful, albeit inexact, business policy tool.

Credit exposure can be defined in many different ways. For example, credit exposure on a loan issued to a customer can be defined in future value terms as the interest and principal cash flows we have been promised on some future dates or as some kind of a single PV concept. For bonds, credit exposure can be defined as the future cash flows from the bond or their total PV. The latter definition will not lend itself to easy aggregation across other securities and contracts of the same issuer.

When applying the concept of credit exposure to forwards, options, and other derivatives, and depending on the structure of the transaction, the cash flows due to be received may not be defined in advance. Consider a long position in an option. If the option ends up in-the-money on the expiry date, then we are owed a cash flow; if it ends up out-of-the-money, then we are not owed a cash flow. Does this mean that if the option is currently out-of-the-money we do not have any credit risk? No, we bought the option, hoping that we might get a cash flow from it. There is a non-zero probability of a positive cash flow if the option is not worthless. We do have credit exposure to the party that sold us the option. If we used the simple logic of discounting cash flows using a credit spread-corrected yield, as we can do with loans and bonds, all out-of-the-money options would have no computed credit exposure. So how else can we define credit exposure?

The answer is not simple. Whatever we do will have to be based on some probabilistic assumptions about how prices or rates are going to move (i.e., our subjective estimate of market risk). It will have to rely on some guesswork. We will have to estimate the expected value or a confidence interval value of the cash flows we are due. Whatever we do will be just a guess or, more technically, a subjective estimate of some random variable. But, we get to choose what variable we want to estimate: the mean, a confidence interval cutoff, or something else.

The most important principle in credit exposure calculations is consistency. We want to treat assets and securities that are essentially the same equally. The credit exposure on a receive-fixed swap should not be any different from the net exposure on a long fixed coupon bond and a short floating-rate bond. The credit exposure on a forward zero should not be any different from the credit exposure on two spot zeroes: one long and one short. We also want the credit exposure on otherwise identical contracts entered into with different counterparties to be identical. After all, the objective is to compute the exposure first and then apply the credit rating of the counterparty to decide whether we are comfortable with it. Lastly, we have to be careful to define credit limits consistently with the definition of exposure we adopt.

Many forwards and derivatives are exchanges of cash flows, and we need to separate the cash flows that we owe from the cash flows that we are owed. We do not have any credit exposure on the first; we have credit exposure on the latter. But is our exposure equal to the full value of the cash flows that we are owed? Suppose we entered into a 1-year foreign exchange (FX) forward to sell GBP 100,000,000 for USD 150,000,000. Our expected cash flows are an outflow of GBP 100,000,000 and an inflow of USD 150,000,000. What if the counterparty to our FX forward defaults and on the maturity date fails to deliver USD 150,000,000. We certainly are not going to rush to deliver our pound sterling obligation under the contract. If the exchange rate moves against us and the counterparty defaults, we will choose not to pay either; if the exchange rate moves in our favor, we will have lost a positive cash flow.

One way to define credit exposure would be as a one-sided confidence interval cutoff of the amount to be owed to us. Suppose today's 1-year forward FX rate is USD1.50/ GBP and the volatility (standard deviation) of the rate is 2%. Based on the bell curve, 68% of the probability lies within ±1 standard deviation, or ±2%, of the central value which we will assume is equal to the forward and 90% of the probability mass lies within two standard deviations or ±4%. The two standard deviation points are thus:

$$1.50(1 - .04) = 1.44 \quad \text{and} \quad 1.50(1 + 0.04) = 1.56$$

At those points, the net cash flows in USD owed to us would be:

At 1.44 $150,000,000 - 100,000,000 \times 1.44 = $ USD 6,000,000

At 1.56 $150,000,000 - 1,000,000 \times 1.56 = $ USD $-$ 6,000,000

We can define the 1.44 point as the 95% confidence interval cutoff. Based on our estimate of volatility, there is a 5% chance that the rate would be at 1.44 and below. At 1.44 we are owed USD 6,000,000. We can define *that* as our credit exposure in future value terms. We can also discount that amount to today to come up with the credit exposure in PV terms. Coincidentally, this would also be the 95% value-at-risk[1] number. Note that if we did not use a confidence interval measure, but simply defined the credit exposure in terms of its expected value, then our FX forward and, in fact, all on-market forwards would have zero credit exposures.

Let us provide another example. This time we look at an interest-rate swap. Suppose we have entered into a 5-year annual interest-rate swap to pay 5.5884% fixed against 12% LIBOR (London interbank offered rate), on a notional principal of GBP 100,000,000. Currently, the 12-month forward, spot zero, and par swap interest rates for different terms, stated in months from today, are as follows:

Table 11.5   Current rates

	Forwards	Maturity	Zeros	Maturity	Swap
0 × 12	5.000 000	12	5.000 000	12	5.0000
12 × 24	5.500 000	24	5.249 703	24	5.2433
24 × 36	5.761 423	36	5.420 001	36	5.4066
36 × 48	6.000 000	48	5.564 702	48	5.5426
48 × 60	5.800 000	60	5.611 720	60	5.5884

Our swap is on-market (i.e., it has a zero PV). How much money is at risk of default? Again we can try to determine a 95% confidence interval measure by considering scenarios where money is owed to us at the five payment dates. We assume that forwards are unbiased predictors of future LIBORs. Suppose the normal volatility of LIBOR rates is 2% per year. This will have to be scaled up by the appropriate number of years to set times. We will be owed money when LIBOR exceeds the fixed rate, since we are paying fixed. We consider two standard deviations up from the forwards.

[1] Value-at-risk is a measure prescribed by the regulators, and used by the majority of banks, in OECD countries to describe their market risk exposure. For a very readable treatment, see P. Jorion, *Value at Risk* (2nd edn), 2000, McGraw-Hill, New York.

Table 11.6 Credit exposure calculation using a two-standard-deviation interval

Time in months		Forward LIBOR	Volatility	95% cutoff	Cash flows		Net CF	Credit exposure	PV credit exposure
Set	Pay				Fixed	Floating			
0	12	5.0000	0.00	5.00	(5,588,397)	5,000,000	(588,397)		
1	24	5.5000	2.00	5.72	(5,588,397)	5,720,000	131,603	131,603	118,802
2	36	5.7614	4.00	6.22	(5,588,397)	6,222,336	633,940	633,940	541,102
3	48	6.0000	6.00	6.72	(5,588,397)	6,720,000	1,131,603	1,131,603	911,212
4	60	5.8000	8.00	6.73	(5,588,397)	6,728,000	1,139,603	1,139,603	867,347
								Total	2,438,463

We compute LIBOR rates that correspond to the 95% interval. We compute the cash flows based on those projected LIBOR rates as well as fixed cash flows. We net the two to get the amounts owed. If positive, we define those as our credit exposures. We also compute the credit exposure in PV terms. The interpretation of that PV number of £2,438,463 is that, based on predicted market movements and in particular the two standard deviation movements, we stand to lose that amount in today's pounds in case of default. It should be said that discounting is not preferred here; it is better to know cash flows at risk for all future dates.

All of the above suggested methods are not based on solid science (i.e., the computed amounts cannot be locked in, arbitraged, paid, or received). They should be viewed simply as "risk scores" for relative exposure comparisons among products and counter-parties. They have no strict monetary interpretation. We cannot even be completely sure that a larger credit exposure number means greater credit risk due to a larger cash flow being exposed.

11.5 CREDIT DERIVATIVES

Credit derivatives, like other derivatives that transfer price or interest rate risk between parties, are structured finance products designed to transfer risk arising from a credit event between two parties (e.g., they may provide exposure to or protection from the default of an issuer). Credit derivatives are forward-like products in that there is a future date and the payout is defined as a net of two flows, at least one of which is credit-related. More often, credit derivatives are option-like products in that there is a trigger event that can take place over a time period and the payout is contingent on the event having taken place. If the event, which can be a default, restructuring, or a credit-rating downgrade, occurs, the credit derivative has a payoff. If the event does not occur, the credit derivative pays nothing.

Similarly to standard options, the payoff of a credit derivative does not have to be fixed, but it can depend on the "severity" or "size" of the event. The "severity" is similar in concept to the notion of credit exposure (i.e., it measures the size of the cash flows lost due to default). This is closely related to the recovery value of the defaulted security. The payoff can also depend on other market variables (prices and rates).

Credit derivatives are very complex credit management tools offering lots of flexibility, but often carrying additional market and credit risks. Their main appeal lies in allowing two parties to transfer the credit risk of a third party. This risk-sharing arrangement can be for a specific time period or can be demarcated by credit events.

Until credit derivatives started trading in the 1990s, the only credit risk management tools at the disposal of bankers were a direct renegotiation with a borrower, diversification of the loan portfolio, or an outright sale of a loan. Credit derivatives allowed the credit profile of a loan portfolio across many dimensions to be customized: length of exposure, selling of some exposure but not all, correlating exposures by blending exposures to like risks, relating the size of loan protection to other market variables, etc.

Basics

Let us consider a *default protection option*. The buyer of the option gets a payout if a specified issuer defaults on or prior to some date. The buyer pays a premium as for any option or insurance product. The default is defined in terms of a *reference security*. The default event is said to take place if the issuer of the reference security fails to pay coupon or any other cash flows specified by the reference security contract. More often than not, the reference security is a bond. If the issuer of the bonds fails to pay on the bond, for the purposes of the default option the default has taken place and the option has a payoff. The payoff is then defined as some amount (say, par) minus the recovery value. The *recovery value* is defined as the price of the defaulted reference security in the aftermarket. For example, if the bond falls in default, but trades at 60 in the aftermarket, the payoff on the option may be defined as 100 minus 60, or 40. The presumption is that the buyer of the protection owns the bond and can recover 60 by selling the bond, and is only compensated for the lost value.

Credit default swap

A default protection option is most often packaged as a *credit default swap* in which the premium is paid periodically as opposed to all upfront. The term of the credit protection and premium payment, called the maturity of the swap, is specified at the outset. As long as the premium continues to be paid, the protection is in place. This is similar to a term life insurance contract without any cancellation rights on both sides.

Let us illustrate. The Kool Kredit Bank has a portfolio of loans to different corporations. Kool Kredit is worried about one particular loan to ABC Corp. which has five more years to maturity. ABC also has some bonds outstanding. Bonds and loans carry cross-default provisions. Kool Kredit selects one of these bonds as a reference security for the default swap it intends to enter into with a credit derivative dealer. In case of ABC's default, the reference security is thought to stand to lose approximately the same percentage of value as the Kool Kredit's loan to ABC.

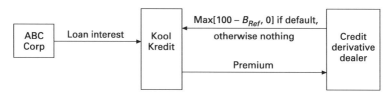

Figure 11.3 Credit default swap used as insurance against loan default (B_{Ref} is the value of the reference bond).

If ABC defaults, then the value of the loan to Kool Kredit will decline from par (100) to the PV of any cash flows post-default. The value of the reference bond will also decline to the PV of any cash flows post-default (i.e., the recovery of the bond). Kool Kredit will receive the difference between par and the recovery value. If Kool Kredit actually owned the reference bond and not the loan, then the credit derivative could have been structured even more simply with a physical-settle provision. Kool Kredit would have the right to put the bond to the dealer in exchange for par. In the slightly more complex mark-to-market arrangement, the recovery value must be defined very clearly. The recovery is typically defined as the bid or mid-price of the bond in the aftermarket. To avoid disputes, an additional provision may be inserted in the contract, specifying that five dealers may be polled to ascertain the bond's aftermarket value.

The International Swaps and Derivatives Association's (ISDA) master documents govern the language of credit derivative contracts. They specifically define the reference entity (reference security), obligation (loan or bond provisions), credit event, and reference obligation. Most trade confirmations include a materiality clause aimed at excluding technical defaults with no change in the reference security's value from the definition of a credit event.

Total-rate-of-return swap

Total-rate-of-return swaps allow banks to obtain default or value loss protection for loans on their books and a subsidy to their cost of funding in exchange for giving up the total return on a loan. The protection-buying bank essentially gives up any cash flows from the loan without having to sell the loan or canceling the loan with the borrower. The protection-selling investor gains access to the return on the loan without having to find his own customers, but bears the risk of default or any event leading to a loss of value of the reference security and has to pay spread over LIBOR as compensation. Total return swaps are perfect examples of credit risk sharing where banks can diminish their exposure to the credit standings of certain borrowers, while non-bank investors can gain exposure and return on loans to certain borrowers.

As an illustration, consider Kool Kredit Bank: instead of buying into a credit default swap, it enters into a total return swap with an investor or dealer. Kool Kredit does not have to involve ABC in the transaction. It agrees to pay any interest and any appreciation in the value of ABC's loan to the dealer. The dealer agrees to pay Kool Kredit LIBOR plus a spread and any depreciation in the value of the reference loan. In effect, the dealer's compensation for providing credit protection is the difference between the interest on ABC's loan passed on to him and the spread over LIBOR he pays. The swap may terminate on any payment exchange date or on a pre-specified credit event. At that point, the two parties would enter into a settlement based on the mark-to-market (par minus the recovery value) of ABC's loan which serves as the reference security for the swap.

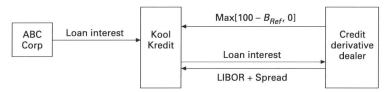

Figure 11.4   Total-rate-of-return swap (B_{Ref} is the value of the reference bond).

The total return swap bundles credit protection with an exchange-of-interest-accrual formula. Credit protection is wide-ranging as the protection provider compensates for any loss of value on the reference security.

Credit-linked note

A credit-linked note is a debt security whose principal repayment depends on the value of a third-party reference security. In case of third-party default, the defaulted security is passed on to the investor in lieu of principal. The enhanced interest rate of the credit-linked note reflects the implicit sale of credit protection by the investor. The issuer of the note is typically a trust set up by a bank arranging the sale of the note. The trust uses the proceeds from the sale of the note to invest in risk-free securities to guarantee the principal of the note if the third party does not default. If the third party defaults, the note is redeemed early at the recovery value of the reference security.

The investor gains a much enhanced interest rate, but bears all the risk of default. The arranging bank acquires protection for its loan or bond portfolio. In case of default of the underlying issuer, the bank receives the excess of the value of the securities held by the trust over the recovery value of the reference security.

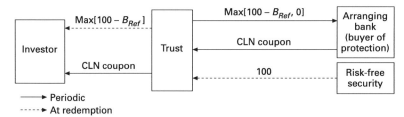

Figure 11.5 Credit-linked note (B_{Ref} is the value of the reference bond).

The credit-linked note bundles a credit default swap with a standard bond obligation. The credit protection premium paid by the arranging bank is passed on to the investor in the form of an enhanced coupon. The protection payout is passed from investors to the bank at redemption. If there are no credit events associated with the reference security, the investor gets a periodic coupon and par at maturity.

Credit spread options

Credit spread options offer payout dependent on the yield differential between default-risky securities and reference benchmarks. The payout is not contingent on any particular credit event. Most credit spread options are structured as put options on the price. The holder of a credit spread option has the right to sell a particular corporate bond at a contingent strike price. The strike price is computed to be the value the corporate bond would have to have on the expiry date so that its YTM would be equal to the YTM on the reference, default-free security plus a spread strike. For example, the buyer of a spread option on ABC's 5-year note struck at a spread strike of 50 bp over the 5-year U.S. Treasury note will face either of two possibilities on the expiration date. If the spread between the YTM on the ABC bond and the Treasury is less than 50 bp, the option expires worthless. If the spread exceeds 50 bp, he sells the ABC bond to the option writer. The price he receives is equal to the PV of the cash flows from the ABC bond discounted at the yield equal to the 5-year Treasury yield plus 50 bp.

Let us illustrate numerically. Suppose 1 year ago we purchased a 1-year European option on the spread between ABC's 6-year bond paying a 5% coupon semi-annually and the 5-year U.S. Treasury issue struck at 55 bp. The principal (face) amount was $100 million. At that time, the ABC bond yielded 5.75% (semi) to price at 96.2392. The reference Treasury off which we were going to calculate the yield spread between the two bonds had not been issued. The then-current 5-year Treasury paying a 5.25% semi-annual coupon yielded 5.23% and priced at 100.1019. The option was described as 3 bp out-of-the-money since the spread at the time of the option purchase was 52 bp. A month ago, the U.S Treasury auctioned off a new 5-year note with a coupon of 5.125%. This note will be used to determine the payoff on the spread option.

Suppose the now 5-year ABC bond is yielding 5.68%. The current market price is 97.0759. The new 5-year Treasury is yielding 5.04% and prices to 100.3716. The yield spread between the two bonds at 64 bp is higher than the strike spread of 55 bp. We will exercise our option to sell the bond at 55 bp over Treasuries (i.e., at a yield of 5.59%). Computing the price of the ABC bond at that yield we obtain 97.4571. Since we can buy the bond for 97.0759 on the open market, the payoff on the option to us is:

$$(97.4571 - 97.0759)/100 * \$100,000,000 = \$381,153$$

Suppose instead that the now 5-year ABC bond is yielding 6.23%. The current market price is 94.7846. The new 5-year Treasury is yielding 5.59% and prices to 97.9958. The yield spread between the two bonds (again at 64 bp) is higher than the strike spread of 55 bp. We will exercise our option to sell the bond at 55 bp over Treasuries (i.e., at a yield of 6.14%). Computing the price of the ABC bond at that yield we obtain 95.1551. Since we can buy the bond for 94.7846 on the open market, the payoff on the option to us is:

$$(95.1551 - 94.7846)/100 * \$100,000,000 = \$370,528$$

The option payout in the two scenarios is not identical, but almost the same. This is because it can be viewed as purely a bet on the spread between the two bonds grossed up by the duration of the bond under consideration. For the last scenario, the duration of the bond computed by blipping the yield from 6.14 to 6.15 is 4.1254. The payout on the option is based on 9 bp (64 – 55). So using the duration approximation, the total payout is:

$$0.041\,254 * 9 * \$100,000,000 = \$371,289$$

Note that nowhere in the calculations did we use the actual price of the Treasury. By comparing the two examples we can also see that the payout is independent of whether interest rates in general go up or down. The only relevant factor is the yield spread between the chosen bond and the reference risk-free security. To emphasize that, spread options are sometimes written by fixing the duration multiplier and defining the payout only with yields.

The fundamental difference between credit spread options and other credit derivatives is that credit events do not explicitly drive the payout, but are rather implicitly incorporated in the payout through a spread differential. The greater the possibility of default of the underlying bond, the greater the spread over risk-free assets is and thus the greater the payout on the spread option is.

Credit options can also be written not on specific underlying bonds, but on the averages of bond yields in a given credit category. These may be used by potential future issuers to hedge against general spread increases till the time of issuance.

11.6 IMPLICIT CREDIT ARBITRAGE PLAYS

We briefly revisit some of the previously described arbitrage relationships to focus on credit considerations. We take the perspective of a corporate debt issuer whose objective is to obtain the lowest cost of financing in the capital market.

Credit arbitrage with swaps

Let us assume that a U.K.-based corporation has a choice of issuing debt in the U.K. or in Australia. Five-year swap rates are 5% in the U.K. and 7% in Australia. Given the corporation's credit rating, the debt can be issued at 60 bp over swap rates in the U.K. Suppose that credit perceptions are different in Australia and the corporation finds investors there willing to accept 45 bp over the swap rates. The corporation would prefer sterling-denominated debt as most of its operations are in the U.K., but the cost differential may push it to do the following.

The U.K. corporation issues a 5-year AUD-denominated bond with a coupon rate of 7.45%. The bond sells at par. The corporation converts the proceeds into GBP to finance its operations. It also enters into a fixed–fixed currency swap receiving 7.45% in AUD and paying 5% plus a margin in GBP. Given the current swap rates, the margin is likely to be a little over 45 bp, but much less than the 60 bp U.K. investors demand. The corporation benefits by obtaining financing at lower cost.

Callable bonds

A U.K.-based corporation currently trades at 80 bp over U.K. government gilts. It believes that 10-year gilt rates will stay at the current 5% level or come down over the next 3 years. It strongly believes that its own credit rating is likely to improve dramatically as it has several new products in the pipeline. The corporation issues 10/2 callable bonds. The bonds have a 10-year final maturity, but can be called at par starting 2 years from today. The YTM on the bonds is 5.95% which is higher than a straight 10-year bullet yield of 5.80%. Suppose 2 years later the credit rating of the corporation improves as predicted to 40 bp over gilts, but gilt rates have stayed at 5%. The corporation may decide to call the bonds and issue new bullet notes at a 5.4% yield. Its overall cost of financing over the 10-year period will be lower than if it had issued bullet bonds at the outset. In fact, the improved credit rating would have made bullet bonds more expensive to retire early as their price would have increased.

11.7 CORPORATE BOND TRADING

The objective of most banking operations, apart from earning fee income for services, is to acquire funds at the lowest possible cost and earning the highest possible rates on its investments. The funds are obtained by offering checking, savings, and certificate of deposit (CD) accounts to retail customers or by borrowing in the wholesale markets through overnight interbank or repurchase agreement (repo) markets. Investments include a variety of consumer and business loans. In this process, banks face two types of risks. The first is the duration mismatch; financing is likely to be short-term, while the investments are likely to be long-term. This then leads to reinvestment and liquidity risk. The second major risk is that of credit exposure to the default by borrowers.

In order to diversify the credit exposure beyond a bank's traditional customer base, the bank may turn to the corporate bond market. This offers exposure to a wider variety of credits and potentially seniority over loans, but comes at the cost of a lower yield.

Corporate bond-trading operations generate two types of profit. The first is simply from inventory turnover through market-making. By charging higher ask prices, paying lower bid prices, market makers pocket the spread. This is not without risk as they hold an inventory of bond positions: those bought for sale and those short-sold for repurchase. This may at times be riskier than stock dealing as corporate bond markets are only liquid for a limited number of better known issuers. The financing required for market making is equal to the financing cost of net inventory plus any margins required. The second type of profit from corporate bond trading comes from credit arbitrage. Credit arbitrage can be implicit or explicit. The first has to do with being net long corporate bonds in the bank's bond portfolio against the general financing from the bank's treasury. Simply by buying bonds the bank is likely to make money in the same way that the bank makes money on its loan portfolio, relative to the cheap financing from deposit taking and overnight operations. This is an easy way to generate profit, but is subject to the same duration and liquidity risk as all the rest of the banking operation. The explicit type of credit arbitrage in corporate bond trading comes from relative value trades within the bond portfolio.

Relative value arbitrage with corporate bonds can take on many forms. It can consist of longs on one credit vs. shorts on another, if we believe that the first will improve and the second will deteriorate. It can consist of longs or shorts on a credit vs. a position in a government security, if we believe that the credit spread over government securities will go down or up. It can also consist of sector and industry tilting of the portfolio, if we believe that the average spread on one industry is going to move differently relative to that on another industry. Relative value arbitrage may also seek to exploit bond maturity selection and reflect a view on the movement of the corporate spreads over time, individually or in aggregate.

In all these strategies, the important factor distinguishing outright speculation from speculative relative arbitrage is whether the portfolio is hedged against the general movement of interest rates or not. This is done implicitly through duration matching of the relative components of the strategy or explicitly by using government securities.

Most corporate bond trading around the world is a cash business. Forwards on corporate bonds are rare and options exist only in the embedded form. Theoretically, there is nothing stopping the markets to evolve to include both forwards and options. Curiously, this has not happened yet. Also surprising is the limited use of credit derivatives by corporate bond traders even though the reference securities underlying many of the derivatives come from the corporate bond markets. Likely, this has to do with the skills gap between that required of a cash bond trader and that of a quantitative derivatives structurer. Also, most corporate bond trading is rarely linked to loan trading even though the two markets have to do with the same risk factors and their integration could lead to better credit diversification. Many banks obtain a bird's-eye view of the total credit exposure at the corporate level through some sort of "credit metrics", but choose not to combine lending and bond trading as the infrastructure in the two markets is different. This is clearly far from optimal.

Index

Printed and bound by CPI Group (UK) Ltd, Croydon, CR0 4YY

24/04/2025

14661408-0001